The Negotiability of Debt in Islamic Finance

The Negotiability of Debt in Islamic Finance

An Analytical and Critical Study

By

Abdulaziz A. Almezeini

BRILL

LEIDEN | BOSTON

Library of Congress Control Number: 2016958374

Typeface for the Latin, Greek, and Cyrillic scripts: "Brill". See and download: brill.com/brill-typeface.

ISBN 978-90-04-34027-5 (paperback)
ISBN 978-90-04-34074-9 (e-book)

Originally published as Volume 1(3) 2016, in *International Banking and Securities Law*,
DOI 10.1163/24056936-12340003

Copyright 2017 by Abdulaziz A. Almezeini. Published by Koninklijke Brill NV, Leiden, The Netherlands.
Koninklijke Brill NV incorporates the imprints Brill, Brill Hes & De Graaf, Brill Nijhoff, Brill Rodopi and Hotei Publishing.
Koninklijke Brill NV reserves the right to protect the publication against unauthorized use and to authorize dissemination by means of offprints, legitimate photocopies, microform editions, reprints, translations, and secondary information sources, such as abstracting and indexing services including databases. Requests for commercial re-use, use of parts of the publication, and/or translations must be addressed to Koninklijke Brill NV.

This book is printed on acid-free paper and produced in a sustainable manner.

Contents

The Negotiability of Debt in Islamic Finance: An Analytical and Critical Study   1
    Abdulaziz A. Almezeini
  Abstract   1
  Keywords   1
  Section 1: Introduction   2
    1.1 *Islamic Finance Growth*   2
    1.2 *Islamic Debt Market*   5
    1.3 *Why is the Islamic Debt Market Illiquid and Non-Diverse?*   7
    1.4 *Does Islamic Law Forbid Trading and Negotiating Debts?*   8
    1.5 *Contribution*   10
  Section 2: Overview of Some Islamic Law and Finance Principles and Concepts   11
    2.1 *Islamic Law Sources*   11
        2.1.1 Quran   12
        2.1.2 Sunnah   13
        2.1.3 Ijma (Unanimity)   15
        2.1.4 Ijtihad (Personal Reasoning)   15
    2.2 *The Islamic Schools of Legal Thought*   17
    2.3 *Islamic Finance Principles*   20
        2.3.1 Riba (Usury)   20
            2.3.1.1 *Riba in Sales*   21
            2.3.1.2 *Riba in Loans*   22
        2.3.2 Gharar (Uncertainty or Speculative Risk)   23
    2.4 *Islamic Financial Transactions*   25
        2.4.1 Musharakah (Partnership)   25
        2.4.2 Mudarabah   27
        2.4.3 Murabahah (Cost-Plus or Markup)   28
        2.4.4 Ijarah (Lease)   29
        2.4.5 Sukuk (Islamic Bonds)   30
  Section 3: Islamic Scholars and the Negotiability of Debt   31
    3.1 *Introduction*   31
    3.2 *Classic Islamic Jurisprudence and the Tradability of Debt*   32
        3.2.1 Sale of Debt for Executed Consideration   32
        3.2.2 Sale of Debt for Executory Consideration   34
    3.3 *Modern Islamic Fiqh (Jurisprudence) Organizations and the Tradability of Debt*   36

- 3.3.1 The Islamic Fiqh Academy in Jeddah   37
- 3.3.2 The Islamic Fiqh Academy in Makkah   39
- 3.3.3 Accounting and Auditing Organization for Islamic Financial Institutions (AAOIFI)   40
- 3.4 *The Effect of the Non-Tradability of Debts on Sukuk Industry*   41
  - 3.4.1 Sukuk Negotiability in the Secondary Market   42
    - 3.4.1.1 *Sukuk Murabaha*   42
    - 3.4.1.2 *Sukuk Salam*   43
    - 3.4.1.3 *Sukuk Istisna*   45
    - 3.4.1.4 *Sukuk Ijarah*   46
    - 3.4.1.5 *Sukuk Musharakah and Mudarabah*   47
- 3.5 *Securitization as an Instrument to Develop Sukuk*   49
- 3.6 *Conclusion*   52

Section 4: Criticizing the Resolutions of Islamic Fiqh Academies Regarding the Tradability of Debts   52
- 4.1 *Introduction*   52
- 4.2 *The Theoretical Foundation of Debt in Islamic Jurisprudence*   53
  - 4.2.1 Property Theory in Islamic Jurisprudence   53
    - 4.2.1.1 *Islamic Fiqh Academy Views on Property*   54
  - 4.2.2 Rights and Obligations Theory in Islamic Jurisprudence   56
  - 4.2.3 Trading Debts (Personal Property Rights) in Islamic Jurisprudence   57
- 4.3 *The Arguments of the Islamic Fiqh Academies to Forbid Trading Debt (Explanation and Discussion)*   58
  - 4.3.1 Riba and the Tradability of Debts   59
    - 4.3.1.1 *Debts Do Not Have Actual Existence*   59
      - Explanation   59
      - Discussion   60
    - 4.3.1.2 *Debt is Equivalent to Money*   62
      - Explanation   62
      - Discussion   63
    - 4.3.1.3 *The Transaction in General is Equivalent to Riba Transaction*   67
      - Explanation   67
      - Discussion   68
  - 4.3.2 Gharar (Uncertainty or Speculative Risk)   70
    - Explanation   70
    - Discussion   71
- 4.4 *Islamic Legal Basis for Permitting the Negotiability of Debt*   73
  - 4.4.1 Istishab (Presumption of Continuity)   73

        4.4.2 Qiyas (Analogical Reasoning)   74
        4.4.3 Maslahah (General Benefit)   75
            4.4.3.1 *Liquidity*   76
            4.4.3.2 *Diversity*   78
Section 5: Conclusion   80
References   82

The Negotiability of Debt in Islamic Finance: An Analytical and Critical Study

Abdulaziz A. Almezeini
Higher Judicial Institute
Al-Imam Muhammad Ibn Saud University, Riyadh
mezeini@mzlawyers.com

Abstract

The challenges posed by the non-liquidity and non-diversity of the Islamic debts market make the market an inefficient tool on contributing to Muslim economic growth. Islamic scholars and experts created sukuk as an Islamic debt instrument to avoid riba (usury), but the sukuk market (especially in the Gulf) still struggles with the prohibition of the trade of debt due to the prohibition of the two Fiqh Academies.

Trading and securitizing debts should be permitted in Islamic law, with one condition, that the debt should be considered low risk. This new rule, the permissibility of trading debts, is supported by three Islamic legal bases, istishab, qiyas, and maslaha, which are recognized by all four Islamic schools of legal thought. Furthermore, permitting the trading of debts is more consistent with the principles and theories of Islamic law than is forbidding it. It is consistent with the obligations theory that debt is a personal right. It is consistent with the mal (property) theory that debt may be sold according to the three Islamic schools of legal thought, all of which consider debt as property. It is consistent with other modern Islamic financial transactions that are permitted by the two Fiqh Academies, such as tawarruq and murabaha.

Keywords

Sukuk – Islamic debt market – Liquidity – Non-liquidity – Islamic jurisprudence – Islamic Fiqh Academy – The obligation theory – Islamic finance – Securitization – Tradability of debt

Section 1: Introduction

Islamic finance is a new, promising, and growing industry that serves Muslims and non-Muslims around the world. Many Western countries host Islamic financial institutions to benefit Islamic businesses in their jurisdictions. Yet, while some aspects of Islamic finance are growing rapidly, others, such as the Islamic debt market, continue to face challenges. The major challenges the market faces includes non-liquidity and non-diversity.

Most Muslim countries have the legal structure to trade debt securities in the primary and secondary markets. These countries allow both kinds of banking and financial systems: conventional and Islamic. However, the Islamic debt market in most Muslim countries is not as attractive and competitive as the conventional debt market.

Islamic bankers have created mechanisms that helped develop the Islamic debt market, while remaining within the bounds of Islamic law. One of those mechanisms is *sukuk*, the Islamic version of a bond. *Sukuk* instruments are structured in such a way as to avoid usury, which is forbidden in Islam. *Sukuk* have been very successful and popular especially within governments in Gulf Countries, which hold many sizeable issues of *sukuk*. Nevertheless, the debt market continues to struggle. The main reason for these problems is the prohibition of trading of debt adopted by contemporary Islamic scholars.

Solving these problems is very important to the economy in general. A developed, tradable and diverse debt market makes the financial market competitive and efficient. A more competitive market is crucial to ensure it is not dominated by only a few banks. The debt market is a critical source of funds that helps companies grow and expand. Moreover, it is an investment vehicle for investors who are looking for stable and predictable income. The availability for reliable investments will encourage the whole economy to grow and develop. Muslim countries need to handle the challenges of the Islamic debt market in order to achieve a strong and growing economy.

This article demonstrates how the growth of the Islamic debt market is restricted by non-liquidity and non-diversity, while other aspects of Islamic finance continue to grow and develop. Because the main cause of the non-liquid and non-diverse debt market is the position of contemporary Islamic scholars regarding the negotiability of debts, this article offers solutions to this problem by analyzing, discussing and criticizing this position. Finally, I propose a methodology for establishing the permissibility of trading debts in Islamic finance.

1.1 *Islamic Finance Growth*

Since its initial development in 1970, the Islamic financial industry has experienced considerable growth not only in Muslim countries but also in the

Western world. From 1970 to 2006, the number of Islamic financial institutions increased from one to around 265 in approximately forty countries with total assets surpassing $262 billion[1] and more than $202 billion in deposits.[2]

During the last decade, the growth rate of the Islamic financial industry exceeded that of the conventional financial industry by an estimated rate of 20–30%.[3] According to a report by HSBC Bank, the compound annual growth rate of the Islamic financial industry for 2006–2009 was 28%. The expected assets for 2010 were $1.003 trillion.[4] In 2012, some Islamic financial experts said the global Islamic finance and banking sector was poised for a year-on-year growth rate of 25%, which would see the industry valued at $5 trillion in 2016.[5]

Oil is one of the main reasons for the rapid growth of the Islamic financial industry. The high price of oil allows for huge liquid assets for the oil-producing countries that are members of the Gulf Cooperation Council (GCC). The governments of these countries invest almost $1 trillion outside the GCC, and the private sector invests $500 billion more. Ninety percent of these transactions go to the United States of America (USA) and European countries.[6] Certain investors and GCC governments require some of these transactions to comply with *Shariah* (Islamic law). The high volume of liquidity and the transactions compliant with *Shariah*, encourage Islamic financial growth in both GCC countries and the Western world.

Three of the largest Islamic financial transactions were required by Muslim governments to comply with *Shariah*. In 2004, "the largest government Islamic bond issuance was by the Department of Civil Aviation of the United Arab Emirates for $750 million."[7] The second largest was by the Bahrain Monetary Agency for $250 million, which was "led by Citigroup, with heavy involvement of the Norton Rose law firm to structure the deal."[8] The third largest issuance was by a Western government, "the German Federal State of Saxony-Anhalt for

---

1 *Islamic Banks: A Novelty No Longer*, BUSINESSWEEK.COM (Aug.7, 2005), *at* http://www.businessweek.com/stories/2005-08-07/islamic-banks-a-novelty-no-longer.
2 Babback Sabahi, *Islamic Financial Structures as Alternatives to International Loan Agreements: Challenges for American Financial Institutions*, BEPRESS LEG. SER. (2004), *at* http://law.bepress.com/expresso/eps/385.
3 JEFFERY WOODRUFF, DEMYSTIFYING CORPORATE *SUKUK* 61 (2007).
4 *HSBC seeks big growth, sukuk pickup in 2010*, REUTERS (Feb. 15, 2010), *at* http://www.reuters.com/article/2010/02/15/us-islamicbanking-summit-hsbc-idUSTRE61E2JD20100215.
5 *Islamic finance industry to hit $5 trillion by 2016*, TRADEARABIA NEWS SERVICE (June 28, 2012), *at* http://www.tradearabia.com/news/bank_219700.html.
6 *Islamic Banking Goes Global*, THE MIDDLE EAST, 2005, at 357.
7 MAHMOUD EL-GAMAL, OVERVIEW OF ISLAMIC FINANCE 13 (U.S. Department of Treasury 2006).
8 *Id.*

€100 million, which was heavily marketed in the Arab countries of the GCC as the first ever Western-government issued Islamic bond."[9]

Now the numbers are booming. In 2012, Arnold & Porter advised Turkey in its first offering of Islamic bonds. The bonds brought in $1.5 billion and they are due in 2018.[10] Again in 2012, Clifford Chance LLP, advised the Saudi Arabian General Authority of Civil Aviation (GACA) in a domestic issuance of an SAR (Saudi Arabian Riyal) of 27.1 billion ($7.2 billion) *sukuk*, due in 2022.[11]

Turning to the private sector, in the early part of 2006 corporate bond issuances totaled $10.2 billion. The most notable was the Dubai Ports issuance of the largest *sukuk* to date: a two-year convertible $3.5 billion bond.[12] In 2005, an estimated $11.4 billion in corporate sukuks were issued, up from $5.5 billion and $4.6 billion in 2004 and 2003, respectively.[13] Sovereign issuances in 2006 totaled $2.7 billion, up from $706 million in 2005, $1.5 million in 2004, and $1.2 million in 2003.[14]

Speaking of the continued growth of the Islamic bond market, Mohammed Dawood, managing director at HSBC Amanah said, "the GCC's *sukuk* issuances are set to reach $30bn–35bn in 2013, up 33 percent from 2012...."[15] Presently, Saudi Arabia's Islamic financial assets make up more than one-quarter of the GCC's total Islamic assets. According to a February 2013 report from Kuwait Financial House, Saudi Arabia issued $10.5 billion in *sukuk* in 2012, a 278% increase over 2011.[16] According to Ernst & Young forecasts, by 2015, "Saudi Arabia's share will grow to more than half [of the GCC's total Islamic assets]...."[17] The rapid growth of Islamic finance is not only in Muslim countries, but also in the Western world, especially in the financial centers of Europe. For example, in the United Kingdom there are five Islamic banks and

---

9   *Id.*

10   *Arnold & Porter Team Assists Turkey with Islamic Bond Offering*, LEGALTIMES (September 26, 2012), *at* http://legaltimes.typepad.com/blt/2012/09/arnold-porter-team-assists-turkey-with-islamic-bond-offering.html.

11   Press Release, Al-Jadaan & Partners and Clifford Chance, LLP, Al-Jadaan and Clifford Chance advise on landmark sovereign and largest ever Saudi *sukuk*, AMEINFO.COM (Jan.23, 2012), *available at* http://www.ameinfo.com/287665.html.

12   EL-GAMAL, *supra* note 7, at 5.

13   *Id.*

14   *Id.*

15   Sara Hamdan, *Interest Rises in Islamic Bonds*, N.Y. TIMES, Feb. 27, 2013, *available at* http://www.nytimes.com/2013/02/28/world/middleeast/interest-rises-in-islamic-bonds.html.

16   *Saudi Arabia: Debate continues over global sharia standards*, OXFORD BUSINESS GROUP (Apr. 9, 2013).

17   ERNEST & YOUNG, RAPID GROWTH MARKET (2012).

seventeen conventional banks providing Islamic services.[18] There are also twenty law firms and four accounting firms providing Islamic professional services.[19] Continually, there are twenty *sukuk* listed on the London Stock Exchange that are raising $11 billion.[20] There are fifty-five institutions that provide education and training in Islamic finance products.[21] In addition, "the UK market for Islamic mortgages has grown to about £500m, some 0.3% of the total UK mortgage market."[22]

Luxembourg is also trying to attract Islamic investments. There are fifteen *sukuk* listed on the Luxembourg Exchange market, for a combined value of €5 billion.[23] Luxembourg is the first non-Muslim country managing significant Islamic funds.[24] There are forty Islamic funds managed by sophisticated international investment companies.[25] With 7%, Luxembourg has the fourth largest percentage of Islamic funds after Kuwait with 9%, Saudi Arabia with 19% and Malaysia with 23%.[26]

1.2 *Islamic Debt Market*

Though Islamic finance has developed over the last ten years, it still faces many challenges that hinder its competition with conventional finance. In Arab countries, which make up a large part of the Islamic world, the financial markets are "suffering from many shortcomings...."[27] These shortcomings include, "the lack of diversification of investment instruments that meet the needs of market operators; the narrowness or the absence of a secondary market where financial papers can be traded thereby restricting their liquidity and the readiness of investors to acquire them."[28]

The limited secondary market and the lack of liquidity are especially hard on the Islamic debt market. According to the International Monetary Fund (IMF),

---

18   Duncan McKenzie, Islamic Finance 2010 8 (2010), *at* www.ifsl.org.uk.
19   *Id.* at 6.
20   *Id.* at 4.
21   *Id.* at 6.
22   *Id.*
23   Yves Mersch, Islamic finance—partnerships opportunities between Luxembourg and the Arab countries, Speech Before the 5th Economic Forum Belgium-Luxembourg-Arab Countries, Brussels, (Nov. 17, 2009).
24   *Id.*
25   *Id.*
26   Ernest & Young, Islamic Funds & Investments Report (2009).
27   Arab Monetary Fund, Contribution of the Arab Monetary Fund to The Development of Arab Capital Markets 27 (2003).
28   *Id.*

the debt market in the Middle East and North Africa (MENA) "stood at US$155.3 billion in 2008, accounting for a meager 0.2% of the total world debt market of US$83.3 trillion in 2008."[29] In 2008, the equity market and bank assets constituted 66.8% of the total MENA capital market of US$2.4 trillion, while the debt market in the region constituted only 6.4% of the total capital market, which is "significantly lower compared to a world average of 37.6% for the debt market representation."[30]

This significant difference indicates that debt instruments are not attractive to Muslim investors who are seeking funds. While there are large sums of money invested in the equity market (both primary and secondary), the debt market is still very undesirable and limited because most of this market is dominated by the public sector. Because of the volume of liquid assets, a more in-depth study of GCC countries is appropriate.

In the primary debt market of 2003–2009, GCC governments issued US$135.1 billion in bonds. They dominated the bond market in the GCC with a 55.6% share.[31] The financial services and real estate sectors, "were the most predominant sectors and issued bonds worth US$47.9 billion and US$18.8 billion, respectively, during the same period."[32]

The secondary market in the GCC is characterized by having a lower trading activity and a lack of transparency.[33] The debt instruments in the GCC markets are thinly traded.[34] In 2008, there were only eighty-five trades executed with a value of SAR1.3 billion (US$345.9 million) in the region. Secondary *sukuk* trading only commenced in Saudi Arabia in June 2009. In 2010, there were only fifty-seven *sukuk* trades on the Saudi Arabian stock exchange (Tadawul), compared to just six trades in 2009.[35]

Moreover, in Saudi Arabia, only a third of *sukuk* issuances are listed on the Saudi Exchange Market.[36] In the Saudi *sukuk* market, "domestic issuers have preferred private placements rather than public issuances."[37] A reason for this preference is the prohibition, adopted by current Islamic scholars, of trading debt in the secondary market. Currently, there are only eight *sukuk* listed on Tadawul (the Saudi Exchange Market).[38]

---

29 NCB CAPITAL, GCC DEBT CAPITAL MARKETS AN EMERGING OPPORTUNITY? 3 (2009).
30 *Id.*
31 BAYINA ADVISORS, THE GCC DEBT MARKET REPORT 35 (2010).
32 *Id.*
33 *Id.* at 10.
34 *Id.* at 19.
35 *Id.*
36 SAUDI HOLLANDI CAPITAL, *SUKUK* MARKET IN SAUDI ARABIA 3 (2013).
37 *Id.*
38 *Id.*

THE NEGOTIABILITY OF DEBT IN ISLAMIC FINANCE 7

Saudi Arabia is the biggest economic and financial market in the GCC. The total value of *sukuk* issues for 2013 in the GCC was $27.453 billion.[39] Saudi Arabia had 60% with total value of $16.518 billion.[40] UAE had 26%, a total value of $7.116 billion,[41] followed by Qatar with a total value of $2.057 billion and Bahrain with a total value of $1.588 billion.[42]

Saudi Arabia, despite having the strongest economy in the region with established exchange markets and a high value of *sukuk* issuances, has only eight listed *sukuk*. This makes the debt market risky because it lacks easy exit strategies. Thus, some of the "debt issues [were] bought by long-term investors planning to hold them to maturity."[43] The Islamic debt market will be more expensive because of the risk factor, making it undesirable to domestic and international investors. As a result, the Islamic debt market is "illiquid, domestic institutional participation is limited, and retail participation is virtually non-existent."[44]

1.3 Why is the Islamic Debt Market Illiquid and Non-Diverse?

An active debt market is very important for the Middle East and Muslim countries for both the public sector and the private sector. It would be "an important step toward more established and diverse financial markets in the region so it will broaden the range of funding sources for corporations and it would present investors, including retail investors, with an important asset class with qualities not found elsewhere."[45] An active debt market is also critical for governments because "a vibrant debt market would offer greater flexibility for fiscal and monetary policy makers."[46]

However, despite considerable efforts by the GCC to push the debt market forward, the debt market remains limited and illiquid. Nevertheless, "the development of a debt capital market in the Gulf is likely to be a drawn-out process and is bound to face some continued resistance on cultural grounds."[47] The cultural grounds referenced above refer to Islam as a religion. The Islamic finance industry is based on Islamic rules that govern Islamic financial transactions.

---

39 ABIR ATAMECH, *SUKUK* QUARTERLY BULLETIN 1Q2013 2 (2013).
40 *Id.*
41 *Id.*
42 *Id.*
43 *Id.* at 22.
44 NCB CAPITAL, *supra* note 30, at 7.
45 *Id.* at 2.
46 *Id.*
47 *Id.* at 26.

There are many restrictions dealing with debt in Islam as a religion. The first important restriction imposed by Islamic law is the prohibition of usury. Usury is issuing debt or a loan, and collecting it back at a premium. Usury is completely forbidden in Islam.[48] Many scholars and experts try to find solutions for Islamic banks in order to avoid usury and make the transactions comply with *Shariah*.[49] This compromise is how *sukuk*, the Islamic version of bonds, was created.[50] This Islamic debt instrument significantly changed the Islamic capital market. In the last ten years, many *sukuk* were issued. It raised the volume of alternative investments in the Islamic capital market.

Though many GCC governments and companies issue *sukuk* as alternative instruments to avoid usury, the secondary market is still illiquid and *sukuk* trading is not as attractive as trading in the equity market. The second rule, the non-negotiability of debt, is the reason for this problem.

1.4 Does Islamic Law Forbid Trading and Negotiating Debts?

Many current Islamic finance scholars assert that it is violative of Islamic law for Muslims to buy or sell any kind of debt in the secondary market. For example, if a company has an account receivable on its balance sheet, it cannot sell this account to a third party. The argument is that debt is non-tradable and non-negotiable according to Islamic law. If an investor holds a debt security in the capital market, he is not allowed to trade this debt on the secondary market because once again these scholars say it is forbidden under Islamic law.

Experts in Islamic finance acknowledge that the prohibition of trading debt is a major hurdle to the development of the Islamic debt market and an obstacle to the existence of the secondary debt market. However, there are few papers and articles that criticize the non-negotiability of debts economically or legally, because it is thought to be a religious principle and cannot be disputed. Debt is approached the same way as usury.

Professor Frank Vogel (former member of Harvard Law School faculty, now an independent scholar and legal consultant in Islamic law)[51] wrote a book in 1998 with Professor Samuel Hayes entitled *Islamic Law and Finance: Religion,*

---

48 See section 2, *Overview of Some Islamic Law and Finance Principles and Concepts*.
49 These scholars who found solutions to avoid usury focus on formalities rather than substantives. In contrast, some scholars who are considering substantives rather than formalities are against Islamic finance industry generally and believe that most of Islamic finance transactions are prohibited. *See* SALEH ALHOSAYYEN, ISLAMIC BANKS, PROS AND CONS (2009).
50 See section 2, *Overview of Some Islamic Law and Finance Principles and Concepts*.
51 Frank E. Vogel, *at* http://frankevogel.net.

Risk and Return. In this book he states, "One almost indispensable resource for accomplishing [the development of Islamic finance] is a secondary market capable of providing acceptable liquidity for investors. There is much debate about what kinds of investments can be traded in a secondary market. Islamic law forbids the sale or trade of financial contracts, which explains why financing of accounts receivable is difficult. On the other hand if a contract or security represents a direct claim on a real asset, it may be sold or traded."[52]

M. Kabir Hassan is a Professor in the Department of Economics and Finance at The University of New Orleans in Louisiana, and the editor of The Global Journal of Finance and Economics.[53] In his paper, "Islamic banking: an introduction and overview," he states that, "For many years Islamic banks were hampered in liquidity management by the absence of an equivalent infrastructure [to conventional bank]. Islamic law has restrictions on the sale of debt that inhibit *Shariah* acceptable secondary markets."[54] In very broad terms, he explains that a secondary market in Islamic finance is not permitted under *Shariah* law.

Ridha Saadallah is a Professor of Economics at the University of Sfax in Tunisia. He previously worked with the Islamic Research and Training Institute of the Islamic Development Bank.[55] He states, "There is a general agreement among the jurists that the sale of debt is not allowed. The rationale usually given for this position is that the sale of debt involves *riba* (interest) as well as *gharar* (excessive uncertainty) both of which are prohibited by the *Shariah*".[56] He indicates that all Islamic scholars adhere to the prohibition of the sale of debt, which causes the illiquid secondary market. A reader with no background in Islamic jurisprudence will believe that trading debt is forbidden in Islamic law because Islamic law forbids usury.

Mohammed Alamin is an expert in Islamic finance and currently the head of the *Shariah* Complaint Department at Unicorn Investment Bank in Bahrain. In his book *Global Sukuk and Islamic Securitization Market*, he has surrendered to that common impression. He says, "Any Islamic debt market will be

---

52 FRANK E. VOGEL & SAMUEL L. HAYES, ISLAMIC LAW AND FINANCE: RELIGION, RISK, AND RETURN 13 (Kluwer Law International 1998).
53 *Contributors* to HANDBOOK OF ISLAMIC BANKING at xi (Kabir Hassan & Mervyn Lewis eds., Edward Elgar 2007).
54 Kabir Hassan & Mervyn Lewis, *Islamic banking: an introduction and overview, in* HANDBOOK OF ISLAMIC BANKING 1, 6 (Kabir Hassan & Mervyn Lewis eds., Edward Elgar 2007).
55 *Id.*
56 Ridha Saadallah, *Trade financing in Islam, in* HANDBOOK OF ISLAMIC BANKING 172, 188 (Kabir Hassan & Mervyn Lewis eds., Edward Elgar 2007).

smaller than the conventional in terms of size. This is based on the *Shariah* principles that prohibit the sale of debts for debt, the non-permissibility to securitize receivables or the *Shariah* insistence in relating debt market to the real economy."[57] He wrote an entire book on his belief that the debt market is significant, and *sukuk* is a smart solution to avoid usury; however, he got stuck on the principle in Islamic law of forbidding the trade of debts.

1.5 Contribution

The goals of this article are to challenge the notion that Islamic law forbids trading debt, and to assert that trading debt is permissible under Islamic law. This article does not claim that 1,400 years of Islamic scholars misunderstood Islamic law. This article offers the perspective that trading debt and financial contract is permissible and consistent with Islamic jurisprudence and Islamic schools of legal thought. In addition, it will distinguish and emphasize the differences between usury and negotiating debt. It will analyze the history of how this idea became a belief and why no one has challenged it. This article establishes new views regarding the negotiability of debt in Islamic finance based on Islamic law sources and methodologies.

This is particularly significant for Western Islamic financial specialists. These specialists do not have direct access to Islamic jurisprudence because of language barriers, terminology, and methodology. This article hopes to remove those obstacles, and provide a new Islamic legal interpretation to Islamic finance specialists with Western legal and financial backgrounds.

Section 2 provides an overview of Islamic law concepts that are important for understanding the explanations and discussions in this article. In addition, Section 2 clarifies the Islamic methodologies and sources necessary to understand the legal basis for permitting debt trade in Islamic law.

Section 3 explains the position of each school of Islamic legal thought on trading debt. Additionally, the differing positions of contemporary Islamic scholars and Islamic law schools will be explored. The resolutions adopted by these organizations, and the negative effects of the resolutions will be analyzed and explained.

Section 4 is the heart of this article. It explains and criticizes the arguments of contemporary Islamic scholars who forbid the trading of debt. It then proposes a new rule, consistent with Islamic fundamentals and principles, which establishes the permissibility of debt trade in Islamic finance.

---

57 Muhammad al-Bashir & Muhammad al-Amine, Global Sukūk and Islamic Securitization Market: Financial Engineering and Product Innovation 29 (Brill 2012).

The views of this article are contrary to the majority; however, it is critical to remove this significant hurdle so the economies of Muslim countries, and Islamic finance in particular, can continue to develop. This article does not intend to challenge Islam as a religion. It challenges an idea that is thought to be a main principle in Islamic finance. Change takes time, but the first step is to change thoughts, ideas, and minds. This article aspires to be the first step to a global change in the Islamic debt market.

Section 2: Overview of Some Islamic Law and Finance Principles and Concepts

The main purpose of this Section is to provide an overview of the principles of Islamic law and finance that are critical to understand the arguments of Islamic scholars regarding the tradability of debts. These principles are also important to evaluate, analyze, and criticize these scholarly arguments.

The first part of this Section is an overview of Islamic law sources, from which Islamic scholars derive Islamic rules. It describes some methodologies that Islamic scholars use to decide if a legal issue falls under Islamic law and whether a legal issue is allowed or forbidden according to Islamic rules.

The second part of this Section clarifies that there are many schools of legal thought under Islamic jurisprudence. Therefore, Islamic scholars often have different opinions regarding each legal issue based on the school of legal thought that he or she belongs to. The negotiability of debt is one of these issues that Islamic schools of legal thought maintain different positions.

The third part explains Islamic finance principles. These principles, *riba* (usury) and *gharar* (uncertainty), control significant legal issues related to finance and commerce, such as the negotiability of debt.

Finally, the fourth part illustrates some transactions that are used commonly in modern Islamic finance, but not in conventional finance. These Islamic commercial transactions are used to avoid usury and uncertainty in modern finance.

2.1   *Islamic Law Sources*

Generally, scholars divide Islamic law sources into two types. The first type consists of divine sources, or primary sources. They are called divine sources because they are from God and the prophet Mohammed. Muslims are obligated to obey these sources.[58] They are also called primary sources because Islamic scholars must attempt to base provisions and rules on these sources

---

58   SHAH ABDUL HANNAN, USUL AL FIQH (ISLAMIC JURISPRUDENCE) 6 (1999).

first.[59] If the provision or rule cannot be based on the primary source then secondary sources are used. Thus, the second type is non-divine sources, or secondary sources.. These are non-divine because they are man-made. They are called secondary because they are used if primary sources are not available.[60] The primary sources are the Quran and the Sunnah.[61] The secondary sources are the Ijma and the Ijtihad.[62] The following section explains all these sources in Islamic law.

2.1.1 Quran

The Quran is the first and the most important source of Islamic law. Muslims define the Quran as "the book, which Allah (God) revealed in his speech to his prophet Muhammad in Arabic, and this has been transmitted to us by continuous testimony"[63] and "which is written between the two covers of the Holy Book."[64]

The Quran constitutes 114 unequal chapters (*Surah*). Each *Surah* contains several parts (*Ayah*).[65] These Ayahs are not equal, either. Some *Ayahs* have 100 words: some only have one.[66]

The Quran was revealed gradually over time.[67] It took twenty-three years to complete the whole revelation. This period is divided into two parts. The first thirteen years is the Makkah part. The prophet Mohammed was in Makkah and lived with non-Muslim Arabs. The next ten years is the Madinah part. The prophet Mohammed moved to Madinah and established the first Islamic state.[68]

The larger part of the Quran was revealed in Makkah, the rest in Madinah. Because Muslims in Makkah lived with non-Muslims, the Makkah part, "mostly deals with beliefs, disputation with unbelievers and their invitation to Islam...."[69] The Madinah part deals more with legal subjects, because Muslims

---

59 *Id.*
60 *Id.*
61 These will be explained later in this part.
62 These will be explained later in this part.
63 ABDUL HANNAN, *supra* note 1, at 6.
64 ṬĀHĀ JĀBIR FAYYĀḌ 'ALWĀNĪ, SOURCE METHODOLOGY IN ISLAMIC JURISPRUDENCE: UṢŪL AL FIQH AL ISLĀMĪ 7 (New rev. English ed. 1994).
65 ABDUL HANNAN, *supra* note 1, at 6.
66 General Knowledge of Holy Quran, *at* http://www.qurannetwork.com/quraninfo.html (The Quran has 6,235 Ayahs, and 77,439 words).
67 *Id.*
68 MOHAMMAD HASHIM KAMALI, PRINCIPLES OF ISLAMIC JURISPRUDENCE 20 (3rd rev. and enlarged ed. 2003).
69 ABDUL HANNAN, *supra* note 1, at 6.

had their own state at that time. Further, the Madinah part deals with legal rules regarding family, society, politics, economics, etc.[70]

The legal material of the Quran is contained in about 500 Ayahs[71] (only 8% of the Ayahs in Quran). These Ayahs were revealed "with the aim of repealing objectionable customs such as infanticide, usury, gambling, and unlimited polygamy."[72] Some Ayahs enforce types of worship to Allah, such as prayer and fasting. Other Ayahs deal with charities, oaths, marriage, divorce, custody of children, fosterage, paternity, inheritance, bequest, relationships between rich and poor, and justice.[73]

Legal Ayahs are limited compared with other subjects and cover various legal fields. They are usually brief with little detail or explanation. For example, prayer, which is the most important worship in Islam, is enforced by three words, "establish regular prayer."[74] Details, such as how to pray and how many times, are not described. Additionally, usury is clearly forbidden in the Quran: "Allah hath permitted trade and forbidden usury."[75] However, the definition of usury, or how Muslims can recognize usury, or how to distinguish between trade and usury is not explained in the Quran. Other sources are needed to derive Islamic rules and provisions, which are not expressed in the Quran. The most important source in Islamic jurisprudence, after the Quran, is the statements of Prophet Mohammed (Sunnah).

2.1.2 Sunnah

Sunnah is the second most important source of Islamic law. The literal meaning in Arabic is "beaten track" or "established course of conduct."[76] According to Islamic scholars, "Sunnah refers to all that is narrated from the Prophet Mohammed, his acts, his sayings and whatever he tacitly approved."[77] Sometimes, the word *Hadith* is used instead of Sunnah. Sunnah and *Hadith* have become synonymous, meaning "conduct of the prophet."[78] Sunnah, however, is usually used for the source in general and *hadith* is used for each single text.

---

70   YAHAYA YUNUSA BAMBALE, AN OUTLINE OF ISLAMIC JURISPRUDENCE 52 (2007).
71   ABDUL HANNAN, *supra* note 1, at 6.
72   *Id.*
73   C. G. WEERAMANTRY, ISLAMIC JURISPRUDENCE: AN INTERNATIONAL PERSPECTIVE 32 (1988).
74   Quran (24:56).
75   Quran (2:275).
76   KAMALI, *supra* note 11, at 58.
77   ABDUL HANNAN, *supra* note 1, at 8.
78   KAMALI, *supra* note 11, at 61.

Islamic scholars classify Sunnah into legal Sunnah and non-legal Sunnah.[79] Legal Sunnah consists of "the prophetic activities and instructions of the prophet as the head of the state and as judge."[80] Non-legal Sunnah "consists of the natural activities of the prophet, such as the manner in which he ate, slept, dressed and such other activities which do not form a part of *Shariah*."[81]

To avoid confusion with the Quran, there was no attempt to record the Sunnah during the lifetime of the prophet Mohammed.[82] About a century after the prophet's death, scholars began collecting and classifying hadiths.[83] Due to the length of this period, scholars should examine these hadiths to be sure they acutally came from the prophet Mohammed. Before the *hadith* were recorded, they were classified into strong and weak.[84] To classify a *hadith* as strong or weak, Islamic scholars trace the provenances of each *hadith* based on an historical prospective. Specifically, Islamic scholars examine all narrators and determine whether or not they are honest and trustworthy. A *hadith* is classified as strong if "it is reported by highly trustworthy or by trustworthy narrator."[85] For example, if a *hadith* was heard directly from the prophet by Ibn Omar (first generation) then Omar told the *hadith* to Nafe (second generation) and finally Imam Malik (third generation) reported the *hadith* in his book, this *hadith* is classified as strong because all reporters are trustworthy according to Islamic scholars historical tracing. On the other hand, a *hadith* is considered weak if one of the reporters is unknown in terms of identity or conduct, a violator of any important practice, or a liar.[86] Strong hadiths are legitimate sources of Islamic law while weak hadiths may not be legitimate sources.[87]

The total number of all hadiths is 11,830.[88] Only 4,400 hadiths are considered strong while the rest are classified as weak.[89] Most hadiths are statements of the prophet. Not all hadiths are legal Sunnah. Some scholars say that there are only 2,000 hadiths that are considered legal Sunnah.[90]

---

79   KAMALI, *supra* note 11, at 110; ABDUL HANNAN, *supra* note 1, at 8.
80   ABDUL HANNAN, *supra* note 1, at 8.
81   Id.
82   WEERAMANTRY, *supra* note 16, at 35.
83   Id.
84   KAMALI, *supra* note 11, at 110.
85   ABDUL HANNAN, *supra* note 1, at 10.
86   Id.
87   KAMALI, *supra* note 11, at 111.
88   Mohammed Alamin, HADITH NUMBER MOHAMMED ALAMIN ARTICLES, *at* http://www.ibnamin.com/.
89   Id.
90   Id.

The Sunnah generally emphasizes details and explains broad topics in the Quran.[91] For example, while the Quran simply says to pray, the Sunnah explains in detail how to pray and how many times Muslims must pray. The Sunnah also explains the concept of usury. It divides usury into many kinds, and distinguishes them. While the Quran merely states that usury is forbidden.

2.1.3   Ijma (Unanimity)

Ijma is the third source of Islamic law. The classical understanding of ijma is "the general [unanimity] among Islamic scholars of a particular age in relation to the legal rule correctly applicable to the situation."[92] Simply put, all the Islamic scholars of one age must have the same opinion regarding a specific legal matter. Unanimity of Islamic scholars on an issue of a particular time is a requirement of ijma, and "the agreement must be expressed by clear opinion of all scholars of the time."[93] According to early Islamic scholars, "only such ijma are considered binding."[94] If there is only a majority opinion, it is not binding.

Islamic scholars use ijma as a limited source for Islamic rules, because "it is extremely difficult to prove."[95] Of course it is difficult to prove that all Islamic scholars in the world have the same opinion on a particular issue. It is even more difficult if there is no text from the Quran or the Sunnah regarding this issue. Usually, provisions that are proven by ijma are also proven by the Quran and the Sunnah. For example, there is unanimity on prayer, fasting, Islamic tax (Zakat), pilgrimage, stealing, killing, etc. These issues are all proven by the Quran and the Sunnah, not only by ijma. On topics without supporting text from the Quran or the Sunnah, there are differing opinions.

2.1.4   Ijtihad (Personal Reasoning)

Practically, Ijtihad is a very important source of Islamic law after the Quran and the Sunnah.[96] The main difference between ijtihad and the revealed sources of *Shariah* is "the fact the ijtihad is a continuous process of development whereas divine revelation and prophetic legislation discontinues after the demise of the prophet."[97] Ijtihad is the main instrument of interpretation

---

91   KAMALI, *supra* note 11, at 78.
92   WEERAMANTRY, *supra* note 16, at 39.
93   ABDUL HANNAN, *supra* note 1, at 19.
94   *Id.*
95   *Id.*
96   KAMALI, *supra* note 11, at 468.
97   *Id.* at 468.

of Islam as a religion, relating it to the changing conditions of real life.[98] Ijtihad is "the methodology which gives Islamic law its adaptability to new situations and capacity to tackle all new issues and problems."[99]

Ijtihad is based completely on personal reasoning. There is no revelation from God to correct the reasoning a scholar uses to deduce an Islamic rule or provision. Therefore, Islamic scholars over the centuries have tried to find methodologies to organize Islamic reasoning. These methodologies help Islamic scholars to derive Islamic rules and provisions if there is no text from the Quran or the Sunnah.[100] The rules derived through ijtihad methodologies are not on the same level of authority as that of the Quran or Sunnah.[101] There is room for differences of opinions. No scholar believes he is the only one who is right.[102] Many methodologies may be used if there is no text from the Quran and the Sunnah, such as *qiyas, maslahah,* and istashab.

1. Qiyas (analogical reasoning): *Qiyas* is a "comparison to establish equality or similarity between two things."[103] Technically, *qiyas* is "the extension of a *Shariah* ruling from an original case to a new case because the new case has the same effective cause as the original case."[104] The original case is regulated by a text of the Quran or the Sunnah. *Qiyas* "seeks to extend the original ruling to the new case."[105] Generally, "the emphasis of *qiyas* is identification of a common cause between the original and new case."[106] For example, the Quran and the Sunnah forbid liquor (the original case). The reason is that liquor is an intoxicant (the effective cause). Islamic scholars extend the provision of the original case (prohibition) to wines (the new case) because they have the same effect (intoxicating).[107]

2. Maslahah (public interest): *Maslahah* literally means benefit or interest.[108] Islamic rules are made in the public's interest, especially in regards to protection of life, religion, intellect, lineage, and property.[109] Practically, "when law cannot be made on the basis of Quran and Sunnah or through *qiyas*, law is

---

98 *Id.*
99 ABDUL HANNAN, *supra* note 1, at 36.
100 *Id.*
101 *Id.*
102 *Id.*
103 BAMBALE, *supra* note 13, at 72.
104 ABDUL HANNAN, *supra* note 1, at 20.
105 KAMALI, *supra* note 11, at 264.
106 *Id.*
107 KAMALI, *supra* note 11, at 268.
108 *Id.* at 351.
109 BAMBALE, *supra* note 13, at 83.

made on the basis of *maslahah* or public interest."¹¹⁰ For example, prisons are not mentioned in the Quran as punishment and were not used by the prophet Mohammed when he ruled the Islamic state. However, when the Islamic empire was growing, the rulers of the empire established prisons to punish criminals as other states and empires were doing at that time. The prisons were in the public interest.¹¹¹

3. **Istishab (presumption of continuity):** *Istishab* means "those facts or rules of law and reason, whose existence or non-existence have been proven in the past and which are presumed to remain so far for lack of evidence to establish any change."¹¹² One kind of *istishab* is the presumption of original absence.¹¹³ Original absence is "a fact or rule which had not existed in the past and is presumed to be non-existent."¹¹⁴ Thus, if there is no rule to forbid eating some kinds of foods, such as an avocado (previously unknown in Arab lands), scholars should continue presuming that eating avocado is not forbidden. It should be allowed based on the presumption of original absence.

2.2   The Islamic Schools of Legal Thought

The textual sources in Islam (Quran and Sunnah) are limited. Most Islamic rules are based on personal reasoning (*ijtihad*), which is a completely human source. As a result, during former centuries of the Islamic empire,¹¹⁵ many schools of legal thought were developed.¹¹⁶

These schools of law are important in Islamic law because "the absence in Islam of council like the councils of the early Christian Church or Buddhism,

---

110   ABDUL HANNAN, *supra* note 1, at 27.
111   *Id.*
112   KAMALI, *supra* note 11, at 384.
113   ABDUL HANNAN, *supra* note 1, at 30.
114   *Id.*
115   *See* WEERAMANTRY, *supra* note 16, at 47 (There is a division in Islam between Sunnis and Shiites. The vast majority of Muslims are Sunni. Shiites constitute 10–15% of the Muslim population (*see* Mapping the Global Muslim Population, *at* http://www.pewforum.org/2009/10/07/mapping-the-global-muslim-population/). Political disputes cause the division. After the Prophet died, Shiites did not recognize the legitimacy of the three Caliphs: Abu Bakr, Omar, and Othman. They recognized only the legitimacy of the fourth Caliph, Ali. In addition, the Shiites believe the Islamic empire from Caliph Ali until Ottoman Empire is illegitimate. On the other hand, Sunnis recognize the legitimacy of all four Caliphs and the whole Islamic empire. The Shiites are isolated and have their own traditions and literature. The four Islamic schools discussed in this chapter are Sunnis. They developed and spread under the rule of the Islamic empire all during history).
116   THE ISLAMIC SCHOOL OF LAW: EVOLUTION, DEVOLUTION, AND PROGRESS 2 (Peri J. Bearman, Rudolph Peters, & Frank E. Vogel eds., Harvard University Press 2005).

wherein doctrinal pronouncements were made with authority, the development of law [in Islam] was thus naturally steered in the direction of juristic activity rather than toward authoritative religious pronouncements."[117] Another important factor is "the absence of a formal priesthood or clergy, [since] the hierarchical structure of the Christian priesthood and the rigid rules of training preceding admission to its ranks had no counterpart in Islam."[118]

These schools evolved in the second and the third centuries of Islam and adopted the Islamic sources and methodologies described above.[119] Their interpretations are not binding.[120] If a judge or a ruler chooses one of their opinions, it is binding as a rule of state, not a rule of God.[121] They are four schools: Hanafi,[122] Maliki,[123] Shafi,[124] and Hanbali.[125]

All schools agree on the principals of Islam (such as praying, fasting, etc.) and the sources of Islamic law (Quran, Sunnah, ijma, and ijtihad). The schools differ in the interpretation of the Quran, the Sunna, and methodologies regarding ijtihad. The Hanafi School is described as the most rational.[126] It is very

---

117 WEERAMANTRY, *supra* note 16, at 46.
118 *Id.*
119 *Id.*
120 THE ISLAMIC SCHOOL OF LAW: EVOLUTION, DEVOLUTION, AND PROGRESS, *supra* note 59, at 148.
121 *Id.*
122 NURIT TSAFRIR, THE HISTORY OF AN ISLAMIC SCHOOL OF LAW: THE EARLY SPREAD OF HANAFISM x (Harvard University Press 2004) (This is the first and earliest school formed by Abu Hanifa (699–767 AD) in Iraq. Abu Hanifa did not write any books on law himself, but his followers recorded his discussions and opinions, which were the basis of this school.
123 THE ISLAMIC SCHOOL OF LAW: EVOLUTION, DEVOLUTION, AND PROGRESS, *supra* note 59, at 41 (The second school of law was founded by Malik bin Anas (d. 795 AD) in Madinah. Malik was a famous scholar at that time. He gathered all his opinions in a book called al-Muwatta (the Leveled Path). This is the basis of the Maliki School. His followers explained, detailed, and added to his book to establish a deep and thoughtful school).
124 The third school was founded by Imam al-Shafi (d. 820 AD). He was originally a follower of Imam Malik, but he later moved to Egypt and established his own school of thought. Imam Shafi wrote the first book on Islamic methodology (Alresalah). He was "a great thinker, had an unusual grasp of principles, and a clear understanding of the judicial problems." Understand-Islam.Org (2009).
125 The fourth school was founded by Imam Ahmad bin Hanbal (d. 855 AD) in Baghdad. Imam Hanbal "did not establish a separate school himself; this was rather done by his disciples and followers." Understand-Islam.Org (2009).
126 George Makdisi, *The Significance of the Sunni Schools of Law in Islamic Religious History*, 10 INT'L J. OF MIDDLE EAST STUD. 1, 3 (1979).

conservative in regards to which hadiths to accept as a source of law. Many hadiths are refused because they are believed to be weak. Hanafi relies heavily on *qiyas* methodology. If there is conflict between a *hadith* and *qiyas*, the Hanafi School sometimes prefers *qiyas* methodology over the *hadith*.[127] The Hanbali School is the most traditional school.[128] It relies heavily on hadiths and traditions. The Hanbali School prefers weak hadiths rather than *qiyas*.[129] The Maliki and the Shafi schools are somewhere in between the Hanbali and the Hanafi.

Sometimes a school has its own methodology. The Hanafi School has *istihsan*, which is "a method of exercising personal opinion in order to avoid any rigidity and unfairness that might result from the literal enforcement of the existing law."[130] The other three schools reject this methodology for being too broad and for possibily undermining traditions. The Maliki School has "the transmitted legal practice of Madinah people"[131] methodology. Since the Prophet lived in Madinah for the last ten years of his life and died there, "a whole generation was able to transmit from a whole generation who had been alive at the time of the Prophet."[132] Thus, Imam Malik relied on the religious practice of Madinah people because he believed it is transmitted from the practice of the Prophet himself. The other three schools reject this methodology, because the companions of the Prophet spread out after his death and not all of them lived in Madinah. This methodology is paramount in the Maliki School as it bases many of its arguments on this methodology.[133]

These differing methodologies have produced a large volume of Islamic jurisprudence literature. There is a debate among the Islamic schools of law on each legal issue. The negotiability of debt is one of the issues on which the Islamic schools have differed. I will explain the various opinions regarding the negotiability and tradability of debt in Islamic law in Section 3.

---

127   Diana Zacharias, *Fundamentals of the Sunnī Schools of Law*, 66 HEIDELBERG J. OF INT'L LAW 491, 495 (2006).
128   Makdisi, *supra* note 69, at 3.
129   Zacharias, *supra* note 70, at 504.
130   KAMALI, *supra* note 11, at 218.
131   *Id.*
132   YASIN DUTTON, THE ORIGINS OF ISLAMIC LAW: THE QUR'AN, THE MUWATTA' AND MADINAN AMAL (CULTURE AND CIVILIZATION IN THE MIDDLE EAST) 61 (Ian R. Netton ed., Curzon Press 1999).
133   Zacharias, *supra* note 70, at 497.

2.3 *Islamic Finance Principles*

In general, Islamic finance is "a prohibition-driven industry."[134] In other words, Islamic law is based on what is prohibited in the Islamic law sources. Thus, bankers and specialists create contracts and engage in transactions that do not include any of the prohibitions. "The instigating factor for prohibition-based contract invalidation can almost always be attributed to the two factors labeled *riba* and *gharar*."[135] Understanding *riba* (usury) and *gharar* (uncertainty) is necessary to comprehend why scholars forbid the negotiability of debt in the current Islamic financial market.

2.3.1 Riba (Usury)

Riba is a grievous sin in Islam. The Quran "vehemently condemns *riba*"[136] in several Ayahs: "O you who have believed, do not consume usury, doubled and multiplied, but fear Allah that you may be successful"[137][;] "Allah has permitted trade and has forbidden interest"[138][;] "O you who have believed, fear Allah and give up what remains [due to you] of interest, if you should be believers. And if you do not, then be informed of a war [against you] from Allah and his messenger."[139] Though the Quran forbids *riba* in several Ayahs, the Quran does not provide a comprehensive explanation of what constitutes *riba*.[140] Interpreters of the Quran define *riba* as "a pre-Islamic practice of extending delay to debtors in return for an increase in the principal."[141] Because this practice existed during the record of revelation, it is the only kind of usury the Quran explicitly forbids.[142] Ibn Hanbal, the founder of the Hanbali School, stated, "this practice (pay or increase) is the only form of *riba*, the prohibition of which is beyond any doubt."[143]

Islamic scholars rely on the Sunnah to define and explain usury. Two main hadiths clarify the rule of *riba*: "Gold for gold, silver for silver, wheat for wheat, barley for barley, dates for dates, and salt for salt, like for like, hand to hand, and any

---

134 Mahmoud A. El-Gamal, Islamic Finance: Law, Economics, and Practice 46 (Cambridge University Press 2006).
135 *Id.*
136 Frank E. Vogel & Samuel L. Hayes, Islamic Law and Finance: Religion, Risk, and Return 72 (Kluwer Law International 1998).
137 Quran (3:130).
138 Quran (2:275).
139 Quran (2:279).
140 Vogel & Hayes, *supra* note 79, at 72.
141 *Id.* at 73.
142 *Id.*
143 *Id.*

increase is *riba*"[144] and "every loan that attracts a benefit is *riba*."[145] Accordingly, Islamic scholars classify *riba* into two kinds: *riba* in sales and *riba* in loans.

2.3.1.1 Riba in Sales

Generally, *riba* is interpreted as "a prohibition of interest charged on loans."[146] This is an oversimplified concept, because "the concept of *riba* applies to more than loans, it applies equally to all transactions be they loan or sales."[147] The first *hadith*, "gold for gold", shows that "the actual reach of the *riba* prohibition goes beyond compensation for lending money."[148] The *hadith* establishes two rules, "that certain goods can be exchanged for each other as long as exchange is present barter. Exchange of goods within a single type is permitted only in equal amounts."[149] The first rule prohibits "all sales within a single type with inequality, with or without delay (*riba* al fadl)."[150] The second rule prohibits "all exchanges with delay among the listed goods with or without equality or identity of type (*riba* alnasia, *riba* of delay)."[151] The *riba* alnasia seems to forbid delayed sales of any of these goods for gold or silver, however, there are other hadiths that prove the prophet purchased on credit, so "delay sales are permitted as long as currency is only one of two considerations."[152]

Although the *hadith* only mentions six kinds of goods (gold, silver, wheat, barley, dates, and salt) Islamic scholars apply the rule to other goods using qiyas[153] (analogy) as a source of Islamic law. The rule is not restricted to these six kinds of goods.[154] Islamic scholars believe these goods were specifically mentioned in the *hadith* because they were the common goods at that time.[155] Hanafi and Hanbali scholars "extended the prohibition to all fungible goods measured by weight or volume, whereas Shafi and Maliki jurists restricted it to monetary commodities (gold and silver) and storable foodstuffs."[156]

---

144 See EL-GAMAL, *supra* note 77, at 50 (Reported by Muslim on the authority of Abu Said Al-Khudriy).
145 See VOGEL & HAYES, *supra* note 79, at 73 (Nail Alwtar).
146 MAHA-HANAAN BALALA, ISLAMIC FINANCE AND LAW: THEORY AND PRACTICE IN A GLOBALIZED WORLD 62 (Tauris Academic Studies 2011) (2010).
147 *Id.*
148 VOGEL & HAYES, *supra* note 79, at 74.
149 *Id.*
150 *Id.*
151 *Id.*
152 *Id.*
153 See page 27.
154 EL-GAMAL, *supra* note 77, at 51.
155 *Id.*
156 *Id.*

A farmer has 100 kg of dates. He wants to sell them to another farmer who has a different kind of dates. The transaction must be in the present, with the same amount of dates (100 kg). What if one party has superior dates and the other party has inferior ones? They want to trade the dates. Must the quantity be equal? According to the rule established by the *hadith*, they must be equal. When approached about this case, the prophet Mohammed said to "[sell] the dates at the best possible market price followed by the procuring of superior dates with the monetary proceeds thereof, this being the most equitable and efficient means to attain the same intended outcome."[157] It is critical to "note that the prophet did not disapprove of the gain made in the exchange of dates but merely of the fact that superior dates were exchanged for inferior dates without impliedly an objective yardstick to assure an equitable exchange."[158]

The meaning and the application of *riba* al fadl may be better understood in light of its context, a barter economy.[159] Economically, *riba* al fadl has "little to do with every day commercial loans and much to do with the encouragement towards engaging in equitable and efficient commercial transactions, which the [*hadith*] exemplifies through an exchange of like for like, equal for equal or alternatively selling the commodity for cash at the best market price and thereafter buying with the cash any other commodity at market price."[160] Further, the *hadith* "[does] not stipulate a fair price or specific price [at] which the buying and selling ought to take place, and leaves such price to be determined by the parties in implied recognition of the inherent equity in mutual consent and the market forces of supply and demand competition."[161]

2.3.1.2   *Riba in Loans*

The most important *hadith* in the modern economy is that every loan that is associated with a benefit is *riba*.[162] The word loan in the *hadith* means "the loan of fungible [assets] including money."[163] "Benefit" in the *hadith* "includes interest on a money loan."[164] This kind of *riba* includes "a pre-Islamic practice

---

157   BALALA, *supra* note 89, at 75.
158   *Id.*
159   *Id.* at 73.
160   *Id.*
161   *Id.*
162   VOGEL & HAYES, *supra* note 79, at 77.
163   *Id.*
164   *Id.*

of extending delay to debtors in return for an increase in the principal...."[165] This practice is banned in the Quran. Many Westerners think *riba* is limited to this kind of transaction, however, that is a misunderstanding of *riba*. Most Islamic jurisprudence is about *riba* in sales, which is used to forbid the sale of debts.

2.3.2 Gharar (Uncertainty or Speculative Risk)

Gharar is the second most important principle in Islamic finance. The Quran only condemns one kind of *gharar*, which is gambling.[166] The Sunnah forbids *gharar* in general, but does not provide a clear definition. It does mention some kinds of *gharar* transactions that clarify the meaning of *gharar*. "The prophet forbade the sale of the pebble and the sale of *Gharar*." "[D]o not buy fish in the sea, for its [sic] *Gharar*." "[T]he prophet forbade the sale of what is in the wombs, the sale of the contents of the udder... the prophet forbade the sale of grapes until they become black, and the sale of grain until it is strong."[167] From these hadiths, Islamic scholars derive a definition of *gharar*. Professor Mustafa Al-Zarqa defines *gharar* as "the sale of probable items whose existence or characteristics are not certain, the risky nature of which makes the transaction akin to gambling."[168]

Most businesses contain some level of risk. Forbidding *gharar* does not mean forbidding all kinds of risks. Professor El-Gamal says, "*gharar* encompasses some forms of incomplete information and/or deception, as well as risk and uncertainty intrinsic to the objects of contract."[169]

Islamic scholars distinguish between major *gharar* and minor *gharar*. Major *gharar* invalidates commercial contracts while minor *gharar* does not.[170] Professor Al-Darir also distinguishes major *gharar* from minor *gharar*. According to his research, there are four conditions for major *gharar* that invalidate a contract:[171]

---

165 *Id.* at 73.
166 (2:219).
167 VOGEL & HAYES, *supra* note 79, at 88.
168 EL-GAMAL, *supra* note 77, at 58.
169 *Id.*
170 BALALA, *supra* note 89, at 40.
171 AL-SADDIQ MUHAMMAD AL-AMIN DARIR, AL-*GHARAR* IN CONTRACTS AND ITS EFFECTS ON CONTEMPORARY TRANSACTIONS page number (Islamic Research and Training Institute 1997).

1. The first condition is that *"gharar* must be excessive to invalidate a contract…,"[172] minor uncertainty about an object of sale does not affect the contract."[173] For example, if a buyer wants to purchase 1000 kg of dates, and the seller provides approximately 1000 kg (the seller knows there is no less than 950 kg and no more than 1050 kg), the contract will be valid. However, if the seller does not know if there is 500 kg or 1000 kg, then it is considered major *gharar* and the contract is invalid.
2. The second condition is that the contract itself "must be a commutative financial contract,"[174] such as selling, leasing, etc. Accordingly, "giving a gift that is randomly determined (e.g., the catch of a diver) is valid, whereas selling the same item would be deemed invalid based on *gharar*."[175]
3. The third condition is that the *gharar* "must affect the principal components"[176] of the contract, such as consideration or goods, in order to invalidate the transaction. For example, if an owner sells a car without determining the price, the contract would be invalid because it contains major *gharar*. It is major *gharar* since the price is unknown and it is a principal component of the contract. If the price and the car are determined, but the service agreement after the purchase is not determined, then the contract is valid.
4. The final condition is "if the commutative contract containing excessive *gharar* meets a need that cannot be met otherwise, the contract would not be deemed invalid based on that *gharar*."[177] For example, the prophet Mohammed and Muslims were dealing with *salam* (advance purchase).[178] *Salam* is "a sale whereby the seller undertakes to provide some specific commodities to the buyer at a future date for an advance, mutually agreed price paid in full."[179] Therefore, "the object of sale does not exist at contract inception…."[180] This is major *gharar*. "[T]hat contract allows

---

172 EL-GAMAL, *supra* note 77, at 58.
173 *Id.*
174 *Id.*
175 *Id.*
176 *Id.*
177 *Id.* at 59.
178 VOGEL & HAYES, *supra* note 79, at 145.
179 Humayon, A. Dar, *Incentive compatability of Islamic Banking*, in HANDBOOK OF ISLAMIC BANKING, 85, 94 (Kabir Hassan & Mervyn Lewis eds., Edward Elgar 2007).
180 EL-GAMAL, *supra* note 77, at 59.

financing of agricultural and industrial activities that cannot be financed otherwise, it is allowed despite that *gharar*."[181]

Islamic scholars agree on the general principles and conditions of *gharar*. The details and application of these general principles and conditions to particular transactions are where different viewpoints emerge.[182]

Economically, *gharar* is forbidden in Islam "to ensure full consent and satisfaction of the parties in a contract...."[183] Islamic financial law requires "full disclosure and transparency and [sic] through perfect knowledge from contracting parties of the counter values intended to be exchanged."[184] The prohibition of *gharar* "protects against unexpected losses and the possible disagreements regarding qualities or incompleteness of information."[185] Accordingly, "all Islamic financial and business transactions must be based on transparency, accuracy, and disclosure of all necessary information so that no one party has advantages over the other party."[186]

2.4   *Islamic Financial Transactions*

Many of the conventional financial transactions are forbidden in Islamic law because they are based on interest. As a result, Islamic scholars turned to traditional Islamic jurisprudence to find acceptable commercial contracts, which Islamic Bankers and specialists developed in order to make them applicable in the modern life. The next section explains some of typical commercial contracts used in the Islamic finance industry.

2.4.1   Musharakah (Partnership)

Musharakah is an Arabic word that literally means "sharing."[187] In business, Islamic scholars define *musharakah* as "a joint enterprise in which all the partners share the profit or loss of the joint venture."[188] *Musharakah* is "often

---

181   Id.
182   VOGEL & HAYES, *supra* note 79, at 91.
183   The rationale of prohibition of *Riba*, The prohibition of Maysir and *Gharar*, Financial Islam—Islamic Finance, *at* http://www.financialislam.com/prohibition-of-riba-maysir-and-gharar.html (last visited Nov. 1, 2013).
184   Id.
185   Id.
186   Id.
187   MUHAMMAD TAQĪ UṣMĀNĪ, AN INTRODUCTION TO ISLAMIC FINANCE 17 (Kluwer Law International 2002).
188   Id.

perceived to be the preferred Islamic mode of financing."[189] Basically, it is "an ideal alternative for the interest-based financing with far reaching effects on both production and distribution."[190]

In *musharakah*, "partners contribute capital to a project and share its risks and rewards."[191] Profits are shared between partners on "a pre-agreed ratio, but losses are shared in exact proportion to the capital invested by each party."[192] For example, A contributes $100,000 and B contributes $300,000. They agree to split the profits evenly, 50% for each partner. This is permissible according to Islamic scholars. In terms of loss, they must share it "in exact proportion to the capital invested by each party," which, in this example, is 25% and 75%.

According to Islamic scholars, it is impermissible to "fix a lump sum amount for any one of the partners, or any rate of profit tied up with his investment."[193] In the previous example, A cannot be assigned $50,000 of profit per month with the rest going to B. The profits must be a pre-determined ratio. In addition, in a *musharakah* contract, profits and losses cannot be prioritized.[194] In other words, no party can be superior "to others in terms of profit distribution or loss allocation, and no pre-fixed return can be promised to any."[195]

In a *musharakah* contract, all partners have the right but not the obligation to participate in the management of the project.[196] This "explains why the profit-sharing ratio is mutually agreed upon and may be different from the [percentage] investment [of each] in the total capital."[197] No one partner can be held liable to guarantee capital or profit to other partners.[198] However, if any "mismanagement and delinquency are proved,"[199] or if there is any kind of breach of the *musharakah* contract,[200] then the responsible partner "may be

---

189   Abbas Mirakhor & Iqbal Zaidi, *Profit-and-loss sharing contracts in Islamic finance*, in HANDBOOK OF ISLAMIC BANKING 49, 51 (Kabir Hassan & Mervyn Lewis eds., Edward Elgar 2007).
190   USMĀNĪ, *supra* note 130, at 17.
191   Mirakhor & Zaidi, *supra* note 132, at 51.
192   Id.
193   USMĀNĪ, *supra* note 130, at 23.
194   Seif I. TAG EL-DIN, *Capital and Money Markets of Muslims: The Emerging Experience in Theory and Practice*, 1 KYOTO BULLETIN OF ISLAMIC AREA STUDIES 54, 58 (2007).
195   Id.
196   Mirakhor & Zaidi, *supra* note 132, at 51.
197   Id.
198   EL-DIN, *supra* note 137, at 58.
199   Id.
200   Id.

held liable to guarantee capital contributions of the other parties"[201] and any damages incurred.

2.4.2   Mudarabah

Mudarabah is another kind of partnership in Islamic law, used for financing purposes.[202] *Mudarabah* is a partnership "where one partner gives money to another for investing it in a commercial enterprise."[203] In other words, the first partner contributes the capital while the other partner manages the business without contributing any capital.[204] If both partners contribute capital then the partnership is considered as *musharakah*, not *mudarabah*.

There are no restrictions on the number of partners contributing capital, or on the number of working partners.[205] Profits must be "shared between the two [or more] parties in accordance with a profit-sharing ratio pre-stipulated at the time of the contract."[206] Profit cannot be a fixed amount or any percentage of the capital employed.[207] There are no restrictions on the profit-sharing ratio in *mudarabah*.[208] It is completely based on the consent of all partners.[209]

"[I]n the absence of infringement, default, negligence or breach of contract provisions by the [working partners]" losses must be borne by the partners who contributed the capital.[210] The partners who contributed capital suffer the loss of their capital. The working partners suffer the loss of their work and efforts.[211] According to Islamic scholars, even if the partners sign a contract agreeing that working partners share losses the stipulation would be invalid.

There are some important differences between *musharakah* and *mudarabah*. In *musharakah*, the capital comes from all partners. In *mudarabah*, the capital only comes from some partners.[212] In *musharakah*, "all partners can participate in the management of the business and can work for it...."[213] In

---

201 *Id.*
202 VOGEL & HAYES, *supra* note 79, at 138.
203 UṣMĀNĪ, *supra* note 130, at 31.
204 *Id.*
205 MUHAMMAD AYUB, UNDERSTANDING ISLAMIC FINANCE 320 (John Wiley & Sons Ltd. 2007).
206 EL-DIN, *supra* note 137, at 57.
207 AYUB, *supra* note 148, at 320.
208 UṣMĀNĪ, *supra* note 130, at 33.
209 *Id.*
210 Mirakhor & Zaidi, *supra* note 132, at 223.
211 *Id.*
212 *Id.* at 30.
213 *Id.*

mudarabah, the partner who contributes the capital "has no right to participate in the management."[214] Only the partner who is responsible for executing the business has the right to manage it.[215] They also differ in terms of profits and loss. "In *musharakah* all partners share the loss to the extent of the ratio of their investment."[216] In *mudarabah*, only the partners who contributed capital suffer the loss.[217] The partner who did not contribute any capital loses only his time and effort.[218] The liability of the partners in *musharakah* is "normally unlimited,"[219] so if the liabilities of the business exceed its assets "the business is liquidated and all the excess liability shall be borne *pro rata* by all the partners."[220] In *mudarabah*, the liability of the partners who contributed the capital is limited to their investment,[221] "unless he has permitted the [working partner] to incur debts on his behalf."[222]

2.4.3 Murabahah (Cost-Plus or Markup)

Murabaha is the most popular Islamic financial instrument. "[M]ost of the Islamic banks and financial institutions use *murabaha* as an Islamic mode of financing."[223] Linguistically, it is derived from the Arabic word "ribh," which means profit.[224] In classic Islamic jurisprudence, *murabaha* is simply a sale. The seller in *murabaha* tells the purchaser expressly what the goods cost the seller and how much profit he is looking to make.[225] That factor distinguishes *murabaha* from other kinds of sales.[226] *Murabaha* is "a trade contract, stipulating that one party buys a good for its own account and sells it to the other party at the original price plus a markup."[227]

In a *murabaha* contract, the seller must inform the buyer of "all items of expense which are included in the cost if these are not known through

---

214   Id.
215   EL-DIN, *supra* note 137, at 57.
216   USMĀNĪ, *supra* note 130, at 30.
217   Id.
218   Id.
219   Id.
220   Id.
221   Id. at 31.
222   Id. at 31.
223   Id. at 65.
224   HANS VISSER, ISLAMIC FINANCE: PRINCIPLES AND PRACTICE 57 (Edward Elgar Publishing 2009).
225   USMĀNĪ, *supra* note 130, at 65.
226   Id.
227   VISSER, *supra* note 168, at 57.

custom"[228] and then "adds some profit thereon."[229] The profit could be a "lump sum or may be based on a percentage."[230] The profit "can be seen as a payment for the services provided by the intermediary, but also as a guaranteed profit margin."[231] The buyer may pay the seller immediately after the contract, delay the payment as a sale on credit, or pay in installments.[232]

Nowadays, *murabaha* is commonly used as a mode of financing.[233] Practically, if a customer wants to buy a car, which costs $100,000, the customer requests the bank to officially purchase the specific car. The customer promises to re-purchase the car from the bank with a markup. The bank determines the markup according to many factors (expenses, administrative fees, etc.), including how many installments the customer needs and how long it will take to pay the full price. The bank determines these factors, the customer agrees, and then the bank purchases the car and sells it directly to the customer. The customer pays the total price in installments as agreed with the bank.[234]

2.4.4   Ijarah (Lease)

Ijarah is an Arabic word meaning, "to give something on rent."[235] In Islamic jurisprudence, *ijarah* means, "to transfer the usufruct of a particular property to another person in exchange for a rent claimed from him."[236] Therefore, the term *ijarah* "is analogous to the English term 'leasing.'"[237] *Ijarah* was not originally a financing contract. Rather it was a sale of usufruct,[238] which means "its rules follow closely the rules for ordinary sales."[239]

In Islamic financing, *ijarah* is "a contract under which a bank buys and leases out an asset or equipment required by its client for a rental fee."[240] During the period of lease, the lessor (bank) owns the asset.[241] The lessor assumes the risk

---

228   VOGEL & HAYES, *supra* note 79, at 140.
229   USMĀNĪ, *supra* note 130, at 65.
230   *Id.*
231   VISSER, *supra* note 168, at 57.
232   *Id.*
233   VOGEL & HAYES, *supra* note 79, at 140.
234   *Ibid.*
235   USMĀNĪ, *supra* note 130, at 109.
236   *Id.*
237   *Id.*
238   VOGEL & HAYES, *supra* note 79, at 143.
239   *Id.*
240   Mirakhor & Zaidi, *supra* note 132, at 52.
241   *Id.*

of ownership and is responsible for insurance and major maintenance,[242] but "has the right to renegotiate the terms of the lease payment at agreed intervals." This is important "to ensure that the rental remains in line with market leasing rates and the residual value of the leased asset."[243]

Some clients want to own the assets at the end of the lease. In this case, Islamic banks use an additional single contract, which is called a "hire-purchase" contract.[244] In this contract, the lessee agrees to pay a prearranged amount of money at the end of the lease to purchase the asset from the lessor.[245] This contract "basically mimics financial leasing practices of conventional finance."[246] The Islamic bank and customer sign the two contracts, the lease and the hire-purchase. "[T]he bank purchases a building, equipment or an entire project and rents it to the client, but with the latter's agreement to make payments into an account, which will eventually result in the lessee's purchase of the physical asset from the lessor."[247]

There are several reasons why more and more Islamic banks are using lease contracts as a mode of financing. First, in a lease contract "the lessor retains legal title to the property being financed, assuring an effective security interest."[248] In other words, Islamic banks retain ownership of the asset, avoiding the risk of customer default (where the customer owns the asset and cannot continue paying the installments). Second, the lease contract includes "flexibility in payment terms and negotiability or transferability."[249] Third, "in some jurisdictions leasing offers tax savings compared with sale,"[250] which minimizes the cost of finance, making lease finance preferable to Islamic banks.

2.4.5   Sukuk (Islamic Bonds)

Sukuk are bonds structured according to *Shariah* principles.[251] Sometimes they are called Islamic bonds, Islamic debt securities, or Islamic trust certificates.[252]

---

242   *Id.*
243   *Id.*
244   Vogel & Hayes, *supra* note 79, at 144.
245   *Id.*
246   Mirakhor & Zaidi, *supra* note 132, at 52.
247   *Id.*
248   Vogel & Hayes, *supra* note 79, at 144.
249   *Id.*
250   *Id.*
251   Muhammad al-Bashir & Muhammad al-Amine, Global Sukūk and Islamic Securitization Market: Financial Engineering and Product Innovation 57 (Brill 2012).
252   *Id.*

Sukuk were created "to meet the requirements of those investors who wanted to invest their savings in *Shariah*-compliant financial instruments."[253] Modern Islamic scholars and bankers focused on creating alternative financial instruments for Muslim investors. *Sukuk* attracts Muslim investors, because they have some of the features of conventional bonds, and but are structured to be complaint with *Shariah* principles.[254]

There are important differences between conventional bonds and *sukuk*. Conventional "bonds are contractual debt obligations whereby the issuer is contractually obliged to pay to bondholders, on certain specified dates, interest and principal."[255] Conversely, "under a *sukuk* structure the *sukuk* holders each hold an undivided beneficial ownership interest in the underlying assets."[256] Therefore, "*sukuk* holders are entitled to share in the revenues generated by the *sukuk* assets as well as being entitled to share in the proceeds of the realization of the *sukuk* assets."[257] In other words, "*sukuk* are based on an exchange of an underlying asset but with the proviso that they are *Shariah*-compliant; that is, the financial transaction is based on the application of various Islamic commercial contracts."[258]

There are different *sukuk* based on the Islamic commercial contracts. For example, there are *sukuk musharakah*, *sukuk murabaha*, and *sukuk ijarah*.[259] The next Section explains these structures in detail. Moreover, it will focus on how non-tradability of debts negatively affects *sukuk* structuring (securitization) and the *sukuk* market (secondary market), even though *sukuk* are based on the exchange of an underlying asset.

Section 3: Islamic Scholars and the Negotiability of Debt

3.1 *Introduction*

This Section serves three purposes. The first purpose is to illustrate the flexibility and diversity of Islamic jurisprudence, especially in regard to the

---

253 Mirakhor & Zaidi, *supra* note 132, at 53.
254 *Id.*
255 Tamara Box & Mohammed Asaria, *Islamic Finance Market Turns to Securitization*, 24 INT. FINANC. LAW REV. July 2005, at 21.
256 *Id.*
257 *Id.*
258 Mirakhor & Zaidi, *supra* note 131, at 53.
259 Islamic commercial contracts such as *musharakah, mudarabah, murabaha* and Ijara which are explained previously.

negotiability of debt. The second is to explain the position of contemporary Islamic scholars regarding such negotiability. The final purpose is to demonstrate how the position of contemporary Islamic scholars negatively affects Islamic finance in general and the *sukuk* secondary market in particular.

The first section of this Section is composed of the opinions and arguments of previous Islamic scholars. There are also explanations of Islamic jurisprudence and the different schools of thought regarding the tradability of debt. Two Islamic Fiqh (jurisprudence) Academies are compared and contrasted,[260] and the standard issued by the Accounting and Auditing Organization for Islamic Financial Institutions (AAOIFI) is explained. These academies and the AAOIFI are universal. Their resolutions and standards are important for Muslims around the world. They are especially important for bankers and lawyers who do not have an Islamic jurisprudence background.

The second section explains how forbidding the negotiability of debts negatively affects the *sukuk* secondary market. The section also shows how this has been an obstacle for the growth of Islamic securitization.

3.2 Classic Islamic Jurisprudence and the Tradability of Debt

When Islamic scholars analyze the tradability of debt, they use the word "sale" because it is the basic contract in trading and the rules of a sale contract are applied generally to other kinds of contracts.[261] In discussing the permissibility of the sale of debts, Islamic scholars have developed two categories: the sale of debt for executed consideration, and the sale of debt for executory consideration. Each category has its own restrictions, types, and provisions.

3.2.1 Sale of Debt for Executed Consideration

There are two types of sale of debt for executed consideration: the sale of debt for executed consideration to the original debtor and the sale of debt for executed consideration to another person. For instance, A borrows $1000 from B. B sells the debt to A for executed consideration. This is the sale of debt to the original debtor. If B sells the debt to C for executed consideration, it is the sale of debt to another person. Each type has its own provisions.

---

260 These two Academies are different from the four Islamic schools of though. They are modern and authoritative. They consist of scholars from all four schools and from different Muslim countries. More details are in the next section.

261 Nabil Saleh, *Definition and Formation of Contract under Islamic and Arab Laws* 5 ARAB L. Q. May 1990, at 101.

THE NEGOTIABILITY OF DEBT IN ISLAMIC FINANCE

The majority of Islamic scholars believe Islamic law permits the sale of debt to the original debtor.[262] There is one condition on this contract. The consideration shall be equal or less than the debt. To be more would be *riba*, which is forbidden in Islamic law.[263] The most important argument concerning this opinion is the freedom of contract in Islamic law. Ibn Taimiah states, "The underlying principle in contracts and [conditions] is permissibility and validity. Any contract or [condition] is prohibited and void only if there is an explicit text [in Quran or Sunnah] proving its prohibition and voiding."[264] Freedom of contract is critical. Islamic scholars repeatedly use this rule as an argument. The majority of Islamic scholars are satisfied with this option for selling debt.

The sale of debt to another person is common, but complicated. There is no shared or majority opinion regarding this type of debt sale. There are three groups with three different opinions on the matter. The first group, made up of the Hanafi and the Hanbali schools, claims this debt sale is completely forbidden in Islamic law.[265] The second group, Maliki, believes it is permitted but with restrictions.[266] The third group, Shafi, believes it is completely permissible in Islamic law.[267]

The first group argues that this transaction contains *gharar* (uncertainty).[268] *Gharar* exists because the person who purchases the debt cannot be sure he will receive it on time, or receive it at all.[269] The prophet Mohammad forbade any sale of *gharar*.[270] Therefore, the sale of debt to another person is prohibited.[271]

The third group arugues an opposite position. The sale is permissible because freedom of contract is one of the main principles in Islamic law.[272] Furthermore, there is no specific text in the Quran or *Hadith* that forbids the sale of debt to another person. No one can forbid something that God does

---

262   Ibn Alqayem, Ealam Almowaqeen 4:105 (Dar Alhadeeth 1993); Mohammed Kurdey, Ahkam Baya Aldayn 97 (1992).
263   *See* page 34.
264   Ibn Taymiah, Majmo'a Al Fatawa 3:474 (King Fahad Center 1994).
265   Alkasaney, Badae'e Alsanae'e 5:182 (Dar Alhadeeth 1996); Ibn Qudamah, Alsharh Alkabeer 5:765 (DarAlhadeeth 1996).
266   Alhattab, Mawahaeb Aljaleel 4:368 (Dar Elfekr 1992) (date of first edition).
267   Alnawaway, Rawdhat Altalebeen 3:224 (Dar Alem Alkotob 2003).
268   Frank E. Vogel & Samuel L. Hayes III, Islamic Law and Finance: Religion, Risk, and Return 64 (Kluwer Law International 1998).
269   *Id.*
270   *See* page 38.
271   *Id.*
272   Alnawaway, *supra* note 8, at 3:224.

not forbid.[273] In terms of risk, any transaction includes risk and that does not mean it is forbidden.[274] The risk in a sale of debt to another person is not major *gharar*. It is classified as regular *gharar*, which is permissible in Islamic law.[275]

The second group chooses a middle ground. Because of freedom of contract, the sale of debt to another person is permissible.[276] However, the parties must avoid any forbidden issues such as *riba* and *gharar*.[277] In order to avoid these forbidden issues, the purchaser must believe the debtor has the ability to pay the debt.[278] The core of the transaction is permissible, and all proposed requirements are issues outside the transaction.

So, two of the four schools of thought believe the sale of debt for executed consideration is permissible. The other two schools believe it is forbidden. Based on their arguments, they are concerned about the uncertainty associated with the transaction, but not with the transaction itself. Thus, if the two parties engaged in the transaction are able to avoid major uncertainty, the sale of debt for executed consideration to another person would be permitted since only major *gharar* is forbidden in Islamic law.

3.2.2 Sale of Debt for Executory Consideration

This is the more complicated and controversial sale of debt for two reasons. First, there is a *hadith* from the prophet Mohammed that forbids the sale of "kali" for "kali". Literally, this *hadith* means "the exchange of two things both delayed" is forbidden.[279] However, this *hadith* has weak authentication.[280] According to Islamic law, if the *hadith* has weak authentication, scholars cannot base their argument upon it.[281] Second, forbidding the sale of two things both delayed "is said to have near universal application"[282] which means, it is not exactly an ijma but it is close to it since the vast majority of Islamic scholars

---

273 Id.
274 See page 38.
275 ALNAWAWAY, *supra* note 8, at 3:224.
276 ALHATTAB, *supra* note 7, at 4:368.
277 Id.
278 Id.
279 The prophet did not use the word *dayn*, which literally means debt. Instead, he used the word delayed, which is different. Some Islamic scholars use the word debt to discuss the provision of delayed consideration. This is one of the main reasons the concept of debt is vague and confusing in Islamic finance.
280 VOGEL & HAYES, *supra* note 9, at 115.
281 See page 23.
282 VOGEL & HAYES, *supra* note 9, at 115.

forbid this kind of transaction. These two elements play a significant role when Islamic scholars analyze the sale of debt for executory consideration.

Islamic scholars separate the sale of debt for executory consideration into three types. The first type is when the debts for both parties have been created in the transaction. In other words, it is the sale of executory consideration for executory consideration.[283] These debts are not due before the transaction. For example, A came to B to purchase a car for $100,000. They agreed that A would pay the money within six months and B would deliver the car after three months. This is called, "Ibtida aldayn by aldayn."[284] According to Islamic jurisprudence, there is unanimous consensus among Islamic scholars that prohibit this sale.[285] Although, the *hadith* that forbids the sale of kali for kali has weak authentication, the meaning of the *hadith* is still applied. In this transaction, A must pay, or B must deliver the car at the time of the transaction to make the contract enforceable. Maliki does exempt one situation. One party may delay the payment or the delivery of goods for three days.[286] These three days are considered close enough to be part of the time of transaction.[287] In short, if two parties create new debt in a transaction, and both considerations are delayed, then Islamic scholars unanimously forbid this transaction under Islamic law.

The second type is the sale of debt for executory consideration to the debtor. For example, A owes B $1000 to be paid after one year. B sells the debt to A for 1000 kg of dates paid after six months. The majority of Islamic scholars believe this transaction is prohibited because it is similar to selling kali for kali, which is unanimously prohibited among Islamic scholars.[288] On the other hand, some scholars, such as Ibn Taimiah and Ibn Alqayyem, believe this type of transaction is permissible because there is no text from Quran or Sunnah that explicitly forbids it. The *hadith*, kali for kali, is weak[289] so it is not a legitimate source for Islamic law provisions. Additionally, the ijma of Islamic scholars only speaks to the first type of transaction (two parties create new debt in a transaction, and both considerations are delayed), so this ijma cannot be

---

283   Again, the concept of debt is unclear which affects the negotiability of debt in Islamic finance. *See* section 4.
284   VOGEL & HAYES, *supra* note 9, at 116.
285   Id.
286   ALHATTAB, *supra* note 7, at 4:368.
287   Id.
288   KURDEY, *supra* note 3, at 97.
289   TAYMIAH, *supra* note 5, at 29:509.

applied to this type.[290] Thus, because of the freedom of contract principle, this transaction would be permitted. Accordingly, while a majority of Islamic scholars forbid the sale of debt for debt to the debtor, some respected scholars believe it is permitted in Islamic law.

The last type is the sale of debt for executory consideration to a person other than the debtor. For example, A owes B $1000. After a year, B sells the debt to C for 1000 kg dates to be paid after six months. The argument regarding this sale is the same as the previous one. The majority forbids the sale because it is similar to selling kali for kali.[291] Again, the minority disagrees, believing the sale is permissible, because the *hadith* is weak and the ijma is limited to the first type of transaction.[292]

In short, two schools of thought permit the sale of debt for executed consideration. The other two schools forbid the sale of debt for executed consideration because of the uncertainty (*gharar*) associated with the transaction. On the other hand, there is only one kind of sale of debt for executory consideration that is unanimously forbidden. The others are forbidden by the majority of Islamic scholars while the minority allows them because the ijma is limited.

The scope of this dissertation is limited to the sale of debt for executed consideration to another person because it is the most common practice in the secondary debt market. Therefore, if there are varied positions among Islamic Schools of legal thought regarding the sale of debt for executed consideration, why then is there an impression among current bankers and lawyers that the sale of debt is completely forbidden in Islamic law?

3.3 *Modern Islamic Fiqh (Jurisprudence) Organizations and the Tradability of Debt*

It is first important to consider the difference between the past and present Islamic legal opinion (fatwa). For better or for worse, Fiqh changes with the times.

In the past, four common, but unorganized, schools of thought generally represented the Islamic Fiqh.[293] Any scholar could add to a school of thought if he followed the main principles of the school.[294] Consequently, the scholars of one school may have had many different opinions and arguments as long as they shared the main principles of the school. These opinions were not

---

290 Id.
291 NASER NASHAWY, BAY ALDAYN 156 (Dar Alfekr Aljame'ey 2007).
292 TAYMIAH, *supra* note 4, at 29:509; ALQAYEM, *supra* note 2, at 4:105.
293 See page 29.
294 Id.

THE NEGOTIABILITY OF DEBT IN ISLAMIC FINANCE

binding unless a judge chose one Fiqh opinion to make a decision. Thus, the Fiqh became binding because it was adopted in a judicial decision, not on the authority of the school of thought.[295] This allowed Islamic jurisprudence to be broad, diverse, and flexible.

Modern Islamic Fiqh is structured by modern organizations. Two Fiqh academies adopt decisions and resolutions in different fields of Islamic jurisprudence. The first academy is in Jeddah and consists of 54 members who are Islamic scholars from different schools and countries.[296] The second academy is based in Makkah and consists of twenty-four members who are Islamic scholars from different schools and countries.[297] Their methodology is to adopt interpretations based on the majority opinion.[298] Their resolutions are understood by non-Islamic scholars to be true Islamic law, without considering the debates behind the resolution. The resolutions attempt to summarize thousands of years of accumulated Islamic jurisprudence in two or three pages. This section analyzes the resolutions related to the negotiability of debts. The standard, issued by the *Shariah*'s Board of the Accounting and Auditing Organization for Islamic Financial Institutions (AAOIFI), which regulates the *sukuk* industry, is also analyzed.

3.3.1 The Islamic Fiqh Academy in Jeddah

On November 19, 1998, the Islamic Fiqh Academy in Jeddah adopted a resolution with number (11/4)101:

> It is not permissible to sell a deferred debt by the non-debtor for a prompt cash, from its type or otherwise, because this results in *Riba* [usury]. Likewise, it is not permissible to sell for a deferred cash, from its type or otherwise, because it's similar to the sale of (kali for kali), which is prohibited in Islam. There is no difference whether the debt is the result of a loan or if it is a deferred sale.[299]

This resolution refers to the sale of debt for cash. The sale of debt for cash has two parts: the sale of debt for prompt cash (executed consideration) and the sale of debt for deferred cash (executory consideration). There are different

---

295 *Id.*
296 Islamic Fiqh Academy in Jeddah, *at* http://www.fiqhacademy.org.sa/.
297 The Muslim World League in Makkah, *at* http://www.mwl-en.com.
298 Islamic Fiqh Academy in Jeddah, *at* http://www.fiqhacademy.org.sa/.
299 Islamic Fiqh Academy in Jeddah, *at* http://www.fiqhacademy.org.sa/qrarat/11-4.htm.

arguments for each part, but the ultimate decision is the same: the transaction is forbidden.

The academy decided the sale of debt for prompt currency is forbidden because it is a kind of usury in sales. It is considered usury in sales because the two considerations are the same type. Debt and cash are both money. The two considerations must be equal and paid at the time of transaction, and in the modern practice of debt sales, the debt is not the same amount as the prompt cash. Therefore, selling debt in this situation is forbidden. This argument is used to support forbidding the sale of debts for prompt currency. Because there is no ayah or *hadith*, the academy uses the argument of *riba* to forbid the sale of debt. As a result, non-experts in Islamic jurisprudence would understand that the sale of debts is forbidden as usury in Islam.

The academy decided the sale of debt for delayed cash is not permissible because it is kali for kali sale. They use the *hadith* without explaining that it is weak, or differentiating between the several kinds of debt sales, or mentioning that there are different opinions among Islamic scholars. Thus, it is implied that the sale of debt for executory consideration is always impermissible.

On June 28, 2006, the academy adopted a new resolution regarding the sale of debt, numbered (17/7) 158:

> Some permissible kinds of . . . sale of debts:
> 1- The sale of debt to a person who is not the debtor if:
>   A. Selling the debt for different and prompt currency, and shall be the price of the day.
>   B. Selling the debt for particular commodity.
>   C. Selling the debt for particular usufruct.[300]

In this resolution, the academy provided more details than the previous resolution written in abbreviated text. Here, the academy mentions some permissible kinds of debt sales. The permissible kinds are based on the *riba* in sales arguments. As explained before, if the two considerations are the same type, then they must be equal and delivered at the time of the transaction, pursuant to Islamic law.[301] Otherwise, it is considered as *riba* in sales.[302] If one consideration is different from the other, the transaction is permissible, even with unequal amounts and delivered at a time other than the time of transaction.[303] The academy emphasizes that if the other consideration is different from the

---

300 Islamic Fiqh Academy in Jeddah, *at* http://www.fiqhacademy.org.sa/qrarat/17-7.htm.
301 *See* page 35.
302 Id.
303 Id.

original debt, then the sale of debt is allowed. Therefore, the sale of debt itself is not a concern in Islamic jurisprudence. The concern is, whether the transaction includes *riba* in sales.

Because debt represents money, the academy considers the debt equivalent to money, and applies the rules and restrictions of *riba* in sales to any transaction that includes the sale of debt. The academy emphasizes that if the type of the consideration is different from the type of debt, then it is allowed.

3.3.2 The Islamic Fiqh Academy in Makkah

On January 10, 2002, the Islamic Fiqh Academy in Makkah adopted an important resolution that still affects the world's Islamic finance industry. The resolution discusses the forms of the sale of debts. There is only one permissible form: "The permissible forms of the sale of credit include the credit selling [sic] to the debtor himself at the present price."[304] This provision is consistent with traditional Islamic jurisprudence. The vast majority of Islamic scholars allow this form and believe it is permissible.[305]

The resolution lists two prohibited forms and gives some practical examples. The first prohibited form is, "[o]ffering the sale of debts to debtor at a deferred price which is more than the debt itself" because "[i]t constitutes a kind of *Riba* (usury), which is prohibited according to *Shariah* (Islamic law)."[306] The second type is, "[o]ffering the sale of debts to a person other than the debtor at a delayed price of similar or other kind" because "[i]t constitutes a form of selling kali for kali (debts for debts), which is prohibited according to the Islamic *Shariah*."[307]

There are several problems with this resolution. First, the resolution connects the sale of debt to the debtor for executed consideration and executory consideration, but the sale of debt to another person for only executory consideration. The resolution does not mention anything about the sale of debt to another person for executed consideration, though such actions are important in modern Islamic finance. Second, the Academy supports the second prohibition with the *hadith* without disclosing that it is a weak *hadith*. Third, the resolution interprets the *hadith*, kali for kali, as debt for debt and that might mislead the reader. Literally, in Arabic language, kali is one kind of debt but

---

304 The Muslim World League in Makkah, *at* http://www.mwl-en.com/2012/05/23/resolutions-of-the-islamic-fiqh-council-16th-session-1422h/.
305 *See* page 53.
306 The Muslim World League in Makkah, *at* http://www.mwl-en.com/2012/05/23/resolutions-of-the-islamic-fiqh-council-16th-session-1422h/.
307 *Id.*

its meaning is coextensive with the meaning of debt.[308] Kali for kali is unanimously prohibited but other kinds of debt, such as the sale of debt for executed consideration, are not mentioned in the kali *hadith*, otherwise prohibited.

Additionally, the resolution lists several practical examples. The most important is securitization. The resolution states, "It is not permissible to securitize debts into securities that may be circulated in secondary market" because "it constitutes a sale of debts to a person other than the debtor in a way that includes *Riba* (usury)."[309] Alternatively, the academy provides a solution to comply with *Shariah*. The solution is "selling them through commodities, provided the buyer takes their delivery at the time of signing the contract, even though the value of the commodity is less than the value of the commercial paper."[310]

The resolution forbids the entire securitization industry. The argument is built on *riba* in sales, similar to the academy in Jeddah when it forbade the sale of debt for cash. The academy in Makkah provides a possible solution of selling debts for commodities. The only advantage of this solution is to comply with the perceived Islamic law, though it does not address the needs of investors and corporations. This resolution cuts off significant business for the Islamic finance industry. It has negative effects on Islamic finance generally, and particularly the Islamic debt market.

3.3.3 Accounting and Auditing Organization for Islamic Financial Institutions (AAOIFI)

The Accounting and Auditing Organization for Islamic Financial Institutions (AAOIFI) is a significant player in the Islamic financial industry. It is "an Islamic international autonomous not-for-profit corporate body that prepares accounting, auditing, governance, ethics and *Shariah* standards for Islamic financial institutions and the industry."[311] It has issued 88 standards: "(a) 48 on *Shariah*, (b) 26 accounting, (c) 5 auditing standards, (d) 7 governance, (e) 2 codes of ethics."[312] The *Shariah* standards translate the traditional language of Islamic law for practitioners, such as bankers and lawyers. The most relevant standard for this article is the *Shariah* standard number 17.

---

308 *See* page 56.
309 The Muslim World League in Makkah, *at* http://www.mwl-en.com/2012/05/23/resolutions-of-the-islamic-fiqh-council-16th-session-1422h/.
310 *Id.*
311 ABOUT AAOIFI, AAOIFI, *at*, http://www.aaoifi.com/en/about-aaoifi/about-aaoifi.html (last visited Jan. 15, 2014).
312 *Id.*

On May 8, 2003, the *Shariah* board of AAOIFI issued standard 17 to regulate Islamic bonds (*sukuk*). This standard clearly states, "It is permissible to securitize assets, usufructs and services, but it is not permissible to securitize debts to be negotiable."[313] The main thrust of the standard is that the *sukuk* must be related to tangible assets, usufructs, or services in order to be negotiable in the secondary market. If the *sukuk* represents debt, it is not negotiable. These standards are written for non-experts in Islamic jurisprudence. These non-experts might get the wrong idea that negotiability of debt is totally prohibited in Islamic law. They would more than likely believe this is a rule in Islamic law based on *riba* (usury) and *gharar* (uncertainty). These restrictions present a significant hurdle to the development of *sukuk* and Islamic securitization.

The two academies based their arguments on the *riba* in sales prohibition (gold for gold and silver for silver). Today, most transactions involve money. These two elements imply that Islamic law forbids the sale of debt. This implication is especially significant for practitioners who do not have any background in Islamic jurisprudence. They will not be able to differentiate between *riba* in sales and *riba* in loan usury. They will believe that the sale of debt is as repugnant as usury. The *Shariah* board of AAOIFI issued standard 17 to confirm the prohibition and stated, "it is not permissible to securitize debts to be negotiable."[314]

3.4 *The Effect of the Non-Tradability of Debts on Sukuk Industry*

Sukuk are financial instruments, created by Islamic bankers and specialists as an alternative to conventional bonds. *Sukuk* were created to avoid *riba*. *Sukuk* comply with traditional Islamic jurisprudence, allowing commercial Islamic transactions to be compliant with Islamic law. There are many kinds of *sukuk*. Each kind is based on an Islamic commercial transaction.[315] *Sukuk* are attractive for governments and companies in the Gulf Corporation Council (GCC) and many entities seeking funds permissible under Islamic law issue *sukuk*.[316]

Although many entities, especially governments, have issued *sukuk*, these instruments have faced several obstacles in the secondary market. As explained in Section 1, while *sukuk* was created to avoid *riba* and make debt instruments

---

313   The *Shariah*'s Board of the Accounting and Auditing Organization for Islamic Financial Institutions Standards for Islamic Banking 240 (2010).
314   The *Shariah*'s Board of the Accounting and Auditing Organization for Islamic Financial Institutions Standards for Islamic Banking 240 (2010).
315   *sukuk murabaha, sukuk salam, sukuk isitsna, sukuk ijarah, sukuk musharak* and *sukuk mudarabah*, etc.
316   *See* section 1, Introduction.

attractive for Muslims, the secondary market is still illiquid and limited. The main reason is the non-tradability of debt in Islamic Finance according to the two resolutions of the Fiqh academies. This Section examines the structure of each kind of *sukuk* and shows how the non-tradability of debt affects whether each *sukuk* is tradable in the secondary market.

Many Islamic bankers search the Western financial industry for instruments compliant with Islamic law in order to develop the *sukuk* industry. Many specialists believe securitization is useful.

3.4.1 Sukuk Negotiability in the Secondary Market

In this section, each *sukuk* structure is explained to show how the non-tradability of debt affects the negotiability of such *sukuk* in the secondary market. It is important to mention here that each *sukuk* is packaged as one deal. Therefore, all parties know in advance all of the procedures, steps and the final result.

3.4.1.1 *Sukuk Murabaha*

As explained in Section 2, in Islamic jurisprudence *murabaha* "is a trade contract, stipulating that one party buys a good for its own account and sells it to the other party at the original price plus a mark-up."[317] The mark-up reflects the services of the seller, or simply a profit margin for the seller. The payment may be in cash or installments.[318] In financing, "*murabaha* is used as a form of a sales contract in which the financial institution or investors buy an asset and then later sell it to the 'borrower' at a marked-up price, which includes a profit component. Payments are made in installments, either on a deferred basis or through upfront payment with deferred delivery."[319]

There are several parties involved in a transaction using *murabaha* to issue *sukuk*. The first party is a company or any business entity that needs funds. The second party is a special purpose vehicle (SPV), created by the company to manage the transaction. Third, a vendor will provide the commodity or the assets. Fourth, the investors will finance the transaction and buy the *sukuk*. The structure of the *sukuk* is described below.

The SPV, which is created by the company seeking funds, issues *murabaha sukuk* to investors and collects funds from investors. The SPV purchases assets

---

317 Hans Visser, Islamic Finance: Principles and Practice 57 (Edward Elgar Publishing 2009).
318 *Id.*
319 Christopher F. Richardson, *Islamic Finance Opportunities in the Oil and Gas Sector: An Introduction to an Emerging Field*, 42 Tex. Int. L. J. 119, 130 (2006).

from the vendor and pays with the proceeds of the sukuk. The company on behalf of the SPV takes delivery of the assets. Then, the company purchases the assets from the SPV on a deferred payment plan and makes payments to the SPV while the SPV passes the payments on to the investors after deducting a service fee.[320]

Although "most of the Islamic banks and financial institutions are using *murabaha* as an Islamic mode of financing,"[321] *murabaha sukuk* are non-negotiable and non-tradable in the secondary market.[322] *Murabaha sukuk* represents "entitlements to shares in receivables from the purchaser of the underlying murababa, they are not negotiable instruments that can be traded on the secondary market because *Shariah* does not permit trading in debt."[323] The Accounting and Auditing Organization for Islamic Financial Institutions *Shariah* standard number 17 clearly determines that muarbaha *sukuk* are not negotiable if the underlying asset is delivered to the end buyer.[324]

3.4.1.2 *Sukuk Salam*

Salam literally means "futures".[325] Islamic scholars consider a contract as *salam* when "a buyer pays in advance for a designated quantity and quality of a certain commodity to be delivered at a certain agreed date and price."[326] The buyer must pay the full price when he signs the contract. The seller must deliver the designated quantity of the commodity on the agreed date. *Salam* contracts were allowed during the life of the prophet Mohammed, particularly for the production of agriculture goods.[327] *Salam* contracts were very important "to

---

320 MUHAMMAD AYUB, UNDERSTANDING ISLAMIC FINANCE 403 (John Wiley & Sons Ltd. 2007).
321 MUHAMMAD TAQĪ USMĀNĪ, AN INTRODUCTION TO ISLAMIC FINANCE 65 (Kluwer Law International 2002).
322 CLIFFORD CHANCE LLP, DUBAI INTERNATIONAL FINANCIAL CENTRE SUKUK GUIDEBOOK 46 (Dubai International Financial Centre 2009).
323 Id.
324 THE SHARIAH'S BOARD OF THE ACCOUNTING AND AUDITING ORGANIZATION FOR ISLAMIC FINANCIAL INSTITUTIONS STANDARDS FOR ISLAMIC BANKING 240 (2010).
325 Said Elfakhani, Imad Zbib, & Zafar Ahmed, *Marketing of Islamic financial products*, in HANDBOOK OF ISLAMIC BANKING 116, 120 (Kabir Hassan & Mervyn Lewis eds., Edward Elgar 2007).
326 Id.
327 USMĀNĪ, *supra* note 62, at 129.

allow farmers access to capital (price of *salam*), with which they can buy seeds, fertilizer, and other materials to grow their crops."328

In modern Islamic finance, *salam* is used for small farmers and traders.329 Pursuant to *salam* agreements, "a trader in need of short-term funds sells merchandize to the [investment] bank on a deferred delivery basis. It receives full price of the merchandize on the spot that serves its financing need at present."330 By the due date, the trader "delivers the merchandize to the [investment] bank [and] the bank sells the merchandize in the market at the prevailing price."331 The price the investment bank pays to the trader is usually less than the market price, so "the transaction should result in a profit for the [investment] bank."332 The structure for issuing *sukuk* using *salam* would be as follows:333

- SPV issues *sukuk*, which represent an undivided ownership interest in certain assets (the "*Salam* Assets") to be delivered by obligor;
- The SPV signs a contract with an obligor to provide commodities and sell it to the end buyers;
- *Salam* certificates are issued to investors, and the SPV receives the *sukuk* proceeds;
- The *sukuk* proceeds are passed on to the obligor, who will deliver the commodity in the future;
- On the agreed date, the SPV receives the commodities from the obligor, then the SPV assigns the obligor as an agent to sell the commodities to the end buyers;
- On behalf of the *sukuk* holders, the obligor sells the commodities for a profit; and
- The *sukuk* holders receive the commodity sale proceeds.

Salam is used by many midsized corporations for liquidity. Using it for *sukuk*, however, is still "rare in comparison to some of the more prevalent structures like *sukuk* al-*ijarah*. The limited use of this structure can be attributed to a

---

328 MAHMOUD A. EL-GAMAL, ISLAMIC FINANCE: LAW, ECONOMICS, AND PRACTICE 82 (Cambridge University Press 2006).
329 MOHAMMED OBAIDULLAH, ISLAMIC FINANCIAL SERVICES 95 (Scientific Publishing Centre, King Abdulaziz University 2005).
330 *Id.*
331 *Id.*
332 *Id.* at 96.
333 SHARIQ NISAR, ISLAMIC BONDS (*SUKUK*): ITS INTRODUCTION AND APPLICATION, *available at* http://www.financeinislam.com/article/8/1/546.

number of factors, namely the non-tradability of the *sukuk*."³³⁴ Thus, "secondary market trading of *Salam Sukuk* is considered impermissible on the grounds that the certificates represent a share in the *Salam* debt [receivables],"³³⁵ which are forbidden according to Islamic scholars. *Salam sukuk* represent the right to receive the commodity in the future, and the right to receive profit by selling the commodity. Because they represent debt, AAOIFI specifies in standard number 17, that *salam sukuk* are not negotiable at all.³³⁶

3.4.1.3   Sukuk Istisna

Istisna literally means "commission to manufacture."³³⁷ In this contract, "the buyer pays the price either in one or multiple installments, and a liability is established on the manufacturer to deliver [in the future] the object of sale as described in the contract."³³⁸ Like *salam*, in *istisna* the seller sells a nonexistent product that he will deliver in the future.³³⁹ There are some differences between *istisna* and *salam*. First, "the subject of *istisna* is always a thing which needs manufacturing, while *salam* can be effected on anything, no matter whether it needs manufacturing or not."³⁴⁰ Second, "it is necessary for *salam* that the price is paid in full in advance, while it is not necessary in *istisna*."³⁴¹ Finally, "the time of delivery is an essential part of the sale in *salam* while it is not necessary in *istisna* that the time of delivery is fixed."³⁴²

In modern Islamic finance, *istisna* is used in "the construction industry, [such as] apartment buildings, hospitals, schools and universities."³⁴³ It is also used in the "development of residential/commercial areas and housing finance schemes"³⁴⁴ and "financing high technology industries such as the aircraft industry, locomotive and shipbuilding industries."³⁴⁵ The structure of *Istisna sukuk* is described below.

---

334   CLIFFORD CHANCE LLP, *supra* note 63, at 34.
335   *Id.*
336   THE *SHARIAH*'S BOARD OF THE ACCOUNTING AND AUDITING ORGANIZATION FOR ISLAMIC FINANCIAL INSTITUTIONS STANDARDS FOR ISLAMIC BANKING 240 (2010).
337   VOGEL & HAYES, *supra* note 9, at 146.
338   EL-GAMAL, *supra* note 69, at 90.
339   *Id.*
340   USMĀNĪ, *supra* note 62, at 136.
341   *Id.*
342   *Id.*
343   AYUB, *supra* note 61, at 269.
344   *Id.*
345   *Id.*

The SPV, which is created by the company looking for funds for a project, issues *sukuk* and sells them to investors. The sukuk represents an undivided ownership interest in the asset that will be manufactured or built in the future. *Sukuk* proceeds are used to pay the builder for building and delivering the future project. When the project is done, the SPV leases the project to the end lessor. The end lessor pays monthly installments to the SPV and the returns are distributed among the *Sukuk* holders.[346] At the end of the lease, the project will be liquidated and proceeds will also be distributed among the *Sukuk* holders.

Although the *istisna* structure seems ideal for financing manufacturing and construction, "the structure of *sukuk* al-*istisna* has not been that widely used."[347] The main reason is "the prevailing view that *sukuk* al-*istisna* are not tradable during the construction period."[348] During the construction period, *sukuk* represented the right to receive the manufactured item in the future, thus it is not tradable according to the two Fiqh Academies. Moreover, when the SPV sells the manufactured item to the end buyer, the *sukuk* are not tradable, because they represent the right to receive the money in the future.[349] Therefore, *sukuk* istsna are very restricted in terms of negotiability in the secondary market.

3.4.1.4 *Sukuk Ijarah*

As explained in Section 2, in Islamic jurisprudence, *ijarah* means "to transfer the usufruct of a particular property to another person in exchange for a rent claimed from him."[350] In Islamic finance, *ijarah* is "a contract under which a bank buys and leases out an asset or equipment required by its client for a rental fee."[351] During the period of lease, the lessor (the bank in this case) owns the asset.[352] The structure for issuing *sukuk* using *ijarah* is as follows:[353]

---

346 Malaysia International Islamic Financial Centre (MIFC), SUKUK USING AL-*ISTISNA'* STRUCTURE, at http://www.mifc.com/index.php?ch=ch_kc_definitions&pg=pg_kcdf_sukuk&ac=236 (last visited Jan. 15, 2014).
347 CLIFFORD CHANCE LLP, *supra* note 63, at 40.
348 *Id.*
349 *Id.*
350 USMĀNĪ, *supra* note 62, at 109.
351 Abbas Mirakhor & Iqbal Zaidi, *Profit-and-loss sharing contracts in Islamic finance, in* HANDBOOK OF ISLAMIC BANKING 49, 52 (Kabir Hassan & Mervyn Lewis eds., Edward Elgar 2007).
352 *Id.*
353 SALMAN SYED ALI, ISLAMIC CAPITAL MARKET PRODUCTS: DEVELOPMENTS AND CHALLENGES 30 (Islamic Development Bank 2005).

- The owner of the asset creates an SPV and sells the assets to the SPV with the understanding that the original owner will lease back the asset from the SPV;
- The SPV then issues ijara *sukuk* for sale to investors, which represent an undivided ownership interest in the underlying asset;
- The *sukuk* sale proceeds provide funds to SPV to pay for the assets purchased from the originator;
- A rent-pass-through structure is adopted by the SPV to pass on the rents collected from the originator-cum-lessee to *sukuk* holders; and
- The *sukuk* contract embeds a put option to the *sukuk*-holders that the originator is ready to buy the *sukuk* at its face value on maturity or dissolution date.

Ijarah sukuk is the most commonly used *sukuk* structure. It is preferable for investors in the Middle East and accepted by *Shariah* scholars.[354] *Ijarah sukuk* represent actual ownership of the underlying asset (which is not a debt or receivable) from the issuance of the *sukuk* until the expiration of the lease. According to AAOIFI *Shariah* standard number 17, *ijarah sukuk* are negotiable and tradable in the secondary market.[355] This is the reason *ijarah sukuk* are the most commonly used *sukuk* by investors in the Middle East. The other kinds of *sukuk*, such as *murabaha, salam* and *istisna*, are non-tradable.

3.4.1.5   Sukuk Musharakah and Mudarabah

In Islamic finance, *musharakah* is "a joint enterprise in which all the partners share the profit or loss of the joint venture."[356] In *musharakah*, "partners contribute capital to a project and share its risks and rewards."[357] Profits are shared between partners on "a pre-agreed ratio, but losses are shared in exact proportion to the capital invested by each party."[358]

Mudarabah is also a partnership. In *mudarabah* some partners contribute capital while other partners manage and prosecute the business without contributing any capital.[359]

---

354   CLIFFORD CHANCE LLP, *supra* note 63, at 13.
355   THE *SHARIAH*'S BOARD OF THE ACCOUNTING AND AUDITING ORGANIZATION FOR ISLAMIC FINANCIAL INSTITUTIONS STANDARDS FOR ISLAMIC BANKING 240 (2010).
356   USMĀNĪ, *supra* note 62, at 17.
357   Mirakhor and Zaidi, *supra* note 66, at 52.
358   *Id.*
359   USMĀNĪ, *supra* note 62, at 31.

In terms of *sukuk* structuring, mushrakah and *mudarabah* are very similar. The major difference is that in *musharakah*, the asset or project is owned by the *sukuk* holders and the originator. In *mudarabah* the asset or project is owned only by the *sukuk* holders. The originator manages the project without being the owner.[360] The structure of *musharakah sukuk* would be as follows:[361]

- SPV issues *sukuk*, which represents an undivided ownership interest in an underlying asset or project;
- The investors subscribe for *sukuk* and pay the proceeds to SPV;
- SPV enters into a *musharakah* arrangement with originator, and the contributions by the SPV and the originator collectively compromise the *musharakah* assets;
- On each periodic distribution date, the SPV and originator shall receive a pre-agreed percentage share of the profits generated by the *musharakah* assets;
- Issuer SPV pays each periodic distribution amount to the investors using the profit it has received from the *musharakah* assets; and
- Upon maturity, any remaining asset would be liquidated and distributed between the SPV and the originator in accordance with the same profit sharing ratios. The SPV then pays such dissolution returns to the investors redeeming the *sukuk* certificates.

Musharakah and *mudarabah sukuk* represent actual ownership of an asset or project from the beginning until maturity. *Musharakah sukuk* are tradable and negotiable in the secondary market, according to the AAOIFI *Shariah* board standard number 17.[362] Although *musharakah* and *mudarabah sukuk* are tradable, they are not commonly used because of the disapproval of Islamic scholars,[363] who believe Islamic banks did not follow the exact requirements and rules set by the AAOIFI.[364]

---

360 Mirakhor and Zaidi, *supra* note 92, at 56.
361 CLIFFORD CHANCE LLP, *supra* note 63, at 21.
362 THE SHARIAH'S BOARD OF THE ACCOUNTING AND AUDITING ORGANIZATION FOR ISLAMIC FINANCIAL INSTITUTIONS STANDARDS FOR ISLAMIC BANKING 240 (2010).
363 CLIFFORD CHANCE LLP, *supra* note 63, at 27.
364 In 2008, the AAOIFI issued a statement criticizing the practice of *musharakah* and *mudarabah sukuk*. It stated that the practice was not in line with Islamic law, because "the credit on the *Sukuk* was based on the credit worthiness of the provider of the purchase undertaking and not the assets underlying the *sukuk*." Norton Rose Fulbright, AAOIFI STATEMENT ON *SUKUK* AND ITS IMPLICATIONS, at http://www.nortonrosefulbright

Thus, three kinds of *sukuk* are completely non-negotiable: *sukuk murabaha*, *sukuk salam* and *sukuk istisna*. Two kinds of *sukuk* are negotiable, *sukuk musharkah* and *sukuk mudarabah*. However, these are not preferable and there are disputes between bankers and Islamic scholars about them. Only *sukuk ijarah* is both negotiable and preferred by Islamic scholars and investors. The resolution of non-tradability of debt adopted by the two Islamic Fiqh Academies and the AAOIFI is the main reason the secondary *sukuk* market is largely illiquid and limited.

3.5 *Securitization as an Instrument to Develop Sukuk*

Islamic bankers and specialists would like to benefit from the Western financial industry, using its financial instruments if they are compliant with Islamic law. Securitization is one technique that may be useful to make the *sukuk* market more liquid and diverse. Zamir Iqbal writes about liquidity and diversity as "some areas of improvement in the banking and capital market sector"[365] that "need immediate attention. . . ."[366] He says:

> Islamic banks are operating with a limited set of short-term traditional instruments, and there is a shortage of products for medium- to long-term maturities. In other words, the secondary markets lack depth and breadth. An effective portfolio management strategy cannot be implemented in the absence of liquid markets, as opportunities for diversification become limited. Since the needs of the market regarding liquidity, risk, and portfolio management are not being met, the system is not functioning at its full potential.[367]

In terms of solutions, Iqbal proposes "offering new products with different risk-return profiles that meet the demand of investors, financial intermediaries, and entrepreneurs for liquidity and safety."[368] He suggests that "securitization is a prime candidate"[369] to achieve that purpose.

.com/knowledge/publications/16852/aaoifi-statement-on-sukuk-and-its-implications (last visited Jan. 15, 2014).
365 Zamir Iqbal, *Challenges Facing Islamic Financial Industry*, 3 J. OF ISLAMIC ECON. BANKING & FIN. 2007, at 1.
366 *Id.* at 5.
367 *Id.* at 3.
368 *Id.*
369 *Id.*

Mohammed Albashir, in his book *Global Sukuk and Islamic Securitization Market: Financial Engineering and Product Innovation*, describes this vision:

> The AAOIFI *Shariah* board has provided some guidelines to help the industry to adhere to its core objectives and strike a [make a balance between the substance and the form]. From a practical point of view, it is believed that securitization is better placed to help in achieving this objective if it is adopted and adapted to Islamic finance principles. This is supported by the fact that most Islamic finance products are based on asset backing, and the concept of asset securitization is particularly amenable to the basic tenets of Islamic finance. Asset securitization describes the process of issuing certificates of ownership as a pledge against existing or future cash flows from a diversified pool of assets to investors. Thus, securitization is highly advocated as the next phase development for the *sukuk* market.[370]

The question is whether securitization will be "the next phase development for the *sukuk* market. . . ." Most Islamic finance products are based on asset backing.[371] Securitization may be an appropriate Islamic finance instrument, because it is also based on asset backing.[372] The essential factor of securiti-

---

[370] Muhammad al-Bashir & Muhammad al-Amine, Global Sukūk and Islamic Securitization Market: Financial Engineering and Product Innovation 244 (Brill 2012).

[371] There are two kinds of sukuk in this context, asset-backed sukuk and asset based sukuk. In asset-backed sukuk, such sukuk "involve granting the investor (sukuk holder) a share of a tangible asset or business venture. In this structure, there is a true sale transaction, where the originator sells the underlying assets to a (SPV) that holds these assets and issues the sukuk backed by them." See, What Is the Difference Between Asset-Backed Sukuk and Asset-Based Sukuk?, Investment & Finance, http://investment-and-finance.net/islamic-finance/questions/what-is-the-difference-between-asset-backed-sukuk-and-asset-based-sukuk.html. On the other hand, the asset-based sukuk "the initial sale of the original assets by the originator to the SPV does not take place, so the ownership of assets remains with the originator of the sukuk." However, "the AAIOFI ((2008)) standards, state that such asset- based sukuk are not Shariah compliant because there is no transfer of assets to the sukuk holders." See, Sweder Wijnbergen & Sajjad Zaheer, Sukuk Defaults: On Distress Resolution in Islamic Finance 7 (2013).

[372] Andreas A. Jobst, *The Economics of Islamic Finance and Securitization*, 13 Journal of Structured Finance, 2007, at 15.

zation is the asset intended to be securitized.[373] The most common type of securitization is the securitization of receivables[374] because "it ensures a continuous flow of income to cover the periodic payments on the securitized assets and usually entails the purchasing of a leased asset, a mortgaged property, unsecured commercial loans or credit card payment systems, which are then securitized and sold on the capital market."[375] Unfortunately, receivables "are a form of debt"[376] according to contemporary Islamic scholars. Debt cannot be securitized and traded in the secondary market, pursuant to the resolution of the Fiqh Academy in Makkah and the AAOIFI *Shariah* standard, which states, "It is permissible to securitize assets, utilities and services, but it is not permissible to securitize debts to be negotiable."[377] Thus, mortgages, credit cards, and car loans, which are typical securitized assets,[378] cannot be securitized and traded.

Theoretically, securitization could be used if the securitized assets are not receivable. Practically, securitization is linked to assets generating money in the future to "ensure a continuous flow of income to cover the periodic payments on the securitized assets."[379] Most of these assets are receivables that cannot be securitized. If Islamic institutions use securitization under the prohibition of trading debts, Islamic securitization will be limited in comparison to conventional securitization.[380] Given that debts are not tradable in Islamic finance, securitization will be very difficult. The obstacles facing securitization

---

373 Jonathan Lipson defines securitization "as a purchase of primary payment rights by a special purpose entity that (1) legally isolates such payment rights from a bankruptcy (or similar insolvency) estate of the originator, and (2) results, directly or indirectly, in the issuance of securities whose value is determined by the payment rights so purchased." Jonathan C. Lipson, *Re: Defining Securitization*, 85 S. CAL. L. REV. 1229, 1231 (2012).

374 MAHA-HANAAN BALALA, ISLAMIC FINANCE AND LAW: THEORY AND PRACTICE IN A GLOBALIZED WORLD 130 (Tauris Academic Studies 2011) (2010).

375 *Id.*

376 Mohammed Obaidullah, *Securitization in Islam*, in HANDBOOK OF ISLAMIC BANKING 191, 195 (Kabir Hassan & Mervyn Lewis eds., Edward Elgar 2007).

377 ACCOUNTING & AUDITING ORG. FOR ISLAMIC FIN. INST., *SHARIAH* STANDARDS No. 17, 4–6 (2003).

378 HALUK GURULKAN, ISLAMIC SECURITIZATION A LEGAL APPROACH 62 (The Institute For Law and Finance at Johann Wolfgang Goethe University 2010).

379 BALALA, *supra* note 114, at 130.

380 Sam R. Hakim, *Islamic money market instruments*, HANDBOOK OF ISLAMIC BANKING 161, 161 (Kabir Hassan & Mervyn Lewis eds., Edward Elgar 2007).

are more than *sukuk*. The non-tradability of debts in Islamic finance affecting the *sukuk* secondary market affects securitization at the root.

3.6 Conclusion

The non-tradability of debts is not an absolute rule in Islamic law. Traditional Islamic jurisprudence classifies the tradability of debts into several types with each kind having its own restrictions and provisions. The most important type is the sale of debt for executed consideration. Two schools of thought permit it in Islamic law. The other schools of thoughts should permit it if there is only minor *gharar* (uncertainty) associated with the transaction. However, the Islamic Fiqh Academies adopted resolutions prohibiting the tradability of debts in the modern economy. The AAOIFI summarized it in a single sentence: "It is permissible to securitize assets, utilities and services, but it is not permissible to securitize debts to be negotiable." This rule negatively affects Islamic finance in general, and the *sukuk* secondary market in particular.

The next Section explains why the Islamic Fiqh Academies forbid the tradability of debts. The resolutions on which they base their arguments are clarified, analyzed, and discussed. It argues that the negotiability of debts should be allowed for several reasons explained in details within the Section. Further, it argues that allowing the tradability of debts is consistent with other Islamic rules, such as *riba* and *gharar*, and consistent with traditional Islamic jurisprudence principles and theories.

Section 4: Criticizing the Resolutions of Islamic Fiqh Academies Regarding the Tradability of Debts

4.1 Introduction

The Islamic Fiqh academies in Jeddah and Makkah set an obstacle to the growth and development of Islamic finance by resolving that the tradability of debt and securitization is forbidden, although no text from the Quran and Sunnah forbids it. The first section of this Section explains how Islamic jurisprudence recognizes debts through two fundamental theories: property and rights in Islamic jurisprudence. The resolutions will be evaluated to determine the extent to which they are compliant with Islamic jurisprudence.

The second section analyzes the arguments of the Fiqh Academies. The Islamic Fiqh Academies forbid trading debt by applying *riba* in sales and *gharar* rules. An analysis of the Academies' arguments for applying the *riba* rule shows it is not applicable. Major *gharar* and minor *gharar* are distinguished. Only major *gharar* is prohibited in Islamic law. Based on Islamic law, there is no reason to forbid debt trading that involves minor *gharar*.

The third section clarifies the legal basis for permitting the trading of debts in Islamic law. Trading debt is permissible in Islamic law based on three methodologies: *istishab* (presumption of continuity), *qiyas* (analogical reasoning), and *maslahah* mursalah (general benefit). This section explains how applying these methodologies would permit trades of debt in Islamic finance. This Section argues that permitting the tradability of debt is consistent with Islamic jurisprudence principles, fundamentals, rules, and concepts.

4.2 The Theoretical Foundation of Debt in Islamic Jurisprudence

4.2.1 Property Theory in Islamic Jurisprudence

The concept of property is "an essential building block of Islamic contract law."[381] Only objects that are considered property may be traded in Islamic law.[382] The Arabic word for property (mal) is mentioned many times in the Quran and Sunnah without a definition. In Islamic jurisprudence "the concept of mal is left wide open on the basis of people's customs and usages."[383] After Islamic schools of law emerged, Islamic scholars contributed to the evolution of Islamic contract law by defining the meaning of mal.

There are two conceptions of mal: the Hanafi school and the majority (Maliki, Shafi, and Hanbali).[384] The Hanafi school defines mal as "non-human things, created for the interest of human beings, capable of possession and transaction therein by free will."[385] The most critical element of this definition is "capable of possession." The Hanafi school requires "mal be physically possessable and preservable."[386] This requirement excludes anything that cannot be physically possessed. Therefore, "all usufructs, debts, mere rights such as the right to development, the right of pre-emption, the right to water, etc., are not considered as mal."[387] The Hanafi school considers only tangible things as mal. Therefore, only tangible things are tradable.

The majority of Islamic schools adopt a different approach. Physical possession is not essential to their conception of mal.[388] The majority defines mal as "[a] thing on which ownership is conferred and the owner when he assumes

---

381 Frank E. Vogel & Samuel L. Hayes, Islamic Law and Finance: Religion, Risk, and Return 94 (Kluwer Law International 1998).

382 Id.

383 Mohammad Islam, *Al-Mal: The Concept of Property in Islamic Legal Thought*, 14 Arab L. Q. 361, 362 (1999).

384 Islam, *supra* note 3, at 363.

385 Id.

386 Vogel & Hayes, *supra* note 1, at 94.

387 Islam, *supra* note 3, at 363.

388 Abdullah Almousa, *The Sale of Rights in Islamic Jurisprudence*, 45 Justice J. Saudi Arabia 170, 188 (2010).

it excludes others from interference...."[389] Additionally, mal has some kind of benefit.[390] Thus, the two requirements for mal are excluding others from interference and benefit. The majority does not require mal to be "physically possessable and preservable."[391] As a result, the majority's conception of mal includes both tangible and intangible things.

There is debate between Hanafi and the majority about whether usufructs and rights are mal. In Islamic jurisprudence, usufructs are "the benefits taken out of material things by way of their utilization which are ostensible, such as residing in a house, riding in a car, the wearing of a cloth and the work of an employee."[392] Rights in Islamic jurisprudence are "what the law recognizes for an individual to enable him to exercise a certain authority or bind others to perform something in relation to him."[393] As explained above, "the Hanafi school recognizes property only in material things which have tangible substance or corpus."[394] The Hanafi school does not recognize usufructs and rights as mal because they cannot be physically possessed. In contrast, the majority recognizes usufructs and rights as mal. The majority definition does not require physical possession.[395]

The groups also differ on whether debt is mal. Since the Hanafi school requires physical possession, they do not consider debt as mal.[396] The majority believes that debt is mal, like all other rights.[397] This disagreement on the definition of mal has affected many other legal issues. One of these issues is the tradability of debts.

4.2.1.1 Islamic Fiqh Academy Views on Property

In 1988, the Islamic Fiqh Academy in Jeddah adopted an important resolution regarding several kinds of financial rights. The academy resolved that business names, corporate names, trademarks, literary productions, and copyrights are tradable pursuant to Islamic law. This resolution has been the cornerstone for modern business in Islamic countries. These rights did not exist before and

---

389 Islam, *supra* note 3, at 365.
390 *Id.* at 364.
391 VOGEL & HAYES, *supra* note 1, at 94.
392 Islam, *supra* note 3, at 366.
393 *Id.*
394 *Id.*
395 Almousa, *supra* note 8, at 188.
396 OSAMAH ALLAHIM, THE SALE OF DEBT AND ITS APPLICATIONS IN CONTEMPORARY LIFE 1/88 (2012).
397 *Id.* at 1/87.

the position of Islamic scholars was unclear. The academy cleared up any confusion, saying, "Business name, corporate name, trade mark, literary production, invention or discovery, are rights belonging to their holders and... can be traded."[398]

In 1986, the Islamic Fiqh Academy in Makkah resolved an important issue regarding copyrights and patents.[399] The academy concluded, "the conditions have changed with the change of time, and there is great difference between then and now, [so] these conditions require new look [sic] that safeguards the right of every person who makes an endeavor."[400] As a result, "it is necessary that author or inventor has a right to what he has authored or invented and this right is his legal ownership, and nobody is allowed to take this ownership without his permission."[401] The Academy emphasized the differences between the past and the present. The newly established provisions were not recognized by earlier Islamic scholars.

The arguments used to permit the trading of these rights are significant. First, "[b]usiness name, corporate name, trademark, literary production, invention or discovery, are rights belonging to their holders."[402] These rights are property and therefore tradable. Second, these rights have "financial value" that did not exist in the past. If people consider a thing valuable, then it is tradable in Islamic jurisprudence, even if the thing had no value before. This two-part argument establishes financial rights which can be traded and sold pursuant to Islamic Fiqh Academies.

---

398   ISLAMIC FIQH ACADEMY (JEDDAH), RESOLUTIONS AND RECOMMENDATIONS OF THE COUNCIL OF ISLAMIC FIQH ACADEMY 89 (1st ed. 2000) ("First: Business name, corporate name, trade mark, literary production, invention or discovery, are rights belonging to their holders and have, in contemporary times, financial value which can be traded. These rights are recognized by Shariah and should not be infringed. Second: It is permitted to sell a business name, corporate name, or trademark for a price in the absence of any fraud, swindling or forgery, since it has become a financial right.").

399   ISLAMIC FIQH COUNCEL (MAKKAH), RESOLUTIONS OF THE OF ISLAMIC FIQH COUNCEL MAKKAH 244 (2006) (The academy noted how much the situation involving these issues has changed, "The transcriber used to spend years in transcribing a large book in order to produce a copy,.... after the advent of the printing press, the issue has become totally different. The author may spend most of his life in writing a useful book and publish it in order to sell it, then another person takes a copy of this book and publishes it by copying [and] the same thing can be said about the inventor.").

400   *Id.* at 245.

401   *Id.*

402   ISLAMIC FIQH ACADEMY (JEDDAH), *supra* note 18, at 89.

Given these two resolutions, the two Fiqh academies support the position of the majority conception of mal (property). They believe mal is not limited to physical possession, as the Hanafi school believes. Mal includes things that have financial value, even if they cannot be physically possessed. Usufructs and rights have financial value, so they are mal. However, one right in Islamic jurisprudence is debt.

4.2.2 Rights and Obligations Theory in Islamic Jurisprudence

The rights and obligations theory is fundamental in Islamic jurisprudence. Most Islamic jurisprudence literature explains and analyzes the rights and obligations in Islamic law. Traditional Islamic jurisprudence is classified according to sources of rights and obligations.[403] Islamic scholars explain each legal provision in each source and discuss the opinions of other schools of law if they adopt different provisions. Contemporary Islamic scholars write about the rights and obligations theory as an introduction to Islamic jurisprudence literature.[404]

Islamic law is a religious law at its core. Islamic scholars divide rights into two major parts: God's rights and people's rights.[405] They discuss the provisions and rules that control and regulate God's rights, such as praying, fasting, and pilgrimaging.[406] Muslims must fulfill these obligations for the satisfaction of God. The people's rights are the rights that people owe each other, such as contractual rights, marriage rights, etc.[407] The people's rights are a big part of Islamic jurisprudence. Many texts from the Quran and Sunna regulate God's rights. This is not the case with people's rights. Thus, there is more room for personal reasoning (*ijtihad*) with respect to people's rights.

People's rights in Islamic jurisprudence are classified into two kinds: property rights and non-property rights.[408] Property rights are those related to property, such as contractual rights, lease rights, etc. Generally, they can be traded.[409] Non-property rights are not related to property, such as marriage rights, custody rights, alimony rights, etc. These cannot be traded.[410] Describing

---

403 Mustafah Alzarqa, Obligations Theory in Islamic Jurisprudence 40 (1st ed., 1999).
404 *Id.* at 10.
405 Almousa, *supra* note 8, at 178.
406 *Id.*
407 *Id.*
408 Alzarqa, *supra* note 23, at 25.
409 Almousa, *supra* note 8, at 178.
410 *Id.* at 179.

property rights as tradable and non-property rights as non-tradable is a generality. There is debate among Islamic scholars as to the details in each provision.

Property rights in Islamic jurisprudence are also divided into two kinds: real rights and personal rights.[411] Real rights are related to things, such as ownership rights and collateral rights.[412] Personal rights are related to people, such as the right to the delivery of goods in a sales contract.[413] Real and personal rights are often combined when performing business transactions.[414] Islamic jurisprudence distinguishes between real rights and personal rights because each category has its own legal provisions. Personal rights are called obligations in Islamic jurisprudence. When Islamic scholars mention the obligations theory, they mean the personal rights theory.[415]

Obligations in Islamic jurisprudence are divided into four categories. The first category is the obligation to deliver fungible property (money or goods).[416] This category is called *dayn*, which literally means debt.[417] The second category is the obligation to deliver a "specific existing thing"[418] (this particular horse or this particular car). This category is called *ayn*.[419] The third category is the obligation to deliver services (under this category, Islamic scholars discuss labor rules).[420] The fourth category is the obligation to refrain from doing something.[421] The first category, *dayn* or debt, is the central subject of this article. As explained previously, Islamic jurisprudence considers debt a personal right to receive any fungible property (money or goods) that must be delivered in the future. How does Islamic jurisprudence deal with the tradability of debt in this broad meaning?

4.2.3   Trading Debts (Personal Property Rights) in Islamic Jurisprudence

Section 3 explained the position of Islamic scholars regarding the tradability of debts. This Section focuses on their position regarding selling debts for executed consideration to a third party because it is the scope of this article. The

---

411   ABDULRAZZAQ ALSANHOURI, RIGHTS SOURCES IN ISLAMIC JURISPRUDENCE 12 (1954).
412   Almousa, *supra* note 8, at 179.
413   ALZARQA, *supra* note 23, at 26.
414   *Id.*
415   *Id.* at 61.
416   ALSANHOURI, *supra* note 31, at 13.
417   *Id.*
418   VOGEL & HAYES, *supra* note 1, at 94.
419   ALZARQA, *supra* note 23, at 84.
420   *Id.* at 85.
421   *Id.*

Hanafi School completely prohibits such a transaction. According to them, debt is not property, so it cannot be sold. The Maliki and Shafi schools permit the sale of debt for executed consideration to a third party. This is consistent with their conception of debt as property. The Hanbali School agrees that debt is property. However, Hanbali prohibits the sale of debt for executed consideration to a third party. They are concerned about the uncertainty (*gharar*) associated with the transaction. They do not have a concern with the transaction itself.

The two Fiqh academies support the majority conception of mal (physical possession is not required) and recognize rights as an independent kind of property. Thus, they resolved that "business name, corporate name, trademark, literary production, invention or discovery, are rights belonging to their holder"[422] and they are tradable because these rights are considered property. Nevertheless, the two Fiqh Academies forbid trading debt although they consider debts as personal rights. The question is why do they prohibit trading debt and securitizing receivable while they permit trading other kinds of rights? The next section clarifies their argument.

4.3 The Arguments of the Islamic Fiqh Academies to Forbid Trading Debt (*Explanation and Discussion*)

As stated in Section 2, Islamic finance is "a prohibition-driven industry."[423] Islamic Law determines what is prohibited in finance and business. Legal issues not prohibited by Islamic law are permitted. In Islamic finance, there are two main principles which Islamic finance tractions must avoid in order to be permissible: *riba* (usury) and *gharar* (uncertainty). There is no text from the Quran or Sunnah that forbids selling debt to a third party. The arguments used by the Islamic Fiqh Academies to adopt the prohibition are based on *riba* and *gharar*.

This section explains the Islamic Fiqh Academy arguments to forbid the sale of debt to a third party and how they apply the rules of *riba* and *gharar* to trading debt. Their arguments are analyzed to determine whether they are consistent with Islamic jurisprudence theories. This section does not criticize the rule of *riba* or *gharar*. They are clearly stated in the Quran and Sunnah. This section merely criticizes the application of these rules to trading debt.

---

422 ISLAMIC FIQH ACADEMY (JEDDAH), *supra* note 18, at 89.
423 MAHMOUD A. EL-GAMAL, ISLAMIC FINANCE: LAW, ECONOMICS, AND PRACTICE 46 (Cambridge University Press 2006).

4.3.1 Riba and the Tradability of Debts

Riba is a terrible sin in Islamic law. Most Islamic finance provisions are based on avoiding *riba*. Most Westerners think that *riba* is simply charging interest on loans. This is incorrect. There are two kinds of *riba* in Islamic law: *riba* in loans (interest) and *riba* in sales (like for like).[424] The Islamic Fiqh Academies forbid the sale of debts representing money to a third part by applying the rule of *riba* in sales.

The Islamic Fiqh Academy in Jeddah states, "It is not permissible to sell a deferred debt by the non-debtor for a prompt cash, from its type or otherwise, because this results in *riba* (usury)."[425] The Islamic Fiqh Academy in Makkah states, "It is not permissible to securitize debt into securities that may be circulated in secondary market" because "it constitutes a sale of debt to a person other than the debtor in a way that includes *riba* (usury)."[426]

According to the *riba* in sales rule, in any sale transaction, if the exchanged considerations are within a single type, they must be equal. If they are not, it is *riba* and prohibited.[427] So, if the exchanged considerations are gold or dollars, then they must be equal and delivered at the same time. If the exchanged considerations are different, gold for dates or money for cars, then no *riba* rule applies. For example, A owes B $1000. B sells the debt to C for $800 cash. The Islamic Fiqh Academies assert that in selling debt for money, the considerations are a single type based on the following three arguments.

4.3.1.1 Debts Do Not Have Actual Existence
Explanation

Some Islamic scholars do not differentiate between debt itself (right to receive money or goods) and what that the debt represents (money or goods), although they do theoretically.[428] If the debt represents money, it is dealt with as if it is money and not as a right to receive money in future. If the debt represents food, it is dealt with as if it is food and not as a right to receive food in the future. For example, A owes B 1000 kg of dates; the value of the dates is $1000.

---

424 See page 33.
425 Islamic Fiqh Academy in Jeddah, *at* http://www.fiqhacademy.org.sa/qrarat/11-4.htm.
426 The Muslim World League in Makkah, *at* http://www.mwl-en.com/2012/05/23/resolutions-of-the-islamic-fiqh-council-16th-session-1422h/.
427 See page 35.
428 Theoretically, they believe that debt is an obligation. In practice, they ignore the independency of debt, just like the Islamic Fiqh Academy in Jeddah, which forbids the trading of debt if the debt represents money and the consideration is cash. *See* page 52.

B sells the debt to C for $800 cash. This transaction would be allowed according to them. If B sold the debt for 800 kg of dates ($800 value), that would be prohibited according to them. Their argument is in the first transaction the considerations are different but in the second transaction the considerations are within a single type. The same concept is applied to debts that represent money. A owes B $1000. B sells the debt to C for $800 cash. This transaction would be prohibited. If B sells the debt for 800 kg of dates ($800 value) then this would be permitted. They ignore that debts are rights to receive (things) in the future and deal with debts as they deal with the subject of the debt directly. Thus, according to them, in trading debts the creditor who sells the debt for money is selling money that the creditor will receive in the future for money he receives now. Essentially, these schools believe that the creditor sells money for money, which is prohibited according to the *riba* in sales rule.

Why do some Islamic scholars ignore the nature of debt as a personal right and deal directly with the subject of the debt that will be received in the future? These Islamic scholars argue that there is no actual existence for the debt itself. In reality, the value of the debt comes from the money that will be paid in the future, not from the debt itself.[429] In other words, the value of debt is completely dependent on the money that will be paid in the future.[430] Debt should be considered money because the two are inseparable. Therefore, the sale of debt to a third party for money should be recognized as money for money, which is prohibited according to the *riba* in sales rule.

Discussion

1. Again, Islamic scholars argue that there is no actual existence for the debt itself. What is actual existence? There are two explanations and each explanation should be discussed. First, if actual existence means physically exist, these Islamic scholars are right. Debt does not physically exist. However, the majority of Islamic schools do not require physical possession for something to be considered mal.[431] Intangible assets, such as rights and debts, are recognized as mal and can be traded. The Islamic Fiqh Academies have confirmed that position and consider modern rights, such as business name, corporate name and trade mark, to be *mal*. The Hanfai School argues that debt does not have actual existence since the Hanafi School requires physical possession. However, it is illogical for other Islamic scholars, who do not require physical possession, to adopt the same argument. Since the majority of Islamic schools

---

429 IBN HAZM, ALMOHALLA 7/452; ALLAHIM, *supra* note 16, at 1/351.
430 *Id.*
431 *See* page 87.

do not require physical possession, debt is considered mal. It is a personal property right and an intangible asset. It is different from cash, which is considered a tangible asset.[432]

Second, if actual existence means abstract existence, this is wrong. According to the obligations theory in Islamic jurisprudence, debt has actual abstract existence and is considered a personal right.[433] For example, in a sales contract, A sells a car to B for $100,000. They agree that A will deliver the car at the time of the contract and B promises to pay the money after one year. In this contract, two obligations are created. Under the first obligation, A must deliver the car and transfer title to B. Under the second obligation, B must pay A, but performance is deferred for one year. This obligation is a debt created by a contract called a credit sale. A owns the debt after finalizing the contract, not the money. The sales contract is legally binding and a new legal relationship is created between the debtor (B) and the creditor (A). The debtor must pay the money after one year and the creditor is entitled to receive the money after one year.[434]

In short, actual existence is not a requirement for a thing to be tradable according to three schools of legal thought and the two Fiqh Academies. Also, according to the obligations theory in Islamic jurisprudence, debt has legal abstract existence and is considered a personal property right.

2. This group of Islamic scholars argues that debt is completely dependent on the money itself. This does not mean the debt and the money have the same provisions. Debt depends on other factors, such time and the solvency of the debtor. These combined factors make debt different from money. Islamic jurisprudence deals with debts and money differently. If someone owns money, the relationship between the owner and the money is considered a real right. The owner can do whatever he wants with the money. In the relationship involving debt, there is no direct relationship between the creditor and the money. The debtor is in the middle. The debtor has the responsibility to pay

---

432   FASB Accounting Standards Codification, 305–310 (In the modern economy, financials deal with debt and receivables as independent kinds of assets, which are different from money. Therefore, in any financial statement, the account receivable is independent from the money account and both of them are assets. When a company wants to sell account receivables, financial banks treat the account differently from the money that the company owns.).

433   *See* page 90.

434   MAHA-HANAAN BALALA, ISLAMIC FINANCE AND LAW: THEORY AND PRACTICE IN A GLOBALIZED WORLD 99 (Tauris Academic Studies 2011) (2010).

the money in the future. That makes a significant difference between debt, as personal right, and money, as a real right, in Islamic jurisprudence.

Two examples will illustrate this difference. In our first example, A purchases 1000 kg dates from B. A receives the dates, but does not have storage. A stores his dates in B's storage. A fire burns B's storage, including A's dates. Thus, A loses his dates and cannot ask B for a replacement if there is not neglect from B.[435] In our second example, A purchases 1000 kg of dates from B, to be delivered after one year. The fire burns B's storage, including the dates owed to A. B still owes 1000 kg of dates to A.[436] In the first case, A had a direct relationship to the dates, but in the second case A had a relationship with B, not with the dates.

Another example may be helpful. A company owes A $1,000,000. The company also owes B $1,000,000. The company bankrupts and has only $1,000,000. Neither A nor B can claim all of the remaining cash. They must share the remaining cash based on the share they deserve, pursuant to Islamic jurisprudence.[437] Neither A nor B as creditors have a direct relationship to the cash owned by the company because A and B merely own debts.

Therefore, Islamic jurisprudence deals differently with the debt (as a right) and the subject of the debt that will be received in the future. Accordingly, in trading debt, the sale of debts for money is different from the sale of money for money. If they are different, different provisions of law should apply.

4.3.1.2 Debt is Equivalent to Money
Explanation

The difference between this argument and the previous one is that the previous one ignores the independence of debt and deals with the debt as if it is money instead of a right to receive the money. On the other hand, this argument acknowledges that the debt is different from the money and considers the debt as a right to receive the money, not the money itself. However, although these scholars acknowledges that debt is different from money, they argue that "debt is equivalent to money, thus a transaction of debt for money is equivalent to a transaction of money for money, attaching all the *riba* rules pertaining to the exchange of money for money."[438] These scholars argue that debt is equivalent to money based on two premises. First, "money and debt are

---

435 ALZARQA, *supra* note 23, at 36.
436 Id.
437 ALZARQA, *supra* note 23, at 34.
438 BALALA, *supra* note 54, at 102.

conceptually equivalent and, therefore, a right to receive money is conceptually equivalent to money."[439] This argument is similar to the previous one, but they try to express it in a way that acknowledges the independence of debt, and gives debt the same legal characteristics as money. The second premise is "money and debt are equivalent in value...."[440] The value of 1000 kg of dates received after one year is equivalent to 1000 kg of dates received now. Also, a $1,000 debt due a year from now is worth $1,000 in cash now. In short, these scholars argue that money and debt are conceptually equivalent and have the same value. The sale of debt for money is equivalent to the sale of money for money. As a result, the *riba* in sales rule should be applied, which results in the prohibition of the transaction.[441]

Discussion

1. The Nature of Money is Different from the Nature of Debt

Understanding the nature of money is critical to deciding whether debts are equivalent to money. The *hadith* that forbids *riba* in sales mentions only six kinds of *riba*.[442] None of them is money. Two of them are gold and silver. Using the *qiyas* methodology, Islamic scholars extend the rule to any kind of money because it has the same cause and effect as gold and silver.[443] The concept of money is not determined by the Quran and *hadith*. Islamic scholars must rely on how specialists determine and define money, and then they apply the *riba* in sales rule. Economists and lawyers define money differently.

Economically, money is "a medium of exchange, a unit of account, and a store of value."[444] "These three functions together distinguish money from other assets in the economy, such as stocks, bonds, real estate [and] art."[445] First, money is a medium of exchange, which "is an item that buyers give to sellers when they purchase goods and services."[446] If a buyer purchases an asset, he is confident that the seller will accept money.[447] Therefore, "to qualify

---

439 *Id.*
440 *Id.*
441 *Id.*
442 *See* page 35.
443 VOGEL & HAYES, *supra* note 1, at 75.
444 N. GREGORY MANKIW, PRINCIPLES OF ECONOMICS 628 (3rd ed. 2004).
445 *Id.*
446 *Id.* at 629.
447 *Id.*

as money, [it] must be the universal means[448] of exchange. . . ."[449] This function "excludes bills of exchange, Treasury bills, straps, postal orders, gold bars, etc., which are objects of purchase and sale and not in universal use as a medium of exchange."[450]

Second, money is a unit of account. This means it "is the yardstick people use to post prices."[451] For example, if someone wants to compare the cost between two cars, he will use money to make the comparison. Thus, "when we want to measure and record economic value, we use money as the unit of account."[452] This function of money excludes other kinds of assets, such as bonds, stocks, and debts. These other kinds of assets are not used as units of account. Their economic values are measured by money.

Third, money is a store of value. It "is an item that people can use to transfer purchasing power from the present to the future."[453] For example, someone sells goods or services and receives money in exchange. He can use this money to buy any kinds of goods now or in the future. However, "money is not the only store of value in the economy."[454] Any person "can also transfer purchasing power from the present to the future by holding other assets."[455]

Legally, money is defined as "all chattels which, issued by the authority of the law and denominated with reference to a unit of account, are meant to serve as universal means of exchange in the State of issue."[456] The legal definition includes two of the functions emphasized by economists: a medium of exchange and a unit of account. However, the legal definition also includes other important characteristics. According to the legal definition, "to qualify as money, a coin or note must be issued by or under the authority of the State."[457] Moreover, the note or coin "must show on its face the amount for which it is effective in law to discharge an obligation"[458] and that "means that when used as currency they are valued in law at their face value, not their

---

448 Universal in one jurisdiction.
449 ROYSTON MILES GOODE & CENTRE FOR COMMERCIAL LAW STUDIES, PAYMENT OBLIGATIONS IN COMMERCIAL AND FINANCIAL TRANSACTIONS 3 (1983).
450 Id.
451 MANKIW, supra note 64, at 629.
452 Id.
453 Id.
454 Id.
455 Id.
456 F. A. MANN, THE LEGAL ASPECT OF MONEY: WITH SPECIAL REFERENCE TO COMPARATIVE PRIVATE AND PUBLIC INTERNATIONAL LAW 8 (4th ed. 1982).
457 GOODE AND CENTRE FOR COMMERCIAL LAW STUDIES, supra note 69, at 2.
458 Id.

intrinsic worth."[459] These two additional legal characteristics, issuance and value, exclude other kinds of assets not issued by the state, and their values are determined by the market.[460]

Economically and legally, the nature of money is different from the nature of debt. Economically, debt is not a medium of exchange or a unit of account. These two functions are critical to the differences between money and other assets. Because debts do not have these functions, they are not equivalent to money. Legally, while debt may be issued by the state, it is not the universal means of exchange. Furthermore, debt value is not determined by the state as is with cash. Debt is not the universal means of exchange and its value is not determined by the state, so it is not equivalent to money.

2. The Value of Money is Different from the Value of Debt

Some Islamic scholars assert that the value of debt has the same value as money (or any property) that will be received in the future. They ignore an important component of any credit transaction, which is time value. Time value means a "dollar paid in the future is worth less than a dollar today."[461] Thus, to "make an investment is to part with money today in exchange for a return payment (or series of payments) in the future."[462] In other words, "cash in hand (liquidity) is worth . . . more than the right to be paid the same amount in the future."[463] Thus, "the translation of the future value into present value" is called the valuation process.[464] Because some people prefer present consumption to future consumption, "future values need to be discounted to make them comparable with present values. . . ."[465] This is called discounting.[466] Time value, valuation, and discounting are considered when determining the value of debt.

---

459   *Id.*

460   Between 1835 and 1866, private banks in the USA used to issue currencies traded among the people. The period is called Free-banking Era. However, the National Bank Act of 1863 ended that era and granted the authority of issuing currencies nationally to the federal government. See Banking Without Regulation: The Freeman: Foundation for Economic Education, http://fee.org/the_freeman/detail/banking-without-regulation.

461   WILLIAM J. CARNEY, CORPORATE FINANCE: PRINCIPLES AND PRACTICE 38 (2nd ed. 2010).

462   *Id.*

463   Balala, *supra* note 54, at 102.

464   CARNEY, *supra* note 81, at 38.

465   Fahim Khan, *Time Value of Money and Discounting in Islamic Perspective*, 1 REV. OF ISLAMIC ECON. 33, 36 (1991).

466   CARNEY, *supra* note 81, at 38.

In Islamic finance, as well as conventional finance, "the time value of money in economic and financial transactions is recognized."[467] So, "in a trade transaction, if the payment of price is deferred, the time value of money will be included in the price of the commodity."[468] Also, "in a leasing contract, time value is an integral part of the rent that parties agree upon."[469] Time value was also recognized by the prophet Mohammed himself. Particularly, the prophet Mohammed exercised the discounting concept in *salam* contracts.[470]

Salam is a sale where "the seller undertakes to supply some specific goods to the buyer at a future date in exchange for an advanced price fully paid at spot."[471] Thus, "the price is cash, but the supply of the purchased goods is deferred."[472] *Salam* is "beneficial to the seller, because he received the price in advance."[473] Further, it is "beneficial to the buyer also, because normally, the price in *salam* used to be lower than the price in spot sales."[474]

Credit sales, *bay al mo'ajal*, are permissible in Islamic law.[475] In these transactions, the seller delivers the goods immediately. The buyer defers payment. The payment is higher than paying "in spot," because of the time value. As explained in Section 2, most Islamic banking finance is based on *murabaha* finance. *Murabaha* finance is built substantively on time value. Islamic banks profit from the difference in value between purchasing goods on the spot and selling them to customers on credit. Accordingly, "Islam does have a concept of time preference."[476]

In modern Islamic finance, "there is no independent Islamic benchmark available to be used for pricing Islamic financial instruments, particularly for pricing the *sukuk*."[477] Time value and the valuation process, however, is recog-

---

467 Fahim Khan, *Islamic methods for government borrowing and monetary management*, HANDBOOK OF ISLAMIC BANKING 285, 295 (Kabir Hassan & Mervyn Lewis eds., Edward Elgar 2007).
468 Id.
469 Id.
470 MUḤAMMAD TAQĪ USMĀNĪ, AN INTRODUCTION TO ISLAMIC FINANCE 129 (Kluwer Law International 2002).
471 Id. at 128.
472 Id.
473 Id. at 129.
474 Id.
475 THE ISLAMIC SCHOOL OF LAW: EVOLUTION, DEVOLUTION, AND PROGRESS 139 (Peri J. Bearman, Rudolph Peters, & Frank E. Vogel eds., Harvard University Press 2005).
476 Khan, *supra* note 85, at 299.
477 Id.

nized in Islamic finance as well as conventional finance. Conventional finance has a well-established process for evaluating this component and "LIBOR[478] is being mostly used as a reference point for pricing these [*sukuk*]."[479] LIBOR is used as a benchmark for *sukuk* if such *sukuk* will be traded internationally. If the *sukuk* will be traded nationally, the interest rate of the local national bank "serves as a benchmark for the government's Islamic securities issued at the national level."[480]

In conclusion, the value of a debt or a receivable is different from money paid on the spot because of the time value. Because of this, the value of receivables is discounted to be less than its face value. Time value and discounting are recognized by conventional finance and Islamic finance. Islamic finance institutions rely on the interest rate (such as Libor) to evaluate Islamic instruments, such as *sukuk*. Debt is not equivalent to money conceptually or in value. Therefore, the rule regarding *riba* in sales should not apply to the sale of debts for money.

4.3.1.3 The Transaction in General is Equivalent to Riba Transaction
Explanation

Some Islamic scholars argue that the general sale of a debt transaction is equivalent to a *riba* transaction because they have the same result. Both exchange money for money with unequal amounts.[481] For example, A owes B $1000 due after one year. B sells the debt to C for $800 cash. After one year, C will receive $1000 in exchange for the $800 that he paid to B. In a *riba* in sales transaction, two considerations of the same kind (gold for gold or silver for silver) are exchanged for different amounts ($1000 for $800). Of course, this is prohibited in Islamic law. Thus, they argue, the same rule should be applied to the sale of debt for money because they have the same result.

The difference between this argument and the previous one is that these Islamic scholars acknowledge that debt is independent from money, and not equivalent to it. They do not focus on the transaction itself, but on the result

---

478 LIBOR (London Interbank Offered Rate) is "a benchmark rate that some of the world's leading banks charge each other for short-term loans. LIBOR is administered by the ICE Benchmark Administration (IBA)." See London Interbank Offered Rate (LIBOR) Definition, INVESTOPEDIA, http://www.investopedia.com/terms/l/libor.asp.
479 Khan, *supra* note 85, at 299.
480 Id.
481 ALLAHIM, *supra* note 16, at 2/526.

of the transaction. Since they have the same result, money for money with the different amounts, the same provision (prohibition) should apply.

Discussion

In this section, the contracts bai al-inah, *tawarruq*, and *murabaha* will be analyzed to determine whether they are *riba*. In bai al inah (sale and buy back), the financier sells goods (which he already owns) to a client as a credit sale while simultaneously buying back the goods from the client at a cheaper price.[482] The goods are not the real subject of the transaction. The purpose of the transaction is for the client to get cash in a way that avoids *riba*. The majority of Islamic schools forbid bai al-inah because it is very similar to *riba* and has the same result.[483] At the end of transaction, the financier pays money to the client, and the client owes the financier more than he paid.

The majority of Islamic schools have developed the tawarrruq transaction as an alternative to facilitate financing without using *riba* or bai al-inah. The term *tawarruq* "is derived from the word al-warq...."[484] Al-warq means derham orthe silver coins of the Islamic empire.[485] Technically, *tawarruq* is "the purchasing of a commodity on credit by the *mutawarriq* (seeker of cash) and selling it to a person other than the initial seller (third party) for a lower price on cash."[486] The majority of Islamic schools permit a *tawarruq* transaction. The Islamic Fiqh Academy in Makkah confirmed that *tawarruq* is permitted.[487] It is not like *riba* because there are three parties in this transaction: the mutawarriq, the seller, and the purchaser. The mutawarriq buys goods from the seller on credit and then the mutawarriq sells the goods to the purchaser and receives cash. According to the majority of Islamic schools, the transaction is different from *riba*, because the source of cash is different from the creditor.[488]

The concept of *tawarruq* has been altered to create *murabaha* financing, with the bank acting as the manager of finance. As explained in Section 2, *murabaha* is the most popular Islamic financial instrument. In a *murabaha* contract, "the bank agrees to buy an asset or goods from a third party [based on the market

---

482 THE ISLAMIC JURISPRUDENCE ENCYCLOPEDIA, 9/96 (Second ed. 1992).
483 Id.
484 IMAN MIHAJAT, THE REAL *TAWARRUQ* CONCEPT ISLAMIC ECONOMIC FORUM FOR INDONESIAN DEVELOPMENT (ISEFID) 5 (2009).
485 Id.
486 Id.
487 ISLAMIC FIQH COUNCEL (MAKKAH), *supra* note 19, at 395.
488 Id.

price], and then resells the goods to its client with a mark-up."[489] If the client needs cash, not goods, the bank sells the goods on behalf of the client to a third party based on the market price (without the mark-up). Then the bank receives the cash and transfers it to the client. The difference between *tawarruq* and *murabaha* is that in *tawarruq* the person who needs cash purchases and sells the goods himself. In *murabaha*, the bank purchases the goods and resells them to the client and then the bank resells the goods on behalf of the client to a third party. These complex transactions are implemented within a few hours. The client does not leave the bank office until all *murabaha* components are finished. At the end of the transaction, he will leave the bank with cash and an obligation to pay to the bank more than what he received. He receives cash equal to the market price but he owes the bank the market price plus the markup. Nevertheless, the *murabaha* transaction is permitted according to the majority of Islamic scholars. The Islamic Fiqh Academy in Jeddah issued a resolution in 1988 to confirm that the *murabaha* transaction is permissible.[490] They argue that a *murabaha* transaction is a real sale contract with multiple parties. Unlike *riba* and bai al-inah, the client receives the cash from a third party, not the bank. Thus, the source of cash is different from the creditor.[491]

The main difference between bay al-inah on the one hand and *tawarruq* and *murabaha* is whether the source of the cash is the same party as the creditor. According to the majority, Bai al-inah is forbidden because the financier is the source of cash and also the creditor. So the sales contract is equivalent and has the same result as a *riba* contract. On the other hand, *tawarruq* and *murabaha* are allowed because the source of cash is different from the creditor. The result of these two transactions is distinct from the result of a *riba* transaction. So, according to the majority of Islamic scholars and the two Fiqh Academies, there is no reason to forbid them.[492]

The argument used to permit *tawarruq* and *murabaha* can also be applied to the sale of debts and receivables. In the sale of debt, there could be three parties and the source of money would be different from the creditor. For example, A sells a car to B for $100,000 due after one year. Then, A sells the debt to C for $90,000. C waits one year and receives $100,000 from B. A is the creditor,

---

489 Abbas Mirakhor & Iqbal Zaidi, *Profit-and-loss sharing contracts in Islamic finance*, in HANDBOOK OF ISLAMIC BANKING 49, 52 (Kabir Hassan & Mervyn Lewis eds., Edward Elgar 2007).

490 ISLAMIC FIQH ACADEMY (JEDDAH), *supra* note 18, at 86.

491 *Id.*

492 ISLAMIC FIQH COUNCEL (MAKKAH), *supra* note 19, at 395.

B is the debtor, and C is the third party. The creditor delivers goods or services on credit to the debtor. The creditor sells the debt to a third party. The third party will wait until the due date and then receives money from the debtor. In each relationship (creditor and debtor, creditor and third party, debtor and third party), none of the parties receives money from the same party he pays money. So, the result of the sale of debt is different from *riba* because in each relationship the source of cash is not the creditor. Therefore, the sale of debt should be permissible, because the argument for *tawarruq* and *murabaha* should also be applied to the sale of debt.

4.3.2 Gharar (Uncertainty or Speculative Risk)
Explanation

Some Islamic scholars try to forbid trading debt using *gharar* (uncertainty or risk). *Gharar*, the second major principle in Islamic finance, is forbidden by *Sunnah*. The Sunnah does not provide any definition or explanation of *gharar*. Islamic schools, however, have set a general rule for *gharar* in financial transactions.[493] There are four conditions that must be present to apply the *gharar* rule. First, the ghrarar must be excessive. Second, the contract must be "a commutative" financial contract, which means not a gift or donation. Third, the *gharar* must affect one of the main components of the contract. Fourth, there is no need for the contract and there is an alternative. If these conditions are present, the contract is forbidden because of the *gharar* rule.[494]

Some Islamic scholars argue that trading debts is forbidden because all four conditions of the *gharar* rule are present in the sale of debts transaction.[495] First, *gharar* exists and sometimes is excessive. The purchaser is not always sure he will receive the money at the time due, or if he will receive the total amount due. The debtor may die or go bankrupt. Second, the sale of debt is a commutative contract. There are at least two parties and the purchaser will be affected by the *gharar*. Third, *gharar* must affect one of the main components of the contract. The debt is a main component of the contract. Forth, usually there is no need for the sale of debt. If the purchaser is looking for profit, there are many permitted ways, other than trading debt. As a result, the *gharar* rule should be applied to trading debt, and it would be a forbidden transaction.[496]

---

493 *See* page 39.
494 *Id.*
495 Alkasaney, Badae'e Alsanae'e 5/148 (2nd ed. 1986); Mohammed Kurdey, Ahkam Bay'e Aldayn 118 (1st ed. 1992).
496 *Id.*

Discussion

Islamic jurisprudence distinguishes between major *gharar* and minor *gharar*. Minor *gharar* is permitted while major *gharar* is not.[497] All commercial and financial transactions include some risk and uncertainty. Only transactions that include high risk and uncertainty, making them akin to gambling, are forbidden in Islamic law. Credit sales are permitted despite the existence of risk. If the risk is considered minor, not major, the transaction will be permissible. If all kinds of risk were forbidden, commercial and business transactions would be very limited. The type of risk involved in the sale of debt is the same type of risk involved in the credit sale transaction meaning it is neither greater nor lesser. If the credit sale transaction is permitted the sale of debts should also be permitted. Otherwise, both of them should be prohibited.

Some Islamic schools permit the sale of debt when certain conditions are met, in order to avoid major *gharar*.[498] The purchaser must believe the debtor has the ability to pay the debt. The purchaser must have full information of the debtor's solvency. Finally, the debtor and the purchaser must not be enemies.[499] The purpose of these conditions is to minimize *gharar* as much as possible. When the Islamic schools first set these conditions, centuries ago, they were deemed appropriate.

Now, there is a sophisticated industry to evaluate debts and examine how much risk is involved. There are special international standards to evaluate debts and distinguish high risk from low risk. These standards could be used to evaluate *gharar* on a case-by-case basis, taking the place of the conditions to avoid major *gharar*.

Each bank and financial institutions has its own risk assessment department, with many getting assistance from rating agencies, to evaluate and assess the risk associated with any particular debt securities. The rating shows how likely the debtor will be able to pay the debt by the due date. Debt securities are classified into different levels. The chart below shows the debts securities rating scale.[500]

---

497   *See* page 39.
498   KURDEY, *supra* note 115, at 111.
499   ALLAHIM, *supra* note 16, at 1/355.
500   Bond Ratings—Series 7, INVESTOPEDIA, *at* http://www.investopedia.com/exam-guide/series-7/debt-securities/bond-ratings.asp (last visited Jul 3, 2014).

Moody's vs. Standard & Poor's Bond Ratings

Bond Rating

Moody's	Standard & Poor's	Grade	Risk
Aaa	AAA	Investment, Highest Quality	Lowest Risk
Aa	AA	Investment, Very High Quality	Low Risk
A	A	Investment, High Quality	Low Risk
Baa	BBB	Minimum Investment Grade	Medium Risk
Ba	BB	Junk, Speculative	High Risk
B	B	Junk, Very Speculative	Higher Risk
Caa	CCC	Junk, Default Possible	Higher Risk
Ca	CC	Junk, Default Probable	Extreme Risk
C	D	Junk, In actual or imminent default	Highest Risk

The first three levels, AAA (lowest risk), AA (lower risk), and A (low risk) would be considered minor *gharar*. In Islamic finance, debts in these three levels would be permissible to trade. The levels Ba or BB and below would be considered major *gharar*. Debts in these levels would not be permissible to trade. The levels Baa or BBB (medium risk) would be controversial. Conservative schools would forbid trading debts classified as Baa or BBB because they would be considered major *gharar*. The more liberal schools would permit trading debts classified at this level because they would be considered minor *gharar*. This modern, sophisticated ranking system can achieve the same result as the conditions required by some Islamic schools to minimize *gharar*.

There is always risk and uncertainty in trading debt. However, this normal risk does not justify the prohibition of all trade of debt. It is unreasonable, impractical, and inconsistent with the *gharar* rule. Since Islamic jurisprudence distinguishes between major and minor *ghrarar*, debts with major *gharar* should be distinguished from debts with minor *gharar*. Because it is more practical and consistent with Islamic finance principles, the Islamic finance industry should rely on the modern credit rating standards to determine the risk of debts and avoid major *gharar*.

4.4   Islamic Legal Basis for Permitting the Negotiability of Debt

Trading debts should be permissible in Islamic law based on three methodologies: *istishab*, *qiyas*, and *maslahah mursalah*. All four Islamic schools of law recognize these methodologies. This section shows how these methodologies could be a basis for permitting the trading of debts in Islamic law.

4.4.1   Istishab (Presumption of Continuity)

As explained in Section 2, *istishab* is a methodology used by all Islamic schools of legal thought to determine whether such a legal issue is prohibited or permitted.[501] In *istishab*, there is a presumption that a rule is still valid because of "lack of evidence to establish any change."[502] For example, the general rule regarding food and drinks in Islamic law is that it is permissible[503] except what is prohibited specifically by Quran or Sunnah, such as pork or alcohol.[504] If there is a new kind of food unknown during the Prophet's life, the presumption is that eating these kinds of food is permissible if there is no specific text from the Quran and Sunnah that forbids it. In short, *istishab* holds that "when there is a ruling in the law, whether prohibitory or permissive, it will be presumed to continue until the contrary is proved."[505]

The general rule for contracts and commercial transactions in Islamic law is that they are presumed permissible if there is no text from the Quran or Sunnah that forbids them.[506] Ibn Taymiiah, a prominent thirteenth century Islamic scholar said, "The underlying principle in contracts and stipulations is permissibility and validity. Any [contract or stipulation] is prohibited and void only if there is an explicit text [from the Quran, the Sunnah or ijma] or a *qiyas* proving its prohibition and voiding."[507] This rule is very important to modern Islamic finance. Most of today's transactions were unknown during the period

---

[501]   See page 28.
[502]   MOHAMMAD HASHIM KAMALI, PRINCIPLES OF ISLAMIC JURISPRUDENCE 384 (3rd rev. and enlarged ed. 2003).
[503]   *Id.* at 386.
[504]   *Id.*
[505]   *Id.* at 388.
[506]   VOGEL & HAYES, *supra* note 1, at 98.
[507]   *Id.*

of revelation. Contemporary Islamic scholars decide whether they are permissible based on the general rules of contracts.[508]

The sale of debt is permitted based on that underlying principle. However, the Islamic fiqh Academies exclude the sale of debt from the general principle of permissibility by applying the *riba* in sales rule. The previous section criticized the arguments for applying the *riba* in sales rule, and argues it is not applicable to debt. Based on *istishab*, the sale of debt should be presumed permissible. There is no text from the Quran or the Sunnah that forbids the sale of debt, and the *riba* in sales rule is not applicable. Debt should be classified by debt rating professionals to minimize *gharar*.

4.4.2 Qiyas (Analogical Reasoning)

If there is no text from the Quran or the Sunnah, *qiyas* is the preferred Islamic legal methodology.[509] As explained in Section 2, *qiyas* is "the extension of a *Shariah* ruling from an original case to a new case because the new case has the same effective cause as the original case"[510] and "the emphasis of *qiyas* is identification of a common cause between the original and new case."[511] For example, the Quran and the Sunnah forbid liquor. The effective cause is that it is an intoxicant. Islamic scholars apply the original case, the prohibition of liquor, to new cases, such as wine, because they are both intoxicating.[512] *Qiyas* is recognized as a source of Islamic laws and rules by all four Islamic schools of law.[513]

Trading debt could be permitted in Islamic law by applying *qiyas* to trading debt and comparing it with *tawarruq* and *murabaha*. As explained in the previous section, the majority of Islamic schools and the two Fiqh Academies accept *tawarruq and murabaha* because the source of cash is from someone other than the creditor. In contrast, the majority and the two Fiqh Academies forbid bai al-inah because the creditor is also the source of cash. The effective cause that makes *tawarruq* and *murabaha* acceptable is that the source of cash is different from the creditor. This effective cause may also exist in the sale of debt. None of the parties receive money from a party who is considered a creditor in the transaction. For example, A sells a car to B for $100,000.

---

508 MUHAMMAD TAQĪ USMĀNĪ, AN INTRODUCTION TO ISLAMIC FINANCE 152 (Kluwer Law International 2002).
509 *See* page 27.
510 SHAH ABDUL HANNAN, USUL AL FIQH (ISLAMIC JURISPRUDENCE) 20 (1999).
511 *Id.*
512 KAMALI, *supra* note 122, at 268.
513 *Id.* at 254.

B promises to pay after one year. A sells the debt to C for $90,000. C waits one year and receives $100,000 from B. A is the creditor, B is the debtor, and C is the third party. The creditor delivers goods or services in a credit sale to the debtor. Then, the creditor sells the debt to a third party and receives money from him. The third party waits until the due date and receives money from the debtor. Thus, in each relationship (creditor and debtor, creditor and third party, debtor and third party), no party receives money from the same party to whom he pays money.

By applying *qiyas*, the permissibility of *tawarruq* and *murabaha* could be extended to the sale of debts for money. The effective cause that makes *tawarruq* and *murabaha* permissible also exists in the sale of debt. The source of cash in these transactions is not the creditor. The *qiyas* methodology shows that the permissibility of trading debt is consistent with other Islamic finance rules and provisions.

4.4.3   Maslahah (General Benefit)

Maslahah is an Islamic Law source adopted by all four Islamic schools of law. It means general benefit or public interest.[514] Islamic schools of law recognize *maslahah* (general benefit or public interest) as an important ground for establishing new rules and laws.[515] Three conditions must be met. First, the benefit must be real. Second, the benefit must be general, not limited to one person or a few people. Third, there can be no conflict with the Quran or the Sunnah.[516] If these conditions are met, the benefit may be established as a law or rule in Islamic jurisprudence. On the basis of *maslahah* Islamic scholars permit currency, establish prisons, and impose agriculture land tax.[517] Many rules related to the state and unknown during the Prophet's life are established based on *maslahah*.

There will be a major public benefit if trading debt is permitted. The economy of the Muslims countries will be grow, develop and be more efficient. Since the financial market is an important part of the economy, a developed and diverse debt market would make the financial market competitive, efficient and not just dominated by a few banks. A diverse debt market facilitates varied sources of fund that assist companies to grow and expand. It also serves as an investment vehicle for investors who are looking for stable and predictable

---

514   KAMALI, *supra* note 122, at 351 (In this context I will use general benefit, to not be confused with interest as charged on loans.).
515   KAMALI, *supra* note 122, at 358.
516   Id.
517   ABDUL HANNAN, *supra* note 130, at 26.

income. However, because of the prohibition of trading debts, Islamic debt market is illiquid and non-diverse and as a result the debt market in Muslims countries is an inefficient tool in contributing to economic growth.

The rest of this section explains how allowing the trading of debts would make the Islamic debt market more liquid and diverse. Liquidity and diversity would allow the Islamic debt market to be attractive to investors and competitive with the conventional debt market.. Muslim economies would be strengthened by providing the benefits of liquidity and diversity to the general public as opposed to a limited group of people. Debt trading does not conflict with any text from the Quran or the Sunnah. Further, *riba* and *gharar* are not applicable to trading debt as explained in the previous section. Therefore, *maslahah* methodology should be applied.

4.4.3.1 *Liquidity*

Saudi Arabia has the strongest economy and financial market in all Muslim countries. The Saudi government established a modern and sophisticated legal structure for trading debt securities. Some conventional bonds are already traded in the Saudi debt market. Despite the effort of the Saudi government, only a third of *sukuk* issuances are listed on the Saudi Exchange Market because of the prohibition of trading debts in the secondary debt market.[518]

The Saudi government has tried many solutions to avoid the non-tradability of debt in Islamic finance. The Saudi General Authority of Civil Aviation (GACA) devised one solution to avoid non-tradability.[519] In October 2013, the GACA issued guaranteed *sukuk* with a total value of SR15.211 billion ($4.056 billion) and a profit rate of 3.21 percent annually.[520] The structure of the *sukuk* is *murabaha*.[521] It is due in 2023.[522] The deal "was 1.9 times oversubscribed with strong demand from a wide range of investors, including banks, sovereign funds, pension agencies, insurance companies and corporations."[523] The funds generated by this *sukuk* "will be used for the construction of the new

---

518 Saudi Hollandi Capital, *supra* note 39 at 3.
519 Abir Atamech, *Sukuk* Quarterly Bulletin 4Q 2013 3 (2014).
520 HSBC and NCB Capital announce completion of SR15bn GACA *sukuk*, Arab News Oct. 7, 2013, *at* http://www.arabnews.com/node/466953.
521 Al-Jadaan advises on largest *sukuk* in the Kingdom of Saudi Arabia, Al-Jadaan & Partners Law Firm, *at* http://www.aljadaan.com/?module=announcements&page=details_en&id=126.
522 *Id.*
523 *Id.*

King Abdul Aziz International Airport in Jeddah."[524] The head of capital markets & corporate finance in the Hong Kong and Shanghai Banking Corporation (HSBC) Saudi Arabia commented: "This *sukuk* has been launched as one single issuance, and in doing so has become the largest single-tranche *sukuk* ever issued in Saudi Arabia."[525] Because it is such a large issuance, the *sukuk* is guaranteed by the Ministry of Finance in Saudi Arabia.[526]

The Saudi government, represented by the Ministry of Finance, was very interested in marketing the *sukuk* among Saudi investors. The government does not necessarily need funds, but it wanted to support and develop the debt market.[527] The debt market in Saudi Arabia, however, is illiquid and investors may avoid purchasing the *sukuk* because of the lack of an exit strategy. The government needed a way around the non-tradability of the *sukuk* in the secondary market. So, the *sukuk* was "approved by the Saudi Arabian Monetary Agency (SAMA) to be eligible for repo arrangements and has also been assigned zero percent risk weighting for capital adequacy calculation purpose."[528] Hence, "investors can hold this *sukuk* as an investment, but also use it as an effective liquidity tool by using it to guarantee cash from the central bank."[529] If an investor needs cash, the government will repurchase the *sukuk* from the investor at a face value (based on the repo-agreement) instead of selling it on the secondary market. This arrangement offers an exit strategy for investors. The *sukuk* is less risky because now investors do not have to hold it until maturity. This solves the problem of liquidity in this particular transaction especially for domestic investors. All theses complicated arrangements are because of the prohibition of trading debt. If trading debt were permitted, the government would encourage the debt secondary market, which would be a healthier and a more efficient and effective option.

The illiquid secondary market is a significant obstacle to developing the debt market in Muslim countries. Saudi Arabia made a huge effort to help the

---

524 ISLAMIC FINANCE NEWS, DEALS OF THE YEAR HANDBOOK 4 (Nazneen Halim, et al. eds., Red Money Group 2013).

525 Saudi Gazette, GACA SUKUK ISSUE HITS SR15.21 BILLION, SAUDI GAZETTE, at http://www.saudigazette.com.sa/index.cfm?method=home.regcon&contentid=20131007182895 (last visited Apr 9, 2014).

526 Id.

527 For the 2013 fiscal year, "total revenue is projected to be around (US $301.6) billions in 2013 and expenditure to be around (US $246.7) billions. As a result, a surplus of SR 206 (US $54.9) billions should be realized." SAUDI MINISTRY OF FINANCE, SAUDI BUDGET FOR 2014 1 (2013).

528 HSBC and NCB Capital announce completion of SR15bn GACA *sukuk, supra* note 140.

529 Id.

debt market by establishing a platform for the trading of debt and finding a solution to promote many *sukuk* deals. However, this kind of solution only works deal by deal. It is not a systemic solution. Moreover, this solution might be attractive to domestic investors, but not international investors. Permitting the trading of debt will be a systemic solution for all kinds of *sukuk* and all types of investors. Most of the current *sukuk* that is unlisted because of the prohibition would be listed and traded, and would provide the secondary debt market with liquidity.

4.4.3.2 Diversity

If the tradability of debt were permitted, the secondary *sukuk* market would be diverse and not limited to a few kinds of *sukuk* as it is now. The *Sukuk* Report 2013, issued by the Islamic Financial Market Organization (IFIM), states that the "*Ijarah Sukuk* structure has been the most popular and widely used structure for International... issuance."[530]

As explained in the previous Section, *sukuk ijarah*, or the prevalent form of international *sukuk* issuances, is preferred by investors because the two Fiqh academies and AAOIFI have approved its trade in the secondary market. There is no religious risk in *sukuk ijarah* because no Islamic scholars oppose its tradability in the secondary market. Solutions, such as the solution used by Saudi Arabia, that are used to solve the tradability problems, might not work with an international issuance.

Though Islamic banks are very important in Islamic finance, they cannot enter the *sukuk* market because of the prohibition on trading debt. Baljeet Grewal, the managing director and vice chairman of the Islamic Financial Services Board (IFCB), said, "As at end-2010,... the Islamic banking sector worldwide is valued at approximately US $850 billion in terms of assets, [so] Islamic banking assets [deposits] represented 83.4% of overall Islamic assets, followed by *sukuk* funds (11.3%) and Islamic funds [equity fund] (4.6%)."[531] Islamic banks do not invest in the *sukuk* market because most of their revenue is considered receivables, which are not tradable pursuant to the two Fiqh Academies.

For example, Al-Rajhi Bank, the biggest Islamic bank in the Middle East and North Africa, had total assets of SR 267,383 million ($71,302 million) at the end of 2012.[532] According to the bank's financial statement, "Net financing accounted

---

[530] THE INTERNATIONAL ISLAMIC FINANCIAL MARKET, IIFM *SUKUK* REPORT 24 (3RD EDITION 2013).

[531] BALJEET KAUR GREWAL, CONSTRAINTS ON GROWTH IN ISLAMIC FINANCE 1 (2011).

[532] ALRAJHI BANK, ALRAJHI BANK ANNUAL REPORT 2012 11 (2012).

for 64.3% of the consolidated total assets of the group as at December 31, 2012, and represents the main driver of revenue and balance sheet growth."[533]

Net financing by products and location as at December 31, 2012, SR million.[4]

Product	Inside KSA	Outside KSA	Provision	Total net Financing	Composition %
Corporate Mutajara	34,422	836	(2,210)	33,047	19.2
Instalment sale	124,595	2,992	(1,826)	125,762	73.1
Murabaha	9,849	3,500	(785)	12,564	7.3
Credit cards	577	3	(12)	568	0.3
Istisnaa	0	0	0	0	0
Total	169,443	7,331	(4,833)	171,941	100.0

Looking at the chart above, "installment [sic] sale is by far the largest financing product overall, accounting for nearly three-fourths of net financing, followed by corporate mutajara."[534] Although the installment sale is the largest financing product and net financing is "the main driver of revenue and balance sheet growth,"[535] Al-Rajhi Bank cannot securitize it and sell it on the secondary market. An installment sale is a receivable, which cannot be securitized and traded according to the Fiqh academies. Securitizing this product may not be a useful financial strategy for the bank, but Islamic bank managers are unable to even entertain the possibility. They must follow the rules set by Islamic scholars. This is true for all Islamic banks around the world, not only Al-Rajhi Bank.

If debts and receivables could be traded in Islamic finance, Islamic banks could securitize their account receivable. Islamic banks would enter the *sukuk* market and contribute to its development. Many kinds of *sukuk* would be issued, so the *sukuk* market would be diverse. International investors would likely be attracted to the *sukuk* issued by Islamic banks because of their solvency. This dynamic would make the *sukuk* market more attractive, diverse, and successful.

---

533   *Id.* at 31.
534   *Id.* at 32.
535   *Id.*

In conclusion, the whole economy of Muslim countries would benefit from the permissibility of trading debts. The Islamic debt market would be more liquid and diverse. It would be an efficient source of funds for new and growing companies and it would be an investment vehicle for investors who are looking for stable and predictable income. The benefits would strengthen and stabilize the economies of Muslim countries and would not conflict with any text from the Quran or the Sunnah. Thus, there are Islamic legal grounds for permitting the trading of debt in Islamic finance.

Section 5: Conclusion

The challenges posed by the non-liquidity and non-diversity of the Islamic debts market make the market an inefficient tool on contributing to Muslim economic growth. Islamic scholars and experts created *sukuk* as an Islamic debt instrument to avoid *riba* (usury), but the *sukuk* market still struggles with the prohibition of the trade of debt due to the prohibition of the two Fiqh Academies.

The two Fiqh Academies have argued that trading debt is forbidden because of *riba* and *gharar* (uncertainty). They apply the *riba* in sales rules for debts, based on three premises: first, the debt does not physically exist, so selling debt for money is considered selling money for money. I have argued, however, that physicality is not required in order to be considered *mal* (property), a position adopted by the majority of Islamic schools of legal thought. Pursuant to the theory of obligations in Islamic jurisprudence, debt has an independent existence as a personal right and it may be tradable. Second, they argue that debt is equivalent to money conceptually and in value. Conversely, I have explained they are different and cannot be equivalent. Debts have characteristics that distinguish them legally from money in Islamic law. Also, since Islamic law recognizes time value, debts and cash have different values. Third, they argue that the result of a transaction in which debts are traded is equivalent to *riba*. Both end with cash being offered for delayed money in a different amount. I have pointed out that in the sale of debt for money, the source of cash is from someone other than a creditor. In a *riba* transaction, the creditor is the same person as the source of cash. Thus, according to the argument I present on opposition to these three premises that the *riba* in the sales rule is not applicable in the trading of debt.

The second argument of the two Fiqh Academies pertains to *gharar*. *Gharar* is a real concern in trading debts. However, as only major *gharar* is forbidden in Islamic law, Islamic finance could rely on the modern debt rating standards to evaluate the riskiness of a debt, which is not uncommon in Islamic finance. Islamic finance institutions rely on LIBOR to evaluate the price and cost of *sukuk*. Thus, if a debt is rated low risk based on the modern debt rating standards, then it should be permissible to securitize and trade it. Low risk is equivalent to minor *gharar* in Islamic law. With this proposal, Islamic finance can avoid *gharar* and benefit from low risk debts and *sukuk*, rather than forbid the entire practice.

Therefore, if *riba* rules are not applicable, and *gharar* can be avoided by the modern, sophisticated debt rating standards, there should be a new rule regarding the negotiability of debt in Islamic finance based on Islamic methodologies and law sources. Trading and securitizing debts should be permitted in Islamic law, with one condition, that the debt should be considered low risk. This new rule, the permissibility of trading debts, is supported by three Islamic legal bases, *istishab*, *qiyas*, and *maslaha*, which are recognized by all four Islamic schools of legal thought.

First, trading debts is permitted in Islamic law based on *istishab* (presumption of continuity). An action is permitted if there is no text in the Quran or the Sunnah forbidding it. This is the general rule that governs all business and commercial transactions in Islamic law. There is no text in the Quran or the Sunnah that forbids trading and securitizing debts; therefore, it should be presumed permissible.

Second, trading and securitizing debts is permitted in by *qiyas* (analogy). *Tawarruq* and *murabaha* transactions are permitted in Islamic law because the source of cash is someone other than the creditor. The reason for permitting *tawarruq* and *murabaha* is also applicable in trading debts. Thus, it should be permitted as well.

Third, trading debts should be permissible based on *maslaha* (general benefit). There are many benefits in permitting the trading of debts. It will make the Islamic debt market liquid and diverse, and thus attractive to international and domestic investors. It will also strengthen and stabilize Muslim economies.

Permitting the trading of debts is more consistent with the principles and theories of Islamic law than is forbidding it. It is consistent with the obligations theory that debt is a personal right. It is consistent with the *mal* (property) theory that debt may be sold according to the three Islamic schools of legal thought, all of which consider debt as property. It is consistent with other modern Islamic financial transactions that are permitted by the two Fiqh Academies, such as *tawarruq* and *murabaha*.

There would be significant positive effects on Islamic finance generally and the Islamic debt market particularly if securitizing and trading debts is permitted. The non-tradability of debts is the main obstacle in developing modern

Islamic finance. Most Islamic financial instruments are structured and built on the non-tradability rule and this has caused major problems. The ability to securitize and trade debts would make the Islamic debt market liquid, diverse, and attractive to both international and domestic investors. Further, it would facilitate the growth and development of Islamic finance, and promote new and creative ways to improve the international and domestic Islamic financial industry. A special financial study would show how the Islamic finance industry would change radically if the prohibition of securitizing and trading debts were repealed.

References

Abbas Mirakhor & Iqbal Zaidi, *Profit-and-loss sharing contracts in Islamic finance*, in HANDBOOK OF ISLAMIC BANKING 49, (Kabir Hassan & Mervyn Lewis eds., Edward Elgar 2007).

Abdullah Almousa, *The Sale of Rights in Islamic Jurisprudence*, 45 JUSTICE J. SAUDI ARABIA 170, (2010).

ABDULRAZZAQ ALSANHOURI, RIGHTS SOURCES IN ISLAMIC JURISPRUDENCE (1954).

ABIR ATAMECH, *SUKUK* QUARTERLY BULLETIN 1Q2013 (2013).

ABIR ATAMECH, *SUKUK* QUARTERLY BULLETIN 4Q 2013 (2014).

ACCOUNTING & AUDITING ORG. FOR ISLAMIC FIN. INST., *SHARIAH* STANDARDS No. 17, 4–6 (2003).

AL-JADAAN & PARTNERS LAW FIRM, *at* http://www.aljadaan.com/?module=announcements&page=details_en&id=126.

AL-SADDIQ MUHAMMAD AL-AMIN DARIR, AL-*GHARAR* IN CONTRACTS AND ITS EFFECTS ON CONTEMPORARY TRANSACTIONS (Islamic Research and Training Institute 1997).

ALHATTAB, MAWAHAEB ALJALEEL (Dar Elfekr 1992).

ALKASANEY, BADAE'E ALSANAE'E (Dar Alhadeeth 1996).

ALNAWAWAY, RAWDHAT ALTALEBEEN (Dar Alem Alkotob 2003).

Andreas A. Jobst, *The Economics of Islamic Finance and Securitization*, 13 JOURNAL OF STRUCTURED FINANCE, 2007.

ARAB MONETARY FUND, CONTRIBUTION OF THE ARAB MONETARY FUND TO THE DEVELOPMENT OF ARAB CAPITAL MARKETS (2003).

ARAB NEWS OCT. 7, 2013, *at* http://www.arabnews.com/node/466953.

Arnold & Porter Team Assists Turkey with Islamic Bond Offering, LEGALTIMES (September 26, 2012), *at* http://legaltimes.typepad.com/blt/2012/09/arnold-porter-team-assists-turkey-with-islamic-bond-offering.html.

Babback Sabahi, *Islamic Financial Structures as Alternatives to International Loan Agreements: Challenges for American Financial Institutions*, BEPRESS LEG. SER. (2004), *at* http://law.bepress.com/expresso/eps/385.

BALJEET KAUR GREWAL, CONSTRAINTS ON GROWTH IN ISLAMIC FINANCE (2011).

Banking Without Regulation: The Freeman : Foundation for Economic Education, http://fee.org/the_freeman/detail/banking-without-regulation.

BAYINA ADVISORS, THE GCC DEBT MARKET REPORT (2010).

Bond Ratings—Series 7, INVESTOPEDIA, *at* http://www.investopedia.com/exam-guide/series-7/debt-securities/bond-ratings.asp (last visited Jul. 3, 2014).

C. G. WEERAMANTRY, ISLAMIC JURISPRUDENCE: AN INTERNATIONAL PERSPECTIVE 32 (1988).

Christopher F. Richardson, *Islamic Finance Opportunities in the Oil and Gas Sector: An Introduction to an Emerging Field*, 42 TEX. INT. L. J. 119, 130 (2006).

Christopher F. Richardson, *Islamic Finance Opportunities in the Oil and Gas Sector: An Introduction to an Emerging Field*, 42 TEX. INT. L. J. 119, 130 (2006).

CLIFFORD CHANCE LLP, DUBAI INTERNATIONAL FINANCIAL CENTRE *SUKUK* GUIDEBOOK (Dubai International Financial Centre 2009).

Diana Zacharias, *Fundamentals of the Sunnī Schools of Law*, 66 HEIDELBERG J. OF INT'L LAW 491, 495 (2006).

DUNCAN MCKENZIE, ISLAMIC FINANCE 2010 (2010), *at* www.ifsl.org.uk.

ERNEST & YOUNG, ISLAMIC FUNDS & INVESTMENTS REPORT (2009).

ERNEST & YOUNG, RAPID GROWTH MARKET (2012).

F. A. MANN, THE LEGAL ASPECT OF MONEY: WITH SPECIAL REFERENCE TO COMPARATIVE PRIVATE AND PUBLIC INTERNATIONAL LAW (4th ed. 1982).

Fahim Khan, *Islamic methods for government borrowing and monetary management*, HANDBOOK OF ISLAMIC BANKING 285, 295 (Kabir Hassan & Mervyn Lewis eds., Edward Elgar 2007).

Fahim Khan, *Time Value of Money and Discounting in Islamic Perspective*, 1 REV. OF ISLAMIC ECON. 33, 36 (1991).

FASB Accounting Standards Codification.

FRANK E. VOGEL & SAMUEL L. HAYES, ISLAMIC LAW AND FINANCE: RELIGION, RISK, AND RETURN (Kluwer Law International 1998).

Frank E. Vogel, *at* http://frankevogel.net.

General Knowledge of Holy Quran, *at* http://www.qurannetwork.com/quraninfo.html (The Quran has 6,235 Ayahs, and 77,439 words).

George Makdisi, *The Significance of the Sunni Schools of Law in Islamic Religious History*, 10 INT'L J. OF MIDDLE EAST STUD. 1, (1979).

HALUK GURULKAN, ISLAMIC SECURITIZATION A LEGAL APPROACH (The Institute For Law and Finance at Johann Wolfgang Goethe University 2010).

HANDBOOK OF ISLAMIC BANKING (Kabir Hassan & Mervyn Lewis eds., Edward Elgar 2007).

HANS VISSER, ISLAMIC FINANCE: PRINCIPLES AND PRACTICE (Edward Elgar Publishing 2009).

HSBC seeks big growth, sukuk pickup in 2010, REUTERS (Feb. 15, 2010), *at* http://www.reuters.com/article/2010/02/15/us-islamicbanking-summit-hsbc-idUSTRE61E2JD20100215.

Humayon, A. Dar, *Incentive compatability of Islamic Banking*, *in* HANDBOOK OF ISLAMIC BANKING, 85, (Kabir Hassan & Mervyn Lewis eds., Edward Elgar 2007).

IBN ALQAYEM, EALAM ALMOWAQEEN (Dar Alhadeeth 1993).

IBN HAZM, ALMOHALLA.

IBN QUDAMAH, ALSHARH ALKABEER (DarAlhadeeth 1996).

IBN TAYMIAH, MAJMO'A AL FATAWA (King Fahad Center 1994).

IMAN MIHAJAT, THE REAL *TAWARRUQ* CONCEPT ISLAMIC ECONOMIC FORUM FOR INDONESIAN DEVELOPMENT (ISEFID) (2009).

Islamic Banking Goes Global, THE MIDDLE EAST, 2005.

Islamic Banks: A Novelty No Longer, BUSINESSWEEK.COM (Aug.7, 2005), *at* http://www.businessweek.com/stories/2005-08-07/islamic-banks-a-novelty-no-longer.

Islamic finance industry to hit $5 trillion by 2016, TRADEARABIA NEWS SERVICE (June 28, 2012), *at* http://www.tradearabia.com/news/bank_219700.html.

ISLAMIC FINANCE NEWS, DEALS OF THE YEAR HANDBOOK (Nazneen Halim, et al. eds., Red Money Group 2013).

ISLAMIC FIQH ACADEMY (JEDDAH), RESOLUTIONS AND RECOMMENDATIONS OF THE COUNCIL OF ISLAMIC FIQH ACADEMY (1st ed. 2000).

Islamic Fiqh Academy in Jeddah, *at* http://www.fiqhacademy.org.sa/.

ISLAMIC FIQH COUNCEL (MAKKAH), RESOLUTIONS OF THE OF ISLAMIC FIQH COUNCEL MAKKAH (2006).

JEFFERY WOODRUFF, DEMYSTIFYING CORPORATE *SUKUK* (2007).

Jonathan C. Lipson, *Re: Defining Securitization*, 85 S. CAL. L. REV. 1229, 1231 (2012).

Kabir Hassan & Mervyn Lewis, *Islamic banking: an introduction and overview*, *in* HANDBOOK OF ISLAMIC BANKING 1, (Kabir Hassan & Mervyn Lewis eds., Edward Elgar 2007).

London Interbank Offered Rate (LIBOR) Definition, INVESTOPEDIA, http://www.investopedia.com/terms/l/libor.asp.

MAHA-HANAAN BALALA, ISLAMIC FINANCE AND LAW: THEORY AND PRACTICE IN A GLOBALIZED WORLD (Tauris Academic Studies 2011) (2010).

MAHMOUD A. EL-GAMAL, ISLAMIC FINANCE: LAW, ECONOMICS, AND PRACTICE (Cambridge University Press 2006).

MAHMOUD EL-GAMAL, OVERVIEW OF ISLAMIC FINANCE (U.S. Department of Treasury 2006).

Malaysia International Islamic Financial Centre (MIFC), SUKUK USING AL-*ISTISNA'* STRUCTURE, at http://www.mifc.com/index.php?ch=ch_kc_definitions&pg=pg_kcdf_sukuk&ac=236 (last visited Jan. 15, 2014).

MOHAMMAD HASHIM KAMALI, PRINCIPLES OF ISLAMIC JURISPRUDENCE (3rd rev. and enlarged ed. 2003).

MOHAMMED KURDEY, AHKAM BAYA ALDAYN (1992).

Mohammad Islam, *Al-Mal: The Concept of Property in Islamic Legal Thought*, 14 ARAB L. Q. 361, 362 (1999).

Mohammed Alamin, *HADITH* NUMBER MOHAMMED ALAMIN ARTICLES, at http://www.ibnamin.com/.

MOHAMMED OBAIDULLAH, ISLAMIC FINANCIAL SERVICES (Scientific Publishing Centre, King Abdulaziz University 2005).

Mohammed Obaidullah, *Securitization in Islam*, in HANDBOOK OF ISLAMIC BANKING 191, (Kabir Hassan & Mervyn Lewis eds., Edward Elgar 2007).

MUHAMMAD AL-BASHIR & MUHAMMAD AL-AMINE, GLOBAL SUKŪK AND ISLAMIC SECURITIZATION MARKET: FINANCIAL ENGINEERING AND PRODUCT INNOVATION (Brill 2012).

MUHAMMAD AYUB, UNDERSTANDING ISLAMIC FINANCE (John Wiley & Sons Ltd. 2007).

MUḤAMMAD TAQĪ USMĀNĪ, AN INTRODUCTION TO ISLAMIC FINANCE (Kluwer Law International 2002).

MUSTAFAH ALZARQA, OBLIGATIONS THEORY IN ISLAMIC JURISPRUDENCE (1st ed. 1999).

N. GREGORY MANKIW, PRINCIPLES OF ECONOMICS (3rd ed. 2004).

Nabil Saleh, *Definition and Formation of Contract under Islamic and Arab Laws* 5 ARAB L. Q. May 1990, at 101.

NASER NASHAWY, BAY ALDAYN (Dar Alfekr Aljame'ey 2007).

NCB CAPITAL, GCC DEBT CAPITAL MARKETS AN EMERGING OPPORTUNITY? (2009).

Norton Rose Fulbright, AAOIFI STATEMENT ON *SUKUK* AND ITS MPLICATIONS, at http://www.nortonrosefulbright.com/knowledge/publications/16852/aaoifi-statement-on-sukuk-and-its-implications (last visited Jan. 15, 2014).

NURIT TSAFRIR, THE HISTORY OF AN ISLAMIC SCHOOL OF LAW: THE EARLY SPREAD OF HANAFISM (Harvard University Press 2004).

OSAMAH ALLAHIM, THE SALE OF DEBT AND ITS APPLICATIONS IN CONTEMPORARY LIFE (2012).

Press Release, Al-Jadaan & Partners and Clifford Chance, LLP, Al-Jadaan and Clifford Chance advise on landmark sovereign and largest ever Saudi *sukuk*, AMEINFO.COM (Jan. 23, 2012), *available at* http://www.ameinfo.com/287665.html.

Ridha Saadallah, *Trade financing in Islam*, in HANDBOOK OF ISLAMIC BANKING 172, (Kabir Hassan & Mervyn Lewis eds., Edward Elgar 2007).

ROYSTON MILES GOODE & CENTRE FOR COMMERCIAL LAW STUDIES, PAYMENT OBLIGATIONS IN COMMERCIAL AND FINANCIAL TRANSACTIONS (1983).

Said Elfakhani, Imad Zbib, & Zafar Ahmed, *Marketing of Islamic financial products*, in HANDBOOK OF ISLAMIC BANKING 116, (Kabir Hassan & Mervyn Lewis eds., Edward Elgar 2007).

SALEH ALHOSAYYEN, ISLAMIC BANKS, PROS AND CONS (2009).

SALMAN SYED ALI, ISLAMIC CAPITAL MARKET PRODUCTS: DEVELOPMENTS AND CHALLENGES (Islamic Development Bank 2005).

Sam R. Hakim, *Islamic money market instruments*, HANDBOOK OF ISLAMIC BANKING 161, (Kabir Hassan & Mervyn Lewis eds., Edward Elgar 2007).

Sara Hamdan, *Interest Rises in Islamic Bonds*, N.Y. TIMES, Feb. 27, 2013, *available at* http://www.nytimes.com/2013/02/28/world/middleeast/interest-rises-in-islamic-bonds.html.

Saudi Arabia: Debate continues over global sharia standards, OXFORD BUSINESS GROUP (Apr. 9, 2013).

Saudi Gazette, GACA *SUKUK* ISSUE HITS SR15.21 BILLION, Saudi Gazette, *at* http://www.saudigazette.com.sa/index.cfm?method=home.regcon&contentid=20131007182895 (last visited Apr. 9, 2014).

SAUDI HOLLANDI CAPITAL, *SUKUK* MARKET IN SAUDI ARABIA (2013).

SAUDI MINISTRY OF FINANCE, SAUDI BUDGET FOR 2014 (2013).

Seif I. TAG EL-DIN, *Capital and Money Markets of Muslims: The Emerging Experience in Theory and Practice*, 1 KYOTO BULLETIN OF ISLAMIC AREA STUDIES (2007).

SHAH ABDUL HANNAN, USUL AL FIQH (ISLAMIC JURISPRUDENCE) 6 (1999).

SHARIQ NISAR, ISLAMIC BONDS (*SUKUK*): ITS INTRODUCTION AND APPLICATION, *available at* http://www.financeinislam.com/article/8/1/546.

ṬĀHĀ JĀBIR FAYYĀḌ 'ALWĀNĪ, SOURCE METHODOLOGY IN ISLAMIC JURISPRUDENCE: UṢŪL AL FIQH AL ISLĀMĪ (New rev. English ed. 1994).

Tamara Box & Mohammed Asaria, *Islamic Finance Market Turns to Securitization*, 24 INT. FINANC. LAW REV. July 2005.

THE INTERNATIONAL ISLAMIC FINANCIAL MARKET, IIFM *SUKUK* REPORT (3RD ed. 2013).

THE ISLAMIC JURISPRUDENCE ENCYCLOPEDIA, (2nd ed. 1992).

THE ISLAMIC SCHOOL OF LAW: EVOLUTION, DEVOLUTION, AND PROGRESS (Peri J. Bearman, Rudolph Peters, & Frank E. Vogel eds., Harvard University Press 2005).

The Muslim World League in Makkah, *at* http://www.mwl-en.com.

The rationale of prohibition of *Riba*, The prohibition of Maysir and *Gharar*, Financial Islam—Islamic Finance, *at* http://www.financialislam.com/prohibition-of-riba-maysir-and-gharar.html (last visited Nov. 1, 2013).

THE *SHARIAH*'S BOARD OF THE ACCOUNTING AND AUDITING ORGANIZATION FOR ISLAMIC FINANCIAL INSTITUTIONS STANDARDS FOR ISLAMIC BANKING 240 (2010).

Understand-Islam.Org (2009).

WILLIAM J. CARNEY, CORPORATE FINANCE: PRINCIPLES AND PRACTICE (2nd ed. 2010).

YAHAYA YUNUSA BAMBALE, AN OUTLINE OF ISLAMIC JURISPRUDENCE (2007).

YASIN DUTTON, THE ORIGINS OF ISLAMIC LAW: THE QUR'AN, THE MUWATTA' AND MADINAN AMAL (CULTURE AND CIVILIZATION IN THE MIDDLE EAST) (Ian R. Netton ed., Curzon Press 1999).

Yves Mersch, Islamic finance—partnerships opportunities between Luxembourg and the Arab countries, Speech Before the 5th Economic Forum Belgium-Luxembourg-Arab Countries, Brussels, (Nov. 17, 2009).

Zamir Iqbal, Challenges Facing Islamic Financial Industry, 3 J. of Islamic Econ. Banking & Fin. 2007.

Printed in the United States
By Bookmasters

BEN JONSON AND ENVY

In the early modern period, envy was often represented iconographically by the image of the Medusa, with snaky locks and a poisonous gaze. *Ben Jonson and Envy* investigates the importance of envy to Jonson's imagination, showing that he perceived spectators and readers as filled with envy and created strategies to defend his work from their distorting and potentially 'deadly' gaze. Drawing on historical and anthropological studies of evil-eye beliefs, this study focuses on the authorial imperative to charm and baffle ritualistically the eye of the implied spectator or reader, in order to protect his works from defacement. Comparing the exchange between authors and readers to social relations, the book illuminates the way in which the literary may be seen to be informed by popular culture. *Ben Jonson and Envy* tackles a previously overlooked, but vital, aspect of Jonson's poetics.

LYNN S. MESKILL is a Lecturer in English at the University of Paris-XIII. She has published articles on Jonson, Shakespeare and Milton in *English Literary History*, *Cahiers Elisabéthains* and the *Revue de la Société d'Etudes Anglo-Américaines*, among others.

BEN JONSON AND ENVY

LYNN S. MESKILL
University of Paris-XIII, France

CAMBRIDGE UNIVERSITY PRESS
Cambridge, New York, Melbourne, Madrid, Cape Town, Singapore, São Paulo, Delhi

Cambridge University Press
The Edinburgh Building, Cambridge CB2 8RU, UK

Published in the United States of America by Cambridge University Press, New York

www.cambridge.org
Information on this title: www.cambridge.org/9780521517430

© Lynn S. Meskill 2009

This publication is in copyright. Subject to statutory exception
and to the provisions of relevant collective licensing agreements,
no reproduction of any part may take place without
the written permission of Cambridge University Press.

First published 2009

Printed in the United Kingdom at the University Press, Cambridge

A catalogue record for this Publication is available from the British Library

Library of Congress Cataloguing in Publication data
Meskill, Lynn S.
Ben Jonson and envy / Lynn S. Meskill.
p. cm.
Includes bibliographical references and index.
ISBN 978-0-521-51743-0
1. Jonson, Ben, 1573?–1637–Criticism and interpretation.   2. Envy in literature.
3. Authorship–Psychological aspects.   4. Authors and readers–England–History–
16th century.   5. Authors and readers–England–History–17th century.   I. Title.
PR2642.E58M47   2009
822′.3–dc22   2009000062

ISBN 978-0-521-51743-0 hardback

Cambridge University Press has no responsibility for the persistence or
accuracy of URLS for external or third-party internet websites referred to
in this publication, and does not guarantee that any content on such
websites is, or will remain, accurate or appropriate.

Contents

List of illustrations		*page* vii
Note on the text		viii
Acknowledgements		ix
1	Introduction	1
	A model of creation	3
	Malevolent eyes: spectators and readers	20
	'Small *Latine*, and lesse *Greeke*'	35
2	An anatomy of envy	42
	The ancient and medieval traditions	42
	Envy in the early modern period	51
	Jonson's *pharmakon*	65
3	Defacement: anxiety and the Jonsonian imagination	75
	Corruptible relics	80
	Literary slander and 'the Epidemicall Infection'	84
	Defacing the 'old Masters'	90
	The envious reader: *Poetaster, Or His Arraignment*	94
4	Sanctuary: Jonson's prophylactic strategy	110
	The poet's sanctuary: 'To Penshurst'	112
	Authority and sanctuary	118
	The envious creator	132
5	Monument: turning the text to stone	139
	'Immortal moniment'	144
	'Borrowing a life of posterity': monument and the court masque	148
	The gorgon gaze of envy: *The Masque of Queenes*	153
	The Medusa of eloquence: *Catiline, His Conspiracy*	177

6 Being posthumous	186
The patched mantle of fame: *The Staple of Newes*	188
Epilogue: fame in the age of print	204
Bibliography	207
Index	226

Illustrations

1 Door detail. Gorgon. Hôtel des Ambassadeurs-de-Hollande, rue Vieille-du-Temple, Paris. *Private collection.*   *page* 32

2 Emblem, 'VIR BONUS INVIDIAE SECURUS', Jean-Jacques Boissard, *Emblematum Liber* (Frankfurt, Theodore de Bry, 1593). *By permission of The Harry Ransom Humanities Research Center, The University of Texas at Austin.*   54

3 Facing pages from *The Masque of Queenes* in Ben Jonson, *Workes* (London, 1616). *By permission of The Huntington Library, San Marino, California.*   156

4 Frontispiece from P. Gérard Pelletier, S.J., *Palatium Reginae Eloquentiae* (Paris, 1641). *By permission of The Bibliothèque Nationale de France.*   181

Note on the text

All quotations from Ben Jonson are from the eleven-volume edition of Jonson's works edited by C. H. Herford, Percy Simpson and Evelyn Simpson (1925–52). I have silently modernized u, v, i, j and scribal contractions as well as the titles of some of Jonson's plays and masques according to common practice. All quotations from Shakespeare's plays are from *The Riverside Shakespeare*, second edition (1997), edited by G. Blakemore Evans and Herschel Baker *et al*.

Acknowledgements

My gratitude goes, first and foremost, to Katharine Eisaman Maus, my dissertation advisor and friend, for her support and counsel during both the initial writing and later revision of this book. Gordon Braden and Claire Kinney, both members of my jury, offered pertinent suggestions for the improvement of the thesis. Of the professors at the University of Virginia whose work shaped my thinking and influenced the elaboration of this book are Alastair Fowler, James Nohrnberg and Jahan Ramazani. At Princeton University, my studies with Glenn W. Most and Froma I. Zeitlin, as well as the intellectual generosity of the late Arthur Hansen, have had a lasting influence on me. My thanks go as well to Karen Newman, whose Brown University class on *Hamlet* left an indelible impression.

This book was mostly written and revised in France. I am particularly grateful to the following colleagues who welcomed me there and invited me to be part of their classes, research groups and conferences, all of which contributed directly to the conception of the initial project: Pierre Iselin, François Laroque, Anne Lecercle, Richard Marienstras and Gisèle Venet. I thank all the members of the various early modern seminars (at Paris IV – Sorbonne, Paris III – Sorbonne Nouvelle, and Paris VII – Denis Diderot) and in particular of the groups *Renaissance(s)* and *Epistémè* (both at Paris III – Sorbonne Nouvelle), professors and graduate students, for their ongoing support of my work and their collegiality. I mention only some whom I have known now for over ten years and who have since become friends and colleagues: Sarah Hatchuel, Pierre Kapitaniak, Sophie Lemercier-Goddard, Ladan Niayesh and Nathalie Vienne-Guérin. My department at the University of Paris XIII (IUT) has been very generous for the past five years in its support of my research – many thanks, most especially, to Claude Andreu, Serge Markovitch, Joseph Cerrato and Bernard Chanez.

This endeavour would not have been possible without the patience and support of friends. John Ash, Philippa Berry, Douglas Bruster, Line

Cottegnies, Laetitia Coussement-Boillot, Marie Couton, Anny Crunelle, Claude Dorey, Anne Dunan-Page, Clifford Endres, Laïla Ghermani, Heidi Brayman Hackel, Mirabeau Buonaparte Lamar Higgins, Sarah Hutton, Jennifer Kirby, Anne-Marie Miller-Blaise, Wayne A. Rebhorn, Elizabeth Scala, Christine Sukic and Gordon Teskey are among those who have supported my work (and the millionth mention of envy) at various stages. Annie Bourgois, Aline Celeyrette, Charlie Condou, Cameron Laux, Laïla Ghermani, Gisèle Venet and most especially, Claude and Maurice Andreu, have provided sustenance and sanctuary in some part of their homes at various moments during the preparation of the manuscript. So did Richard Wilson, who invited me to speak at Lancaster and do research there when I was living close to the Bosphorus, but far from a library suitable for my needs. Gordon McMullan has also been very generous in inviting me to speak in London and having me sample his internationally famed dinners during my trips to London and the British Library.

The librarians and staff at the Bibliothèque Nationale de France, the British Library, the Bodleian, the Harry Ransom Humanities Research Center and the University of Lancaster have been very generous with their time and their resources. I am also very grateful to the Bibliothèque Nationale de France, The Harry Ransom Humanities Research Center and The Henry Huntington Library for the use of the images from their collections which I have included in this book. I would like to extend a special thanks to Elizabeth Cullingford and to the Department of English at the University of Texas at Austin which welcomed me as a visiting scholar. Both Casey Caldwell and Lilia Beaman deserve special mention for their material help.

A part of Chapter 5 has appeared in *ELH* 72 (2005) and part in a journal published by the University of Paris VII – Denis Diderot, *Les Cahiers de Charles V*, in a special issue entitled *Silent Rhetoric: The Rhetorics of Silence in Early Modern Literature*, edited by Laetitia Coussement-Boillot and Christine Sukic (2008). A portion of Chapter 3 is taken from a paper 'Slanderous Reading and the Case of Ben Jonson' which I gave at the University of Paris X – Nanterre in June 2007 and which is included in *Language and Otherness in Renaissance Culture*, edited by Ann Lecercle and Yan Brailowsky (Nanterre: Presses Universitaires de Paris X, 2008). I thank all the editors concerned for permission to re-use this material.

I am grateful to Vicki Cooper at the Press for her initial efforts on behalf of the book. Sarah Stanton, who took over as my editor, has been extremely kind and efficient. Many thanks go to Rebecca Jones and Tom

O'Reilly for being immensely helpful through the various stages of the completion of the book. I would especially like to thank my 'extraordinary' readers. I am particularly grateful for the perceptiveness of my anonymous readers for Cambridge University Press, all of whose incredibly stimulating and generous suggestions were key in transforming the book. My deepest debts are to Karen Britland and Line Cottegnies, both of whom read the entire manuscript more than once; their painstaking editorial work, and judicious and incisive comments have been invaluable. All remaining errors and infelicities are entirely my own. Finally, I would like to thank my family for their support and love. This book is, as they know, also very much for them.

CHAPTER I

Introduction

Ben Jonson has been accused of envy from at least the late seventeenth century, if not before. Tradition has it that John Dryden first interpreted Jonson's comment that Shakespeare had 'smalle *Latine*, and lesse *Greeke*' as 'sparing and invidious'.[1] Nicholas Rowe's statement that Jonson 'could not but look with an evil Eye upon any one that see'd in Competition with him' is typical of the way a number of eighteenth-century Shakespeare editors painted Jonson as ungenerous, ungrateful and even malevolent.[2] Moreover, Rowe places Jonson's 'evil Eye' in direct contrast to Shakespeare's generous one in narrating the story of how Shakespeare read an early play of Jonson's: 'Shakespeare *luckily cast his Eye upon it*, and found something so well in it as to engage him first to read it through, and afterwards to recommend Mr. *Johnson* and his Writings to the Publick' (my emphasis).[3] In telling the tale of how Shakespeare helped the young Jonson get his start in the theatre, Rowe deftly holds up Shakespeare's charitable reading eye against Jonson's envious one. In a fascinating section entitled 'Proofs of Ben Jonson's Malignity, from the Commentators on Shakespeare' in the introduction to his edition of Jonson's *Works*, William Gifford presents

---

[1] Alexander Pope refers to this tradition when he writes: 'I cannot for my part find any thing *invidious* or *sparing* in those verses, but wonder Mr. Dryden was of that opinion' (my emphasis). Edmond Malone (ed.), 'Mr. Pope's Preface', *Plays and Poems of William Shakespeare in Ten Volumes* (London, 1790), vol. I, p. 89. John Freehafer has suggested that it was not Dryden, but Leonard Digges who first spotted a slur in Jonson's judgement concerning Shakespeare's knowledge of the classical languages. John Freehafer, 'Leonard Digges, Ben Johnson [*sic*], and the Beginning of Shakespeare Idolatry', *Shakespeare Quarterly* 21 (Winter 1970), 63–75; p. 66. Jonson's description of Shakespeare's Latin and Greek is to be found in his elegy to Shakespeare: 'To the memory of my beloved, the AUTHOR MR. WILLIAM SHAKESPEARE: And what he hath left us', which first appeared in 1623 in the Shakespeare First Folio. *Ungathered Verse* (xxvi), Herford and Simpson, vol. VIII, p. 391 (line 31). All references to Jonson's works will refer to 'Herford and Simpson' and include the volume, page and, when appropriate, line number.
[2] Nicholas Rowe, 'Some Account of the Life, *Etc.* of Mr. *William Shakespear*' in *The Works of Mr. William Shakespeare in Six Volumes* (London, 1709), vol. I, p. xiii.
[3] *Ibid.*, p. xiii.

I

readers with choice examples of Jonson's 'supposed hostility to Shakespeare' handed down from one Shakespeare editor and commentator to another. Gifford writes that 'of all calumniators [of Jonson] Mr. Malone is the most headlong', but he seems to take particular delight in quoting Charles Macklin's virulent description of Jonson: 'He was splenetic, sour, over-run with envy, – the tyrant of the theatre – perpetually uttering slights and malignities against the lowly Shakespeare, whose fame was grown too great for his envy to bear.'[4] There were, however, other early critics, like Gifford, who understood that Jonson's 'envy' was, in part, an editorial invention and a useful cornerstone in the literary sanctification of Shakespeare. In *Specimens of the English Poets*, Thomas Campbell refers to 'the established article of literary faith that [Jonson's] personal character was a compound of spleen, surliness and ingratitude'. He argues that Shakespeare's fame was constructed even out of Jonson's supposed envy:

> The fame of Shakespeare himself became an heirloom of traditionary calumnies against the memory of Jonson; the fancied relics of his envy were regarded as so many pious donations at the shrine of the greater poet, whose admirers thought they could not dig too deeply for trophies of his glory among the ruins of his imaginary rival's reputation.[5]

Campbell shows the extent to which the construction of a cult of Shakespeare went hand in hand with a Jonson envious of his rival. Every unsavoury anecdote or veiled allusion served as a 'pious donation' to the 'shrine' of Shakespeare's fame. Out of the ashes of Jonson's reputation, Shakespeare's phoenix rises. As early as 1819, Campbell offers a corrective to any simplified opposition of Shakespeare to Jonson, yet, almost two centuries later, the myths of envy, as well as the archaeological hunt for more 'relics', are as widespread as ever.

This powerfully evocative myth of Jonson's envy of Shakespeare is most probably the reason why scholars have not examined in any detail Jonson's frequent references to envy and its cognates. Envy has been so visibly associated with Jonson's personal envy that it has been nearly impossible to disassociate the tradition of the envious man from any examination of the persistent thematic issues derived from envy in Jonson's works. In other words, the *topos* of envy has been so *visible* as a critical term to describe Jonson's personal animosities and malicious nature that envy within the

---

[4] William Gifford, *The Works of Ben Jonson, With Notes Critical and Explanatory and a Biographical Memoir in Nine Volumes*, ed. F. Cunningham (London: Bickers and Son, 1875), vol. I, pp. cciv, ccxiii.
[5] Thomas Campbell, *Specimens of the English Poets*, 7 vols. (London: John Murray, 1819), vol. III, pp. 142–3.

works themselves has been rendered *invisible*. While the biographical subject and the presence of envy in his texts are not unrelated phenomena, there needs to be a clearer division between envy as a biographical characteristic ascribed to Ben Jonson and textual manifestations of a preoccupation with envy. The life and temperament of the author might indeed produce the works of Ben Jonson, but they are by no means sufficient to explain them.

A MODEL OF CREATION

This image of a Jonson envious of Shakespeare exists side by side with two other images, both in their way quite contradictory to that of the splenetic rival. The first is the legendary *persona* of the convivial playwright, the frequenter of taverns and drinker of sack, whom contemporaries and later critics alike referred to amiably as 'Ben'. This image is in part due to Jonson's own efforts at immortalizing and publicizing himself as well as to the way he was remembered in poems appended to his works and those in the collection, *Jonsonus Virbius*, commemorating his death. At the same time, Jonson has also been perceived as a neo-Stoic, virtuous and 'centred' moralist.[6] Clearly, he modelled himself upon the classical authors as guides to literary decorum and moral probity. He was almost certainly influenced by Sidney's argument in *An Apologie for Poetrie* (1595) that poetry in its larger sense of 'fiction' was necessarily linked to the teaching and understanding of virtue.[7] Yet, to read Jonson as writing primarily for the reformation of public and court morals has perhaps prevented our appreciating fully his self-interested programme as a writer.[8] Jonson may indeed have wished

---

[6] Thomas Greene, 'Ben Jonson and the Centered Self', *SEL* 10 (1970), 325–48.
[7] Sir Phillip Sidney, *An Apologie for Poetrie* (London, 1595). See the following passages for the association of poetry with virtue: 'But even in the most excellent determination of goodnes, what Philosophers counsel can so redily direct a prince, as the fayned *Cyrus* in *Xenophon*? Or a vertuous man in all fortunes, as *Aeneas* in *Virgil*?', sig. D4; 'I think it may be manifest, that the Poet with that same hand of delight, doth draw the mind more effectually, then any other Arte dooth, and so a conclusion not unfitlie ensueth: that as vertue is the most excellent resting place for all worldlie learning to make his end of: so Poetrie, beeing the most familiar to teach it, and most princelie to move towards it, in the most excellent work, is the most excellent workman', sig. F2; '... the ever-praise-worthy Poesie, is full of vertue-breeding delightfulnes', sig. L2ᵛ.
[8] Martin Butler notes Jonson's self-interested calculations concerning his own posterity with regard to his role as courtly panegyrist: 'Jonson [in his 'Epistle to Master John Selden'] professes to feel untouched by the revelation that his poems sometimes praised men more than they deserved, but he was demonstrably disinclined to allow his own writings to testify against him in this way, since when he compiled the collected edition of his works he excluded at least two panegyrics lauding men who had fallen from favour since the poems were written, the Earl of Somerset and Sir Edward Coke.' Martin Butler, 'Ben Jonson and the Limits of Courtly Panegyric' in Kevin Sharpe and Peter Lake (eds.), *Culture and Politics in Early Stuart England* (Basingstoke: Macmillan, 1994), pp. 91–115; p. 96.

to see himself as embodying the role of the *didaskalos*, the ancient term for playwright in ancient Greece; but his canny self-representation in prologues, for instance, should not deter us from excavating other motives and other pressures which may have influenced and shaped his art.⁹ Jonson's virulent response to attacks on *The New Inn* (1629), for instance, would seem to reveal a keen interest in the reception of his works in the public mart not to mention it being at odds with the 'centred' self, philosophically writing poems in imitation of Horace.¹⁰ Within the limits of the masque genre he was certainly bound to praise the courtiers participating in masques and the politics of their royal patrons. Yet, the image of the writer as proselytizer of virtue and reformer of court manners is problematic in light not only of the sheer fantasticalness of many of the anti-masques or most of the characters in *Bartholomew Fair* (1614), but also, as Bruce Boehrer has argued, the writer's fascination with the scatological and the crude.¹¹ And, as with Rabelais, the carnivalesque aspect of much of Jonson's work may be seen as the reverse of the sombre, almost misanthropic face that emerges in a play like *Volpone* (1606).

It is this darker aspect of Jonson that both Edmund Wilson and William Kerrigan brought more fully to light, providing a necessary antidote to the image of a morally upright poet and playwright.¹² Wilson's attempt to understand the psychological sources of Jonson's literary production from a Freudian standpoint led him to identify Jonson as an obsessive 'anal-erotic'. Though not perhaps his most remarkable piece of criticism, Wilson's essay owes its notoriety to his temerity in opposing the pervasive image of Jonson as a virtuous and ethical writer. Harold Bloom comments approvingly on Kerrigan's essay: '[D]issenting from our modern portrait of Jonson as sane and virtuous, [he] returns us to the reality of the poet's abiding melancholy.'¹³ Both Wilson and Kerrigan took what

---

⁹ Graham Ley, *A Short Introduction to the Ancient Greek Theater*, rev. edn (Chicago: University of Chicago Press, 2006), p. 14.

¹⁰ See Jonson's 'An Ode. To himself', *Underwood* (xxiii), Herford and Simpson, vol. VIII, p. 174. 'Come leave the lothed stage, / and the more lothsome age' (lines 1–2). Dates in parentheses of Jonson's plays and masques in the text will refer to the date of *performance*, which in certain cases coincides with the date of first publication. I will refer to publication dates when the discussion involves the *printed* text specifically.

¹¹ Bruce Thomas Boehrer, *The Fury of Men's Gullets: Ben Jonson and the Digestive Canal* (Philadelphia: University of Pennsylvania, 1997).

¹² Edmund Wilson, 'Morose Ben Jonson', *The Triple Thinkers* (New York: Charles Scribner's Sons, 1948), pp. 213–32; William Kerrigan, 'Ben Jonson Full of Shame and Scorn', *Ben Jonson: Studies in the Literary Imagination* 6 (April 1973), 199–218.

¹³ Harold Bloom (ed.), *Modern Critical Interpretations: Ben Jonson* (New York: Chelsea House Publishers, 1988), p. 2. One could argue that this approach reinvokes, under another name, the

might be called a *sinister* approach to Jonson. The present book may be said to inscribe itself in such an approach. I will be arguing that *envy* and *envious* are words the writer uses to describe the way the spectator will *look at* and the reader will *read* his work. Scholars of Jonson have referred to the way the writer anticipates his reception and the means he uses to control it in what Gérard Genette has termed the paratext.[14] I would like to show that the source of this anxiety for Jonson lies in a very specific authorial image of the spectator and reader.[15] The writer's perception is that the audience's *vision* is naturally *depraved*, so that they *see* obliquely and thus necessarily distort, pervert and deform the meaning of the text.

This image of the misreader may very well reflect the way Jonson read or misread those writers who preceded him. It would seem, at first glance, that Harold Bloom's 'anxiety of influence', which posits an often troubled relationship between strong writers and the (father) ghosts of the literary past, may be useful in understanding certain aspects of Jonson's anxious relationship with previous literary giants and their monuments. According to Bloom:

Poetic Influence – when it involves two strong, authentic poets, – always proceeds by a misreading of the prior poet, an act of creative correction that is actually and necessarily a misinterpretation. The history of fruitful poetic influence, which is to say the main tradition of Western poetry since the Renaissance, is a history of anxiety and self-saving caricature, of distortion, of perverse, willful revisionism without which poetry as such could not exist.[16]

Yet, there are a number of problems with the Bloomian model with regard to Jonson. First, the usefulness of this model for the early modern period remains a vexed question. Thomas Greene, for instance, does not see it as adequately describing the relationship between the humanist poet and the classics of antiquity: 'The humanist poet is not a neurotic son crippled by a Freudian family romance, which is to say he is not in Harold Bloom's terms Romantic. He is rather like the son in a classical comedy who displaces his

---

envious Jonson depicted by Rowe, Dryden and Malone. But I will be referring to the 'abiding melancholy' *manifested in the texts*, not in the poet himself. The key is to separate, again, the man from the texts and a biographically focused study from a textual one.

[14] Gérard Genette, *Seuils* (Paris: Editions du Seuil, 1987).
[15] Certain terms, such as 'anxiety', borrowed from the the realm of psychoanalysis, but which have become appropriated by literary criticism to describe textual phenomena, will be used in this book.
[16] Harold Bloom, *The Anxiety of Influence: A Theory of Poetry* (Oxford: Oxford University Press, 1973), p. 30.

father at the moment of reconciliation.'[17] On the other hand, while Greene argues for the inappropriateness of Bloom's 'Romantic' model for an early modern author, Thomas Cartelli sees Bloom's omission of Jonson from the ranks of strong, anxious poets as an odd oversight: 'Harold Bloom contends that Jonson had "no anxiety as to imitation" (p. 27) and thus fails to register a most interesting case-study in the politics of influence. Indeed, Jonson's chronic imitation of his Roman masters conceivably served as a defensive buffer against the competing influence of his contemporaries upon his work, and constituted a complex strategy by which he might maintain distinction in his ongoing battle for recognition.'[18] Yet, the problem with Bloom's model lies deeper than this argument suggests since the anxiety with which recent Jonson scholars are particularly concerned is with what Lucy Newlyn has called the 'anxiety of reception'.[19] Newlyn sees the weakness in Bloom's model in its singular orientation toward the relationship poets have to the 'past', but, she points out:

[A]nxieties experienced by writers centre as much on the future as on the past – not just because an author's status, authority, and posthumous life are dependent on readers, but because writing exists in dialogue with others whose sympathies it hopes to engage.[20]

Newlyn's account has the virtue of attempting to see both sides of readerly reception: reception by the writer of past authors as reader as well as the anxiety experienced by the writer with regard to his or her own future reception by readers. Newlyn thus suggests a model in which the relationship writers have with their future is indicated by their relationship, as readers, to the past:

writers are peculiarly alive to their own status as readers, and as often as not this leads to an awareness of their revisionary relationship to the materials that they read. Such awareness brings with it, as an inevitable cost, the apprehension that all writing – including their own – is contingent, provisional, open to reconstruction. Potentially, then, the writing-reading subject is divided in its response to the release of subjectivity which occurs in acts of interpretation. Writers who are *robustly revisionary* in relation to past authors can be prescriptive when it comes to imagining their own reception; and this equivocation with respect to interpretative

---

[17] Thomas Greene, *The Light in Troy: Imitation and Discovery in Renaissance Poetry* (New Haven: Yale University Press, 1982), p. 41.
[18] Thomas Cartelli, '*Bartholomew Fair* as Urban Arcadia, Jonson Responds to Shakespeare', *Renaissance Drama*, n.s. 14 (1983), 151–72; p. 160.
[19] Lucy Newlyn, *Reading, Writing, and Romanticism: The Anxiety of Reception* (Oxford: Oxford University Press, 2000).
[20] *Ibid.*, p. vii.

freedom is sometimes reflected in the way they *imagine or theorize the reader's role* [my emphasis].[21]

What Newlyn terms here as 'robustly revisionary' was called, in antiquity and later in the Renaissance, *aemulatio*. According to Wayne A. Rebhorn: 'In Renaissance rhetorical and educational theory, emulation is classified as a form of imitation, an identification with one's model at the same time that one attempts to surpass it... emulation means identification with another person, a model, or an ideal; it can indicate a form of brotherhood or comradeship or even love. On the other hand, it simultaneously means rivalry; it is a competitive urge that... can also, when taken to an extreme, entail feelings of hatred and envy.'[22] If, as Newlyn suggests, there is a correspondence between the way an author reads the past and the way he or she expects to be read in the future, then a certain type of 'revisionary' writer might well imagine the reader's role as informed by envy and contentiousness.[23]

Rather than considering, as others have already done, Jonson's imitation and transformation of past writers, I intend to focus on his perception and conception of his own audience.[24] While Jonson's own reading habits and his conception of his reader are necessarily associated, the aim in this book is to consider the nature of the reciprocal relationship between author and reader in which Jonson perceives the reader's role as being one dominated by invidiousness. As a direct result of this image of his audience and reader, Jonson's writings are marked by a *rhetoric of discontinuity* in which the creation and production of text is, in part, catalyzed by rupture in response to

---

[21] *Ibid.*, pp. vii–viii.
[22] Wayne A. Rebhorn, 'The Crisis of the Aristocracy in *Julius Caesar*', *Renaissance Quarterly* 43 (1990), 75–111. Also cited in Rona Goffen, *Renaissance Rivals: Michelangelo, Leonardo, Raphael, Titian* (New Haven: Yale University Press, 2002), p. 4. See G. W. Pigman III on the problematic association of *aemulatio* with 'envy, strife and contentiousness' in 'Versions of Imitation in the Renaissance', *Renaissance Quarterly* 33 (1980), 1–32; p. 24.
[23] In his essay on the 'Uncanny', Freud describes the device of projection specifically with reference to envy in a very similar manner: 'Whoever possesses something at once valuable and fragile is afraid of the envy of others, in that he projects onto them the envy he would have felt in their place.' Sigmund Freud, 'The Uncanny (1919)' in *The Standard Edition of the Complete Psychological Works of Sigmund Freud*, ed. James Strachey, 24 vols. (London: The Hogarth Press, 1955), vol. XVII, pp. 217–56; p. 240. Cited in Alan Dundee, 'Wet and Dry, the Evil Eye: An Essay in Indo-European and Semitic Worldview' in *Interpreting Folklore* (Bloomington: Indiana University Press, 1980), pp. 93–133; p. 100.
[24] See, among others, Robert C. Evans, *Habits of Mind: Evidence and Effects of Ben Jonson's Reading* (Lewisburg: Bucknell University Press, 1995) and *Jonson, Lipsius and the Politics of Renaissance Stoicism* (Wakefield: Longwood Academic, 1992); A. W. Johnson, *Ben Jonson: Poetry and Architecture* (Oxford: Clarendon Press, 1994); James Riddell and Stanley Stewart, *Jonson's Spenser: Evidence and Historical Criticism* (Pittsburgh: Duquesne University Press, 1995).

the perceived appearance of an invidious gaze. The Jonsonian text is generated by and through a series of engagements with the spectator's and later, the reader's, imagined queries or objections. At times, these engagements take the form of strategies to 'ward off', 'avert', 'trick' or 'appease' that same gaze through the use of marginalia and other paratexts, but also through a momentary arresting of the flow of narrative to turn toward perceived and imaginary objections. In emphasizing an inherent discourse of almost ritual conflict I would like to note that I do not imagine a perfect, peaceful scenario of writing without this outside gaze. In other words, this eye is one which the writer must 'battle' and 'baffle', but at the same time it is a gaze that uncovers a lack that must be filled. As such, the envious spectator both presents a form of danger to the writer but also, paradoxically, serves as the source or engine of *copia*. In writing not just *against*, but in *response to* a judging spectator or reader (ready to uncover authorial weakness or spur the writer to emulative feats) envy emerges as a generative force. It is therefore an envious muse, withholding and inspiring at the same time.

The separation of the writing and reading selves within the paradigm of envy may be described as the division of the writing 'I' in conjunction with and in conflict with an envious 'eye'. Rather than a paradigm of 'usurpation' described by Georges Poulet and Maurice Blanchot in which the very integrity of the writing subject is placed into question, we find in Jonson's works evidence of a continuous oscillation between the 'I' or the 'we' of the writer and the source of oblivion, imagined as the curious and potentially malicious spectator or reader.[25] This 'I', it must be noted in advance, is not that of the historical writer, but rather the 'I' of his poetic voice. The marker, 'I', or some kind of reference to the writer of the text throughout the masque marginalia, for example, attests to the authorial consciousness of the existence of another person. At times this person is one with whom the writer can identify (a reader like himself), but, as we have seen in the problematic slipperiness of the idea of emulation, this other person can simultaneously become a curious and even potentially malicious reader to whom the writer must explain, justify or excuse himself. The masque marginalia is generated out of the oscillation between the authorial 'I' and a curious 'eye': 'This *Dame* I make to beare the person of *Ate*, or Mischiefe (for so I interpret it) out of Homer's description of her: *Iliad*.'[26] Or: 'There wants not inough, in nature, to authorize this part of our

---

[25] For her commentary on Poulet and Blanchot, see Newlyn, *Reading, Writing, and Romanticism*, pp. vii–viii.
[26] *The Masque of Queenes*, Herford and Simpson, vol. VII, p. 286 (line 95 n. *n*).

fiction, in separating *Niger*, from the *Ocean*'.[27] We will discover the extent to which this movement between author and imagined reader is generative of text, not just in the margins, but within the texts themselves.

'The design of the whole'

Twenty years ago, Stephen Greenblatt astutely urged critics to 'abjure' romantic ideas of solitary genius, motiveless art and transcendent representation: 'This book argues that works of art, however intensely marked by the creative intelligence and private obsessions of individuals, are the products of collective negotiation and exchange.'[28] At the present critical moment we are not so much in danger of losing sight of the material and social forces which shape literary works as we are in danger of losing sight of the textual traces of the phantasmagoria of the individual or individuals who wrote them. While the present study seeks to distance itself from a literary-biographical reading of Jonson and envy, it will aim to recuperate the way the text is indeed marked by 'the creative intelligence and private obsessions' of an author. These traces can best be distinguished in examinations of a whole *œuvre*. Yet, many scholars of Jonson limit themselves to a particular genre or period of Jonson's work. This, of course, is a natural enough impulse as well as, often, an editorial necessity. Indeed, one of the positive legacies of Foucault's questioning of what an author is has been a useful interrogation of our assumptions about the *nature* of authorship and *what* even constitutes the authorial *œuvre*: does it consist of the works the author has published himself, his drafts (*brouillons*), his notes, the appointments written in the margin of his notebook (*carnet*) or even the odd laundry list?[29] Yet, Foucault's important interrogations, as well as a renewal of interest in the material circumstances of the production of literary works, including performance, have both had the side-effect of contributing to the fragmentation of Jonson's corpus. Jonson's works increasingly figure in thematic studies for the purpose of illuminating a socio-historical trend to which they can lend an appropriate quotation. He has become the subject for a chapter in a book on the early modern period rather than a viable

---

[27] *The Masque of Blacknesse*, Herford and Simpson, vol. VII, p. 172 (line 118 n. *l*).
[28] Stephen Greenblatt, *Shakespearean Negotiations: The Circulation of Social Energy in Renaissance England* (Oxford: Clarendon Press, 1988), p. vii. For his list of 'abjurations' to literary critics, see p. 12.
[29] Michel Foucault, 'Qu'est-ce qu'un auteur?' in Arnold I. Davidson and Frédéric Gros (eds.), *Philosophie: Anthologie* (Paris: Gallimard, 2004), pp. 290–318; pp. 295–6. For a version in English: 'What is an Author?' in Josue Harari (ed.), *Textual Strategies: Perspectives in Post-Structuralist Criticism* (Ithaca: Cornell University Press, 1979).

subject as an author of a distinct, complex and interrelated body of work. Monographs dedicated to themes and subjects which traverse the poems, masques and plays have been increasingly rare in the growing specialization of both Jonson and early modern studies, although there are some notable exceptions.[30]

It is this kind of fragmentation and specialization that T. S. Eliot inveighed against in his conception of how to read Ben Jonson. It was Eliot who reawakened interest in Jonson in the twentieth century in his short essay, 'Ben Jonson', in *Elizabethan Dramatists*. He attempted to find a new perspective on the author who had the misfortune to have been 'damned by the praise that quenches all desire to read the book; to be afflicted by the imputation of the virtues which excited the least pleasure'.[31] He was convinced that to understand Jonson truly, more classical scholarship or historical understanding of the period was *not* what was required of Jonson's readers:

his poetry is of the surface. Poetry of the surface cannot be understood without study; for to deal with the surface of life, as Jonson dealt with it, is to deal so deliberately that we too must be deliberate, in order to understand ... The immediate appeal of Jonson is to the mind; his emotional tone is not in the single verse, but in *the design of the whole*. But not many people are capable of discovering for

---

[30] Without doubt, the new *Cambridge Edition of the Works of Ben Jonson*, edited by David Bevington, Martin Butler and Ian Donaldson will go a long way to remedying this situation. Once the entirety of Jonson's production is easily available in a modern and digitally word searchable format, considerations of Jonson's work across genres will inevitably multiply. Literary biographies tend naturally to cut across generic lines and traverse periods: Marchette Chute, *Ben Jonson of Westminster* (New York: E. P. Dutton and Co., 1953), Rosalind Miles, *Ben Jonson: His Life and Work* (London: Routledge and Kegan Paul, 1986), David Riggs, *Ben Jonson: A Life* (Harvard: Harvard University Press, 1989) and W. David Kay, *Ben Jonson: A Literary Life* (Basingstoke: Macmillan, 1995). In non-biographical studies of Jonson's works, both Katharine Eisaman Maus and Bruce Thomas Boehrer, for example, have cut across generic divisions and, in the case of Maus, dealt with Jonson's *œuvre* in its quasi-entirety. See Maus, *Ben Jonson and the Roman Frame of Mind* (Princeton: Princeton University Press, 1984) and Boehrer, *The Fury of Men's Gullets*. Recently, Tom Lockwood in *Ben Jonson in the Romantic Age* (Oxford: Oxford University Press, 2005) has examined the reception of Jonson's works in the nineteenth century. Other studies which have traversed generic boundaries in the study of Jonson are: Alexander Leggatt, *Ben Jonson: His Vision and His Art* (London: Methuen, 1981), Jongsook Lee, *Ben Jonson's Poesis: A Literary Dialectic of Ideal History* (Charlottesville: University of Virginia Press, 1983) and Michael McCanles, *Jonsonian Discriminations: The Humanist Poet and the Praise of True Nobility* (Toronto: University of Toronto Press, 1992). Robert C. Evans in *Ben Jonson and the Politics of Patronage* (Lewisburg: Bucknell University Press, 1989) goes so far as to defend his decision to focus almost exclusively on Jonson's poems by noting the relative lack of scholarship on the poems: 'the dramas and entertainments have been the object of some of the richest and most provocative criticism devoted to Jonson over the last several decades, whereas the poems have only recently begun to attract the same kind of intensely sustained scrutiny'. He notes that to have ignored the masques and plays completely from his discussion of the poems 'would have opened me – and rightly so – to charges of neglecting crucial aspects of [Jonson's] life and art' (pp. 10–11).

[31] T. S. Eliot, 'Ben Jonson', *Elizabethan Dramatists* (London: Faber and Faber Ltd., 1963 [1934]), pp. 67–82; p. 67.

themselves the beauty which is only found after labour; and *Jonson's industrious readers have been those whose interest was historical and curious, and those who have thought that in discovering the historical and curious interest they had discovered the artistic value as well*. When we say that Jonson requires study, we do not mean study of his classical scholarship or of seventeenth-century manners. We mean intelligent *saturation in his work as a whole*; we mean that in order to enjoy him at all, we must get to the centre of his work and his temperament, and that we must see him unbiased by time, as a contemporary [my emphasis].[32]

In his desire to consider Jonson as a 'contemporary', 'unbiased by time', Eliot's essay may easily be dismissed as radically outmoded. Yet, it seems that Eliot may also have been very perspicacious in suggesting that an overemphasis on scholarship could have the effect not of illuminating the text, but rather the opposite: of burying it in historical detail. A consideration of Jonson through a 'saturation in his work as a whole' may be perceived as returning to an older style of criticism, yet it seems that it is precisely such saturation that can bring into focus a repetitive theme and motif such as envy in the whole of the writer's work. The present book intends to consider how and why the Jonsonian *œuvre* is marked by an obsession with 'envy'. To answer these questions, the representation of envy will need to be considered in its cultural, anthropological and historical dimension. Only by recognizing envy's historical association with the eye and the gaze can we understand Jonson's obsessive references, well documented by scholars, to looking, spying and judging as part of a coherent system of apprehending and protecting the literary work against public and private scrutiny.[33] Only then can we begin to see it, not merely as an iconographical image or the humour of a malcontent, but as the motor of a system of literary creation. This book will read envy in Jonson's works, never divorced from the culture of the sixteenth and early seventeenth centuries, but nevertheless as part of an intricate system of a body of literary works with a certain textual and intellectual integrity.

The problem of envy

Before turning to Jonson and the representation of envy in his work, I would like to consider briefly the way the subject of envy has been broached generally. One finds discussions of envy most frequently in the fields of

---

[32] *Ibid.*, pp. 68–9.
[33] See Gabriele Bernhard Jackson, *Vision and Judgement in Ben Jonson's Drama* (New Haven: Yale University Press, 1968) and William W. E. Slights, *Ben Jonson and the Art of Secrecy* (Toronto: University of Toronto Press, 1994).

psychology, moral philosophy, sociology and economics. Envy is, first and foremost, a social phenomenon. It is, consequently, also an economic and a moral one. It is about 'keeping up with the Joneses', moving up the corporate ladder, but also the problem of justice and the equal distribution of wealth. At the end of the revised edition of *A Theory of Justice*, John Rawls acknowledges that his original model of social justice was incomplete in that it overlooked *envy* as a factor in the process of selecting principles of justice:

> Throughout I have assumed that the persons in the original position [position from which deliberators select principles of justice] are not moved by certain psychological propensities (§25). A rational individual is not subject to envy... since envy is generally regarded as something to be avoided and feared, at least when it becomes intense, it seems desirable that, if possible, the choice of principles should not be influenced by this trait. Therefore, for reasons both of simplicity and moral theory, I have assumed an absence of envy... Nevertheless these inclinations do exist and in some way they must be reckoned with... I shall discuss the problem of envy as an illustration of the way in which the special psychologies enter into the theory of justice.[34]

Having acknowledged the importance of such an 'irrational' emotion in the conception of a theory of social justice, Rawls goes on to confront what he then calls 'The Problem of Envy' in a section appended to the revised edition of his book.[35] In scientific journals, models of 'envy-free' allocations in relation to the 'zero-sum' game of economic penury abound.[36] The word 'envy' in America has become synonymous with consumerist desire in which people possess 'shoe envy' or (in New York City) 'apartment envy', a form of emulative rivalry for luxury goods.[37] Envy is commonly defined as pain at the sight of another's prosperity.[38] The German word 'Schadenfreude',

---

[34] John Rawls, *A Theory of Justice*, rev. edn (Oxford: Oxford University Press, 1999), pp. 464–6.
[35] *Ibid.*, p. 464.
[36] See, among others, D. K. Foley, 'Resource Allocation and the Public Sector', *Yale Economic Essays* 7 (1967), 45–198; H. Varian, 'Equity, Envy, and Efficiency,' *Journal of Economic Theory* 9 (1974), 63–91; H. Varian, 'Distributive Justice, Welfare Economics, and the Theory of Fairness', *Philosophy and Public Affairs* 4 (1975), 223–47; R. Young, 'Egalitarianism and Envy', *Philosophical Studies* 52 (1987), 261–76.
[37] See Thorstein Veblen, *The Theory of the Leisure Class: An Economic Study of Institutions* (New York: Macmillan, 1915 [1899]). See particularly Chapter II, 'Pecuniary Emulation', where Thorstein discusses the importance of 'invidious comparison' as an incentive for conspicuous consumption (pp. 22–34).
[38] See Aristotle, *Rhetoric*, II.x. Aristotle, *The Art of Rhetoric*, trans. John Henry Freese (London: William Heinemann, 1926), II.x.10. and Kant's definition in *The Metaphysics of Morals* (1797): 'Envy is a propensity to view the well-being of others with distress, even though it does not detract from one's own. [It is] a reluctance to see our own well-being overshadowed by another's because the standard we use to see how well off we are is not the intrinsic worth of our own well-being but how

on the other hand, describes the strange delight many feel at the sight of another's failure or defeat, a feeling akin to, but not the same as envy.[39] The world of art, like the halls of academe, is, and has been, well known as a hotbed for envious relationships. Alexander Pushkin wrote his play *Mozart and Salieri* in 1826, one year after Salieri's death when rumours of his confession to having poisoned Mozart out of envy were still in the air. Pushkin's play would become the basis of Peter Shaffer's *Amadeus*, very successfully adapted for the screen by Milos Forman in 1984.

The number of envious characters in early modern literature, not just in Jonson, would seem to encourage us to see envy as a universal passion. Iago, in Shakespeare's *Othello*, is emblematic of the destructive power of envy, which ends in the deaths, not only of its purported victims, but the envier himself. Milton's Satan is not only referred to frequently as filled with envy, but is even represented as wondering if God himself may not have been envious.[40] In his work on envy in both Spenser's *The Faerie Queene* (1596) and *The Shepheards Calendar* (1579), Ronald B. Bond has illuminatingly considered Spenser's representations of envy both in terms of physical 'vision' and within the political context of the envious atmosphere of the court of Queen Elizabeth I.[41] Yet, however 'universal' a passion it may seem, representations of envy need to be examined in their cultural and historical context for us to understand the power attributed to it in the Renaissance long before it became weakened in current usages. It is a concept with a rich ancient and medieval history that has roots in philosophy, theology, medicine and the visual arts. In the introduction to *Envy, Spite and Jealousy: The Rivalrous Emotions in Ancient Greece*, the editors note a lack of historical and contextual work on what they have called the 'rivalrous emotions':

After a long dry spell, the cross-cultural, interdisciplinary study of the emotions has become a lively subject for research over the past twenty or thirty years...To date, however, there has been no comprehensive treatment of the rivalrous emotions

---

it compares with that of others.' *The Cambridge Edition of the Works of Immanuel Kant: Practical Philosophy*, trans. M. Gregor (New York: Cambridge University Press, 1996), p. 459.

[39] Joseph Epstein, *Envy: The Seven Deadly Sins* (New York: Oxford University Press and The New York Public Library, 2003), p. 69.

[40] Satan wonders at God's interdiction to eat of the tree of knowledge: '...knowledge forbidden? / Suspicious, reasonless. Why should their Lord / Envy them that?' John Milton, *Paradise Lost*, ed. Alastair Fowler (London: Longman, 1968), p. 225 (IV.515–17).

[41] Ronald B. Bond, 'Vying with Vision: An Aspect of Envy in *The Faerie Queene*', *Renaissance and Reformation*, n.s. 8 (1984), 30–8 and 'Supplantation in the Elizabethan Court: the Theme of Spenser's February Eclogue', *Spenser Studies* 2 (1981), 55–65; see also R. B. Gill, 'The Renaissance Conventions of Envy', *Mediaevalia et Humanistica*, n.s. 9 (1979), 215–30.

such as envy, jealousy, emulation and malicious spite in ancient Greece, at least since the slender volume by Peter Walcot entitled *Envy and the Greeks: A Study of Human Behavior* (1978).[42]

This collection includes essays on Greek society, politics and literature. Another recent collection, from France, includes essays that further enlarge the scope of literary treatments of envy.[43] Many of the essays are inspired by psychoanalytic investigations into envy, following the work of Melanie Klein.[44] Others provide an historical and European context for an examination of envy in early modern England.[45] In the introduction to this volume, Fabrice Wilhelm remarks on the absence of any comprehensive treatment of envy equivalent to Raymond Klibansky, Erwin Panofsky and Fritz Saxl's magisterial work on melancholy, *Saturn and Melancholy*:[46]

Scientific rigor would have demanded a history of envy to precede an analysis of its literary representations. It is certain that beyond a certain continuity of definition, envy has psychological and social implications that are different in Classical Athens, at the beginning of monachism, at the time of the creation of the great universities of the Middle Ages, in the seventeenth century or the nineteenth. But there exists no work on envy comparable to that which Panofsky devoted to melancholy.[47]

---

[42] David Konstan and N. Keith Rutter (eds.), *Envy, Spite and Jealousy: The Rivalrous Emotions in Ancient Greece* (Edinburgh: Edinburgh University Press, 2003), pp. 1–2. In classical studies, where articles and essays on the subject are numerous, Peter Walcot's *Envy and the Greeks: A Study of Human Behaviour* (Warminster: Aris and Phillips, Ltd., 1978) provides an extremely useful introduction to the subject with a mine of examples from Greek authors in the fields of both politics and literature. See also David Konstan, *The Emotions of the Ancient Greeks: Studies in Aristotle and Classical Literature* (Toronto: University of Toronto Press, 2006).

[43] Fabrice Wilhelm (ed.), *L'Envie et ses figurations littéraires* (Dijon: Editions Universitaires de Dijon, 2005). See also Pascale Hassoun-Lestienne (ed.), *L'Envie et le désir: les faux frères* (Paris: Autrement, 1998).

[44] In the field of psychoanalysis, Melanie Klein's *Envy and Gratitude: A Study of Unconscious Sources* (London: Tavistock Press, 1957) is still the point of reference on the subject.

[45] See Edith Karagiannis-Mazeaud, 'Sur la rime vie / Envie: Jalons pour une histoire de l'Envie et de ses représentations au XVIe siècle: Ronsard, Du Bellay, Jodelle, Peletier du Mans' in Wilhelm (ed.), *L'Envie et ses figurations littéraires*, pp. 95–118 and Gilles Polizzi, 'L'Enfant désallaité: Envie et création dans la fiction humaniste de la première Renaissance', in *ibid.*, pp. 119–45. Mazeaud's essay describes the frequency with which envy is mentioned among the Pléiade poets. Polizzi's essay considers envy and the act of creation in Rabelais.

[46] Raymond Klibansky, Erwin Panofsky and Fritz Saxl, *Saturn and Melancholy: Studies in the History of Natural Philosophy, Religion and Art* (London: Nelson, 1964).

[47] 'La rigueur scientifique aurait voulu qu'une histoire de l'envie précédât une analyse de ses représentations littéraires. Il est bien certain qu'au-delà de la permanence définitionnelle, l'envie a des implications psychologiques et sociales différentes dans l'Athène classique, aux débuts du monachisme, au moment de la création des grandes universités du Moyen Age, à l'âge classique ou au XIXe siècle. Mais il n'existe pas de travaux sur l'envie comparables à ceux que Panofsky a consacrés à la mélancolie'. Wilhelm (ed.), *L'Envie et ses figurations littéraires*, p. 12.

Introduction

To underline his point that a substantial historical work on envy is necessary, Wilhem all but dismisses Helmut Schoeck's *Envy: A Theory of Social Behavior*, noting that while the book may be useful in the fields of anthropology or sociology, it has little to say, for instance, about the key role of the early Church fathers in the construction of the Western concept of envy and omits completely the work of Melanie Klein in his chapter on psychoanalysis.[48] D. L. Cairns goes so far as to call Schoeck's book 'nauseating'.[49] Despite its flaws, Schoeck's *Envy* remains a starting-point for inquiries into the subject, with chapters dedicated to an examination of this emotion in the realms of political science, psychoanalysis, behavioural science and philosophy.[50]

A particular case has to be made for René Girard's *A Theatre of Envy*, first published in 1990, which might appear to be to Shakespeare what this book intends to be to Jonson.[51] Girard argues that Shakespeare had his own vocabulary for *mimetic desire*, such as 'suggested desire', 'jealous desire' and 'emulous desire'. According to Girard, 'the essential word is "envy", alone or in such combinations as "envious desire" or "envious emulation"'.[52] Yet, Girard's emphasis on the concept of mimetic desire is different from the kind of envy which I will be considering. Girard's 'theatre of envy' is defined in terms of the 'triangulation of desire' in which two characters, of the same sex, pursue the same object, one of the opposite sex. Girard describes how, in *Two Gentlemen of Verona*, Valentine loves Sylvia and, as a result of mimetic desire, Proteus, his best friend, is inflamed with love for Sylvia as well. It is true that mimetic desire mimics, *in form*, the relationship between the envier and his rival, in which the desired thing is subordinate to the *someone* who enjoys the privileged relationship with it. Yet, throughout his book, Girard's emphasis is on envy as mimetic, triangulated desire rather than on envy as *invidia*, what Fabrice Wilhelm has termed the specific envy of 'the philosophical and theological tradition'.[53]

---

[48] Helmut Shoeck, *Envy: A Theory of Social Behavior* (London: Secker and Warburg, 1966).
[49] D. L. Cairns, 'The Politics of Envy: Envy and Equality in Ancient Greece' in Konstan and Rutter (eds.), *Envy, Spite and Jealousy*, pp. 235–52; p. 235.
[50] A key essay is George M. Foster, 'The Anatomy of Envy: A Study in Symbolic Behavior', *Current Anthropology* (April 1972), 165–202. I am indebted to this essay for the title of Chapter 1 of the present book.
[51] René Girard, *A Theater of Envy: William Shakespeare* (Oxford: Oxford University Press, 1991). Originally published as *Shakespeare: les feux de l'envie* (Paris: Bernard Grasset, 1990). All references will be to the English version.
[52] *Ibid.*, p. 4.
[53] Wilhelm also differentiates his work and that of his colleagues in *L'Envie et ses figurations littéraires* from that of René Girard in the following terms: 'Nevertheless, his [Girard's] conception of envy, which he identifies with mimetic desire, is not that which is the legacy of the philosophical

This is the envy of Satan for Adam and Eve and the first cause of the Fall. This is the passion that was to become one of the seven deadly sins in the medieval period and is depicted in the Renaissance emblem tradition, following the description in Book II of Ovid's *Metamorphoses*, as a decrepit woman, eating her heart out, with vipers emerging from her mouth or as a kind of fury or Medusa.⁵⁴

Envy and jealousy

To clarify further the envy that will be the subject of this book it will be helpful to differentiate it not only from 'mimetic desire' but also from jealousy, the passion with which it is most often confused, especially in ordinary parlance.⁵⁵ A simple way of considering the difference would be to say that 'one is jealous of what one has, envious of what other people have'.⁵⁶ The seventeenth-century moralist La Rochefoucauld is careful to differentiate between the two passions:

La jalousie est en quelque manière juste et raisonnable, puisqu'elle ne tend qu'à conserver un bien qui nous appartient, ou que nous croyons nous appartenir; au lieu que l'envie est une fureur qui ne peut souffrir le bien des autres.⁵⁷

(Jealousy is in some way proper and reasonable, since it only tends to guard a good that is ours, or that we believe belongs to us, while envy is a rage that cannot abide the good of others.)

The English adjective 'jealous' is derived from the Greek *zélos* via the Latin *zelos*, which originally meant 'emulation' and 'zeal'. The *Oxford English Dictionary* thus defines *jealous* as:

Zealous or solicitous for the preservation or well-being of something possessed or esteemed; vigilant or careful in guarding; suspiciously careful or watchful; troubled

and moral theological tradition and constitutes the subject of the present conference' (p. 13, my translation).

⁵⁴ See Emblem LXXI 'Invidia' of Andrea Alciati. The *subscriptio* reads: 'A filthy woman who chews the flesh of vipers, whose eyes hurt, and who devours her own heart; emaciated and grayish, she carries a throny staff in her hand: this is how Envy is to be pictured.' Andrea Alciati, *A Book of Emblems: The* Emblematum Liber *in Latin and English,* trans. and ed. John F. Moffitt (London: McFarland and Company, Inc., 2004), p. 90.

⁵⁵ The reason for this confusion may stem from the taboo that seems to surround envy, particularly in modern times. Both jealousy and even emulation, the other 'passions' with which envy is (rightly) often confused, are still both more 'positive' and more likely to be admitted as a motivation than envy.

⁵⁶ Epstein, *Envy*, p. 4. George Crabb in *English Synonymes* notes: 'We are jealous of what is our own; we are envious of what is another's. Jealousy fears to lose what it has; envy is pained at seeing another have that which it wants for itself.' Cited in Cairns, 'The Politics of Envy', p. 239 n. 12.

⁵⁷ *Maxime 28* in La Rochefoucauld, *Maximes, 1678* (Paris: Bordas, 1992), p. 13 (my translation).

by the belief, suspicion, or fear that the good which one desires to gain or keep for oneself has been or may be diverted to another; resentful towards another on account of known or suspected rivalry.[58]

Envy, on the other hand, comes from the Latin 'invidia', derived from *invidere*, a verbal form compounded from *in-* ('upon') plus *videre* ('to see'), and so: 'To look maliciously upon; to feel displeasure and ill-will at the superiority of (another person) in happiness, success, reputation, or the possession of anything desirable; to *regard* with discontent another's possessions or advantages.' (*OED* s.v. 'envy' *v.* 1) While a traditional formula to distinguish envy from jealousy is to claim that envy involves two people, jealousy three (hence the association of jealousy primarily with love triangles), it is clear that both envy and jealousy involve a triadic relationship. The difference between the two passions involves rather the relative importance of any one of the three elements to another. Both jealousy and envy involve a pair of individuals whose relationship is mediated, or structured, by an intervening property or object. The mediating property is 'possessed' by one member of the dyad; the other member does not possess it, but wishes to. It is this desire that creates the feeling of envy in the latter person, making him an envier. The difference between envy and jealousy is that jealousy focuses on the *desired object* (whether a person, possession or abstract quality) whereas envy focuses on the *possessor* of the desired object.[59] The good or possession is the trigger, but not the target of envy, whereas the possession is of superior importance to the jealous person, who fears losing what he possesses, be it his lover or his unblemished reputation.

Distinguishing envy from jealousy, when we do not completely distinguish them today, involves, implicitly, conceiving of their differences in historical terms. These differences are, of course, dependent upon epoch, language and culture. David Konstan argues that because the Greeks lacked a term that answers to the English 'jealousy' or the Italian 'gelosia', they may not even have experienced jealousy in the modern sense.[60] That the early modern period did, in fact, acknowledge two separate emotions is evident in their different iconologies, which would have been familiar to Jonson and his contemporaries. In Ripa's *Iconologia*, 'Gelosia' is pictured as a young and beautiful woman whose dress is covered in eyes and ears,

---

[58] *OED* s.v. 'jealous' *a.* 3, 4. [59] See Cairns, 'The Politics of Envy', p. 239 n. 12.
[60] David Konstan, 'Before Jealousy' in Konstan and Rutter (eds.), *Envy, Spite and Jealousy*, pp. 7–27; p. 8.

signifying the desire to see and hear each action of the beloved.⁶¹ In the early modern period, the figure of Fame was often depicted covered in eyes, mouths and ears, following Virgil's description in Book 4 of the *Aeneid*. Gelosia holds a branch of thorns in her right hand signifying the jealous person's self-inflicted pain and jealousy's eternal vigilance is represented by a cock perched on her left arm. 'Invidia', on the other hand, is not illustrated in Ripa.⁶² 'She' is described as an old, ugly, pale woman ('Donna vecchia, bruta, e pallida)'. Ripa notes that Invidia is an ancient enemy of virtue ('antica inimicitia con la virtù'), following in its train, ready to spray venom into souls ('sempre à spargere il veleno') since she is constantly thinking of how to do evil to another. She has humble origins, represented by the rags she wears ('mal vestita'), but she never attempts to reach high things, and is thus linked to idleness and sloth. She is possessed of a sharp tooth and a sideways glance ('con occhio torto in disparte'). She both freezes ('ghiaccio') and burns ('bagnasi di sudore') at the same time at the sight of another's happiness.⁶³ Ripa's 'Gelosia' and 'Invidia' are clearly very different. Yet, what they share is the fact that both are eternally vigilant and fascinated with the sight of an object that can only give them pain.

The present study could well have considered the representation of a jealousy/envy split in Jonson's works by considering the jealous Thorello in *Every Man in His Humour* (1598), recognized as a model for Shakespeare's Othello, and the humour of 'envy' in the figure of Macilente in *Every Man Out of His Humour* (1599). One could read Ben Jonson's *Catiline, His Conspiracy* (1611) as a subtle exploration of the difference between jealousy and envy. Cicero's zeal and vigilance to protect Rome might well be opposed to the Catilinian envy of a decadent aristocrat begrudging an inferior plebian his chance to rise in the ranks. This fear and hatred of the rival who comes from a lower social stratum, or the young upstart, could be seen as an illustration of what

---

⁶¹ Cesare Ripa, 'Gelosia', *Iconologia* (Padua, 1611), p. 195.
⁶² *Ibid.*, 'Invidia', pp. 262–3. While 'Invidia' is not accompanied by an image, the illustration of 'Peccato' in the 1611 edition of the *Iconologia* (p. 133) resembles, in many respects, the description of 'Invidia'. There are, nevertheless, important differences. According to Virginie Bar, Ripa's 'Peccato' is 'presented as a horrible young man, naked, blind and blackened, walking on rocks along a cliff, water serpents mixed in his hair, snakes entwining his body and a third reptile eating out his heart'. Virginie Bar, *La Peinture allégorique au Grand Siècle* (Dijon: Editions Faton, 2003), p. 351 (my translation). Bar argues that the image identified as Envy in Nicholas Poussin's painting entitled *Le Temps soustrait la Vérité aux atteintes de l'Envie et de le Discorde* ('Time protecting Truth from the Attacks of Discord and Envy') is actually the figure of Ripa's 'Peccato' or 'Sin'. For an interesting discussion of Ripa's 'Peccato' with regard to Shakespeare, see Raymond B. Waddington, 'Moralizing the Spectacle: Dramatic Emblems in *As You Like It*', *Shakespeare Quarterly* 33 (Summer 1982), 155–63; see particularly pp. 159–60.
⁶³ All references are from 'Invidia' in Ripa, *Iconologia*, p. 262.

Cairns describes as 'top-down *phthonos* [envy]' on Catiline's part. In other words, the complex and unusual envy described by Aristotle in the *Rhetoric*. According to Cairns, Aristotle argues that:

[T]he superior individual (for example a tyrant or a god) does not envy others from a position of equality or near-equality; he is jealous of his privileges *vis-à-vis* those who are greatly inferior; and his jealousy would be assuaged not by the elimination of inequality between himself and them, but by its maintenance or enhancement; the *phthonos* [envy] of superiors denies equality between the patient and the target of the emotion, but enforces it between the target and everyone else. Again, this facilitates recognition... that, in the politics of envy, both mass and elite are driven by negative emotions of a comparable nature.[64]

On the other hand, rather than separate the two emotions, Lily B. Campbell suggests that jealousy is a secondary passion, *derived* from envy: 'Jealousy was, in the thinking of the Renaissance, not one of the simple or elementary passions but a derivative or compounded passion. It is a species of envy, which is in turn a species of hatred... It is this curious mingling of love and hatred with grief or fear that we see in jealousy.'[65] Despite clear differences, the two share, in the words of Lacey Baldwin Smith, a certain tendency toward 'paranoia'.[66] Interestingly enough, Smith finds his own definition of this neurosis in Jonson's *Every Man In His Humour*, where Thorello describes his jealousy as: 'a pestilence' that 'doth infect... the braine', the 'blacke poyson of suspect'.[67] In taking the phrase, 'the blacke poyson of suspect', as a description for his paranoid 'mode of cognition', Smith mentions neither the play, the author, the character speaking nor the situation. In deciding to divorce this phrase from the sexual intrigue of Jonson's play, he may, in fact, have wished to emphasize the common, generalized state of watchful and careful *vigilance* that jealousy, paranoia and envy share:

The central feature of the paranoid cognitive response to life is not simply suspicion, 'the black poison of suspect', it is the conviction that things are never as they appear to be – a greater and generally more sinister reality exists behind the

---

[64] Cairns, 'The Politics of Envy', p. 242.
[65] Lily B. Campbell, *Shakespeare's Tragic Heroines: Slaves of Passion* (Magnolia, MA: Peter Smith, 1960), p. 148.
[66] Lacey Baldwin Smith writes apropos his own use of the term 'paranoia': 'To burden a century with a medical term which is at best imprecise even in its clinical usage, to impose a disease of the individual upon the collective mentality of a kingdom, and to describe Tudor England as paranoid is to risk the legitimate wrath of both historian and psychiatrist... Obviously, the sixteenth century was not clinically paranoid... it did manifest many of the symptoms of what Richard Hofstader has describes as "the paranoid style" of thought and David Shapiro the paranoid "mode of cognition".' Lacey Baldwin Smith, *Treason in Tudor England: Politics and Paranoia* (London: Pimlico, 2006), p. 36.
[67] Ben Jonson, *Every Man In His Humour*, Herford and Simpson, vol. III, p. 330 (II.iii.59–60; 69).

scenes – and the corollary that what is standing hidden in the wings, prompting, manipulating, but always avoiding exposure to the footlights, is the presence of evil…The paranoid man, therefore, is ever vigilant and on his guard.[68]

Smith describes the central feature of the paranoid state of mind as based not just in 'suspicion', but in the belief in the 'presence of evil', 'hidden in the wings, prompting' and 'manipulating'. Against this hidden evil the paranoid man is on his guard. Smith thus describes the state of Tudor England as a regime based on a paranoia nourished in Gloriana's court, filled with envious backbiters and spies, against whom every courtier needed to defend and protect him or herself.

MALEVOLENT EYES: SPECTATORS AND READERS

In turning to Jonson, one is struck by the way references to envy pervade the writer's works. In the preface to *The Masque of Blacknesse* (1605; first print edition 1608), Jonson cites *Ignorance* and *Envie* as the two great enemies to the posterity of the masque. The anti-masque character, Night, in *The Masque of Beauty* (1608), is described as envious. Likewise, the witches of *The Masque of Queenes* (1609) are motivated by envy. In an Ode, the poet invokes Pallas Athene to make 'Gorgon Envye yield' and famously begins 'To Penshurst' by stating that it was not built for 'envious show'.[69] Despite what might be considered a certain critical mass of such references, when scholars have considered envy in the works of Jonson, they have tended to focus almost exclusively on two instances: the humourous malcontent, Macilente, in *Every Man Out of His Humour*, or the masque-like monster 'Envie' in the Induction to *Poetaster* (1601).[70] Both are allegorical, tangible

---

[68] Smith, *Treason in Tudor England*, pp. 36–7.
[69] See 'Ode', *Ungathered Verse* (xlviii), Herford and Simpson, vol. VIII, p. 421 (line 41) and 'To Penshurst', *The Forrest* (ii), *Ibid.*, p. 93 (line 1).
[70] For a discussion of Macilente as a 'malcontent' in relation, particularly, to the medieval sources of Jonson's emblematic figure of envy see Charles Read Baskervill, *English Elements in Jonson's Early Comedy* (New York: Gordian Press, Inc., 1967), pp. 158–69. See also James D. Redwine, Jr, 'Beyond Psychology: The Moral Basis of Jonson's Theory of Humour Characterization', *ELH* 28 (1961), 316–34; M.A. Harris, 'The Origin of the Seventeenth-Century Idea of Humours', *MLN* 10 (1895), 44–6; Henry L. Snuggs, 'The Comic Humours: A New Interpretation', *PMLA* 62 (1947), 114–22; Allan H. Gilbert, *The Symbolic Persons in the Masques of Ben Jonson* (Durham: Duke University Press, 1948), entry on 'Envy'. Recent work on the emotions or passions in early modern studies includes Gail Kern Paster, Katherine Rowe and Mary Floyd-Wilson (eds.), *Reading the Early Modern Passions: Essays in the Cultural History of Emotion* (Philadelphia: Pennsylvania University Press, 2004). For discussions of the emblematic figure 'Livor' ('Envie' in the 1616 Folio) in *Poetaster* see, among others, Matthew Steggle, *Wars of the Theatres: The Poetics of Personation in the Age of Jonson* (English Literary Studies: University of Victoria, 1998) and Lindsay M. Kaplan, *The Culture of Slander in Early Modern England* (Cambridge: Cambridge University Press, 1997).

embodiments of envy. Both are studied, for the most part, in isolation, within readings of the individual plays in which they appear rather than as examples of a larger authorial engagement with envy. Aside from these punctual analyses of envious 'characters', envy in Jonson has been considered, for the most part, in terms of the playwright's rivalrous relationships with his contemporaries.[71] Recently, however, Ian Donaldson, in 'Looking Sideways: Jonson, Shakespeare, and the Myths of Envy', has explored the mythology behind Jonson's historical envy of Shakespeare.[72] This article represents an important first step toward a fuller discussion of envy in the works themselves. Donaldson points out that Jonson makes references to envy with 'intriguing and significant frequency'.[73] He reminds the reader of the writer's use of the emblematic representations of envy from handbooks such as Ripa's *Iconologia* and notes Jonson's familiarity with Renaissance perspective theory and the way paintings (or a perspective stage), viewed from an oblique angle, become distorted. It is according to these laws that the King, viewing the court masque from the mathematical centre, could enjoy the masque at 'a true angle of vision'.[74] Donaldson cites Jonson's poem, 'In Authorem', in the dedication to Nicholas Breton's *Melancholike Humours*, to show how the poet applied these rules of perspective to describe how readers could read books from the *wrong* angle:

> Look here on *Bretons* worke, the master print:
> Where, such perfections to the life doe rise.
> If they seem wry, to such as looke asquint,
> The fault's not in the object, but their eyes.[75]

Jonson here, according to Donaldson, 'declares if Breton's readers cannot see the beauties of his work, then the blame must lie not with the work, but with the readers themselves: they are simply not observing it aright, but looking sideways, "asquint"'.[76] The poem's suggestive portrait of

---

[71] For the rivalrous relationships between playwrights during the 'War of the Theatres' see James Shapiro, *Rival Playwrights: Jonson, Shakespeare, Marlowe* (New York: Columbia University Press, 1991) and James P. Bednarz, *Shakespeare and the Poets' War* (New York: Columbia University Press, 2001). For Jonson's rivalrous relationships with his fellow playwrights and desire to distinguish himself from them, see also George W. Rowe, *Distinguishing Jonson: Imitation, Rivalry, and the Direction of a Dramatic Career* (Lincoln: University of Nebraska Press, 1993).
[72] Ian Donaldson, 'Looking Sideways: Jonson, Shakespeare, and the Myths of Envy', *Ben Jonson Journal* 8 (2001), 1–22.
[73] *Ibid.*, p. 2.
[74] *Ibid.*, 4. See also Stephen Orgel, *The Illusion of Power: Political Theater in the English Renaissance* (Berkeley: University of California Press, 1975).
[75] Ben Jonson, 'In Authorem', *Ungathered Verse* (ii), Herford and Simpson, vol. VIII, p. 362 (lines 5–8).
[76] Donaldson, 'Looking Sideways', p. 1.

readers who read 'sideways', or *askance*, is not developed further; instead, Donaldson turns his attention to his putative topic, the myth of Jonson's envy of Shakespeare, and, with it, a more biographically inflected discussion. Yet, in Jonson's lines 'on *Breton's* work' we are privy to a tug-of-war of hermeneutic responsibility between author and reader in which the writer accuses the reader of an act of misprision. 'Fault' is correctly glossed in one sense as 'blame', but in this context, it also implies that the reader's curious gaze *creates* a fissure or a stain in the text that did not exist in the writing of it. The writer attributes this stain or fault to the 'beam' in the reader's own eye.[77] In placing responsibility for the misinterpretation of the text squarely on a reader who, voluntarily or involuntarily, *looks at things awry*, the writer describes the act of reading as a form of ocular malevolence.[78]

These lines show that for Jonson, there exist readers who read books *obliquo oculo*, or *enviously*. Jonson here represents the act of looking and reading as equivalent to what Francis Bacon called an 'Act of *Envy*'.[79] In anticipation of future criticism and censure, the writer may be seen to engage in textual strategies and rituals in order to censure apotropaically his own work before it falls under the gaze of the malicious spectator or envious reader. Richard Burt, for instance, has shown how 'Jonson undertook to reform the public theatres by aligning himself with the court censor, internalizing its interpretive categories and practices'.[80] I will be discussing this internalization of the censor in terms of the poet's apotropaic rituals to ward off the *eye*, not just of the official censor, but the invidious eye he imagined of his audience and reader who would deform his work.[81]

---

[77] Matthew 7.3: 'And why beholdst thou the mote that is in thy brother's eye, but considerest not the *beam* that is in thine own eye? Thou hypocrite, first cast out the beam out of thine own eye; and then shalt thou see clearly to cast out the mote out of thy brother's eye' (my emphasis). In Matthew, this passage is introduced by the following verses: 'Judge not, that ye be not judged. For with what judgement you judge, ye shall be judged' (7.1–2); see also Luke 6.42 in the King James Bible.

[78] See Bushy's speech on looking 'awry' in *Richard II*: 'Like perspectives, which rightly gaz'd upon, / Show nothing but confusion; *ey'd awry*, / Distinguish form. So your sweet majesty, / *Looking awry* upon your lord's departure, / Find shapes of grief more than himself to wail' (my emphasis; II.ii.18–22). Charles R. Forker notes the difference implied between 'eyed awry' and 'looking awry'. The first refers to what one is supposed to do in order to see an anamorphic painting correctly: look at it from an angle or eye it 'awry'. The second, 'looking awry', describes the Queen's perverse misreading of her 'lord's departure' in which she creates shapes and forms, or, in the vocabulary of Jonson's poem, finds 'faults', where there are none. It is against the reader who *looks* awry that Jonson is writing; yet, like Shakespeare, he plays on the paradox of anamorphosis in which to see correctly one must *eye wrongly* (London: The Arden Shakespeare, 2002).

[79] Sir Francis Bacon, 'Of Envy', *The Essayes or Counsels, Civill and Morall* (London, 1629), p. 40.

[80] Richard Burt, *Licensed by Authority: Ben Jonson and the Discourses of Censorship* (Ithaca: Cornell University Press, 1993), p. 4.

[81] The word 'apotropaic' comes from the Greek *apotropein*, to turn away. It is a ritual or an object whose function is to turn aside evil. 'Apotropaism' is the performance of a magic ritual or incantatory formulas in order to avert or overcome evil.

Submitting to scrutiny

Jonson's suspicion concerning the way his text would be 'eyed' is one he shares with a host of Renaissance authors at a time when appearing in print was still a source of much anxiety. The fear of visibility and exposure is something the psychologist R. D. Laing sees as a basic drive in all living beings:

> In a world full of danger, to be a potentially seeable object is to be constantly exposed to danger. Self-consciousness, then, may be the apprehensive awareness of oneself as potentially exposed to danger by the simple fact of being visible to others. The obvious defence against such a danger is to make oneself invisible in one way or another... Quite often... the individual feels that his greatest risk is to be the object of another person's awareness. The myth of Perseus and the Medusa's head, the 'evil eye', delusions of death rays and so on are I believe referable to this dread.
>
> Indeed, considered biologically, the very fact of being visible exposed an animal to the risk of attack from its enemies, and no animal is without enemies. Being visible is therefore a basic biological risk; being invisible is a basic biological defense. We all employ some form of camouflage.[82]

That visibility presents a risk is, I believe, key in understanding Ben Jonson's works. The risk of placing oneself first before a theatrical audience in a public arena and then, later, before the inquisitive and judging eye of the reading public was, paradoxically, one the playwright not only accepted, but actively sought. Jonson rejected the option, which, as Harold Love has shown, was still very much available to him, of 'publishing' himself, like his contemporary John Donne, in manuscript form, which would have exposed him only to members of a coterie or his friends.[83] Instead, not only did he write for a public and court audience, but he also actively chose print. Furthermore, he was not only content to publish (or be published) in quarto, but he chose to expose himself to the gaze of readers in a lavish folio in 1616. Yet, Joseph Loewenstein writes that Jonson presents himself as a man 'ambiguously engaged with the literary marketplace'.[84] And

---

[82] R. D. Laing, *The Divided Self: An Existential Study in Sanity and Madness* (Harmondsworth: Penguin Books, 1965), pp. 109–10.

[83] Harold Love, *The Culture and Commerce of Texts: Scribal Publication in Seventeenth-Century England* (Amherst: University of Massachusetts Press, 1993). Notwithstanding Jonson's clear interest in print, Joseph Loewenstein points out 'it is important to remember that Jonson's non-dramatic works, as well as his masques, seem to have had a fairly wide circulation in manuscript'. *Ben Jonson and Possessive Authorship* (Cambridge: Cambridge University Press, 2002), p. 2 n. 5.

[84] Joseph Loewenstein, 'The Script in the Marketplace' in Stephen Greenblatt (ed.) *Representing the English Renaissance* (Berkeley: University of California Press, 1988), p. 273.

Stanley Fish argues that Ben Jonson published his works even in defiance of all but a very small readership:

> [M]ore starkly than any other poem we have examined, the epistle to Squib displays the determined reticence of an art that *refuses to submit itself to scrutiny and judgement*. Both the action it performs and the actions it reports look inward toward the already constituted community of observers and readers. Jonson writes the poem only in order to be (apart from Squib from whom he is indistinguishable) *its only reader* [my emphasis].[85]

I would suggest that the opposite is the case. Jonson's poems of praise, like all of his work, are written very much with an eye to their being scrutinized and judged, as their own author scrutinized and judged them and everything he wrote and read. While, perhaps, in an imaginary, best of all possible worlds, they would be read and praised without such scrutiny, the writer cannot and does not refuse to be pried open. While Fish may very well be suggesting that Jonson writes the poem to be 'its only reader', *metaphorically*, the fact that this state of affairs is patently not the case in bibliographic terms makes these kinds of statements problematic. Fish's corollary assertion that Jonson and Squib are 'indistinguishable' is perhaps a way of describing the strange fact that the 'person' who has survived in this poem is the poet, especially a poet such as Jonson who, as we shall see, often put his own posterity in the forefront. Fish may very well be reacting to the distorting effect Jonson's frequent autobiographical focus on himself has upon reading. The 'bulk of Ben', at times, may efface its subject by incorporating it. This, however, to my mind, is not quite the same as asserting that the author and the reader are the 'same' or 'indistinguishable' in the act of reading. The whole problem with print, in the late sixteenth and early seventeenth centuries, was, indeed, at best, its embarrassing, at worst, dangerous, ability to disseminate. Jonson's mistrust of the reader's ability to understand him does not necessarily translate into a decision to choose stoic withdrawal. We might well need to consider Jonson's 'engagement with the marketplace' in terms of strategic and well-considered defence mechanisms to protect his work from both spectator and reader.

I would argue that Jonson is active in finding ways of meeting, anticipating and diverting envious curiosity by confounding and baffling it or camouflaging the object of its gaze. This image of Jonson is coherent with

---

[85] Stanley Fish, 'Authors-Readers: Jonson's Community of the Same' in Greenblatt, *Representing the English Renaissance*, pp. 231–64; p. 253. See 'An Epistle to Master Arth: Squib' *Underwood* (xlv), Herford and Simpson, vol. VIII, p. 216.

the punctually obsessive proofreader at Stansby's press, an active participant in the book trade and, as a result, in the strategies and rituals necessary to manipulate and elicit certain responses from readers.[86] The extent of Jonson's investment in both the competitive book market of his own day and in that of a future generation can best be measured by his constant reference to the reader who will judge his work. That this engagement results in a strange hybrid of discourses should not be at all surprising. Jonson may perhaps best be understood in this respect when compared to Montaigne, moving between two conflicting discourses that existed simultaneously at a critical period of transition between a world of humanist values and pragmatic, bourgeois ones.[87] Jonson's construction of his envious readers combines multiple aspects of a world whose values were changing and, significantly enough, whose readers were changing. His envious reader or readers may be seen as symptomatic of the age in which he lived and wrote.

Like other writers of the period, Jonson shows himself to be extremely conscious of the risks involved in the performance of his plays or in sending his text into the world where it would meet the gaze of strangers, rather than just friends, many of whom did not share the same values or the same education as himself. Yet, he willingly accepted this risk and in doing so invested in the means of camouflaging and protecting his work at every turn. The spectators and readers who are implicated in Jonson's works, whether in prologues, dedications or poems of praise are sometimes classically educated in the humanist tradition and 'understanders', who may indeed be part of a 'community of the same'. Yet, Jonson's readers are, more often than not, *not* the 'same', nor even similar. In fact, they are all too often very different and, as such, need to be dealt with accordingly. They are doubting, critical, mistrustful, sceptical, easily bored, prejudiced, sometimes practically illiterate (at least, in his eyes) and, it must be added in the case of so many of the poems and masques, at least in performance, often of a completely different social class from that occupied by the poet.[88]

Nevertheless, underlying these differences in class, education and appreciation, the implied audience in Jonson's texts are at some level all marked by a certain level of inquisitiveness, an eagerness to 'see' and to 'look', as

---

[86] For Jonson as a close proofreader see Mark Bland, 'William Stansby and the Production of *The Workes of Beniamin Jonson*, 1615–16', *The Library*, Sixth Series, 20 (March 1998), 1–33; p. 19.

[87] With regard to this 'transition', see Philippe Desan (ed.), *Humanism in Crisis: The Decline of the French Renaissance* (Ann Arbor: University of Michigan Press, 1991), pp. 10–17.

[88] In this book, I will be referring to Jonson as 'writer', 'author', 'playwright' and 'poet'. In print, the masques present a peculiarly ambiguous generic case in their mixture of poetry and dramatic dialogue (among other things), a mixture I will be discussing later. I have, for this reason, used 'poet', 'masque writer' and 'author' to stand in for 'Jonson' when discussing the masques.

well as to 'look into', although the nature and form of this 'inquisition' differs from one reader to another. Fish takes the title of his essay, 'Authors-Readers: Jonson's Community of the Same', from the line 'So with this Authors Readers will it thrive' of the poem 'In Authorem' prefacing Nicholas Breton's *Melancholike Humours*, the same discussed by Donaldson above.[89] In contrast to Donaldson, Fish does not examine Jonson's use of the word 'asquint' in terms of envy, even though it was frequently associated with envy in the early modern period. Nevertheless, Fish's argument that a real hermeneutical gap between author and reader is expressed in the idea of looking 'asquint' will be an important one for the present study of envy; when Fish sees 'asquint' as describing the 'gap' or 'distance' between author and reader, he is describing precisely what Jonson implies in the idea of 'envy'. What is less fruitful in Fish's argument is the notion that the gap between the squinting, censuring reader and author of the poem is quite neatly and hermetically sealed in the creation of a composite figure of an 'author-reader'. It is my belief that for Jonson a hermeneutical or envious distance between writer and reader is *inherent* and that the existence of a perfect identity (what Fish refers to as 'sameness') between authors and (even certain ideal) readers is *not* implied by Jonson except as a kind of hyperbolic image of praise. For Fish, the conflation of author and reader into one portmanteau *persona* by the end of each poem completes the circle of interpretation, bringing its reader and author into a kind of symmetrical understanding by creating (or forcing) an identity between them. I would argue that the gap between author and reader, emblematized by the idea of envy, is necessarily and always co-existential with the act of interpretation. The labour of convincing and persuading readers is always about to take place in a future and unknown time with unknown readers. Only through an elaborate set of rituals, such as those to be described in this book, can, at best, a *modus vivendi* between author and his audience be reached. The idea that Jonson wished to be read by members of a select club and had to 'put up' with either the ridiculous, fashion-following gentleman or the plebian ignorance of the rabble does not account for what appears to be Jonson's textual engagement with his epoch's new readership.

Jonson distinguishes between different sets of readers, carefully fleshing out the image of an envious misreader in doing so. While again, there are varying degrees of reading generosity or lack of it, oppositions between readers and the kind of reading they do are often created for the purpose

---

[89] Ben Jonson, 'In Authorem', *Ungathered Verse* (ii), Herford and Simpson, vol. VIII, p. 362 (line 12). Subsequent references to this poem will be included in the text.

of isolating or identifying the envious. In the poem 'In Authorem' we find that 'this Author's Readers' (line 12) are opposed to 'such as looke asquint' (line 7). Jonson describes another reader as 'an ill man' who 'dares not securely looke / Upon it [a goode Booke], but will loath, or let it passe, / As a deformed face doth a true glasse'.[90] Just as the 'fault' or 'beam' is not in the object but in their own eyes, as we saw above, so too the 'deformation' they see is their own deformity.

Readers are also described in a poem entitled 'A Vision of Ben Jonson, On the Muses of His Friend M. Drayton'. This poem quite sarcastically predicts a bright future for Drayton's poem, *The Battle of Agincourt*, in the modern literary marketplace:

> An *Agincourt*, an *Agincourt*, or dye.
> This booke, it is a *Catechisme* to fight,
> And will be bought of every Lord or Knight
> That can but reade; who cannot, may in prose
> Get broken peeces, and fight well by those.[91]

Here, the buyers of the book are either the semi-illiterate lord or knight 'that can but read' or a perfect illiterate. While one could see this pathetic readership as merely a negative reflection on Drayton and his poetry, these readers are also Jonson's. In the preface to the published edition (in quarto) of the masque *Hymenaei* (1606) Jonson describes the spectators of his masque in performance as eaters:

> I am contented, these fastidious *stomachs* should leave my full tables, and enjoy at home, their cleane emptie trenchers, fittest for such ayrie tasts: where perhaps a few *Italian* herbs, pick'd up, and made into a *sallade*, may find sweeter acceptance… For these mens palates, let not me answer, O *Muses*.[92]

But he *has* answered, and at length. These, too, are Jonson's readers, if not his 'ideal' ones, and his work is not only addressed to them, but constructed through his depiction of them and his continual anticipatory responses to them. I have placed the word *ideal* in quotation marks to show that I take Heidi Brayman Hackel's point concerning the way reader-response theorists have described the reader in fairly abstract terms as 'mock', 'ideal', 'model', 'implied', 'encoded', 'informed' and 'super': terms

---

[90] Ben Jonson, 'On the Author, Worke, and Translator', *Ungathered Verse* (xxiv), Herford and Simpson, vol. VIII, p. 389 (lines 8–10).
[91] Ben Jonson, 'The Vision of Ben Jonson, On the Muses of His Friend M. Drayton', *Ungathered Verse* (xxx), Herford and Simpson, vol. VIII, p. 398 (lines 70–4).
[92] Ben Jonson, *Hymenaei*, Herford and Simpson, vol. VII, pp. 209–10 (lines 23–9).

which she argues need to be grounded in a historical account of readers and the act of reading.[93] Hackel's study aims to respond to the gap in 'theory' by 'tracking historical readers, who linger in material traces in early modern books and in other documentary records'.[94] The hunt for readers in archives and in the margins of their books is, as she and David Scott Kastan argue, an important next stage in the process of exorcizing the 'ghost of the reader' which has been haunting literary studies.[95] In a section of her book devoted to prefatory letters in early modern works, Heidi Hackel highlights a shift in writers' attitudes toward readers:

> The prefatory letters to the Zoili [the emblem of the malicious and carping critic in the early modern period] signal a tremendous shift in early modern attitudes towards readers. First of all, attempts at control over access to books have yielded to admonitory letters contained *within* the books. No longer identified in advance and held at bay, the *bad reader now already possesses the book and has in fact begun to finger the preliminaries*. Robert Herrick imagines these readers infiltrating even more deeply into his book when he addresses epigrams in the middle of his volume 'To Momus' and 'To my ill Reader'. This new access for the bad reader, whether real or imagined, issues in a heightened guardedness in the prefaces and marginalia in Elizabethan books... While the presence of these prefatory letters reveals a perceived loss of control over readership, the content of many of these letters points to a *new confidence that bad readers can be won over*. Though the letters often merely try to *banish bad readers*, some suggest new strategies to the Zoili, inviting them to read on without malice... while prefaces tried to 'shun' such readers at the 'doore', printed marginalia completed this effort to control and direct reading [my emphasis].[96]

Jonson's descriptions of readers confirm Hackel's remarks concerning the new dangers presented to the author by the 'bad' new reader. She sees the danger of readerly 'infiltration' and 'access' resulting in 'a heightened guardedness' in prefaces, letters to ill readers and the citation of authorities in the margins, what Hackel calls simply 'marginalia'. Authorial control is most evident in the paratexts. While Jonson is a classic example, perhaps *the* example, of an early modern author who makes ample use of liminal texts to 'control and direct reading', I would like to show that this desire to guard and direct does not confine itself to notices and marginalia, but is an

---

[93] Heidi Brayman Hackel, *Reading Material in Early Modern England: Print, Gender and Literacy* (Cambridge: Cambridge University Press, 2005), pp. 6–7.
[94] *Ibid.*, pp. 6–7.
[95] *Ibid.*, p. 60 n. 10. In her note, Hackel cites Umberto Eco: 'Undoubtedly the universe of literary studies has been haunted during the last years by the ghost of the reader' (*The Limits of Interpretation* (Bloomington: Indiana University Press, 1990)), p. 46.
[96] *Ibid.*, pp. 124–5.

integral part of the generation of the whole work, of which the paratexts are only one dimension. Furthermore, Jonson's figuration of the malicious reader goes far beyond the *topos* of *captitio benevolentiae* described here by Hackel. The feeling that the bad reader could be won over may be too optimistic with regard to Jonson. The relationship between the writer and the envious reader is one, not of persuasion and reformation into 'gentleness', but of vigilant fear and suspicion. The reader is, naturally and constitutionally, filled with that natural depravity that defines enviousness. The reader cannot help but misread, if only because he or she inhabits a fallen world. One of the changes from a prelapsarian to a postlapsarian universe in *Paradise Lost* is illustrated by the new 'obliquity' of the poles.[97] Human depravity in moral terms is reflected by a depravity in physical terms.[98] The skewing of the poles is a consequence, at the macrocosmic level, of the appearance of sin in the world, and a telling metaphor for the Adamic inability to see as clearly as in the prelapsarian paradise. In other words, the obliquity of the universe testifies to the impossibility of hermeneutic coincidence or Cratylitic seamlessness between, among other things, writerly intention and readerly interpretation. The figure of the envious spectator and reader can be seen to structure Jonson's imagination; the writer's effort to address the envious is thus an integral part of the texture of the work. Moreover, the envious reader is everywhere because the reader is in the writer himself, looking at himself, watching himself in the act of writing.

Baffling scrutiny

Etymologically, 'invidia' is related to the invidious gaze or the malicious or evil eye. Both the ancient and medieval traditions that inform Jonson's representations of envy, as well as a rich contemporary discourse, focus on the power attributed to the eye to harm. In the early modern period, envy, like love, was imagined in terms of rays emanating from the eye itself, following the Greek theory of extramission, but this 'ray' was also a metaphor for the harm envy could wreak on reputation in the form of slander and calumny. For a long time there existed a controversy concerning whether vision was the result of emissions *from* the eye or the reception of light

---

[97] 'Some say he bid his angels turn askance / The poles of earth twice ten degrees and more / From the sun's axle; they with labour pushed / Oblique the centric globe.' John Milton, *Paradise Lost*, p. 543 (x.668–71).
[98] The French word *dépravé* still conserves the early modern use of the word 'depraved' to mean skewed, oblique and deformed.

rays *into* the eye. The idea that the eye emitted rays toward an object was attributed originally to the Pythagoreans; the notion that the eye received small images of objects, *species* or *simulacra*, transmitted in a sort of atomic flux was attributed to Democritus and later Lucretius. Jean-Baptiste della Porta in *De Refractione* (1593) and later Kepler in *Ad Vitellionem paralipomena, quibus astronomiae pars optica traditur* (1604) may be said to have 'closed' the scientific debate officially in opting for vision based on reception into the eye.[99] Both beliefs continued to exist simultaneously, though, at least at a metaphoric and figurative level. John Donne's 'The Extasy', for instance, makes use of the older idea of eyes emitting rays and studies on perspective, like that of Abraham Bosse in the first half of the seventeenth century, instruct painters to use the idea of visual rays implicitly starting from the painter's eye (what he also calls a *visual pyramid*) to project geometric figures on flat surfaces.[100] The effects of the evil eye in the early modern period were conceived as being emitted *from* the eye, because the harm was localized in the agent whose gaze affected its victim. In the Petrarchan tradition, it was the beloved who was believed to be possessed of such dangerous powers of vision, as we see in Maurice Scève's *Délie* (1544) where the poet calls his lover 'Mon Basilisque', 'My Basilisk', referring to the mythical beast with powers of mortal fascination similar to those of the Medusa. The lover's gaze acts like a sword, 'with her piercing eye, transfixing my body'.[101] On the other hand, in his masques, Jonson attributes to the eye a corresponding thaumaturgical power to cure. The King's gaze is compared to the sun, a large eye, whose beams 'shine day, and night, and are of force / To blanch an AETHIOPE, and revive a *Cor's*. / His light scientiall is, and (past mere nature) / Can salve the rude defects of every creature.'[102] A similar conceit in *The Essex House Masque* informs Prometheus' injunction that the audience help him to animate stones by looking at them: 'Calmely looke and with desire / Add to the fire. / Which your breathinges must fan higher' (lines 192–4). The Argument to this masque refers to the deadly power of Pallas Athena who possesses the Gorgon's head whose looks can kill: 'Revenging Pallas with her Gorgons head / Meets the rebellion: and doth looke them dead'

---

[99] See Margaret Llasera, *Représentations scientifiques et images poétiques en Angleterre au XVIIe siècle: à la recherche de l'invisible* (Paris: CNRS Editions, 1999), p. 54.

[100] See Philippe Hamou (ed.), *La Vision perspective (1435–1740): l'art et la science du regard de la Renaissance à l'âge Classique* (Paris: Editions Payot & Rivages, 1995), pp. 229–32.

[101] Cited by Leonard Forster, *The Icy Fire: Five Studies in European Petrarchism* (Cambridge: Cambridge University Press, 1969), p. 37.

[102] Ben Jonson, *The Masque of Blacknesse*, Herford and Simpson, vol. VII, p. 177 (lines 254–7).

(lines 12–13).[103] Within the hyperbolic language of love poetry and masque conceit, eyes can both kill and cure.

The belief in both the miraculous and the noxious power of vision is also expressed in critiques concerning the optical instruments of the epoch, particularly the 'Optic tube' of Galileo, which would become one of John Milton's metaphors for knowledge as well as sin in *Paradise Lost*. In a theological metaphor inspired directly by the new science, Milton compares Satan to one of the solar spots (*maculae solis*) discovered by Galileo: 'There lands the fiend, a spot like which perhaps / Astronomer in the sun's lucent orb / Through his glazed optic tube yet never saw.'[104] Jonson participated in the period's fascination with the power of vision, representing its power both to cure and fearing the nefarious effects upon his own work of the gaze of the reader who, to all intents and purposes, face to face with the book, becomes a potentially powerful and deadly gazer.

The sixteenth-century Gorgon heads carved on the doors of the Hôtel des Ambassadeurs-de-Hollande on rue Vieille-du-Temple in Paris remind us that, in the Occident, the Medusa of the petrifying glance was believed to have been possessed of a powerful apotropaic power to ward off the evil eye. The *gorgoneion*, the head of the Medusa mounted in the breastplate of Minerva, was the 'earliest example which we can positively assert to be a prophylactic charm against the fatal glance which she was believed to have possessed'.[105] Considered one of the most efficacious of amulets, it was the first prophylactic device worn by men in battle, to absorb the angry glance of an enemy and then *baffle* their malignity.[106] Indeed, 'a charm would prove doubly effective if, in deflecting the evil glance, it simultaneously caused shame and confusion on the part of the beholder'.[107] To divert, shame and confuse: these were the weapons of those grotesque and hideous faces or

---

[103] Text of *The Essex House Masque* in Timothy Raylor, *The Essex House Masque of 1621: Viscount Doncaster and the Jacobean Masque* (Pittsburgh: Duquesne University Press, 2000), pp. 23 and 17, respectively.

[104] Milton, *Paradise Lost*, p. 179 (III.588–90). For a discussion of this passage as a description of the entrance of envy and sin into the world see my 'Optique et Anamorphose dans *Le Paradis Perdu* de John Milton', *Revue de la Société d'Etudes Anglo-Américaines des XVIIe et XVIIIe Siècles* 61 (November 2005), 53–70.

[105] Frederick Thomas Elworthy, *The Evil Eye: The Origins and Practices of Superstition* (New York: The Julian Press, Inc., 1958), p. 146.

[106] Ibid., p. 158. Elworthy claims as well that the idea of masks becoming popular as protectors is rooted in their power to protect the wearer from the evil eye. Actors in classical times adopted a mask to hide their features, most likely from the general dread of the evil eye, lest among the crowd, gazing upon the performer, some may have possessed that fatal influence which Heliodorus records respecting the daughter of Calasiris (p. 158).

[107] S. A. Callisen, 'The Evil Eye in Italian Art', *The Art Bulletin* 19 (September 1937), 450–62; p. 453.

Illustration 1. Door detail. Gorgon. Hôtel des Ambassadeurs-de-Hollande, rue Vieille-du-Temple, Paris.

masks protecting the entrances to homes from malicious intruders or their bearer in battle from death. These weapons were based on those used by the Egyptians and the Greeks:

> On the homeopathic principle that like cures like, carved eyes were worn in necklaces, and eyes were worked into the design of amulets, cut into gems and painted on vases by Egyptians, Etruscans and Greeks to stop the evil eye. On the center of medals and gems was cut an eye surrounded by threatening animals, such as a snake, scorpion, dog, panther, and lion, and by cutting implements, such as swords and daggers... The popularity of the apotropaic eye symbol has persisted into modern times, reinforced by the association with the protecting eye of God and providence... The earliest known Greek amulets against fascination were carved heads of the Medusa, not only because they were hideous enough to arrest the evil eye, but also because the Medusa herself had wielded an eye so powerful that it turned men to stone, and the reminder of this might give pause to an ordinary fascinator.[108]

---

[108] Edward S. Gifford, Jr, MD, *The Evil Eye: Studies in the Folklore of Vision* (New York: Macmillan, 1958), p. 68.

While the widespread dissemination of such beliefs and practices might appear preposterous to us today, the amplitude of current evil eye beliefs might make us pause. Various cultures continue to guard themselves against curiosity and envy using physical objects, ritual gestures and charms. The 'evil eye' bead is placed upon the threshold to protect against the entrance of the evil eye even today in modern, republican Turkey. The people of Mediterranean and South American cultures are on perpetual watch against creating the tiniest access or passage for evil through unseemly happiness, love or pride in one's own accomplishments. Spontaneous outbursts of praise, moments of revelling in one's good luck or one's skill, are inevitably accompanied by watchfulness and vigilance in the form of a phrase such as 'may the evil eye not touch it', followed, in a number of cultures, by a knock on wood. The first and most basic defence against the evil eye is simply to hide the object that might be envied. Barring that, any object or gesture which gives rise to an obscene idea is thought to be especially effective against envious fascination. Part of the apotropaic function of amulets is to draw the harmful glance toward an object that will be unaffected, so these prophylactic objects should be striking in appearance, of a bright colour, glitter, and be of extreme grossness, or odd, in order to attract, startle and generally divert attention away from the potential victim toward the object itself. For this reason anything 'strange, odd, or uncommon, as likely to attract the eye, was considered most effectual' against fascination.[109] Thus, hand gestures, still widely used in Italy, such as the 'horned hand' (*mano cornuta*), the fig hand (*mano fica*), and the open hand are all apotropaic, as are all phallic images.[110] Some remedies for the evil eye have involved, even in the twentieth century, forms of sympathetic magic: 'In the Scotch Highlands if a stranger looks admiringly on a cow the people still believe she will waste away from the evil eye, and they offer him some of her milk to drink, in the belief that by so doing the spell will be broken and averted.'[111] These ritual gestures, punctual interventions, many of a

---

[109] Elworthy, *The Evil Eye*, p. 148.
[110] Amica Lykiardopoulos, 'The Evil Eye: Towards an Exhaustive Study', *Folklore* 92 (1981), 221–30; p. 227.
[111] Elworthy, *The Evil Eye*, p. 9. For a discussion of evil eye beliefs in Scotland, see John Gregorson Campbell, *Witchcraft and Second Sight in the Highlands and Islands of Scotland: Tales and Traditions Collected Entirely from Oral Sources* (Glasgow: James MacLehose and Sons, 1902), pp. 55ff. In Brittany, in the 1950s, if farm animals were sick and sorcery suspected the farmer believed he could 'give the hair of the animals' to the magician who would undo the spell of the evil eye. Hairs, considered metonymically for the animal, were gathered with tweezers on a particular side of the animal at a particular time of day and given to the sorcerer to cure. See Christophe Auray, *Magie et sorcellerie dans les fermes bretonnes* (Rennes: Editions Ouest-France, 2006), p. 116.

daily nature, were and are in a number of cultures symptoms of a complex system of continuous exchange between rivals, neighbours and servants to protect themselves from the harm of fascination and the danger of becoming a victim of the malevolent gaze.[112] These beliefs are of varying degrees, from flat-out credulity to a superstitious desire to put oneself in the best possible position with regard to a providential universe. Evil eye beliefs and practices must be seen as a series of daily Pascalian wagers in which it is always better (and with very little effort on one's own part) to appease the envious eye by throwing salt over one's shoulder, uttering a necessary incantation or following the prescribed ritual. Evil eye superstitions can be seen as a means of social control in which individuals play a double role of fascinating in order to avoid being fascinated. According to Tobin Siebers: 'Protocol requires that one should avoid casting the evil eye all the while protecting oneself from being fascinated by using amulets or rites that deflect or neutralize it.'[113]

Between the writer of a printed book and the strangers who will become its readers, no face-to-face ceremony of protection by the owner or ritual dispraising by the possible envier is possible to assure the writer that the reader will not cast an evil eye upon the text.[114] In other words, there is no way the writer can knock on wood as he presents the book to his reader, nor can he denigrate, in a low whisper, the value of the object he dares to expose to the gaze of a stranger before revealing his treasure. The reader, similarly, cannot mutter politely before staring and curiously prying into the volume of the poet's thoughts.[115] The danger the reader presented to

---

[112] George M. Foster divides behaviours to protect against the evil eye into four types: concealment, denial, the 'sop' (symbolic sharing) and true sharing. He argues that these types fall into a continuum of preferred choices in the order he has listed them. For instance, 'people prefer' first to *conceal* whatever properties they possess that might be envied, but barring this option, or, upon discovery, they will then choose to *deny* that anyone would have reason to envy them. When this denial is 'deemed inadequate' (is not accepted by the envier), they will be forced to participate in a *symbolic sharing* of the desired object in the form of a 'sop', the sharing of some miniscule portion of the thing envied. Finally, if the sop proves insufficient, people who continue to fear the envy of others will be forced into true sharing, the distribution of a significant part of the possession for which they are envied. It is important to note that, while he claims a certain universality, Foster's examples are culled from contemporary cultures and from predominantly poor, subsistence societies or groups where neighbourly envy is focused on food, children and health ('The Anatomy of Envy', pp. 175–82). Nevertheless, this caveat in mind, his examples and conclusions are rich and thought-provoking.

[113] Tobin Siebers, *The Mirror of Medusa* (Berkeley: University of California Press, 1983), p. 40.

[114] 'Ritual dispraising' is mandatory when pronouncing compliments, often feared for their power to attract the evil eye. Siebers, *ibid.*, p. 43.

[115] The evil eye is believed to be present not only when someone *praises* something, but also when one inquires into something with curiosity or stares fixedly at the object in question.

the book was, as we shall see, often a very real danger for the early modern writer. It was, therefore, the role of the writer to anticipate possible harm and censure, by ensuring that the text was defended properly against the reading eye. We cannot, of course, hope to imagine evil eye beads decorating books or amulets appearing out of nowhere from the printed page to conjure the envious eye of the reader approaching the text.[116] There is no image of a Gorgon gracing the frontispiece of each book, as they graced the doors and portals of so many houses and rooms in the early modern period. Yet, I would argue, the fact that these kinds of behavioural rituals do not exist between writers and their readers in such familiar forms does not imply that writers did not feel the need for some kind of similar protection against the reading eye. When a reader is 'invited' to step through the frontispiece of a book, the defenses the writer erected in anticipation of this visitor are not material, behavioural, sculptural or architectural – they are necessarily literary.

'SMALL *LATINE*, AND LESSE *GREEKE*'

When Jonson writes about the '*envious* weather' that would blow apart the 'flowers' of the author Thomas Palmer, or wonders if any defender of the 'worke' of John Beaumont can build a barrier, 'where Envy hath not cast / A Trench against it?'; or if he finds fault with those who look at Nicholas Breton's work 'asquint', or tells John Selden that he will 'defend / Thy gift 'gainst *envie*', clearly we are dealing with a writer who perceived the danger of envy as almost consubstantial with the act of reading (my emphasis).[117] When he assures a friend that his praise 'Faire Æmulation, and no Envy is', the writer is equally aware of the potential danger he

---

[116] That said, images of 'grotesques' in the decorative borders of early modern books may well have been intended to serve this kind of apotropaic function. I thank Victoria Bladen for bringing to my attention the grotesques camouflaged in the decorative borders of my copy of a 1540 French emblem depicting *The Calumny of Apelles*. For the emblem, see the 'Catalogue' Engraving 19.A in Jean-Michel Massing, *Du texte à l'image: la calomnie d'Apelle et son iconographie* (Strasbourg: Presses Universitaires de Strasbourg, 1990). This emblem will be discussed further in Chapter 3.
[117] 'From *The Sprite of Trees and Herbes*, by Thomas Palmer', *Ungathered Verse* (i), Herford and Simpson, vol. VIII, p. 361 (lines 1; 8); 'On the honor'd Poëms of his honored Friend, Sir John Beaumont, Baronet', *Ungathered Verse* (xxxii), *ibid.*, p. 401 (lines 13–14); 'In Authorem', *Ungathered Verse* (ii), *ibid.*, p. 362 (line 7); 'An Epistle to Master John Selden' *Underwood* (xiv), *Ibid.*, p. 161 (lines 78–9). It should be noted that all the examples I give here are Jonson's addresses to other writers in response, as a reader, to their books. For Jonson's reading 'habits' see Robert C. Evans, *Habits of Mind: Evidence and Effects of Ben Jonson's Reading* (Lewisburg: Bucknell University Press, 1995).

runs in praising others.¹¹⁸ It might be time to come back to where I began: the curiously fraught relationship between Ben Jonson and Shakespeare in critical history. It is in the context of Jonson's obsession with the potential danger posed by the envious or oblique gaze to *deprave* in the act of reading (and, by extension, writing) that we must return to his famous elegy to Shakespeare in the 1623 Folio. In possibly one of the strangest openings in the history of panegyric, Jonson addresses the dead:

> To draw no envy (*Shakespeare*) on thy name,
> Am I thus ample to thy Booke, and Fame:¹¹⁹

The poem opens with a ritual denial. We may see this liminal negation as an example of an apotropaic gesture against the evil eye. The poet, as reader of Shakespeare's book, assures him that in complimenting it, and praising it 'amply', he has no intention of *drawing* the evil eye to Shakespeare's 'name'. It must be understood that the 'evil eye' was not necessarily the eye of the praiser. It was believed in antiquity and in the early modern period that praising something in public inevitably risked drawing any eye toward the subject of praise. It was for this reason the Roman victor returning in triumph would wear a *fascinus* or counter-charm to protect him from the public's gaze. Bacon attests to a similar belief in the early modern period when he writes:

[T]he Stroke, or Percussion of an *Envious Eye* doth most hurt ... when the *Party envied* is beheld in Glory, or Triumph; For that sets an Edge upon *Envy*; And besides, at such times, the Spirits of the *person Envied*, doe come forth, most into the outward Parts, and so meet the Blow.¹²⁰

The 'Party [potentially] envied' is indeed Shakespeare, 'beheld in Glory', with the publication of his works in folio. It is therefore appropriate for Jonson to assure Shakespeare (and, of course, the reader) that the ample praise of the book to follow is not intended to 'draw', like a magnet, the general gaze of 'envy' to Shakespeare's name. It must be remembered that Jonson has been commissioned, of all the friends of Shakespeare, to write the lead poem for the First Folio. We see the early modern poet tiptoeing

---

¹¹⁸ Ben Jonson, 'To the Author, Writer and Translator', *Ungathered Verse* (xxiv), Herford and Simpson, vol. VIII, p. 389 (line 22). It is significant that Jonson needs to modify the word 'Æmulation' with 'faire' in order to distinguish it from 'Envy'. This ambiguity between emulation and envy will be discussed at more length in Chapter 2.
¹¹⁹ Ben Jonson, 'To the memory of my beloved, the AUTHOR MR. WILLIAM SHAKESPEARE: And what he hath left us', *Ungathered Verse* (xxvi), Herford and Simpson, vol. VIII, p. 390 (lines 1–2). Subsequent references to the poem will be included in the text.
¹²⁰ Bacon, 'Of Envy', *Essayes*, pp. 40–1.

through a kind of visual minefield, for as writer of the present poem, Jonson may also be seen as enviable. It is his elegy that comes first in the triumphal procession. Moreover, his poem, physically, comes first, occupying the 'outward Parts', most exposed to view and criticism. We can see, then, this initial denial of envy as a kind of ritualistic knocking on wood in the act of praising as protecting both Shakespeare, the person praised, as well Jonson, the praiser. Jonson approaches the book and effects a ritual dispraising to assure Shakespeare that he does not intend to draw him into harm's way in the act of complimenting him. At the same time, the writer of this elegy needs also to defend *himself*, and his poem, against those unknown readers (readers intimately associated with Shakespeare or with a vested interest in being associated with his name), who very well might envy Jonson, chosen to write the first elegy to Shakespeare. Jonson interestingly defends himself against these envious readers by accusing them of being misreaders of Shakespeare:

> While I confesse thy writings to be such,
> As neither *Man*, nor *Muse* can praise too much.
> 'Tis true, and all men's suffrage. But these wayes
> Were not the paths I meant unto thy praise:
> For seeliest Ignorance on these may light,
> Which, when it sounds at best, but eccho's right;
> Or blinde Affection, which doth ne'er advance
> The truth, but gropes, and urgeth all by chance;
> Or crafty Malice, might pretend this praise,
> And think to ruine, where it seem'd to raise. (lines 3–12)

Jonson is here carefully distinguishing himself and his praise from that of the three characters who also praise, but whose praise can actually 'hurt' and even 'ruin' their object: the ignorant, the blindly affectionate and the maliciously crafty. This description of three types of readers testifies to a coterie world of strong alliances and acts of hypocritical manipulation; a world in which literary 'merit' took a back seat to internal patronage politics, social climbing and cronyism. At the same time, it brings into focus the importance of reading and readers in the creation of a legitimate literary posterity: 'These are, as some infamous Baud, or Whore, / Should praise a Matron; What could hurt her more?' (lines 13–14).

While one might understand Jonson's interest in distinguishing himself, as a reader of Shakespeare, from these 'bawds' or 'whores' (i.e. bad readers who threaten to make Shakespeare's posterity a bastard one), one might still ask, why does he engage in such an elaborate ritual? Why does he make so public a gesture? A gesture which, ironically enough, will bring in its train the opposite interpretation, that he is the soul of invidiousness itself? I would suggest that Jonson might very well have believed himself to be suspected at the time of harbouring envious feelings toward Shakespeare and felt the need to defend himself from this calumny. In *Timber* he writes how the Players accused him of malevolence:

> *I remember*, the Players have often mentioned it as an honour to *Shakespeare*, that in his writing, (whatsoever he penn'd) hee never blotted out line. My answer hath beene, Would he had blotted a thousand. Which they thought a malevolent speech. I had not told posterity this, but for their ignorance, who choose that circumstance to commend their friend by, wherein he most faulted.[121]

In his studied and, at times, overzealous defence of Jonson, William Gifford claims that no sign of jealousy or rivalry was ever hinted at between Jonson and Shakespeare in their own lifetimes and that this 'legend' was the sole construction of the eighteenth century and Shakespeare's (evil) editors.[122] The above testimony from Jonson shows that this was not the case. He was openly accused of 'malevolence' by the 'Players' and he feels the need to 'tell posterity' about it in order to defend himself. He might very well have considered the poem dedicated to Shakespeare as an ideal opportunity to defend himself against accusations for posterity and he took occasion by the forelock. The anthropologist George Foster considers a particular category of defences used by those suspected of envying others:

> We now turn to those cultural devices used by people who feel *they may be suspected of envy, or whose position or situation is such that they may reasonably be suspected of envy*...They consist largely of symbolic expressions calculated to reassure the *listener* that actual or implied praise does not in fact mean envy, or that the recipient of the gesture need not fear the initiator of the action [my emphasis].[123]

In the poem to Shakespeare, then, we can hear Jonson speaking to his contemporary accusers as well as to a listening posterity, all the while addressing (and reassuring) the 'recipient' of his praise, Shakespeare. Jonson ably exploits the opportunity to write the elegy as a means to settle old scores as well as defend his own poetic name before the judgement of posterity. That Jonson 'told posterity this' (again) in his poem to Shakespeare is eloquent testimony of his belief in Shakespeare's true and lasting greatness because he saw in Shakespeare's fame the power to protect him in the future. The appearance of the name 'Shakespeare' in the middle of the *first* line of the poem ('To draw no envy (*Shakespeare*) on thy name')

---

[121] Ben Jonson, *Timber, or Discoveries*, Herford and Simpson, vol. VIII, p. 583 (lines 647–53).
[122] Gifford, *The Works of Ben Jonson*, p. cxciv. [123] Foster, 'The Anatomy of Envy', p. 182.

may be understood, not necessarily as an apostrophe of one poet to his 'beloved', nor as the insidious mention of the envy of the writer for his rival, but as the invocation of a powerful talisman to ward off the envy of both contemporary and future readers (and accusers). Jonson transforms Shakespeare into his own personal amulet. He associates the name twice with the pronoun 'my' in the poem: 'My *Shakespeare*, rise…' (line 19); '*My* gentle *Shakespeare*' (line 56), making Shakespeare a personal, prophylactic device; by describing, as many have noted, his own artistic method, Jonson protects himself from derision by associating it with the artistic method of *his* Shakespeare. Jonson, then, is at once preeminently enviable and at the same time fascinates the envious public gaze by brandishing the name of 'Shakespeare' which he turns into an actual weapon: 'shake a Lance' / …at the eyes of Ignorance' (lines 69–70). Here we see how, literally, Shakespeare's very name becomes a kind of linguistic charm that will serve to ward off the envy of the ignorant. Just as Jonson, in the Preface to *The Masque of Queenes*, to be discussed in more detail later, claims Prince Henry's 'understanding' as a weapon with which to 'decline the stiffnesse of others originall Ignorance', so too he uses Shakespeare's powerful name to shake a 'lance' against those who will threaten his own name in posterity.[124]

The chapter which follows, *The Anatomy of Envy*, is intended to give the reader a brief history of the concept of envy to contextualize Jonson's conception of it. Chapter 3, *Defacement*, describes the ways in which the early modern writer may have imagined or perceived his texts as being *marred* by the reading eye. The defacing gaze of the envious spectator and reader is perceived *metaphorically* as capable of spoiling or corrupting texts. *Defacement* is the fear the writer has of his work (and thus his reputation) being misread, misapprehended and even perverted by the reader, a fear which lies, as I have argued, behind his elegy to Shakespeare and his adroit conversion of Shakespeare into a talisman against these readers. What defaces the text, within the Jonsonian phantasmagoria, is the envious gaze of, first, the spectator, in the case of the masques and the plays, and then the reader, in a second instance, when the work appears in print. Readerly envy (or even readerly ignorance, which for Jonson is a form of envy) begrudges the poet his due, by perverting (or missing) the text's meaning. In order to protect and defend his creation from the defacing gaze of envy, and, because he identifies himself to such an extent

---

[124] See Jonson's dedication of *The Masque of Queenes* to Prince Henry, Herford and Simpson, vol. VII, p. 281 (lines 38–40). This dedication will be discussed in more detail in Chapter 5.

with his creation, to protect his own name and fame, the poet builds or flees to a *sanctuary*.

Chapter 4, *Sanctuary* and Chapter 5, *Monument*, are dedicated to considering the writer's strategies to defend his literary production from defacement. *Sanctuary* is a *temporary* refuge for the poet to shelter himself from envy. The playwright seeks to create a sanctuary for his work to protect it even from the gaze of his contemporaries, for the actual performance of the play or the masque, or for the patron or aristocrat to whom he dedicates a poem of praise. The need for a sanctuary expresses the writer's fear of being suspected of having commited a *crime* and so in need of the protection of a refuge that possesses an intrinsic virtue. *Monument* explores the way in which the writer's vigilant gaze to protect and defend his own work leads to his turning, again *metaphorically*, his own work into stone. I read Jonson's *The Masque of Queenes* as a key document in the elaboration of Jonson's Gorgon gaze upon his own work in anticipation of the reader's gaze. The homeopathic logic of the Medusa, that like cures like, reveals the extent to which, within a logic that perceives the act of reading as necesssarily envious and thus necessarily harmful to the writer's creation, the best protection against envy is an apotropaic form of literary self-envy. The appearance of the figure of the Gorgon in Jonson's texts must be seen as part of the logic of building a monument as memorial and protection against envy. *Monument* may be seen as a form of sanctuary, but may be distinguished from it *temporally*. Monument establishes sanctuary for the poetic work and the poet for *eternity*. It thus provides a place for the performance text to have a secondary afterlife in another form. Through the printing and publication of his stage works and with the prologues, prefaces, narrations, glosses, commentaries, stage directions and marginalia he adds to or even weaves through the original performance text (which we can never recover in full), the writer prepares a monument for a future generation. The division I am drawing between sanctuary and monument, and the means employed by the writer to create a sanctuary for the text or to monumentalize it, is never a rigid one. The process of monumentalization can at times be seen as a form of sanctuary and vice versa. For the purposes of the present study, however, I have decided to establish a division, to separate as much as possible the varying levels and kinds of poetic defenses against the envious gaze, a consequence of the temporal variation in spectators and readers the poet anticipates will judge his work. In the final chapter, *Being posthumous*, I look at the first play written by Jonson after the publication of his 1616 Folio and his extended absence from the public stage. In *The Staple of Newes* (1625) Jonson may be seen to be writing from beyond the grave, a spectre out of his own monument to himself. By the time the play was written, many of his previous works had already become classics of the previous epoch. The *Staple* bears witness to Ben Jonson attempting to write in the shadow of his own sepulchre.

CHAPTER 2

An anatomy of envy

THE ANCIENT AND MEDIEVAL TRADITIONS

The roots of envy in the early modern period can be traced to the classical and Christian traditions, both of which reveal a deep interest in this emotion. The classical tradition may be said to begin with Hesiod in *Works and Days*. In this work the ancient author contends that there exists not one, but two forms of envious 'strife' in the world:

> So there was not just one birth of Strife after all, but upon the earth there are two Strifes. One of these a man would praise once he got to know it, but the other is blameworthy; and they have thoroughly opposed spirits. For the one fosters evil war and conflict – cruel one, no mortal loves that one, but it is by necessity that they honor the oppressive Strife, by the plans of the immortals. But the other one gloomy Night bore first; and Cronus' high-throned son, who dwells in the aether, set it in the roots of the earth, and it is much better for men. It rouses even the helpless man to work. For a man who is not working but who looks at some other man, a rich one who is hastening to plow and plant and set his house in order, he envies him, one neighbor envying his neighbor who is hastening toward wealth: and this Strife is good for mortals.[1]

Hesiod is the first to distinguish between a 'praiseworthy' envy and a 'blameworthy' envy: one a healthy rivalry leading even the laziest to industry, the other a destructive desire that fosters conflict and war. The early modern period would call the one, *emulation* and the other, *envy*. Yet, in his subsequent description of the emulative rivalry which encourages men to work, Hesiod emphasizes the hatred and envy [*phthonos*] between those of the same profession engaged in surpassing one another: 'And potter is angry with potter, and builder with builder, and beggar

---

[1] Hesiod, *Theogony, Works and Days, Testimonia*, ed. and trans. Glenn W. Most (Cambridge: Harvard University Press, 2006), pp. 87–9 (lines 11–24).

begrudges [*phthonos*] beggar, and poet poet.'² In *his* translation of these lines in *The Anatomy of Melancholy* (1621), Robert Burton uses both 'emulation' and 'envy' to render Hesiod's meaning: 'A Potter *emulates* a Potter; / One Smith *envies* another: / A beggar *emulates* a beggar; / A Singing man his brother' (my emphasis).³ In Burton's translation, the difference between emulation and envy is all but erased; they are alternating aspects of the same *contentiousness*, which, Burton claims, is ubiquitous: 'Every society, corporation, and private family is full of it, it takes hold almost of all sorts of men, from the Prince, to the Plowman, even amongst Gossips it is to bee seene; scarce three in a company, but there is siding, faction, emulation ... jarre, private grudge, hart-burning in the midst of them.'⁴ George Chapman's 1618 verse translation of these same lines seems similarly to conflate emulation and envy: 'The Neighbour, doth the Neighbour, aemulate: / The Potter, doth the Potters profit hate; / The Smith, the Smith, with spleene Inveterate: / Beggar, maligns the Beggar, for good done; / And the Musition, the Musition.'⁵ Chapman's 'loose' translation includes 'hatred', 'malign' and 'spleen' as synonyms for the Hesiodic strife that is 'good' for mortals. We might well consider Jonson's 'To the Reader' opposite Shakespeare's portrait in the First Folio in light of Hesiod's two strifes: 'the Graver had a strife / With nature, to out-doo the life'.

Plutarch, in Philomen Holland's 1603 translation, concluded, like Hesiod, that envy existed between equals and neighbours:

they beare envie unto such onely as seeme to prosper and to live in better state than their neighbours: by which reckoning it should seeme that envie is a thing indefinite, much like unto a disease of the eies *Ophthalmia*, which is offended with the brightnesse of any light whatsoever ... envie is properly between man and man.⁶

---

² Hesiod, *ibid.*, p. 89 (lines 25–6). See also G. W. Pigman's translation of these lines and his commentary concerning the negative language with which Hesiod describes emulation, 'Versions of Imitation', pp. 16–17. Pigman translates the Greek *phthonos*, not as 'begrudge' but as 'envy'. According to Glenn W. Most, 'Hesiod puts envy into the very centre of the account of the fundamental conditions of human existence he provides in the *Works and Days*.' Glenn W. Most, 'Epinician Envies' in Konstan and Rutter (eds.), *Envy, Spite and Jealousy*, pp. 123–42; p. 130.
³ Robert Burton, 'Aemulation, Hatred, Faction, Desire of Revenge', *The Anatomy of Melancholy* (Oxford, 1621), p. 137 (Part I. Sec. 2. Memb. 3. Subs. 8).
⁴ *Ibid.*, p. 137.
⁵ George Chapman, *The Georgicks of Hesiod: Translated Elaborately out of the Greek* (London, 1618), p. 2. I have omitted footnote markers 17 and 18 which appear in the body of Chapman's text and which refer to his marginalia.
⁶ Plutarch, 'On Envie and Hatred' in *The Philosophie Commonlie called, The Morals, Written by the learned Philosopher Plutarch of Chaeronea, Translated out of Greek into English* (London, 1603), pp. 234–6.

Plutarch interestingly compares envy to 'Ophthalmia', a disease of the eyes which cannot bear the 'brightnesse of any light'. The metaphor here is in keeping with the important connection between the phenomenon of envy and vision throughout classical literature. Aristotle, in the *Rhetoric*, describes envy as a kind of pain at the *sight* of the good fortune of others and he elaborates as follows:

> Nearly all the actions or possessions which make men desire glory or honour and long for fame, and the favours of fortune, create envy, especially when men long for them themselves, or think that they have a right to them, or the possession of which makes them slightly superior or slightly inferior. And it is evident whom men envy... They envy those who are near them in time, place, age, and reputation... and those with whom they are in rivalry... for no man tries to rival those who lived ten thousand years ago, or are about to be born, or are already dead; nor those who live near the Pillars of Hercules; nor those who, in his own opinion or in that of others, are either far inferior or superior to him; and the people and things which one envies are on the same footing... whence the saying, 'Potter (being jealous) of potter'. And those who have succeeded with difficulty or have failed envy those whose success has been rapid. And those whose possessions or successes are a reproach to themselves... And those who either have or have acquired what was naturally theirs or what they had once acquired; this is why the older man is envious of the younger one.[7]

This passage from Aristotle is important because it includes a number of elements which will be repeated in the early modern period as truisms concerning envy. Aristotle singles out 'glory', 'honour' and 'fame' as inevitably attracting the envy of others. He notes, like Hesiod, whom he cites, that people envy their equals, but he adds that they envy those, who with the same means and the same opportunities at their disposal, have achieved more, in less time and with apparently less effort. Pindar, writing odes on the victors of athletic competitions and wars, also shows himself to be keenly aware of the danger of envy for those deserving glory and honour.[8] In the *Rhetoric*, Aristotle distinguishes envy (*phthonos*), righteous indignation (*nemesis*), and malice (*epichairekakia*). According to Edward B. Stevens:

---

[7] Aristotle, *The Art of Rhetoric*, trans. John Henry Freese (London: William Heinemann, 1926), pp. 239–41 (II.x.10).

[8] Glenn W. Most notes the importance of Pindar in the study of envy in antiquity: 'But it is to Pindar that the true votaries of Greek envy know they must turn, for no other Greek author invokes envy as frequently and as prominently as he does... Pindar declares that it is his central activity as an epinician poet to ward off the blame of the envious so that the merited success of the athletic victor can shine in the light of the praise that is its due.' Most, 'Epinician Envies', p. 133.

The first of these is the general term and may be used to designate either of the other two. The fundamental emotion is that of begrudging someone something, whether the prize is one which we ourselves do not have but should like to have (*phthonos*), or one the unmerited possession of which raises our indignation (*nemesis*), or one which we are maliciously or, it may be, justly, pleased to see another person lose or fail to acquire (*epichairekakia*).[9]

The connection between envy and a disease of the eye in Plutarch appears in Horace's use of the phrase *obliquo oculo*, literally, the 'oblique eye', to describe envy in *Epistles* 1.14.37.[10] In Book II of the *Metamorphoses*, Ovid's portrait of Envy was a powerful image of horror seen through the eyes of the goddess Minerva, who seeks Envy in her cave to wreak vengeance on Aglauros. In George Sandys' 1621 translation, Minerva gazes at the monstrous figure of Envy:

> There saw she Envie lapping Vipers blood;
> And feeding on their flesh, her vices food:
> And, having seene her, turn'd-away her eyes.
> ...
> Shee [Envie] only laught, when shee sad sights beheld,
> Her ever-waking cares exil'd soft sleepe:
> Who lookes on good successe, with eyes that weepe.[11]

Ovid writes that Envy looked at the goddess, 'askance' (*obliquo*), which Sandys translates 'with a wicked eye'.[12] While her own pain comes from looking at 'good successe', her gaze, like Medusa's, was believed to be implicitly harmful and dangerous to others. As a result, people in classical antiquity felt the need for protective devices against the 'wicked eye' of envy. There is indeed ample archaeological evidence of amulets and talismans against the evil eye in Greek culture, more plentiful, André Bernard suggests, than we might suspect in a culture vaunted for its 'rationality' and

---

[9] Edward B. Stevens, 'Envy and Pity in Greek Philosophy', *The American Journal of Philology* 69 (1948), 171–89; p. 171. In *The Nicomachean Ethics*, Aristotle discusses the relative differences between these passions in terms of a mean between extremes: 'Righteous Indignation (*nemesis*) is the observance of a mean between Envy (*phthonos*) and Malice (*epichairekakia*) ...The righteously indignant man is pained by undeserved good fortune; the jealous man (*phthonos*) exceeds him and is pained by all the good fortune of others; while the malicous (*epichairekakia*) man so far falls short of being pained that he actually feels pleasure.' Aristotle, *The Nicomachean Ethics*, trans. H. Rackham (London: William Heinemann, 1926), p. 105 (II.vii.15).
[10] Horace, *Satires, Epistles and Ars Poetica*, trans. H. Rushton Fairclough (Cambridge: Harvard University Press, 1926), pp. 340–1.
[11] Ovid, *The First Five Bookes of Ovids Metamorphosis*, trans. George Sandys (London, 1621), p. 55.
[12] *Ibid.*, p. 56.

'enlightenment'.[13] According to Martin Jay, Greek culture's relationship to 'vision' itself was very ambiguous:

> Although one can certainly find a more positive attitude toward the actual eyes in Greek philosophy, most notably in Aristotle's defense of induction and the power of sight to discriminate among more pieces of information than any other sense, it is thus apparent that Greek culture was not as univocally inclined toward celebrating vision as may appear at first glance. Indeed, a certain anxiety about vision's malevolent power is expressed in many of the central Greek myths, most notably those of Narcissus, Orpheus, and Medusa. And the all-seeing Argus, nicknamed Panoptes, is ultimately undone by Pan, whose enchanting music lulls him to sleep... The frequent existence of apotropaic amulets and other devices to disarm the evil eye (which the Greeks called the *baskanos opthalmos*) also suggests how widespread the fear of being seen existed here as elsewhere.[14]

This Greek fear of vision and the myths that represented the harm emanating from the eye were inherited from the Greeks by the Romans, who were as preoccupied with *invidia* as the Greeks with *phthonos*. In the *Eclogues*, Virgil's shepherd believes his animals can be harmed by someone looking at them: 'Nescio quis teneros oculus mihi *fascinat* agnos' ('some evil eye is bewitching my tender lambs').[15] This ancient belief in the power of the fascinating gaze to physically harm would survive intact in the early modern period.

The Church fathers were prolific in their writings on envy since it was the passion they associated with the devil. Cyprian, bishop of Carthage and author of a treatise in Latin 'On Jealousy and Envy' (*de Zelo et Livore*) describes envy as the vice consubstantial with the devil and the first cause of the fall of man.[16] Slander and calumny, motivated by envy, are also associated with the devil, as the Greek for slander, *diabolos*, amply testifies. In the Old Testament, it is most probably Saul who epitomized the envious man well into the early modern period. In his homily 'On Envy', St Basil 'stresses how Saul was irrationally possessed by envy'.[17] The Vulgate version of 1 Samuel 18.9 relates that Saul, after hearing David praised above him, 'was accustomed to look at David with eyes that were not straightforward'.[18] In

---

[13] André Bernand, *Sorciers grecs* (Paris: Fayard, 1991), pp. 11–12.
[14] Martin Jay, *Downcast Eyes: The Denigration of Vision in Twentieth-Century French Thought* (Berkeley: University of California Press, 1993), pp. 27–8.
[15] Virgil, 'Eclogue III', *Eclogues, Georgics, Aeneid I–VI*, trans. H. Rushton Fairclough (Cambridge: Harvard University Press, 1999), p. 47 (line 103).
[16] Cited in Walcot, *Envy and the Greeks*, p. 93.
[17] Vasiliki Limberis, 'The Eyes Infected by Evil: Basil of Caesarea's Homily, "On Envy"', *The Harvard Theological Review* 84 (April 1991), 163–84; p. 166.
[18] Cited in Allan H. Gilbert, *Dante's Conception of Justice* (New York: AMS Press, Inc., 1965), p. 124.

Mark 7.22, the King James Bible translates as 'envy' what was originally in the Greek *ophthalomos poneros* or 'evil eye'.[19] According to the Evangelists, Pilate believed that Christ had been betrayed out of envy (Matthew 27.18 and Mark 15.10). Christ would become the foremost victim of envy in the theological literature and St Basil uses him as an example to emphasize the paradox at the heart of envy, which rejects and hates outright all that is beneficial:

> Why was he [Jesus] envied? Because of the miracles … The dead were raised, and the giver of life was slandered … Demons were destroyed and the smiter was plotted against. And finally they handed the joy of life over to death, and they whipped the liberator of humanity, and they condemned the judge of the universe.[20]

Christ, it seems, was aware of the divisive power of this passion. Cyprian writes of how his disciples asked him which of them would be the greatest, to which Christ replied: 'the least among you all is the one who will be great' (Luke 9.48). Cyprian interprets this remark saying 'by His reply He cut off all rivalry. He tore out and broke away every cause and material of gnawing envy'.[21] Augustine's discussion of envy in *The City of God* aimed to construct a model of Christian virtue which contrasted sharply with the old Roman ideals of virtue as 'glory'.[22] Basil similarly attempts to reconcile the importance of public honour for the members of his small Christian community with the Christian virtues of charity and patience. He does this, according to Vasilikos Limberis, by making Christian virtues and Christian beliefs the supreme form of protection against the evil eye, the redoubtable accessory, for these communities, to all forms of praise and glory.[23] Peter Brown has argued that rather than repressing certain superstitious practices like those to protect against the evil eye, 'the Christian church offered an explanation of misfortune that both embraced all the phenomena previously ascribed to sorcery, and armed the individual with weapons of satisfying precision and efficacy against suprahuman agents'.[24]

Envy would ultimately be included in the list of the so-called 'seven deadly sins'. In the fourth century, Evagrius of Pontus, 'father of the

---

[19] Cited in Walcot, *Envy and the Greeks*, p. 87.
[20] Cited in Limberis, 'The Eyes Infected by Evil', p. 167.
[21] Cited in Walcot, *Envy and the Greeks*, p. 93. [22] *Ibid.*, p. 95.
[23] Limberis, 'The Eyes Infected by Evil', pp. 175ff.
[24] Peter Brown, 'Sorcery, Demons, and the Rise of Christianity from Late Antiquity into the Middle Ages' in Mary Douglas (ed.), *Witchcraft, Confessions, and Accusations* (London: Tavistock, 1970), p. 28. Cited in Limberis, 'The Eyes Infected by Evil', p. 179.

seven cardinal sins', taught the elements of the ascetic life using a list of sins describing those temptations against which the desert fathers struggled.[25] Interestingly, *invidia* does not appear in the original list, perhaps, hypothesizes Morton Bloomfield, because of its 'connection with property', which of course was not an element of temptation (to the same extent as gluttony or lust) for those leading an hermetic life.[26] St Thomas in the *Summa Theologica* notes that envy is caused chiefly by the sight of others' material possessions and Dante, in the *Purgatorio*, later represents the envious with their eyelids sewn together with wire to prevent them from seeing the goods of others in order to envy them.[27] Envy enters the official list of the seven sins when, in the fifth century, Gregory the Great in his *Moralia* added envy (*invidia*) to the sins in the third place, after pride (*superbia*) and anger (*ira*). This order was subject to change and envy would often find its place just after pride in the medieval period, perhaps, Bloomfield suggests, as a result of a shift from an agrarian to mercantile economy.[28]

In *The Canterbury Tales*, Chaucer creates an image of envy that synthesizes the philosophical and theological traditions. The Parson places 'envye' after 'pride' and learnedly cites both Aristotle and Augustine: 'After pryde wol I speken of the foule synne of Envye, which that is, as by the word of the Philosophre, "sorwe of oother mannes prosperitee"; and after the word of Seint Augustyn, it is "Sorwe of oother mennes wele, and joye of othere mennes harm".'[29] The Parson identifies envy as a sin specifically against the Holy Ghost: its 'malice' is opposed to the 'bountee' of the Holy Spirit.[30] In Chaucer we find some of the elements that would characterize early modern envy: the false exterior of the envious man who hypocritically hides his envious nature and envy as the worst of the seven deadly sins. The Parson avows: 'Certes, thanne is Envye the worste synne that is. For soothly, alle othere synnes been somtyme oonly agayns o special vertu, / but certes Envye is agayns alle vertues and agayns alle goodnesses. For it is sory of alle the bountees of his neighebor, and in this manere it is divers from alle

---

[25] Morton W. Bloomfield, *The Seven Deadly Sins: An Introduction to the History of a Religious Concept, with Special Reference to Medieval English Literature* (Michigan: Michigan State University Press, 1967 [1952]), p. 57.
[26] *Ibid.*, p. 59.
[27] Allan H. Gilbert, *Dante's Conception of Justice* (New York: AMS Press, Inc., 1965), pp. 123–4.
[28] Bloomfield, *The Seven Deadly Sins*, pp. 95–6.
[29] Geoffrey Chaucer, 'The Parson's Tale ('Sequitur de Invidia'), *The Canterbury Tales*, in Larry D. Benson (ed.), *The Riverside Chaucer* (Oxford: Oxford University Press, 1987), p. 303.
[30] *Ibid.*, p. 303.

othere synnes.' He concludes with the truism that would become typical in comparisons between envy and the other deadly sins: 'For wel unnethe is ther any synne that it ne hath *some delit in itself*, save oonly Envye, that evere hath in itself angwissh and sorwe' (my emphasis).[31] The remedy for envy is love, both of one's enemy and of one's neighbour: 'Certes, thanne is love the medicine that casteth out the venym of Envye fro mannes herte.'[32] As in Ovid's *Metamorphoses*, Envy is implicitly perceived as a poison and so in need of a 'medecine'.

Contemporary with Chaucer's *Tales*, John Gower's *Confessio Amantis* devotes its second book to Envy, which comes, as in Chaucer, after the dialogues devoted to Pride. The envious man is described as one who burns perpetually: 'Whan that he wot another levere / Ort more vertuous than he, / which passeth him in his degré.'[33] This image of burning would become a commonplace to describe the passion and rage of the envious as in an emblem by George Wither whose image is that of a volcano.[34] Gower's discourse on Envy is divided into sections such as 'The sin of Envy', 'A description of Spite', or 'The worse part of Envy: Detraction' in which 'the tongue resounds in the air with poisonous speech, just as rumor flies away; in scandal to another'. In the *Mirour de l'Omme*, Gower anatomizes each of the seven deadly sins in a kind of allegorical 'drama'. In a pre-Miltonic incest story, the Devil, 'in his malice', conceives a daughter named Sin upon whom he engenders Death.[35] Sin and Death in turn engender seven daughters, namely the seven deadly sins, whom Satan sends off to wreak havoc in the World. Envy is described as having a 'fine appearance' which hides her 'ill will'.[36] She is the hypocritical 'counselor' to the world, an advisor to Kings. Envy's daughters are divided into 'Detraction', 'Sorrow-for-Other's-Joy', 'Joy-for-Other's-Grief', 'Supplanting' and 'False-Semblance', all described in terms relevant to the political and social milieu of the period, with homely details concerning every kind of person from the gossipy housewife to the intriguing courtier.[37] Gower's detailed 'genealogy' of Envy is extremely useful in that many of the fundamental attributes and beliefs concerning envy in the early modern period, as well as the close ties between envy, slander,

---

[31] *Ibid.*, p. 303.   [32] 'Remedium Contra Peccatum Invidie', *ibid.*, p. 305.
[33] John Gower, *Confessio Amantis*, ed. Russell A. Peck and trans. Andrew Galloway (Kalamazoo: Medieval Institute Publications, 2003), vol. II, p. 55 (Book 2, lines 6–8).
[34] George Wither, *A Collection of Emblemes, Ancient and Moderne* (London, 1635), p. 97.
[35] John Gower, *Mirour de l'Omme*, trans. William Burton Wilson (East Lansing: Colleagues Press, 1992), p. 6.
[36] *Ibid.*, p. 6.   [37] *Ibid.*, pp. 40–54.

gossip and rumour, are clearly established in this extremely influential piece from the late fourteenth century.[38]

Sixteenth-century mystery and miracle plays, in keeping with the theological tradition, would represent the devil's envy as the predominant motive for tempting Adam and Eve. In the 'Cowpers' production of the Fall, Satan enters the scene 'troubled at God's intention to take on him the nature of man': 'The kynde of man he thoght to take, / And theratt hadde I grete envye, / But he has made to hym a make, / And harde to her I wol my hye.'[39] In the *Chester Mystery Cycle*, Adam blames Eve for being the vehicle for Satan's envy, explaining to God: 'My lycourouse wyfe hath bynne my foe; / the devylls envye shente mee alsoe.'[40] However, it is the envy of Cain for his brother Abel that would become a frequently used human image of envy's power to divide men in the early modern period. In one early mystery play, Cain describes his own envy as a form of sudden petrification at the sight of God's acceptance of his brother, Abel's, better offering:

> Out, out! How have I spent my good?
> To see this sight I am neare wood.
> . . . .
> My semblant for shame shakes
> For envy of this thinge.[41]

---

[38] In *Assembly of the Gods*, John Lydgate follows the model of Prudentius in the *Psychomachia*, by describing a battle between Vices and Virtues on the plain of 'Microcosmos'. Lydgate also translated *The Pilgrimage of the Life of Man* from the French of Guillaume de Deguileville (1330), a book that would become incredibly influential in England and the source for John Bunyan's *Pilgrim's Progress*. The cataloguing of the seven deadly sins is something we find in Stephen Bateman's *A Christall Glasse of Christian Reformation* (London, 1569) and in Spenser's *The Fairie Queene* (1596), probably the last apparition of the seven deadly sins together in the old medieval order before becoming satirized and ironized in works such as Thomas Dekker's *The Seven Deadly Sins of London* (1606). In traditional iconography of the virtues and the vices, Envy often appears surrounded by acolytes Calumny and Slander. The virtue normally associated with Envy was Charity. In the oldest manuscript concerning the seven deadly sins, dated 1390, envy is represented as a monk seated on a dog (ms. 400 BnF). We find in a manuscript painted for Louise de Savoie, Envy seated on a dog, facing Charity. The dog will be an attribute of envy up until the fifteenth and sixteenth centuries. On the other hand, envy is also feminine and particularly from the fourteenth century onwards appears in the guise of Ovid's portrait. In each of these works, up to and including Spenser, envy is described in its iconographical attributes, associated with the wolf and the dog, as well as those animals such as the basilisk, associated with a noxious gaze. Herod would become, in the medieval period, one of the emblematic figures of envy: his envy of Christ, whom he saw as threatening his own power, led to the 'massacre of the innocents'.

[39] 'Man's disobedience and fall from Eden' in Lucy Toulmin Smith (ed.), *York Plays: The Plays Performed by the Crafts or Mysteries of York on the Day of Corpus Christi in the 14th, 15th, and 16th Centuries* (New York: Russell and Russell, 1885), p. 22 (lines 12–15).

[40] 'Adam' in R. M. Lumiansky and David Mills (eds.), *The Chester Mystery Cycle* (London: Oxford University Press, 1974), p. 28 (lines 353–4).

[41] 'Cain', *ibid.*, p. 36 (lines 569–70; 575–6).

It is 'envy of this thinge' that pushes Cain to murder Abel.

It is significant that the seven deadly sins became associated with the cult of death in the fifteenth and sixteenth centuries. William Dunbar's *The Dance of the Sevin Deidly Synnis* (1507) is a version of the Dance of Death except that each 'death' figure is a different sin. In 1522, St Thomas More, in his treatise on 'Last Things' notes that it was through the 'enticement' of his daughter Envy that Satan 'set upon our first parents in paradise'.[42] He describes envy as a 'sore torment & a very consumpcion', a sickness that drinks up the moisture of the body and 'consumeth the good bloode, so discoloreth the face, so *defaceth the bewty*, so *dysfigureth the visage* leaving it al bony, leane, plae, and wan' (my emphasis).[43] More's conception of envy as defacing and disfiguring the physical appearance of its victim is one that will inform Jonson's image of the threat posed by envy to the writer's text. The only remedy for this defacing envy, as for all the sins described by More, is the 'remembrance of death'.[44] This too would be the remedy for Jonson and his contemporaries: a clear vision of death, made tangible in the *memento mori* of the printed book, the means to ensure the writer's own posterity in the face of corruption.

ENVY IN THE EARLY MODERN PERIOD

The gruesome portrait of Envy in Book II of Ovid's *Metamorphoses* was well known in the Renaissance and provided the ekphrastic model for an early modern iconography. In the emblem books, Envy is depicted as a woman with a pallid visage, wasted body, oblique gaze, surrounded by snakes. According to this tradition, the figure of Envy is characteristically pale and lean. The Latin *Livor*, often another substantive for envy at the time, reflects this key feature of envy, namely its pale, corpselike color. In Golding's translation, Ovid paints her as follows: 'Her lyppes were pale, her cheekes were wan... Her body leane as any Rake.'[45] In the words of Robert Burton: 'It crucifies their soules, and withers their

---

[42] St Thomas More, 'Last Things' in *The Complete Works of St. Thomas More*, ed. Anthony S. G. Edwards et al. (New Haven: Yale University Press, 1997), vol. 1, p. 159.
[43] *Ibid.*, p. 158. [44] *Ibid.*, p. 160.
[45] Ovid, *The Fyrst Four Bookes of P. Ovidius Nasos worke intitled Metamorphosis, translated out of Latin into English meter by Arthur Golding Gentleman*, trans. Arthur Golding (London, 1565), sig. Civ^v. In George Sandys' version: 'Her body more then meger; pale her hew', *The First Five Bookes*, p. 55. In Thomas Dekker's *Troia-Nova Triumphans. London Triumphing* (London, 1612), 'Envy' is introduced, at the beginning of 'The Third Device', as 'pallid, meagre and leane, her body naked, in her hand a knot of Snakes, crawling and writhen about her arme' (lines 280–2).

bodies, makes them hollow-ey'd,^b pale & leane, and gastly to behold.'[46] Abraham Cowley describes her as: 'that hideous monster, meagre, fell; / That skeleton, is belch't up too from Hell'.[47] This characteristic thinness of envy is due to its self-martyring sorrow at the sight of another's prosperity: 'When he beholds another doing well, / He wastes away, he suffers tortures fell.'[48] In Ovid, 'In seekyng to anoy: / And worke distresse too other folke, her selfe she dooth destroy. / Thus is shee torment too her selfe.'[49] The sight of another's 'fatness', in other words, makes envy 'lean'. Envy is, in this logic, self-consuming, as Cowley writes: 'Malicious men did their own bodies pine, / To see their neighbours plentifully dine.'[50] John Davies offers an insightful psycho-physiological explanation for envy's leanness: '*Envie* therefore the *hart* doth macerate, / Because the *Tongue* dares not the *griefe* disclose, / That makes the *griefe* still on the *hart* to grate, / Which the *leane looke* alone in silence shows.'[51] So, while Envy is perceived to waste away, this emaciation is very much due to an active self-consumption. Burton quotes antiquity: '*As a moth gnaws a garment*, so saith *Chrysostom doth envy consume a man*'.[52] This wasting and eating away is necessarily associated with unhealthiness and disease. Like melancholy, according to Burton, envy is a kind of 'rotting of the bones'.[53] It was imagined as a disease that ate itself, metaphorically, from the inside out. Stephen Bateman associates envy with bodily corruption in his third description of Envy:

But envie tormenteth himself when he seeth any good thing happen unto another. And the most harm falleth upon himself. It holdeth the heart and mind in great melancholy, and maketh colour to waxe pale. It drieth the body oft to sigh.[54]

The passion of envy is conceived of as a disease or a corruption and thus, as we shall see, in need of a cure, a remedy or an antidote. Ovid speaks of Envy's noxiousness: 'Her breast with gall, her tongue with poyson sweld... Her

---

[46] Burton, 'Envy, Malice causes', *The Anatomy of Melancholy* (Oxford, 1621), p. 136 (Part I. Sec. 2 Memb. 3 Subs. 7).
[47] Abraham Cowley [attributed to], 'The Brazen Age', *The Foure Ages of England* (London, 1648) p. 22.
[48] *Ibid.*, p. 136. [49] Ovid, *The Fyrst Four Bookes*, trans. Golding, sig. Civ^v.
[50] Cowley, *The Foure Ages*, p. 23.
[51] John Davies, *Microcosmos* (London, 1603), p. 196. The marginal note states the proverbial truism: 'The envious are ashamed to bewray their envie.'
[52] Burton, *The Anatomy of Melancholy*, p. 136.
[53] *Ibid.*, p. 136. Samuel Gott attests to the harmful effects of the passions on a person's health: 'Excess of Affections, especially Malignant, as Fear, Grief, Envy, Malice, and all Anxiety of mind, destroyes the body more then that of Food.' Samuel Gott, *An Essay of the True Happiness of Man* (London, 1650), p. 32.
[54] Bateman, 'Of Envie', *A Christall Glasse of Christian Reformation*, sig. G4.

cancred hand upon her [Aglauros's] brest she lay'd, / And crooked thornes into her heart convay'd, / and breath'd in baneful poyson.'[55] The mere breath of an envious person could even have fatal effects upon the weak, as we see in the frontispiece of Johannes Christian Frommand's *Tractatus de Fascinatione*, in which the breath of an old woman puts a child in his mother's arms into a faint, or kills it.[56] In the *Sylva Sylvarum*, Bacon writes:

> As for *Envy*, that emitteth some *Maligne* and *Poysonous Spirits*, which taketh hold of the *Spirit* of Another... But yet if there be any such *Infection* from *Spirit* to *Spirit*, there is no doubt but that it worketh by *Presence*, and not by the *Eye* alone, Yet most Forcibly by the *Eye*.[57]

Bacon testifies to the noxious effects of mere 'Presence' all the while underlying the primacy of the eye.[58]

In his popular commonplace book of 1657, *The English Parnassus*, Joshua Poole lists the following adjectives under the entry 'Envie':

> Pale, lean, swelling, snarling, blue-eyed, squint-eyed, restless, killing, stabbing, cutting, wounding, sullen, snaky, viperous, poysonous, blear-eyed, self-eating, self-consuming, self-torturing, self-martyring, black-mouthed, muttering, whispering, lean-fac't, carping, censorious, repining, undermining, snake-haird, burning, flaming, boyling, revengefull, malicious, spightful, cancred, subtle, sly, crafty, heart-gnawing, deadly, mortall, jealous, cruell, calumnious, detracting, pernicious, out-rageous, proud, disdainfull, haughty, crooked, biting, currish.[59]

A number of envy's attributes listed by Poole are associated with snakes. In medieval and Renaissance painting, we find examples of the allegorical figure of Envy represented with snakes coming out of the mouth of the envious person to sting another or to sting its host in the breast or, even more startlingly, in its own eye, as in Giotto's painting of *Invidia* in the Scrovegni Chapel at Padua.[60] The snakes in Envy's hair testify to the way

---

[55] Ovid, *The First Five Bookes*, trans. Sandys, pp. 55–6.
[56] Johannes Christian Frommand, *Tractatus de Fascinatione* (Nuremberg, 1674).
[57] Francis Bacon, *Sylva Sylvarum: Or, A Naturall History* (London, 1651), pp. 205–6.
[58] *Ibid.*, p. 206.
[59] Joshua Poole, *The English Parnassus*, 1657 (Menston: The Scolar Press Limited, 1972), p. 89. Many of the elements in this list will be discussed later in this chapter and in the following ones. Thomas Elyot defines 'Invidia' as 'envy, hatred, ill will' in *The Dictionary of Sir Thomas Eliot Knight* (London, 1638) and Edward Phillips lists the neologism, 'eyebite' (under 'EY'), defining it as 'to *fascinate or bewitch* by a certain evil influence of the eye'. Edward Phillips, *The New World of English Words*, 1658 (Menston: The Scolar Press Limited, 1969). The idea of 'biting' is present in the term 'backbiting', which Thomas Wilson defines as an 'evill tongue', which is the same as 'slander'. *The Arte of Rhetorique*, 1560, ed. G. H. Mair (Oxford: Clarendon Press, 1909), p. 117.
[60] For a discussion of Giotto's painting in relation to other contemporary representations of the 'tongue', see Jesse M. Gellrich, 'The Art of the Tongue: Illuminating Speech and Writing in Later

Illustration 2. Emblem, 'VIR BONUS INVIDIAE SECURUS', Jean-Jacques Boissard, *Emblematum Liber* (Frankfurt, Theodore de Bry, 1593).

it was given the attributes of the Gorgon Medusa in the early modern period.[61] Jean-Jacques Boissard depicted Envy as an old woman with live snakes in her hand and snakes for hair. In his emblem 'Invidiae descriptio', Geffrey Whitney poses and answers questions concerning the attributes of *Invidia*: 'And what declares, her eating vipers broode? / That poysoned

---

Medieval Manuscripts' in Colum Hourihane (ed.), *Virtues & Vices: The Personifications in the Index of Christian Art* (Princeton: Department of Art and Archaeology, 2000), pp. 93–119.

[61] Jean Clair, *Méduse: contribution à une anthropologie des arts du visuel* (Paris: Gallimard, 1989), p. 105.

thoughtes, bee evermore her foode … And what is mente by snakes upon her head? / The fruite that springes, of such a venomed braine.'[62] A stunning native English Medusa, cross-eyed, open-mouthed, with four snakes twining around its head, can be found in a central position on the Jacobean screen in the Great Hall of Knole, the country house of the Sackville family. Whether Jonson was connected to the family and its home is difficult to say. Jonson wrote an Epistle, *Underwood* 13, to Edward Sackville and Anne Clifford, the wife of Richard, Edward's son, danced in Jonson's masques at court and seems to have appreciated the author for she owned a copy of the 1616 Folio.

Cornelis Cort, in *The Painter of Truth*, after Federico Zuccari, depicts Envy as a skeletal woman lying in a fetal position in a kind of cavelike tomb with live snakes emerging from her mouth. In the background of the painting are Furies with brands in their hands and snakes emerging from their heads and twining about their naked arms.[63] The radiant figure of Truth, at which the painter gazes, is positioned above the writhing figure of Envy, in the same attitude traditionally adopted for the defeat of vices crushed under the feet of their opposite virtue. Similarly, the head of a Medusa underneath the figure of Fame and her globe, in Battista del Moro's 'Fame', can be read as a figure of envy, the obstacle to Fame.[64] Envy and Virtue were often represented together in the early modern period. In Rubens' ceiling in Whitehall, Envy, in the form of a dragon, is pierced by the spear of Virtue. Walter Devereux's motto on the Montacute House portrait reads 'Virtutis comes Invidia' ('Envy (is) the companion of Virtue'). The destiny of the courtier reminds us of what Aristotle had known, that to possess glory and honour was to become susceptible to the dangerous envy of others. Devereux's portrait testifies to the belief that virtue is always shadowed by envy.

Envy and the evil eye

In the essay, 'Of Envy', Francis Bacon emphasizes that aspect of envy we have already noted in the classical and theological traditions, namely its harmful and dangerous gaze:

---

[62] Geffrey Whitney, *A Choice of Emblemes And Other Devises* (Leyden, 1586), p. 94. See also *Veritas temporis filia*: 'Three furies fell, which turne the worlde to ruthe, / Both Envie, Strife, and Slaunder, heare appeare' (p. 4).
[63] Clair, *Méduse*, fig. 33.
[64] John Peacock, *The Stage Designs of Inigo Jones: The European Context* (Cambridge: Cambridge University Press, 1995), p. 241.

There be none of the affections which have been noted to fascinate or bewitch, but love and envy. They both have vehement wishes; they frame themselves readily into imaginations and suggestions; and they come easily into the eye, especially upon the presence of the objects; which are the points that conduce to fascination, if any such thing there be. We see likewise, the scripture calleth envy an evil eye; and the astrologers call the evil influences of the stars evil aspects; so that still there seemeth to be acknowledged, in the act of envy, an ejaculation or irradiation of the eye.[65]

Bacon states that both envy and love share the ocular power to 'fascinate or bewitch'. He describes the 'Act of Envy' as an 'ejaculation or irradiation of the eye'. The eye was believed to send its rays *toward* its object in order to see and so the belief that the envious gaze was a harmful 'irradiation' is an extension of this belief in the physical properties of the gaze. Bacon specifies that the envious eye is 'of greatest Force, when the *Cast of the Eye is Oblique*'.[66] John Aubrey concurs with him when he writes: '[T]he Glances of Envy and Malice, do shoot also subtilly; the Eye of the Malicious person does really Infect (and make Sick) the Spirit of the other.'[67] What Ronald B. Bond has called Bacon's 'biophysics of envy' was part of the thinking of the period.[68] As we have seen, Bacon testifies, as well, to the early modern belief that a person in the midst of being showered with honours was perceived to be particularly magnetic and attractive to the envious eye. Later in the seventeenth century, Thomas Pierce is of the same opinion, describing what Bacon termed 'rays' as 'darts' aimed at a 'Mark':

The *greater* any man is, the more he is *expos'd* as *the Butt of Envy*; he is by so much the fairer *Mark*, to be singled out and *shot* at, with *Darts* of *Mischievousness*, and *Malice*, as well as Envy. A Truth so *experimented* and *known* throughout the Annals of all the World, that the great *Emperours* of the *East* were almost *All murder'd*; nor were there many of the *West*, who were not *cut off* by *Fraud*, or *Fury*.[69]

In 'On the Power of the Imagination', Montaigne attributes this ocular power to fascinate and bewitch to witches: 'And as to witches, it is said that

---

[65] Bacon, *Essayes*, p. 40. [66] Bacon, *Sylva Sylvarum*, p. 205.
[67] John Aubrey, *Miscellanies Upon the Following Subjects* (London, 1696), p. 147.
[68] Bond, 'Vying with Vision', p. 31.
[69] Thomas Pierce, *The Law and Equity of the Gospel, or, The Goodness of our Lord as a Legislator* (London, 1686), p. 633. George Villiers, second Duke of Buckingham, mused on the destructive nature of envy, wounding and conspiring against 'Merit' and 'Desert': 'The blackest wound of Merit, and the Dart, / That secret Envy points against Desert.' *Poetical Reflections on a Late Poem entitled Absalom and Achitophel By a Person of Honour* (London, 1682), p. 4.

they possess offensive and harmful eyes.'⁷⁰ Aubrey concurs that witches had 'evil Eyes' and that children were particularly susceptible to fascination:

> Infants are very sensible of these Irradiations of the Eyes: In Spain, France, Etc. In Southern Countries, the Nurses, and Parents, are very shy to let People look upon their young Children, for fear of Fascination. In Spain, they take it ill if one looks on a Child, and make one say, God Bless it. They talk of *mul dé ojos*. We usually say, Witches have evil Eyes. ⁷¹

Bacon had said the same, writing that 'the Act of *Envy*, had somewhat in it, of *Witchcraft*'.⁷² In fact, the casting of the evil eye was a type of *maleficium*. In *Religion and the Decline of Magic*, Keith Thomas describes these early modern beliefs:

> [A] witch ... could mysteriously injure other people. The damage she might do – *maleficium*, as it was technically called – could take various forms. Usually she was suspected of causing physical injury to other persons, or of bringing about their death. She might also kill or injure farm animals or interfere with nature by preventing cows from giving milk, or by frustrating such domestic operations as making butter, cheese or beer ... The manner in which the witch actually exercised this occult power was also believed to vary. Sometimes her evil influence was conveyed through physical contact: the witch touched her victim or gave out a potent, but invisible, emanation from her eyes. In this case he was said to have been 'fascinated' or 'overlooked'. Alternatively the witch pronounced a curse or malediction which in due course took effect. Here the victim was said to have been 'forspoken'.⁷³

The witch had the power to harm through touch, the gaze and the spoken spell. This kind of power was regularly perceived as a property of the feminine and often attributed to an old woman or the malicious village crone, who acted as she did out of 'envy and malice'.⁷⁴ Toward the con-

---

⁷⁰ 'Et quant aux sorciers, on les dit avoir des yeux offensifs et nuisans.' Michel de Montaigne, 'De la force de l'imagination', *Essais*, ed. Pierre Michel (Paris: Gallimard, 1965), vol. 1, p. 169.
⁷¹ Aubrey, *Miscellanies*, pp. 147–8. The belief that witches possessed an envious or evil eye is even mentioned by the sceptical Reginald Scot as being widespread and tenacious: 'The Irishmen addict themselves wonderfully to the credit and practice hereof; insomuch as they affirme, that not onelie their children, but their cattell, are (as they call it) eybitten, when they fall suddenlie sicke, and tearme one sort of their witches eybiters.' Reginald Scot, *The Discoverie of Witchcraft* (1584), p. 51 (Book III, chap. xv).
⁷² Bacon, *Essayes*, p. 47.
⁷³ Keith Thomas, *Religion and the Decline of Magic: Studies in Popular Beliefs in Sixteenth- and Seventeenth-Century England* (London: Penguin Books, 1971), p. 519.
⁷⁴ John Webster testifies to the 'supposed' power of witches to fascinate and poison: 'it is taken sometimes for envy and malice, because those that were supposed to use Fascination, did direct it to one Creature more than another through their envious minds ... And so was accounted a kind of eyebiting; whereby (as the Vulgar believed) children did wax lean, and pined away, the original whereof

clusion of the essay, 'Of the Power of the Imagination', Montaigne cites Pliny's description of women from Scythia who possessed the power to kill with an angry look. He describes the 'vertu éjaculatrice' (the ejaculating faculty) of female turtles' and ostriches' gazes, as well as the poisonous glance of witches, like the glances which 'fascinated' Tityrus' lambs in the *Eclogues*, concluding with a story relating how women 'transmit marks of their fancies to the bodies of the children they carry in their womb'.[75] Montaigne here joins together the presumed power of the evil eye to fascinate and bewitch with the sixteenth-century medical belief, studied by Paré among others, that women were capable of *imprinting* images from their own imaginations on the unborn bodies of their children. The Renaissance belief that pregnant women could deform the embryo in their womb through what Marie-Hélène Huet calls the 'double influence of the mother's imagination and the contemplation of images' was for Montaigne perfectly analogous to the distorting and perverting power of the malevolent eye.[76]

The cure for envy

According to Alan Macfarlane, a number of African tribes such as the Lovedu, the Azande and the Gisu had, well into the twentieth century, two forms of 'counter-action' to the harm of witches. First, they believed in 'mystical' counter-action, which includes medicines, charms, dances and amulets, and secondly, in 'practical' counter-action, which consisted of simply avoiding giving a witch a motive for bewitching one, avoiding old people in general and not being boastful or jealous of one's own possessions. Since envy is perceived as a basic motive of witches, people fear to be conspicuously successful among those in the same tribe.[77] This description of African tribal customs for protection against witchcraft may well be useful in understanding similar rituals in early modern England. Here too we find two forms of 'counter-action' to the harm of envy, which we

---

they referred to the crooked and wry looks of malicious persons, never examining the truth of the matter of fact, whether those children that pined away, had any natural disease or not, that caused that macilency or pining away.' John Webster, *The Displaying of Supposed Witchcraft* (London, 1677), p. 20.

[75] '[N]ous voyons par experience les femmes envoyer aux corps des enfans qu'elles portent au ventre des marques de leurs fantasies.' Montaigne, *Essais*, vol. 1, p. 169.

[76] Marie-Hélène Huet, *The Monstrous Imagination* (Cambridge: Harvard University Press, 1993), p. 13.

[77] Alan Macfarlane, *Witchcraft in Tudor and Stuart England: A Regional and Comparative Study* (London: Routledge and Kegan Paul, 1970), pp. 219–20.

might also call the 'mystical' and the 'practical'. The plots of a number of early modern court masques, entertainments and pageants of the period turn symbolically on the defeat of Envy or an envious character by the powerful gaze of the King or the Queen, or some avatar, such as 'Virtue' or 'Fame'. The 'mystical' counter-action to envy may be seen in the belief in the medicinal harmonies of music, as well as in the performance of certain patterns in dances by the masquers to purge the effects of the envious individuals of the anti-masque. In the *Magnificent Entertainment* of 1603, celebrating the ascension of James I to the throne of England, Dekker's 'Invidia' is defeated by 'Vertue': 'At whose immortall brightnes and true light, / *Envies* infectious eyes have lost their sight.'[78] The power of Virtue, or the King, to purge the infection of Envy was, as we have seen above, an encomiastic *topos* that found its source in the Petrarchan conceit of the 'dazzling' power of the beloved's eye. It was this power attributed to Queen Elizabeth's gaze to purge men of their humours that rid Macilente of his envy in the epilogue of Jonson's *Every Man Out of His Humour*. The envious Macilente approaches the Queen, who attended the actual performance, and proclaims that he is suddenly purged of all envy:

> Never till now did object greet mine eyes
> With any light content: but in her graces,
> All my malicious powers have lost their stings.
> Envie is fled my soule, at sight of her,
> And she hath chac'd all black thoughts from my bosome,
> Like as the sunne doth darkenesse from the world.[79]

In the Queen, the power to fascinate and injure becomes the mystical power to cure. When Petrarch puns on how his beloved Laura's Medusa-like gaze turns him into a stone or 'petra', we see the problematic imbrication of the beloved and the monstrous Gorgon.[80] Similarly, the 'sight' of the Queen problematically serves both as a beneficial and protective *gorgoneion*, but also as a power of such strength as to throw others into a state of awe and terror. It is for this reason that the gaze of the monarch can be seen as an example of a *pharmakon*, possessing both the power to kill and to cure by looking.[81]

---

[78] Thomas Dekker, *The Magnificent Entertainment* (London, 1603), lines 1433–4.
[79] Epilogue to *Every Man Out of His Humour*, Herford and Simpson, vol. III, p. 599 (lines 1–6).
[80] Petrarch, '*Rime Sparse* 197' in *Petrarch's Lyric Poems: The 'Rime Sparse' and Other Lyrics*, trans. Robert M. Durling (Cambridge: Harvard University Press, 1976).
[81] Jacques Derrida, 'Plato's Pharmacy' in *Dissemination*, trans. Barbara Johnson (London: Continuum, 1981 [1972], pp. 67–154.

While the encomiastic notion of the monarch's ability to quell envy was appropriated for a flattering epilogue or a court masque, the very real problems posed by envy at court contributed to more practical assessments of the situation. According to Louis Montrose: '[L]ife within the Elizabethan court and on its margins was characterized by intrigue, backbiting, and bribery; by intense competition for personal and political influence, office, prestige, and income.'[82] Within this paradigm of Elizabethan court culture:

> The successful politician … had to remain alert lest a rival seek to displace him in the prince's favour by spreading falsehoods and insinuations. Absence from the privy chamber, even from the ante-room of kings, could prove fatal, for the household of the prince was no different from that of lesser personages throughout the kingdom: malice and tale-bearing permeated them all. Envy, suspicion, enmity, and lies were reported at all levels of society as clients and servants sought to win favour by discrediting or destroying their colleagues and adversaries.[83]

The fortunes of courtiers were often hostage to the envy of their immediate rivals. In Ulpian Fulwell's *The Eyghth Liberall Science* (1576), a series of dialogues concerning the means men employ to advance their fortunes in the world, flatterers and sycophants are encouraged to beware of the envious:

> He that lives at Court …
> Let him be sure of this,
> If Fortune chance to frowne,
> Envy in time will turne the wheele
> And throw him head-long downe.[84]

One could argue that envy at court was simply more acute because the stakes were so high. Edmund Spenser described the 'hell' of the 'suitor' in need of patronage: 'To fawn, to crouch, to wait, to ride, to run, / To spend, to give, to want, to be undone.'[85] With such intimate and painful knowledge of the Tudor court, it is probably no accident that in his Eclogue 'February', Spenser dissents from the view that the Queen was magically capable of overcoming the envy that surrounded her simply by gazing on it.[86] According to Ronald B. Bond, the Eclogue 'furnishes the queen with

---

[82] Louis Adrian Monstrose, 'Celebration and Insinuation: Sir Philip Sidney and the Motives of Elizabethan Courtship', *Renaissance Drama*, n.s. 8 (1977), 3–35; p. 5.
[83] Smith, *Treason in Tudor England*, p. 154.
[84] Cited in Samuel Chew, *The Pilgrimage of Life* (New Haven: Yale University Press, 1962), pp. 61–2. Pierre Boaistuau makes it clear that envy is not a parasite of the mediocre. Pierre Boaistuau, *Le Théâtre du Monde*, ed. Michel Simonin (Genève: Droz, 1981), p. 211 (lines 1121–7).
[85] Muriel St Clare Byrne (ed.), *Lisle Letters*, 6 vols. (London, 1983 [Chicago, 1981]), vol. VI, p. 3. Cited in Smith, *Treason in Tudor England*, p. 15.
[86] Bond, 'Supplantation in the Elizabethan Court', p. 60.

a reminder to be *vigilant* lest envious slander blight her policy or subvert her most devoted counsellors'.[87] Blighting envy is represented by the 'faded Oake' envious of the 'Primrose', who drops 'canker-wormes' on the young flower's 'branches' out of 'spight', the result of which its 'fresh florets' are 'defast'.[88] Spenser's counsel may indeed be seen as of the 'practical' sort of counter-actions against envy. The poet's advice to the Queen with regard to envy does not propose a magic cure to its existence among her counsellors, it requires rather that the Queen be observant, watchful and provide herself with a network of spies to anticipate the faction, sedition and treason perceived to be motivated primarily by envy. Daniel Fischlin has argued that the 'Rainbow Portrait' of Queen Elizabeth I, in a robe covered in eyes and ears, is an image of such vigilance.[89]

And she was right to cover herself in eyes and ears. Peter Ramus describes people most likely to be envious as those: 'That are within a little of the highest.'[90] He lists those things men envy in others, such as glory and fortune, before suggesting certain Machiavellian tactics for defeating one's enemies: 'He therefore that would not have his Enemy prevail...must...make his Adversary appear such, as are above described, to be subject to the Envy of others.'[91] In other words, since there is no use in denying its presence in court, men who would be successful must arm themselves and one of the most effective arms is, in fact, to attract envy toward one's enemy. Francis Bacon gives the same advice to those in high, public positions and natural victims of envy: 'the wiser sort of great persons bring in ever upon the stage somebody upon whom to derive the envy that would come upon themselves'.[92]

This pragmatic, even Machiavellian, approach espoused by Spenser, Ramus and Bacon may be considered the result of the conviction, dating from antiquity, that there was, in fact, no real cure or remedy for envy. Boaistuau and Burton both cite Marcus Aurelius with regard to men's ultimate powerlessness before the envy of other men: '*I have read*, saith Marcus Aurelius, *Greek, Hebrew, Chaldee authors, I have consulted with*

---

[87] Ibid., p. 60.
[88] Edmund Spenser, 'February', *The Shepheards Calendar* in *The Faerie Queen[e]: The Shepheards Calendar: Together with the Other Works of England's Arch-Poët* (London, 1611), p. 6.
[89] For examinations of the significance of eyes and ears in this portrait see Daniel Fischlin, 'Political Allegory, Absolutist Ideology, and the "Rainbow Portrait" of Queen Elizabeth I', *Renaissance Quarterly* 50 (Spring 1997), 175–206, and Joel Fineman, *The Subjectivity Effect in the Western Literary Tradition: Essays Toward the Release of Shakespeare's Will* (Cambridge: Harvard University Press, 1991).
[90] Peter Ramus, 'Of Envy', *A Compendium of the Art of Logick and Rhetorick in the English Tongue* (London, 1651), p. 209.
[91] Ibid., p. 210.   [92] Bacon, *Essayes*, p. 30.

many wise men, for a remedy for envy, I could find none, but to renounce all happiness, and to be a wretch and miserable for ever.'[93] This resignation before the power of envy would become, as Walcot has noted, adopted and transformed by St Augustine and St Basil into the pursuit of the Christian life and the 'heavenly city of God'. Individual virtue was to be a shield against envy. However, both the Stoic and the Christian solutions were inadequate and effectively incompatible with a society based on ambitious desire for glory, riches and fame. In *The Nature and Mischief of Envy* (1693), Jonathan Blagrave is dubious concerning the efficacy of 'virtue' to defeat envy, despite Christian and Neo-platonic philosophical ideas:

First, There is no mans Innocency, no man's Vertue that can secure him from the direful strokes of Envy. Nay, many times the more Innocent, the more Religious, useful and beneficial a man is in his place and station, Envy encreases the more against him.

Secondly, There is no Man so great or powerful, or of so secure an Estate or Fortune, but the Violence of Envy hath been capable of overthrowing him. Sometimes a private Envy hath been able to do it; but a common Envy hath seldom fail'd of accomplishing any Mans ruine.[94]

Blagrave first claims that 'Vertue', far from being a shield against envy, actually draws envy towards it. John Davies similarly shows that the envious gaze is most attracted by what is noble: 'For *envies eies* pry most of al on *praise,* / The noblest *goods, goods* of the noblest *Minde* / They most envie.'[95] Envy's violence, its ability to accomplish any man's 'ruine' may indeed have served as justification for those in positions of power to be less than 'virtuous' and even cunning for their own protection. The message between the lines of treatises such as Blagrave's is ultimately a very individualistic one: namely the need to protect oneself at all costs because the danger presented by envy was particularly deadly and insidious.

Envy and emulation

This chapter began with Hesiod's distinction between what the early modern period would call emulation and envy. In the early modern period, the idea was that if envy could not be defeated, it could be deflected, perhaps,

---

[93] Burton, *The Anatomy of Melancholy*, p. 137 (Part I. Sec. 2 Memb. 3 Subs. 7). See also Boaistuau, *Le Théâtre du Monde*, pp. 211–12 (lines 1129–39).
[94] Jonathan Blagrave, *The Nature and Mischief of Envy* (London, 1693), pp. 2–4.
[95] Davies, *Microcosmos*, p. 194.

into its more positive counterpart, virtuous emulation. Robert Burton's translation of Hesiod, as we have seen, was clearly circumspect concerning the differences between the two, although he admits (briefly): 'Honest emulation in studies, in all callings is not to be disliked, 'tis *ingeniorum cos*, as one calls it, the whetstone of wits: As *Themistocles* was roused up with the glory of *Miltiades*; *Achilles* trophys loved *Alexander*: but when it is immoderate, it is a plague, and a miserable paine.'[96] For Aristotle, in both emulation and envy, the viewer feels pain at the sight of something 'good' and it is in this initial viewing that emulation shows its problematic association with the contentiousness that marks envy. Yet, Aristotle explains the very important difference in their manner of subsequently reacting to this pain:

Let us assume that emulation is a feeling of pain at the evident presence of highly valued goods, which are possible for us to obtain, in the possession of those who naturally resemble us – pain not due to the fact that another possesses them, but to the fact that we ourselves do not. Emulation therefore is virtuous and characteristic of virtuous men, whereas envy is base and characteristic of base men; for the one, owing to emulation, fits himself to obtain such goods, while the object of the other, owing to envy, is to prevent his neighbour possessing them.[97]

This difference between emulation and envy was appropriated by the early modern period which saw emulation as spurring the 'envier' to great deeds and envy as a source of a self-destructive melancholy. While Burton sees the dangers of 'immoderate' emulation ending in misery, others were more optimistic about distinguishing the two. According to Peter Ramus: '*Emulation* is griefe arising from that our Equals possess such goods as are had in honour, and whereof we are capable, but have them not; not because they have them, but because not we also.'[98] Envy cannot bear that another possesses something good, whereas emulation is the desire to possess (and willingness to strive for) what the other possesses. Again, Blagrave, at the end of the seventeenth century, shows how the two passions originate from the same 'sight', but with very different consequences:

There is indeed a Commotion, that arises in Mens Hearts upon the like occasion of seeing the Prosperity or Honour of another, which they think themselves capable of; that is very different from Envy, and is term'd by the Moralists Emulation;

---

[96] Burton, *The Anatomy of Melancholy*, p. 139 (Part I. Sec. 2 Memb. 3 Subs. 8).
[97] Aristotle. *Rhetoric*, p. 243 (II.x.11).
[98] Ramus, 'Of Emulation', *A Compendium of the Art of Logick*, p. 210.

& is that Vertue, which St. Paul exhorts to in those words, *Let us consider one another to provoke unto Love and to good Works*, Heb. 10.24. Which doth not like Envy covet the Reward, but the work too.⁹⁹

Envy ponders the destruction of the other who possesses a good or quality while emulation considers how it may achieve and even surpass the other's achievement. While both passions were often described as arising from very personal and originally painful experiences, the social, political and historical implications of their difference were not lost on the moralistic writers of the early modern period. All 'action' arising from either passion could have either beneficial or noxious effects on society as a whole. Given that the tangible consequences of envy were believed to be at the root of both sedition and war, the conquest of this passion was certainly important at the level even of the nation itself. For John Davies in *Microcosmos* (1603), faction was blamed on envy and malice, as was the desire to expand and conquer.¹⁰⁰ George Whetstone attributed war to envy.¹⁰¹ On the other hand, the positive consequences of emulation were seen in the historical accomplishments of every age. Emulation is the 'Spring and Rise of all Noble and Worthy Actions' according to Blagrave who cites Caesar's emulation of Alexander from Plutarch:

> And Caesar, when he read the Actions of Alexander, wept to think he was past his Age before he had done anything memorable. These great Men (Themistocles and Caesar) had no ill will to the persons they emulated; nor did they go about to lessen, but rather magnify'd their Deeds; and never griev'd that others did well, but that they had not done the like themselves.¹⁰²

Caesar 'wept' when he read 'The Actions of Alexander'. Caesar's suffering comes from reading about Alexander's exploits which Caesar feels he should have accomplished at that point in his career. Plutarch is careful to specify that Caesar's emulation is not envious. Instead, he sees Caesar's emulation as having the effect of 'magnifying' Alexander's deeds; Caesar's readerly emulation makes Alexander greater. The effect of having one's 'actions' recorded, as Alexander's were by Plutarch (and Achilles' by Homer), means that they are not only memorialized, but they serve as a model for emulation and thus, *future* action. If a 'reader' such as Caesar, a good reader,

---

[99] Blagrave, *The Nature and Mischief of Envy*, p. 7.
[100] Davies, 'Envy and Empire be Inseparate', *Microcosmos*, p. 113.
[101] George Whetstone, *The English Myrror. A Regard Wherein al estates may behold the Conquests of Envy* (1586). Whetstone argues that envy is the 'originall of Paricide, and other inhumane murders' and sees it as the motive behind all wars.
[102] Blagrave, *The Nature and Mischief of Envy*, p. 8.

intending no 'ill will' toward Alexander's name, could have the effect of *magnifying* the deeds of his predecessor, the opposite was also believed to apply: the future reader could well possess the means of diminishing the substance of an author's work.

JONSON'S *PHARMAKON*

For the early modern period, the 'envious' represented, of course, a much larger and more hetereogenous group than those diabolical people possessed with the power to 'overlook' their neighbours. They were critics and judges, spies and gossips, squinters and slanderers. While envy is often figured in the period as devouring her own heart, it is also represented with the viperous, stinging tongue emerging from her mouth, wrapped around her arms or writhing in her hair. This iconography shows envy both in its disastrous, self-destructive isolation, but also in its vindictive power to harm. Thomas Dekker's 'Envy' commands her viperous brood: 'Adders *shoote, hysse speckled Snakes... Calumny spit.*'[103] As we have seen, the idea of 'shooting' often refers to the gaze of envy in the period: the snake representing the percussive darting of both the eye and the tongue, the eyebite and the backbite. Envy is located in the imbrication of eye and tongue, and it is this that constitutes its pervasive and unstoppable power.

The Latin poet Catullus' lines on the number of kisses the poet will give his love, 'quae nec pernumerare curiosi / possint nec mala fascinare lingua' ('which shall not be counted by curious eyes / nor bewitched by an evil tongue') is translated by Ben Jonson as follows:

> That the curious may not know
> How to tell them as they flow,
> And the *envious*, when they find,
> What their number is, be pined [my emphasis].[104]

Jonson sums up Catullus' *mala fascinare lingua* in the word 'envious'. The Latin verb *fascinare*, equivalent to the Greek *baskainein*, can be translated as 'to be jealous', but also, more actively, 'to bewitch' or 'to cast the evil eye'.[105] In Jonson's translation of Catullus, the 'envious' are not only those

---

[103] Dekker, 'The Speech of Envy', *Troia-Nova Triumphans* (lines 297; 302).
[104] 'To the Same [To Celia]', *The Forrest* (vi), Herford and Simpson, vol. VII, p. 103 (lines 19–22).
[105] Walcot, *Envy and the Greeks*, p. 79. 'But 'to be jealous' is not the basic meaning of *baskainein*, which in fact means 'to bewitch' or, more specifically, 'to cast the evil eye', so that in Plato's *Phaedo*, when Socrates has been lavishly praised by a companion for his skill in argument, he utters the

who look with a fascinating eye, but also those who bewitch with an evil tongue. Casting a spell was a combination of looking with malicious intent and reciting curses or even spells or charms to harm an object. The eye and the tongue were both aspects of envy.[106]

Envy's power to deface and destroy works and reputations was believed to come, then, from the double action of the fascinating eye and the evil tongue. What Catullus writes about kisses applies as well to poems. The Neo-Latin poet Johannes Secundus understood this, when he entitled his cycle of poems the *Basia*, or *Kisses*. Those who are envious are envious of the poet's poems. What is at stake for an early modern writer is finding a means of protecting his poems from those who would search into them, count them and become infuriated when they 'see' and learn how many the poet has written. Envy represents here the malice of the reader (in Catullus' poem, the reader as rival writer) and the power of this malice to 'cast an evil eye'. The Greek lyric poet Callimachus, in the preface to the *Aetia*, rails against those evil-minded critics who have called into question the genre within which he worked, the epigram: 'Get out you deadly race of *Baskania* for the future judges verse on the basis of its art, not its length!'[107] This talismanic curse against the evil eyes of his critical readers (who judged Callimachus for not writing epic) is an attempt to protect the work apotropaically and the author's reputation in future times.

The Renaissance *topos* of attributing criticism and misreading to the malignant, over-curious or envious reader was widespread. In the English literary tradition, envy often appears as part of the poetic convention of an exordium. In their prologues and prefaces, many early modern writers employed strategies to anticipate censure and thus defend in advance their works and reputations against the misreading eye of the reader. They would regularly enjoin spectators to look well on their play and avoid

---

following warning, 'don't be boastful in case some evil eye (*baskania*) overturns the subsequent argument... the Latin verb *fascinare* being the equivalent of the Greek *baskainein*' (pp. 79–80).

[106] Matthew W. Dickie notes with regard to the classical tradition that 'it is by no means certain that when a Greek or a Roman attributed some misfortune to the action of *Baskania, phthonos, fascination, invidia*, or *livor*, he invariably imagined that the harm done had been effected by the *eyes* of the envious party... we must be careful not to assume that... the notion of the power of the eyes to harm was always to the fore.' Matthew W. Dickie, 'Invidia', *The Classical Review*, n.s. 49 (1999), 363–4; p. 364.

[107] Cited in Walcot, *Envy and the Greeks*, p. 79. 'In another epigram (21, verse 4) Callimachus wrote, as it were, his own epitaph, proudly proclaiming that his own song was 'stronger than the evil eye (*baskania*)'. *Ibid.*, p. 78.

judging it, as Sir Philip Sidney writes, with 'severer eyes'.[108] They would urge their reader not to envy the writer his due by perverting the meaning of the work, nor gaze with such curiosity as to uncover strange meanings or monstrous conceits unintended by the author. The Prologue of Thomas Dekker's *The Wonder of a Kingdom* (1636) speaks for the 'Poet', who 'knows what Iudges sit to Doome each Play, / (The Over-curious Critick, or the Wise) / the one with squint; 'Tother with Sunn-like eyes, / Shootes through each scaene'.[109] In his *Defence of Rhyme* (1603), Samuel Daniel refers to critics who do nothing but 'deprave', or distort, the texts they read.[110] George Chapman writes in 'The Preface to the Reader' to his translation of Homer (1611): 'I know, the curious, and envious, will never sit downe satisfied. A man may go over and over, till he come over and over; and his paines be onely his recompence.'[111] John Harington is particularly vehement in his description of the readers of his time:

> [W]e live in such a time in which nothing can escape the envious tooth and back-biting tongue of an impure mouth, and wherein every blind corner hath a squint-eyed Zoilus that can look aright upon no man's doings (yea, sure there be some that will not stick to call Hercules himself a dastard, because, forsooth, he fought with a club and not at the rapier and dagger).[112]

Harington concludes his harangue claiming that 'knowledge hath no foe but the ignorant'.[113] From just this sampling we see that readers are described as having eyes that 'squint' and 'shoot' or 'deprave', literally, bend what they see out of shape. They are also perceived as never satisfied, ignorant and sharp-toothed, implying calumny and slander. According to Heidi Brayman Hackel, such prefaces often represent envious and carping critics 'as physically monstrous: Thomas Lodge calls them "squinteyed asses", and John Banister attributes to them "the tongue of the horsleech, the eye of the cockatrice, the talents of a tyger"'.[114] I would argue that these grotesque representations can be seen as the literary equivalent of an obscene and fascinating apotropaic gesture. They represent a literary

---

[108] Sir Philip Sidney, 'To My Deare Ladie and Sister, the Countess of Pembroke', *The Countess of Pembrokes Arcadia* (London, 1590), sig. A3ᵛ.
[109] Thomas Dekker, *The Wonder of a Kingdom* in *The Dramatic Works of Thomas Dekker*, ed. Fredson Bowers (Cambridge: Cambridge University Press, 1958), p. 577 (lines 2–5).
[110] Samuel Daniel, Preface, *A Defence of Ryme* (London, 1603), n.p.
[111] George Chapman, 'Preface to the Reader', *The Iliads of Homer, Prince of Poets* (London, 1611), sig. A4ᵛ. The original 1609 edition does not include this expanded prefatory material.
[112] John Harington, 'A Preface, Or Rather a Briefe Apologie of Poetrie', *Orlando Furioso in English Heroical Verse* (London, 1591), sig. iiᵛ.
[113] Ibid., sig. iiᵛ.   [114] Hackel, *Reading Material*, p. 123.

equivalent to a kind of 'amuletic logic' in which like cures like.[115] Of course, the reader's gaze could not be 'cured' simply by calling him (or her) ignorant or an 'ass'. This is not the point. The point is that if we understand that this conventional *topos* possesses roots in a certain kind of apotropaic or prophylactic charm, we may begin to understand certain literary gestures (particularly those of Ben Jonson) in the period as rooted in this kind of logic.

Just as epics invoked the poetic Muse in order to aid the poet in undertaking the work, so, too, the appearance of envy in the exordium of a number of Renaissance poems and prefaces is conventional, and one could argue, the inverse of the poetic invocation to the Muse. In these *exordia*, envy is called forth and exorcized, at least nominally, in the poet's paratextual remarks. The writer can be seen to portray himself not only as having given birth to his work, but also as a parent protecting his child from the gaze of strangers. In the prefatory poem to *The Shepheards Calendar*, entitled 'To His Booke', Spenser speaks to his book with the following words:

> Goe, little Booke: thy selfe present,
> As child whose parent is unkent,
> To him that is the president
> Of noblesse and of chevalrie:
> And if that Envy barke at thee,
> As sure it will, for succoure flee
> Under the shadow of his wing.[116]

The poet sends his book, like a child, into a hostile world where Envy, in the form of the reader, lies in wait. The writer instructs his book to seek the protective 'wing' of the one who is 'the president / Of noblesse and of chevalrie', the poem's dedicatee and patron, Sir Philip Sidney. Under the aegis of Sidney, the book may enter the world. Spenser's line, 'If that Envy barke at thee', conjures up the image of a monstrous dog, the animal traditionally associated with envy in the medieval period and which will become transformed in Spenser's own Blatant Beast in *The Faerie Queene*.[117]

Implicit in Spenser's prefatory poem, the written word, from the hand of its creator to its reception by the dedicatee, is almost sure to encounter

---

[115] Siebers, *The Mirror of Medusa*, p. 8.
[116] Edmund Spenser, 'To His Booke', *The Shepheards Calendar* in *The Faerie Queene[e]: The Shepheards Calendar* (London, 1611), sig. [A1ᵛ] (lines 1–7).
[117] For the first mention of the Blatant Beast, see *The Faerie Queene*, *ibid.*, p. 303 (Book VI, Canto 1, 7).

monstrous 'Envy'. Yet, the book does not stand ready to battle envy. No defenses are posited, no weapons described. Rather, the poet encourages the book to *flee* and find refuge with a powerful member of the literary court. Moreover, he instructs his book to introduce itself as the child of an unknown (but also illiterate) father and to say (*if asked*) that it was only a shepherd swain who sang the poems while he was feeding his flock. Wendy Wall argues that the poem opens by portraying 'the text as a bastard, a wandering poem whose author-father is 'unkent' or unknown. Yet, she notes that 'the query of origins concludes with the writer's promise to 'name' himself and thus rescue this poem from bastardy after the text has been well-received – when it is 'past jeopardee'.[118] The problem of bastardy is surely implied in these opening lines, but the poem never states that the author, 'Immerito', plans on revealing himself. He simply states that when the child is 'past' the monstrous barking Envy, he should return: 'Come tell me what was said of mee, / And I will send more after thee.' The child is clearly not a bastard, he is only told to 'present' himself as one. I would argue that the appearance of bastardy, base-birth and shame are all aspects in a conventional ruse to camouflage the value of a very precious thing. The exhortation to flee and find refuge is another version of the parental advice to avoid direct inquiry and to obfuscate if pressed to reveal himself. The poet anticipates the hostile gaze and warped judgement by creating a picture of himself and his creation as low and unenviable in an effort to deflect the envy of the reader through denial and denegation. The preface can thus be seen as doubly protected by its apotropaic signature: 'Immerito'. Spenser's care to address envy is evident again in the 'Letter to Raleigh' appended to *The Faerie Queene*. In the 'Letter', as in the prefatory poem to *The Shepheards Calendar*, Spenser implicitly follows up on Aristotle's assertion that people are not envious of those who lived in the past to choose a hero safe from envy:

I chose the historie of King *Arthure*, as most fit for the excellencie of his person, beeing made famous by many mens former workes, and also furthest from the daunger of envie, and suspicion of present time. In which I have followed all the antique Poets historicall ... By example of which excellent Poets, I labour to pourtraict in Arthure.[119]

---

[118] Wendy Wall, *The Imprint of Gender: Authorship and Publication in the English Renaissance* (Ithaca: Cornell University Press, 1993), p. 236.
[119] Edmund Spenser, 'A Letter of the Authors', *The Faerie Queene* in *The Faerie Queen[e]: The Shepheards Calendar* (London, 1611), pp. 1–1ᵛ.

Spenser avoids the envious gaze of the contemporary reader by placing his epic in a mythical British past. His hero is a legendary King whose antiquity and greatness place him comfortably out of the reach of envy.

So, in keeping with the literary commonplaces set out by the great classical rhetoricians and poets, and conscientiously imitated by the scholars and poets of the Renaissance and Enlightenment, an invocation and banishment of envy, formulaic in nature, had become an almost required feature of any learned work by Jonson's time. But while he pays a similar debt, such concerns are endemic for him, informing the substance of his work in a fashion that distinguishes it from other writers. Jonson's prefaces invariably resonate with the recurrence of envy, in some other form, throughout the rest of the work. It is interesting, for example, that not only does the Preface to *The Masque of Blacknesse* enumerate the dangers Envy and Ignorance pose to the poet's work, but the *plot* turns upon the fact that poets have begrudged and envied black women any praise of their beauty. In the 'sequel' to *Blacknesse*, *The Masque of Beauty*, performed three years later on Twelfth Night 1608, the main villain turns out to be envious Night, whose anger at whiteness fuels the plot. Jonson prefaces the masque by indicating the 'limits' imposed upon him by the Queen to write a sequel to the previous masque:

> it was her Highnesse pleasure... and command, that I should thinke on some fit presentment, which should *answere the former*, still keeping them the same persons, the daughters of NIGER, but their beauties *varied*, according to promise, and their time of absence excus'd, with foure more added to their number [my emphasis].[120]

Four (added) sisters are kept prisoner on an island by the sorceress, who wishes to revenge herself upon the original twelve black sisters from *The Masque of Blacknesse*, who had, by the time of the second masque ('according to promise') blanched themselves in moonlight and a substance called 'rosmarine':

> Night *envi'd*, as done^e in her despight,
> And (mad to see an Aethiope washed white)
> Thought to prevent in these; lest men should deeme
> Her colour, if thus chang'd, of small esteeme.
> And so, by *malice*, and her *magicke*, tost
> The Nymphes at sea, as they were almost lost,
> Till, on an Iland, they by chance arriv'd,

---

[120] Ben Jonson, *The Masque of Beauty*, Herford and Simpson, vol. VII, p. 181 (lines 2–8).

> That^f floted in the mayne; where, yet, she had giv'd
> Them so, in charmes of darknesse, as no might
> Should loose them thence, but their chang'd Sisters sight.

e Because they were before of her complexion.
f To give authoritie to this part of our fiction, Plinie had chap. 95. of his 2. book. *Nat. Hist. de Insulis fluctuantibus.* & Card. lib. I. *de rerum variet.* cap. 7. reports one to be in his time knowne, in the Lake of Loumond, in Scotland, to let passe that of Delos, &c.[121]

The Renaissance association of envy with witchcraft finds an apt characterization in Jonson's masque witch, Night. Her malice and her magic go hand in hand. The envious witch has the power to conjure up 'charmes of darknesse' to hold the masquers enthralled. The only way for the charm to be broken, significantly enough, is through 'their chang'd Sisters sight'. The spell placed upon the nymphs by envy may only be broken by the *sight* of, or the vision of the whitened sisters. The logic involved in Night's spell is based on the homeopathic principle in which like cures like. These previously 'cured' sisters become a cure for the remaining (magically imprisoned) black sisters. Yet, the phrase 'their chang'd Sisters sight' is ambiguous. It may imply that the almost iconic *image* of the whitened sisters will break the charm of darkness surrounding the nymphs (and permeating them). Yet, it could also be read as meaning that one active *look* from the eyes of the whitened sisters could undo the charm placed upon them by envious Night.

This emphasis on 'sight' is key to our understanding the implications of the charm because the changed sisters serve as cure in exactly the same way the Medusa is said to poison. Even the ancient sources for the story of Perseus and Medusa differed as to whether a glimpse of the Medusa could turn one into stone or whether the gorgon had to look at you and cross your gaze. This same issue is evident in Jonson's ambiguous phrasing concerning the breaking of Night's charm. The 'blanched' sisters could well be 'Medusas' imported by the poet from the previous masque to baffle the witch of the present masque. In other words, Jonson has created, through his play on whiteness and blackness in these two masques a kind of narrative *pharmakon*.[122] The change from blackness to whiteness in the

---

[121] *Ibid.*, pp. 183–4 (lines 80–9 and marginal notes *e* and *f*).
[122] I am referring here to Jacques Derrida's discussion of Plato's use in the *Phaedrus* of the Greek word *pharmakon* as both 'remedy' and 'poison' (among other things) to describe the invention of writing. I cite from Barbara Johnson's translation of Derrida's original French: 'The common translation of *pharmakon* by remedy [*remède*] – a beneficient drug – is not, of course, inaccurate... Its translation by 'remedy' nonetheless erases, in going outside the Greek language, the other pole reserved in the word *pharmakon*. It cancels out the resources of ambiguity and makes more difficult, if not

first masque serves as a kind of cure for the envy of poets who slander black skin; by becoming white, the Ethiopian princesses can baffle the gossip and tales poets have spread denigrating the colour of their skin over the centuries. In other words, it is not a colour that is important, but rather the change from one to another which serves as an apotropaic charm. It is the transformation from one thing to another that is curative and protective, not any of the original elements in themselves. Yet, in the second masque, *The Masque of Beauty*, this cure of blackness is hinted at as the opposite of a cure. The change to whiteness is in fact a poison, the drug of artifice and ephemerality. We see that the change to whiteness in *Beauty* lays the emphasis on 'change'. Even though the change is justified as being for the 'better', it is nevertheless one more turn of the wheel of colour, one more narrative trick, one more way to write one more masque for a Queen who wished them 'the same persons' but 'varied'.[123] And this poisonous change, this variation, is represented by 'their chang'd Sisters sight', the image of the Medusa. It is Night, who in her dark constancy appears less terrifying than the perpetual motion machine of women chasing after whiteness or turning each other white.

It will be made increasingly clear in the following chapters how much of Jonson's work is in some fashion fuelled by envy. Sometimes, envy is literally embodied in a masque character such as Night in *The Masque of Beauty*, Hecate or Terror in *The Masque of Queenes*. The envious character provides the blocking force with which the plot must resolve itself. On the other hand, envy is projected by the writer onto the reader against whom, or in response to whom, the author must create a defence in the form of marginalia, explanations and citation of ancient authorities. In both the quarto and the folio edition of certain masques of Jonson's, notes appear in the margins horizontally across from the footnote marker in the text and, in many cases, surround the text thus interrupting or breaking it up. At the point where the reader's eye encounters the letter marker, it moves from the text either directly to the left (if the text is on the left-hand page) or right margin (which sometimes flows over the border and under) in order to read the note, before continuing its journey through the main body of the text. In my own quotation of Jonson's passage from *The Masque of Blacknesse*, I have placed, out of formatting necessity, the marginal notes

---

impossible, an understanding of the context ... the King's reply presupposed that the effectiveness of the *pharmakon* can be reversed: it can worsen the ill instead of remedy it.' Jacques Derrida, 'Plato's Pharmacy', *Dissemination,* trans. Barbara Johnson (London: Continuum, 1981), pp. 99–100.

[123] Ben Jonson, *The Masque of Beauty*, Herford and Simpson, vol. VII, p. 181 (lines 6 and 7).

under the main text, but the reader must always imagine them directly beside the main text, distracting and interrupting the eye in the course of its reading the body of the text. The superscription is a signifier of the appearance of the readerly gaze upon the writer's text. It provides the site for the silent vocalization of the questions (more or less innocuous) implicitly asked by the reader while reading. It is thus the site where the reader appears in the imagination of the writer in the act of writing, or in the act of rereading. Note *e* above, for instance, is a response to the implied question 'Why was Night envious?' The question strangely is neither a sign of readerly perplexity nor a challenge. In fact, the marginal note here is an attempt by the masque writer to defend his narrative design in the face of the constraints (he feels) have been placed upon him. He needs to explain why Night was envious in order to help the reader remember the story from the previous masque and justify the narrative thread he has created between the two masques. The note, oddly enough, marks a gap, precisely the gap between two masques performed three years apart and now, in writerly retrospection, embodied in an interruption in the text. The text is interrupted in order to be sewn back together again by way of explanation and justification. Note *f*, which gives 'authoritie', can also be read in response to an imagined question: 'What is your classical source for the existence of this island?' But, again, even while the footnote marker implies a curious reader somewhere, waiting for explanation, justification or just more information, the footnote marks the moment that the eye of the writer turns back upon itself and looks at itself. The writer derives immense pleasure in interrupting his text at various moments. This pleasure is a form of self-display. It is also obviously a visual pleasure for the writer who imagines the impression the text will produce in the reader's mind as he is creating it. The split between the writing and the reading self creates a knot in the text. The text folds back upon itself, making a loop from the main body to the marginal note back to the place where it first left off. The self-sting of Envy's snake, emerging from Envy's mouth and then stinging itself, may here be likened to this fold of the text, heralded by the superscription. These letters in superscript are just one, typographically very visual, symptom of the writer's perception of his own curious gaze upon his work. The writing of prefaces, descriptions, commentary and marginal notes are in response to what the writer sees as the outcropping of questions and desires on the part of the reader, but it must be clear that these signs of curiosity emerge out of the writer himself.

The Jonsonian process of literary creation therefore involves a split in the writer, who turns his gaze upon his own text in anticipation of the gaze of the reader and proceeds to defend the text against his own envy. For, like the *pharmakon*, this writerly envy is both the remedy and the poison. It is at the origin of more writing and at the same time the constant discovery of lack. This cleavage in the authorial task, between creation and judgement, manifests itself most visually in the printed masque. The digression to authority or justification in turn engenders the marginalia and commentary that flows around the text and which, in turn, serves to build a monument. At the same time, it could well be argued that such specularity is one of the hallmarks of the writing self. In *The Mirror and the Text* (1989), Lucien Dällenbach cites a fragment from André Gide's *Journal* in which he describes the process of *watching* himself in the act of writing:

> I am writing on the small piece of furniture of Anna Shackleton's that was in my bedroom in the rue de Commailles. That's where I worked; I liked it because I could see myself writing in the double mirror of the desk above the block I was writing on. I looked at myself after each sentence; my reflexion spoke and listened to me, kept me company and sustained my enthusiasm.[124]

Gide looks at himself 'in between each sentence', seeing the reflection in the mirror keeping him 'company'. Four centuries before, Sir Philip Sidney, in Sonnet 34 of *Astrophil and Stella*, records a dialogue between his writing self and an objecting voice, censuring the poet in his poetic enterprise; the poet reprimands himself: 'Peace, foolish wit, with wit my wit is mard. / Thus write I while I doubt to write.'[125] The irony, of course, is that out of this 'marring' of wit emerges a sonnet, a miniature monument of a self-study of the writer in the process of writing. Ben Jonson's specularity is therefore not new to him, nor is this specularity unique in the way the oscillation between a writing and either narcissistic (like Gide) or judging (like Sidney) self creates a fertile field of the imagination, either by holding the poet in a state of 'fervour' or, which may not be so different, in a state of 'friction' with writer and writer as reader. As we have noted with regard to the ancient notion of *aemulatio*, a certain competion or strife was a necessary condition for creativity. I would suggest that Jonson creates the conditions for such strife, a situation to 'whet' his own wit, in the figure not of a gentle reader, but an envious one.

---

[124] Lucien Dällenbach, *The Mirror in the Text*, trans. Jeremy Whiteley and Emma Hughes (Cambridge: Polity Press, 1989). 'C'était là que je travaillais; je l'aimais, parce que dans la double glace du secrétaire, au-dessus de la tablette où j'écrivais, je me voyais écrire; *entre chaque phrase je me regardais*; mon image me parlait, m'écoutait, me tenait compagnie, me maintenait en état de ferveur.' Lucien Dällenbach, *Le Récit spéculaire: essai sur la mise en abyme* (Paris: Editions du Seuil, 1977), p. 71.

[125] Sir Philip Sidney, *Astrophil and Stella* in *Sir Philip Sidney* ed. Katharine Duncan-Jones (Oxford: Oxford University Press, 1989), p. 166 (lines 11–12).

CHAPTER 3

Defacement: anxiety and the Jonsonian imagination

> COTTA. Mean time, give order, that his books be burn't,
> To the *Ædiles*.
>
> (*Sejanus, His Fall*, 1603)[1]

The Masque of Blacknesse marks a decisive moment in Ben Jonson's career. It is the first time that Jonson collaborated with Inigo Jones and Queen Anne to whom the masque is dedicated and whose name 'ANNE' appears prominently on the title page of the Quarto in 1608. The poet wrote a masque 'Of Blacknesse': 'because', explains the writer to his reader, 'it was her Majesties will, to have them *Blackmores* at first'.[2] The masque, shaped in part by this constraint of the Queen's, drawn and constructed by a new set-designer, a rival artist, marks a crisis, as well, in Jonson's perspective on 'envy'. In the preface to the masque, Jonson meditates on the problematic ephemerality of the genre in which he is writing and describes envy as *defacement*:

The honor, and splendor of these *spectacles* was such in the performance, as could those hours have lasted, this of mine, now, had been a most unprofitable worke. But (when it is the fate, even of the greatest, and most absolute births, to need, and borrow a life of posteritie) little had been done to the studie of *magnificence* in these, if presently with the rage of the people, who (as a part of greatnesse) are privileged by custome, to deface their *carkasses*, the *spirits* had also perished. In dutie, therefore, to that *Majestie*, who gave them their authoritie, and grace; and, no lesse than the most royall of predecessors, deserves eminent celebration for these solemnities: I adde this *later hand* to redeeme them as well from Ignorance, as Envie, two common evills, the one of *censure*, the other of *oblivion*.[3]

---

[1] Ben Jonson, *Sejanus, His Fall*, Herford and Simpson, vol. IV, p. 408 (Act III, lines 465–8).
[2] Ben Jonson, *The Masque of Blacknesse*, Herford and Simpson, vol. VII, p. 169 (lines 21–2).
[3] *Ibid.*, (lines 1–14).

In these, the first lines of the preface, Jonson seeks to justify the publication of a court masque. The preface is complex syntactically and rich in innuendo.[4] The poet refers to his work in banking terms and elliptically suggests what benefits 'that Majestie, who gave them their authoritie, and grace' will accrue as a result of the poet's decision to publish the masque. These issues of profit and posterity will be considered later.[5] What is striking here is the anxiety the poet expresses about the fate of the spectacles' 'spirits'. This concern is conveyed particularly in the way he refers to the custom of the masquing aristocracy to pull down the stage-sets at the end of one night's performance. The ephemerality of this art, which lives for only a few hours, serves as a vehicle for the poet to reflect on poetic *defacement*: '[I]f presently with the rage of the people, who (as a part of greatness) are privileged by custome, to *deface* their carkasses, the *spirits had also perished*' (my emphasis). Shakespeare described this phenomenon of physical and symbolic ruin in *The Tempest* as leaving 'not a rack behind'.[6] Both Shakespeare and Jonson play on tearing down the architectural frame, the 'rack' or the 'carkass' and tearing up the body. While he may only be describing a masque decor, the painted slats, the backdrop or costumes, the poet uses the word 'carkasses' to describe the physical 'body' of the masque.[7] In this Neo-platonic metaphor, repeated later in the preface to *Hymenaei*, the poet's part of the masque, his 'invention', is perceived as the 'soule'.[8] In *The Masque of Blacknesse*, the defacement of corpses is perceived as a kind of state-authorized barbarity like the mutilation of the body of a criminal (or martyr) after death. Jonson may be seen trying to mitigate this image of defilement with the parenthetical remarks: 'as a part of greatnesse' and 'privileged by custom'. Nevertheless, the idea of defacement rests in all its negative and irreligious horror.

---

[4] Richard C. Newton, among others, has discussed the difficulties of Jonsonian syntax: 'One of the most notable characteristics of Jonson's poetic personality ... is his peculiar habit of making negative statements and excluding possibilities and interpretations from his verse, when to all appearances he either is or ought to be making positive assertions and enriching their complexity and depth. Sometimes this habit is quite obvious; at other times and rather more continuously it is unobtrusively imbedded in the texture of the verse.' Richard Newton, 'Ben/Jonson: The Poet in the Poems' in Alvin Kernan (ed.), *Two Renaissance Mythmakers: Christopher Marlowe and Ben Jonson* (Baltimore: The Johns Hopkins University Press, 1977), pp. 165–95; p. 166.

[5] In Chapter 4.   [6] William Shakespeare, *The Tempest* (IV.i.156).

[7] He may also be describing the physical *body* of the Queen, who may be said to have 'defaced' herself in wearing black make-up on her face and arms. Dudley Carleton writes that the blackface on the Queen and her ladies 'became them nothing so well as their red and white, and you cannot imagine a more ugly Sight, then a Troop of lean-cheek'd Moors'. He adds that when the Spanish ambassader kissed the Queen's hand 'there was Danger it would have left a Mark on his Lips'. Cited in Herford and Simpson, vol. X, p. 448.

[8] Ben Jonson, *Hymenaei*, Herford and Simpson, vol. VII, p. 209 (line 7).

This destruction becomes a metaphor for the extinction of all traces of the masque's and, by extension, the Prince's, and by further extension, the poet's 'magnificence'. The threat of the spirit or 'soule' perishing, of being erased along with the decor, provides the author with the justification and drive to comment, describe, add notes, surround his text with fragments from sources and authorities and print and publish his work, a process he describes as adding a 'later hand'.[9]

While the two sentences which make up the bulk of these lines are (most certainly intentionally) complex, Jonson clearly draws an analogy between the 'rage of the people', which defaces 'carkasses', and the 'ignorance' and 'envy' (of the people) which 'censure' and consign to 'oblivion' ('spirits'). The 'rage' that moves the courtiers is equivalent to the 'envy' that moves the censurer: the official, court censor, surely, but also the future critical reader of the masque text now in print. 'Ignorance' is represented in tandem with 'Envie', implicitly possessing equivalent active powers of ruin.[10] Jonson's comparison of the fate of bodies and the fate of poetic invention in this preface gives us a glimpse into his definition

---

[9] Jonson's reference to 'that Majestie, who gave them their authoritie, and grace' could refer to King James I, who as the primary spectator of the Queen's masque confers upon it that authority that belongs supremely to him. The subsequent reference to 'the most royal of predecessors', referring to Queen Elizabeth, would again imply the King as the successor of Elizabeth I. A few lines later, as well, Jonson refers explicitly to Queen Anne: '*her* Majesties will'. Nevertheless, the term 'that Majestie' in the preface is highly ambiguous. It is Anne's name that appears on the title page of the Quarto as performer ('personated'); her name also appears on the title page of the holograph of *The Masque of Queenes* as well, with the adjective 'absolute' attached; however, the subsequent 'dedication' of this same masque is to Prince Henry. Furthermore, the reference to Elizabeth I is fascinatingly ambiguous, as she could be considered the 'royal predecessor' of Anne *as* '*Queen*'. This reading is even more possible in light of the fact that, as Ann Rosalind Jones and Peter Stallybrass have noted: 'Elizabeth's old clothes were also recirculated as masque costumes' (p. 26) and there was every chance that Anne was dressed in her predecessor's clothing for the masque performance. While I believe that 'Anne' may well be the most immediate object referred to in this preface, I do think that Jonson was clearly interested in leaving ambiguous which royal he is referring to as a means of flattering both sovereigns at the same time, by keeping the gender of 'Majestie' ambiguous. For this reason I have chosen to use the more neuter word 'Prince' to refer to the symbolic possessor of monarchical power. See Ann Rosalind Jones and Peter Stallybrass, *Renaissance Clothing and the Materials of Memory* (Cambridge: Cambridge University Press, 2000).

[10] Garret A. Sullivan describes the slumped figure of Oblivion in the frontispiece to Raleigh's *History of the World*. He is: 'phlegmatic, inactive, lethargic. The image compellingly represents a notion of forgetfulness as *inactivity*. Moreover, that inactivity is effeminizing, the male figure having fallen into an emasculated, Circean lassitude, his prone body attesting to the loss of the rectitude (both physical and ethical) that is associated with idealized masculinity. In contrast, History's is a noticeably active body; she literally steps on Death and Oblivion' (my emphasis). According to Sullivan, Oblivion represents 'a notion of forgetfulness as *inactivity*'. This image of Oblivion can usefully be placed in contrast to Jonson's conception of both Ignorance and Envy. While Oblivion is inactive, for Jonson, Ignorance and Envy – the active *causes* of Oblivion – are both capable of destroying, ruining and defacing. See Garret A. Sullivan, Jr, *Memory and Forgetting in English Renaissance Drama: Shakespeare, Marlowe, Webster* (Cambridge: Cambridge University Press, 2005), p. 32.

of envy and its power. Censure defaces and oblivion is, in some respects, the final degree of defacement, the ruining or blotting out of something to the extent that it ceases to be recognizable. In the poet's representation of envy's effects on poetic 'spirit', 'Envie' has the power to deface poetic invention.

I would argue that to fully appreciate Jonson's anxiety of reception and his investment in controlling it, we should see his writing as propelled by this fear of the 'defacement' of the text by the reader. While defacement refers to the anxiety concerning the fate of his *ephemera*, the masques and plays, it also refers, in a second stage, to the writer's apprehension that the text will be misread, misunderstood and, as a result, deformed. What defaces the text, within the Jonsonian phantasmagoria, is ignorance and envy. The play or masque can be forgotten, but, even if it survives, it can also be destroyed through misreading and slander. Malicious envy, even unintended by the ignorant, begrudges the author his due by dismembering the text's meaning. The courtiers are 'privileged by custome' to tear away; the reader too is privileged by custom to think as he pleases, judge, censure and rip apart, metaphorically and even physically. Defacement therefore refers to an aggregation of authorial concerns. These include the fear of the *physical destruction* of the authorial work (at the fore in Jonson's preface to *Blacknesse*), but also harm to the meaning of the work through *censorship* as well as damage to poetic reputation and fame by *slanderous misreading*.

As we have seen above, Francis Bacon in his essay, 'Of Envy', describes the physical harm that can be caused by the 'Stroke' or 'Percussion' of the 'Act of *Envy*', which he compares to 'an Ejaculation, or Irradiation of the Eye'.[11] Bacon's early modern description of the physical violence of the envious gaze gives us a tangible image of the metaphorical harm caused by misreading as Jonson imagined it. In the same way the 'envious and foul disease' of smallpox defaces the visage of one of Jonson's patrons, so too the malice and ignorance of the reader metaphorically defaces poetic creation.[12] In 'An Execration upon *Vulcan*', the god of fire is described as able to destroy with his burning looks, taking: 'envious care and paine, / To ruine any issue of the braine …' with the poet wondering if 'I had deserv'd … thy *consuming lookes* / Perhaps, to have beene burned

---

[11] Bacon, *Essayes*, p. 40.
[12] Ben Jonson, 'An Epigram. To the small Poxe', *Underwood* (xxxiv), Herford and Simpson, vol. VIII, p. 188 (line 1).

with my bookes' (my emphasis).¹³ The 'fire', which broke out in a corner of Jonson's desk, becomes yet another opportunity for the poet to rail at length, but also to reflect upon the nature of the forces of defacement and on the fragility and metamorphic nature of his 'issue' or posterity. Similarly, 'envious censors' are invited 'with their broadest eyes' to 'look through and through me', like the narrator in Scève's *Delie*, caught in the blazing gaze of his Basilisk lover.¹⁴ Jonson describes the 'consuming lookes' and the 'broad eyes' of the envious in the same violently physical terms he uses in the preface to *The Masque of Blacknesse*. The poet imagines himself 'burned' at the stake as a blaspheming heretic; he imagines the censors, in an age before the X-ray, as thrusting steel 'through and through me'. These images of the defacement of the body are one early modern writer's representation of the fate of his work at the hands of the reader. Without a doubt, this image of the reader is a pessimistic and dark one. It is this vision of the reader whom he seeks, but intends to control, that propels the poet to extend the talismanic and prophylactic function of the ritual exorcism of envy in contemporary prefaces right into the text itself, creating characters and inserting passages whose function is to protect and defend the text from the envious reading eye. And, while looks consume and shoot darts, so too can speech. Slander blots and defaces the poet's work through calumny, detraction, defamation, denunciation, gossip, rumour, evil-speaking and censure. Jonson writes in an ode 'To Himself':

> Are all th'*Aonian* springs
> Dri'd up? lyes *Thespia* wast?
> Doth *Clarius* Harp want strings,
> That not a Nymph now sings?
> Or droop they as disgrac't,
> To see their Seats and bowers *by chattring Pies defac't*? [my emphasis]¹⁵

The noise, the tongues and the 'chatter' of censurers have the same effect on poetry as censuring looks. Both are sources of defacement.

---

[13] Ben Jonson, 'An Execration upon *Vulcan*', *Underwood* (xliii), Herford and Simpson, vol. VIII, p. 203 (lines 13–14; 17–18).
[14] Ben Jonson, Prologue to *Every Man Out of His Humour*, Herford and Simpson, vol. III, p. 430 (lines 62–3).
[15] Ben Jonson, 'An Ode. To himself', *Underwood* (xxiii), Herford and Simpson, vol. VIII, p. 174 (lines 7–12).

CORRUPTIBLE RELICS[16]

The idea of defacement and the action of defacing have a rich and complex history in the sixteenth and seventeenth centuries.[17] First, it implies physical damage. In a person, it is the disfiguring and marring of beauty; in architecture, the ruin and destruction of cities and monuments. In a book, the ink blot, the addition of interlinear lines, notes scribbled in the margins or, as we see in copies of certain texts of Jonson's and other early modern readers, the equivalent of a second text, inhabiting the interstices of the previous one.[18] This may be seen as 'defacement' in its most benign form, the marks of careful and interested reading. The branding of books with ownership marks is another form of harmless defacement, although behind both kinds of marks is a tacit assertion on the part of the reader of their possession of both the book and its contents. Of course, this kind of *appropriation* of one person's work by another was and is viewed sociably as a type of mutual cooperation on the part of both author and reader. Yet, this cooperation is not without its darker side, for, in a certain light, the act of marking up a page, the sign of close engagement, can also be seen as evidence of a certain strange desire to master and tame the contents of the book, making it submit to the logic of the reader. Even less benign are forms of censorship such as 'bisking', in which a passage has been cancelled by overprinting with an inked block. The erasure, 'damasking' and cancellation of former marks and traces all serve to mar the appearance of the text or traduce its original integrity.[19] Ernest Gilman describes the

---

[16] Peter D. McDonald describes Jerome McGann's *words* given at a conference on 24 March 1982 as 'only the *corruptible relics* of extraordinarily complex and always ephemeral occasions'. In 'Implicit Structures and Explicit Interactions: Pierre Bourdieu and the History of the Book', *The Library*, Sixth Series, 19.2 (1997), 105–21; p. 105.

[17] According to the *OED*: '*Deface*, v. 1. To mar the face, features, or appearance of; to spoil or ruin the figure, form or beauty of; to disfigure. 2. To destroy, demolish, lay waste. 3. To blot out, obliterate, efface (writing, marks) b. *fig.* To blot out of existence, memory, thought, etc.; to extinguish. 4. To destroy the reputation or credit of; to descredit, defame.'

[18] Robert C. Evans, David McPherson, James A. Riddell and Stanley Stewart have all described how Jonson read and responded to other writers, using marginal flowers and hands to point to passages of particular interest as well as adding marginalia, which included commentaries, notes and even diagrams. See Robert C. Evans, *Jonson, Lipsius and the Politics of Renaissance Stoicism* (Wakefield: Longwood Academic, 1992); James A. Riddell and Stanley Stewart, *Jonson's Spenser: Evidence and Historical Criticism* (Pittsburgh: Duquesne University Press, 1995); David McPherson, 'Jonson's Library and Marginalia: An Annotated Catalogue', *Studies in Philology, Texts and Studies Series*, 71.5 (1974).

[19] The importance of preserving this original integrity or 'wholeness' is evident in Humphrey Moseley's preface to his monumental edition of the complete works of Beaumont and Fletcher. The editor claims that his edition (London, 1647) is both exhaustive and accurate: 'Now you have both All that was *Acted*, and all that was not, even the perfect full Originalls without the

iconoclastic defacement, not only of images, but also of books after the dissolution of the monasteries in the 1530s: 'idolatrous books, if they were not destroyed, were...liable to be *defaced* ... methodically *scoured* of both images and text' (my emphasis).[20] Apart from such ideological cleansing of books, the process simply of printing a book exposed the text to defacement, as authors and printers were well aware. Typographical and orthographical errors in the printing of works, especially in a printing-house such as William Stansby's where Jonson's 1616 Folio was printed, was a well-known phenomenon:

The complexity of the conditions of production in Stansby's printing-house has implications that bear upon the printing history of Jonson's *Workes*. The evidence is also extensively corroborated. Some authors, it is true, were less than complimentary...Thomas Coryate commented that 'many errors have been committed ... Most of which ascribe I pray thee (candid Reader) to the negligence of the Corrector, and not to my unskilfulnesse' ... Likewise, John Hull offered no errata but shifted responsibility for the errors: 'Gentle Reader, there be faults escaped in the Printing, wee doe intreate you not to impute them, to the ignorance of the Author, but the haste of the Printer.'[21]

Mark Bland points out that Stansby or his corrector would indeed take responsibility for some 'faults ... committed by me in the Printing'.[22] At other times, the printer and publisher would acknowledge mistakes, but justify them: 'some things have escaped, others beene mistaken, partly by the absence of him who penned this Treatise, partly by the unleageablenesse [*sic*] of his hand in the written copy'.[23] Jonson, on the other hand, could comport himself as the model author in relation to his printer:

He lived a few hundred yards from the printing-house, and so revises could have been delivered (as they were for Purchas) when he was unable to attend. What is evident from the quantity of fastidious proof-corrections made from the revise as stop-press corrections is that Jonson was intimately involved in the production of his *Workes* and that he proof-read closely. It is both the thoroughness with which he amended the punctuation that argues for Jonson's involvement, and the exacting and varied ways in which punctuation marks were exploited for their dramatic

---

least mutilation' (sig. A2**ᵛ). See Line Cottegnies, 'Modernité du XVIIème siècle: la naissance de l'écrivain en Angleterre', in *Confluences* VI: *Ecriture(s) et modernité* (Nanterre: Université Paris - X Nanterre, 1993), pp. 57–76; pp. 74–5.

[20] Ernest B. Gilman, *Iconoclasm and Poetry in the English Reformation: Down Went Dagon* (Chicago: University of Chicago Press, 1986), p. 11. See pages 5–10 for Gilman's 'brief chronicle of a hundred years of English iconoclasm' (p. 10).

[21] Bland, 'William Stansby', p. 8.   [22] *Ibid.*   [23] *Ibid.*

and rhetorical effects – exemplified by the differing principles of punctuation that control the language of Caesar, Cicero and Fulvia in *Catiline*.[24]

Bland's description of Jonson's 'fastidiousness' testifies to a desire to control the final product, or at least parts of it, to the greatest extent possible. This careful proofing of copy is, as we shall see, the last stage, for a number of the works if not all, of a continuous effort on the part of the writer to protect the work. Bland argues that Jonson's 'involvement' serves to heighten 'dramatic and rhetorical effects'. This argument for the poet's interest in the 'orality' of his work leads Bland to argue that Jonson should not be seen primarily as a poet of the 'page', but of the 'stage'.[25] I think that Jonson's desire to control the oral and 'dramatic' aspect of his text does not imply that he is not a poet of the page. It is, indeed, through the medium of print that Jonson felt he could control the 'voice' of the future actor and cut down on, what is well known in music, the 'deformation' of the sounds he intended.

In addition to the errors of the printing-house, the censor's marks may be seen as another example of the visible signs of defacement, from the point of view of the writer at least. The censor's damasking and cancels are all eloquent reminders of possible injury to a text, just as the cutting off of ears, branding of thumbs and other such marks of discipline and punishment may be said to deface bodies. On the other hand, as a number of recent scholars have noted, this torture chamber (or Foucauldian) vision of early modern censorship must be considered both exaggerated and incomplete.[26] The fact that Jonson himself was waiting to become Master of Revels, a post he held in reversion, has served scholars as an example of the interiorization of the censor's practice by a writer. Yet, this useful anecdote needs to be supplemented with a more global picture of how the coveted position of censor is part of the fabric and construction of Jonson's working methods. It is worthwhile to consider the extent to which Jonson *defaces* his own poetic creation in his own too anxious solicitude to respond to the curious or envious gaze he imagined reading his texts. The discontinuity of the Jonsonian text, pockmarked by footnotes, citations from authorities, asides, digressions, sudden explanations, defences and justifications as well, as we shall see, the insertion of characters for

---

[24] *Ibid*, p. 19.   [25] *Ibid*.
[26] Richard Burt, for one, takes issue with the critical account of censorship which has often 'relied on images of the cropped ears of William Prynne and severed hand of John Stubbes, of book burnings, imprisoned authors, and shattered printing presses ... defining it exclusively as a negative exercise of power centered on the court'. Burt, *Licensed by Authority*, p. 1.

this same purpose, bears witness to its defacement by the writer himself; the writer is the first corrupter of his own text and as such is its first (and perhaps most effective) censor.

Moreover, the physical spoiling of the text is closely linked in the notion of defacement to the destroying of credit or the disparaging of a person's reputation and name. When Sidney writes in *An Apologie for Poetrie*, that poetry 'hath had even the names of Philosophers used to the defacing of it' he is referring to the way philosophers have defamed and slandered poetry, beginning, of course, with Plato in the *Republic*.[27] Shakespeare's *Richard II* is preoccupied with slander's effect on a name. In the very first scene, Mowbray accuses Bolingbroke of being a 'slanderous coward, and a villain' since Bolingbroke has publicly called him 'a traitor and a miscreant'.[28] When Bolingbroke, now King Henry, is presented with the proofs of Richard's murder he tells his henchman: 'Exton, I thank thee not, for thou has wrought / A deed of slander with thy fatal hand / Upon my head and all this famous land' (v.vi.34–6). Richard dies in the body, but Henry's name receives a blow for all time and Henry's words are prophetic, as only the audience can appreciate, of how slander will stain his name in posterity.[29] Slander here acquires the historical dimension that is its most damning feature; it is a spot that is never wiped clean: a mark, like the mark of Cain, that is always present, even in one's descendants. Speaking like a woman protecting her virtue, the aristocratic Mowbray tells his King that: 'The purest treasure mortal times afford / Is spotless reputation; that away, / Men are but gilded loam or painted clay' (1.i.177–9). Hamlet too is preoccupied even at the moment of his death with the fate of his name: 'Horatio, I am dead, / Thou livest. Report me and my cause aright / To the unsatisfied … O God, Horatio, what a wounded name, / Things standing thus unknown, shall I leave behind me!'[30] His dying wish is that Horatio should 'tell [his] story' (v.ii.328) to the 'unsatisfied', those who doubt, question, pry and disbelieve. Only through Horatio's representation of him can

---

[27] Sidney, *Apologie*, sig. B2.
[28] William Shakespeare, *The Tragedy of King Richard the Second* (1.i.61; 1.i.39). Subsequent references to the play will be included in the text.
[29] According to Marjorie Garber: 'In "real" time – the time of the audience, the time of the performance – [Shakespearean prophets] are, so to speak, looking backward, at events that have already taken place. In dramatic time – the context of the plays in which they appear – they are looking forward at anticipated events in the future. The result is a remarkable theatrical illusion, hindsight masquerading as foresight.' Marjorie Garber, '"What's Past Is Prologue": Temporality and Prophecy in Shakespeare's History Plays' in Barbara Kiefer Lewalski (ed.), *Renaissance Genres: Essays on Theory, History and Interpretation* (Cambridge: Harvard University Press, 1986), pp. 301–31; p. 308.
[30] William Shakespeare, *The Tragedy of Hamlet, Prince of Denmark* (v.ii.338–40; 344–5).

Hamlet's name be healed. These examples speak to a number of aspects of slander that implicitly inform Jonson's idea of its defacing harm. In Shakespeare, slanderous defacement is described as a wound and a stain, whether of blood or of a woman's virtuous reputation. Here, Jonson too, like his contemporaries, uses a panoply of words to express the harm that awaits poetic invention and the name and fame of the writer. Words such as 'blot', 'raze' and 'corrupt' express, often in very material terms, the fear of defacement and effacement (or oblivion) implicit in the Jonsonian idea of envy and of textual defacement.

LITERARY SLANDER AND 'THE EPIDEMICALL INFECTION'

While slander is primarily associated with the tongue and orality, its iconographic and literary imbrication in envy reveals the engine that was believed, since antiquity, to drive it. In 'On Not Being Quick to Put Faith in Slander', the ancient writer Lucian describes, in an ekphrasis, a painting by Apelles, the most famous ancient Greek painter; in the painting, Calumny drags her victim by the hair before a man (usually identified as a judge or king) with enormous ears who strains forward to listen to her calumny. It is significant that Slander is literally led by *Envy* to the man sitting on the throne.[31] Grasping Slander tightly by the hand and guiding her toward the man with enormous ears, eager to hear what she has to say, is the 'pale, ugly man who has a piercing eye and looks as if he had wasted away in long illness; he may be supposed to be Envy'.[32] The intimate relationship between envy and slander is one that pervades medieval and early modern literature.[33] Before Jonson, the poet most attuned to the problem of slanderous defacement was Spenser.[34] The image of 'Envy barking' in his prefatory poem to *The Shepheards Calendar* is the envious reader possessed of a slandering tongue. Envy's bark is portrayed in *The*

---

[31] Lucian, *Lucian* (I), ed. A. M. Harmon (Cambridge: Harvard University Press, 1913), p. 365.
[32] *Ibid.*, p. 366. It is noteworthy that Envy is male in Lucian. In earlier medieval depictions as well, Envy is male, a monk riding upon a wolf or a dog. Later, in the Renaissance, under the influence of the Ovidan representation in Book II of the *Metamorphoses*, Envy would be represented primarily as female, but in many representations (as with representations of the Medusa) Envy possesses a strangely androgynous face, half woman, half man. See 'Envy' in Chew, *Pilgrimage*, pp. 109–11.
[33] Richard Dutton has shown Lucian's work to be a probable source of Shakespeare's *Comedy of Errors*: '*The Comedy of Errors* and *The Calumny of Apelles*: An Exercise in Source Study' in Richard Dutton and Jean E. Howard (eds.), *A Companion to Shakespeare's Works, Volume III, The Comedies* (Oxford: Blackwell Publishing, 2003), pp. 307–19.
[34] Spenser criticism reflects the poet's preoccupation with the court and the envious and competitive world it represented. See the work of Ronald B. Bond, cited above.

Fairie Queene in all its monstrousness. The Blatant Beast would become, for Jonson and others, *the* image of defacement.³⁵ This apocalyptic monster appears in Book VI, the last of Spenser's epic. It is the household pet of the couple, Envy and Detraction, a beast of 'a thousand tongues', filled with 'spight' and 'malice', the 'plague' and 'scourge' of men.³⁶ The Beast is tied up by Calidore for a while, but eventually escapes his cage in the epic, loosed upon the world to wreak havoc forever. The Beast having escaped, Spenser's epic work ends in a mournful self-reflexive recognition of the power of slander to deface the poet's work. The last stanza of the epic becomes a coda to literary slander:

> Ne may this homely verse, of many meanest,
> Hope to escape his venemous despite,
> More then my former writs, all were they clearest
> From blamefull blot, and free from all that wite,
> With which some wicked tongues did it backbite,
> And bring into a mighty Peeres displeasure,
> That never so deserved to endite.
> Therefore do you my rimes keep better measure,
> And seeke to please, that now is counted wise mens treasure.³⁷

The 'blamefull blot' is the mark that resembles the damasking or cancellation of the censor. Backbiting tongues have placed Spenser in danger with a 'mighty Peer'. When Spenser writes of 'venemous despite' and 'wicked tongues' that 'backbite' he is primarily talking about those who had slandered the poet by finding dangerous political meanings in his writings. Spenser was, in fact, accused by James VI of Scotland of defaming his mother, Mary, Queen of Scots, in his portrait of the hypocritical witch and temptress, Duessa. Besides being accused of disseminating political opinions and meanings in their 'fictions' (in other words, propagating slander and sedition), poets were often submitted, mostly by their rivals, to

---

³⁵ James Nohrnberg notes 'the frequent imagery of defacement throughout the legend. "Deface" is often opposed to "grace" in the rhymes. The marking or mutilation of buildings, for example, might qualify as a form of discourtesy [Book VI of *The Fairie Queene* was the book of 'Courtesy']: the Blatant Beast is guilty of this kind of aesthetic offense at VI.xii.25.' James Nohrnberg, *The Analogy of The Faerie Queene* (Princeton: Princeton University Press, 1976), p. 688 n. 63. See Jonson's reference to the 'blatant beast' in 'To my Detractor', *Ungathered Verse* (xxxvii), Herford and Simpson, vol. VIII, p. 408: 'I pitty thee, poore Curre … thou art, a *blatant beast* / by barking against mee' (my emphasis, lines 7–10).
³⁶ Edmund Spenser, *The Faerie Queene*, p. 303 (VI.i.8–9). According to Nohrnberg, 'The Beast shares its tongues with Virgil's Fama, full of tongues, and its teeth with Ovid's "biting Envy", which rants and rails at the roman poet in an envoi.' Nohrnberg, *Analogy*, p. 688.
³⁷ Spenser, *The Faerie Queene*, p. 352 (VI.xii.41).

accusations of plagiarism, surprisingly frequent in an age which had only recently begun to use the word plagiary in its present meaning.[38]

It is in relation to the representation and problem of slander that we begin to understand the full effect of the defacement the author imagines by the censure and the misprision of the envious reader. Slander is the oral chatter, the 'winged tongue', the rumour that taints reputation and blots a person's name in the eyes of posterity.[39] Slander has the power to deface reputation and consign a name to oblivion and is, as such, a kind of symbolic murder. M. Lindsay Kaplan has delved into what legal historians term spoken or written 'defamation' in the early modern period, including the ambiguous status of satire, often considered the equivalent of calumny from the 'victim's' point of view, but, as Puttenham suggests, more like 'well deserved reproch' from the satirist's point of view.[40] Others have focused on the vexed question of slander and women's sexual reputation. Yet, what might be termed 'literary' slander should be seen as an extension of such slanderous enunciation: here, the misrepresentation and false statement which define slander are made by the whisperer in a theatre or by the reader of a text. False attribution or calumny is disseminated and propagated by the spectator or reader among his peers, his contemporaries and posterity – through conversation, teaching, reviews, the writing of articles, notes, editions, introductions and a host of more insidious means aided by a thick network of rumour, gossip and scholarly backbiting. Poetic reputation is thus squarely in the hands of the reader, who, at every turn, is apt to misconstrue the text, or maliciously misrepresent it for his own ends. The literary fortunes of a writer may be said to depend on the baleful effects of slanderous reading, in which envy, as the reading eye, works in tandem with slander, the misrepresenting tongue. Envy and detraction work together in the reader to deform meaning and pervert the destiny of the author and the legitimacy of his work.

When *he* discusses slander, Jonson often uses words associated with the eye and emphasizes the power of envy to deform, pervert and deprave what

---

[38] The first use recorded in the *OED* of the term to denote one who plagiarizes or 'steals' from another is Jonson's *Poetaster* (1601).

[39] George Wither depicts slander as a winged tongue with the motto 'No heart can think, to what strange ends, / The Tongue unruely Motion tends.' Wither, *A Collection of Emblemes*, p. 42.

[40] M. Lindsay Kaplan, *The Culture of Slander in Early Modern England* (Cambridge: Cambridge University Press, 1997). George Puttenham writes: 'Wherefore the Poets, being in deed the trumpetters of all praise and also of slaunder (not slaunder, but well deserved reproch)'. Here Puttenham has translated 'fama' in both its good sense and in its bad, but decided to add a caveat, because the idea of 'slander' is too strong for what a poet attempts to do in satire. George Puttenham, *The Arte of English Poesie* (London, 1589), p. 28 (chap. XVI).

it sees. In other words, the misrepresenting power of slander, its power to 'wrest' and 'pervert', is attributed by Jonson to the envying and envious eye. Allan H. Gilbert notes how Jonson's perception of slander is unusually centred on the visual and described in terms of the look or the eye:

> In *Hymenaei*, Slander is 'squint-eyd', and in *Queens* she is said to boast 'her oblique looke' (128). One expects her to be characterized also by the tongue, as in Spenser's Blatant Beast in *FQ* 6.12.27, or Ripa's *Detrattione*. The references to the eye are fitting for Envy, and indicate that Jonson thought of Slander as essentially envious.[41]

Although Gilbert sees Jonson's characterization of slander in terms usually reserved for envy, Jonson's conflation of the two (which we have already seen in his translation of Catullus' *mala fascinare lingua* as 'envy') has precedent in the visual arts. In Lucian's ekphrasis, Envy pulls Calumny toward the seated figure. Most representations of *The Calumny of Apelles* in the pictorial tradition represent two figures, Envy and Calumny, juxtaposed, closely connected, yet, for the most part, separate entities.[42] Yet, we find in one version from 1600, the figure of Calumny invested with *the* attribute of envy, namely the irradiating eye. In this engraving the two figures are very much separate ('Invidia' can be seen on the left-hand side of the engraving tripping up 'Innocentia' while 'Calumnia' stands at the centre before the king). The description attached to the image notes the fact that rays of light are pictured emerging from Calumny's eyes: 'Calumnia ardentes habet oculos.'[43] In another representation of *The Calumny of Apelles*, we find the figure of Envy seemingly 'absent' until we realize that the figure of Slander incorporates the figure of Invidia since she is invested with the snaky head of a Medusa, associated in the iconography of the early modern period with Envy.[44] The figure of Envy rising in the opening of Jonson's *Poetaster* is itself a similar combination of Envy and Slander. She

---

[41] Allan H. Gilbert, *The Symbolic Persons in the Masques of Ben Jonson* (New York: AMS Press, Inc., 1967), p. 219.
[42] For discussions of this pictorial tradition see David Cast, *The Calumny of Apelles: A Study in the Humanist Tradition* (New Haven: Yale University Press, 1981) and Jean-Michel Massing, *Du texte à l'image: la calomnie d'Apelle et son iconographie* (Strasbourg: Presses Universitaires de Strasbourg, 1990).
[43] Massing, *Du texte à l'image*, pp. 393–4, Engraving 30.A. The artist is unidentified. Massing notes with regard to the representation of Calumny in this particular engraving: 'la Calomnie est représentée avec des faisceaux de lumière sortant de ses yeux' [Calumny is represented with rays of light coming out of her eyes] (p. 394).
[44] *Ibid.*, p. 431, Engraving 51.A. The artist is Andrea Comodi, but the date is uncertain. Massing puts it before 1638. Massing notes that even though Calumny is represented *as* Invidia, she is still identifiable (as Calumny) because she holds Calumny's characteristic torch.

is a mixture of the attributes of the eye of envy 'cracke ey-strings, and your balles / Drop to earth; let me be ever blind. / I am prevented' and the misrepresenting tongues of slander:

> Help me to damne the Authour. Spit it foorth
> Upon his lines …
> …
> … that he may see you arm'd
> With triple malice, to hisse, sting, and teare
> His worke, and him; to forge, and then declame,
> Traduce, corrupt, apply, enforme, suggest.[45]

Envy and slander are completely intertwined, complementing each other, performing the same function in perfect unison. The eye that sees and deforms is calumnious. 'Envie' possesses a slanderous eye. This monster, a mixture of the attributes of slander and envy, is the image of the reader for Jonson and the embodiment of the threat of *defacement* which he continually calls *envy*.

As we have seen, Samuel Daniel describes readers who 'check us with a show of what it would do in another kind, and yet do nothing but *deprave*' and John Harington mourns, 'we live in such a time in which nothing can escape the envious tooth and back-biting tongue of an impure mouth, and wherein every blind corner hath a squint-eyed Zoilus that can look aright upon no man's doings'.[46] Daniel's use of the word 'deprave' and Harington's reminder that Zoilus is 'squint-eyed' give us an idea of how Jonson perceived the envious reader as capable of 'deforming' the text, a perception evident in those poems in which the act of 'looking' is metaphorically compared to the viewing of an anamorphic perspective. When Jonson refers to the reader as one who looks 'asquint' his poem 'In Authorem', he is implicitly referring to the viewing of an anamorphic image, or, in the French, an image *dépravée*.[47] As we have seen, in the conclusion of some of his poems, the poet puts a twist on the analogy with an anamorphosis; we, the reader, discover that the deformation that defines an anamorphic image, lies not in the text/painting, but rather in the eye of the reader. This depravation appears as a consequence of looking at the text, not only 'awry', from a

---

[45] Ben Jonson, Prologue to *Poetaster*, Herford and Simpson, vol. IV, p. 204 (lines 28–30; 46–54).
[46] Samuel Daniel, Preface, *A Defence of Ryme* (London, 1603), n.p. (my emphasis); John Harington, 'A Preface, Or Rather a Briefe Apologie of Poetrie', *Orlando Furioso in English Heroicall Verse* (London, 1591), sig. ii^v.
[47] Jurgis Baltrusaitis entitles his series on anamorphosis: *Les perspectives dépravées* (Paris: Flammarion, 1995).

certain angle, but also enviously or 'askance'. All readers, in other words, are potentially capable of deforming and misreading a text, unless they 'look well' upon the work, or make sure to 'eye it directly' instead of taking it from the oblique angle.

Yet, how does this misprision by the envious or the ignorant reader really constitute a 'defacement' of the text? If the 'fault' lies with the reader and not the text what real harm does this reader present to the writer? One could argue that the envious reader offered no harm to the writer because the writer did not write for him or her. Jonson, who so scrupulously differentiated between the 'Reader in Ordinary' and the 'Reader Extraordinary' in his dedication of *Catiline, His Conspiracy* and who in the epigraph to the 1616 Folio, claimed that he did not mind 'only a few readers' seems clearly dismissive of this reader. Nevertheless, the envious reader is quite capable of defacing the writer's work for the very simple reason that in the social world of readers, the 'good' reader and the 'bad' reader are in continuous contact with each other and occupy the same spaces. It is through the *exchange*, through rumour and gossip, that the depraved image is passed on to others. The reader is not hermetically sealed off, either alone in a theatre or even alone with a book. The perversion of the text by one spectator or reader with a 'fault' in his eye is liable to contaminate the judgement of another. Jonson describes the effects of the slanderous eye in a model of infectious spectatorship: in the Induction to *Bartholomew Fair*, he urges the spectators to judge for themselves and not be contaminated by anyone sitting next to them. The Scrivener reads out the 'ARTICLES of Agreement, indented, between the *Spectators* or *Hearers*, at the *Hope* on the Bankeside, in the Countyr of *Surrey* on the one party; And the *Author of Bartholomew Fayre*'.[48] The articles call for the spectators to censure the play in proportion to how much they have paid for their seats and '[I]t is also agreed, that every man heere, exercise his owne Iudgement, and not censure by *Contagion*, or upon *trust*, from anothers voice, or face, that sits by him.'[49] In *Timber, or Discoveries*, Jonson similarly refers to slander as a highly infectious disease:

The Writer must lye, and the gentle Reader rests happy, to heare the worthiest workes misinterpreted; the clearest actions obscured; the innocent'st life traduc'd; And in such a licence of lying, a field so fruitfull of slanders, how can there be matter wanting to his laughter? Hence comes the *Epidemicall* Infection. For how can

---

[48] Ben Jonson, *Bartholomew Fair*, Herford and Simpson, vol. VI, p. 15 (lines 64–7).
[49] *Ibid.*, p. 16 (lines 97–8).

they escape the contagion of the Writings, whom the virulency of the calumnies hath not stav'd off from reading?[50]

The 'contagion' and 'virulency' of this infection is 'contained' in *Bartholomew Fair* in the drawing up of a legal contract between author and spectator before the performance. In *Timber*, the poet muses on the epidemics of reading and the inevitable contagion of the unimmunized reader by viral calumnies.

DEFACING THE 'OLD MASTERS'

The act of writing is fraught with the peculiar danger of defacement, by the printer, the censor and the slanderer, whether spectator or reader. There is also the risk of defacement at the hands of the writer himself, inhabited by the censoring eye which he turns ruthlessly upon his own text, even from the moment of its conception. In *The Advancement of Learning* (1605), Francis Bacon discusses the 'quarrel' between the Ancients and the Moderns, the pitting of old beliefs against new discoveries, Aristotelian truths against new insights into the mechanics and motions of nature. He compares antiquity to the Titans, resentful of the new Olympians coming into their power. He paints the young Olympians as cruelly egotistical. He describes the tense relationship between novelty and antiquity in terms of envy and defacement: 'Antiquity *envieth* there should be new additions, and Novelty cannot be content to add, but it must *deface*.'[51] The old feel a kind of bitterness that they should be bettered, but Bacon represents this as a necessary, if painful, aspect of knowledge. At the same time, he chides those who would advance learning in the present for not admitting that they see further only because they stand on the shoulders of giants. They are not content to 'add', but they must also 'deface'.

If imitation is the greatest form of flattery, then many of Ben Jonson's passages in *Timber* are our best proof of his admiration for Bacon. Jonson goes to him, for instance, to get his *matter* concerning antiquity's envy of the new:

It was well noted by the late L. St *Alban*, that the study of words is the first distemper of Learning: Vaine matter the second: And a third distemper is deceit, or the likenesse of truth; Imposture held up by credulity. All these are the Cobwebs

---

[50] Ben Jonson, *Timber, or Discoveries*, Herford and Simpson, vol. VIII, p. 572 (lines 288–96).
[51] Francis Bacon, *The Two Bookes of Francis Bacon, Of the Proficience and Advancement of Learning* (London, 1605), sig. F4ᵛ.

of Learning, and to let them grow in us, is either sluttish or foolish ... Let *Aristotle*, and others have their dues; but if wee can make farther Discoveries of truth and fitnesse then they, why are we envied? Let us beware, while we strive to add, we do not diminish, or deface; we may improve, but not augment ... We must ... awake Antiquity, call former times into question; but make no parties with the present, nor follow any fierce undertakers ... but gently stirre the mould about the root of the Question.[52]

The quandary inherent in Jonson's phantasmagoria of the act of writing finds here a lucid formulation. Whatever the new author writes threatens to traduce some former text: as a modern writer you are bound to deface ancient texts. The idea of steering a course and augmenting must give way to following in the wake of your predecessors and improving: 'We must ... awake Antiquity, call former times into question; but make no parties with the present, nor follow any fierce undertakers.' Giving birth is itself a possible transgression against the ancients. Moreover, to write implies the defilement of the temple of the literary father. These 'fathers' include the ancients, but also, interestingly, a recent 'father' such as Francis Bacon, the 'late L. St *Alban*'. Because he continually finds himself indebted to previous writers either for inspiration or authority or both, Jonson finds the danger of defacement everywhere, both of defacing and of being defaced. Steering a middle course between calling former times into question and not being a part of a fierce 'party' or faction is the lot of the early seventeenth-century writer. This 'middle course', between adding and defacing, may be seen in Jonson's approach to the masque. As Evelyn A. Tribble reminds us, Jonson's first attempt to provide an exegesis for one of his own works was in the publication of *His Part in the Entertainment for James I* (1603).[53] Jonson's 'program' to 'frame himself within the humanist, classical context' is carried out in the margins of the page:

Jonson's first pageant, a dialogue between the Genius of the City and Tamesis (the Thames) is glossed so as to emphasize its affiliations with the classical past as much as with the English present. The keys appear before the glossed word, thus ensuring that the reader's eye is continually directed toward the margins ...These five lines *engender* a margin full of commentary, beginning in the right margin and continuing onto the foot of the page, framing the speech.[54]

---

[52] Ben Jonson, *Timber, or Discoveries*, Herford and Simpson, vol. VIII, p. 627 (lines 2090–113).
[53] Evelyn A. Tribble, *Margins and Marginalia: The Printed Page in Early Modern England* (Charlottesville: University Press of Virginia, 1993), pp. 133–4.
[54] *Ibid.*, p. 135.

The texts Jonson cites in his margins serve as the basis of his work, supporting it, visually on the page, and figuratively as defence, explanation and authority. His work is visually and figuratively 'grounded upon Antiquity'.[55] In doing so, Jonson may be seen as adding, improving and building a monument, using the foundation stones of antiquity to build his own work on the work of previous generations. Yet, Thomas Dekker saw the nature of Jonson's monument building in a very different way. In Dekker's opinion, Jonson's use of erudition to explicate an entertainment was tantamount to putting 'Genius … on the rack', executing and killing the 'spirit' of the living conceit while at the same time shredding and cutting up antiquity:

To make a false flourish here with the borrowed weapons of all the old Masters of the noble Science of Poesie, and to keepe a tyrannical coyle, in anatomizing Genius, from head to foote, (onely to shew how nimbly we can carve up the whole messe of the Poets) were to play the Executioner, and to lay our Cities household-God on the rack, to make him confesse how manie paire of Latin sheetes, we have taken and cut into shreds to make him a garment. Such feates of Activitie are stale and common among Schollers.[56]

For Dekker, turning an entertainment into a kind of scholarly and erudite tome is comparable to early modern forms of torture. Classical authors are 'carved up' and 'cut into shreds' and then patched together every which way. Genius is described as 'anatomized', her entrails running out of her cut-up body and spilling over into the margins of the printed page. Dekker sees the text's reaching back to antiquity as, in effect, a version of stealing capitals from ancient monuments to build a doorway or stones from a ruin to pave one's kitchen. In his *Entertainment* and then later in *The Masque of Blacknesse*, Jonson may be seen to 'add' antiquity in the margins, yet, we see that this 'adding' involves precisely the 'diminishing' and 'defacing' he and Bacon warn against, since the process, as Dekker perceived it, necessarily involves 'dis-limbing', a form of cutting or tearing apart.[57]

The problematic relationship between monument and defacement, between laying the foundation for something new and carving up antiquity may find its ultimate expression in the strange scene of birth

---

[55] *Ibid.*, pp. 140–1. Jonson, *Hymenaei*, Herford and Simpson, vol. VII, p. 209 (line 16).
[56] Thomas Dekker, *The Magnificent Entertainment* (London, 1604), sig. A4. Cited and discussed in Tribble, *Margins*, pp. 139–40.
[57] See Shakespeare's *The Tragedy of Antony and Cleopatra* for defacement imagined using the idea of 'dis-limbing': 'That which is now a horse, even with a thought / The rack *dislimns*, and makes it indistinct / As water is in water' (my emphasis, IV.xiv.9–11).

at the opening of Jonson's 'To The Immortal Memory and Friendship of That Noble Pair, Sir Lucius Cary and Sir H. Morison'. In the first stanza of this poem we find a number of the terms Jonson associates with the threat of defacement, not least of which is the figure of Hannibal, the master defacer and 'razer' of Rome. The infant of Jonson's poem turns away from the prospect of Hannibal's razing 'rage', not unlike the defacing 'rage' of the courtiers who tore down masque sets, by re-entering the womb of its mother:

> Brave Infant of *Saguntum*, cleare
> Thy comming forth in that great yeare,
> When the Prodigious *Hannibal* did crowne
> His rage, with razing your immortall Towne.
> Thou, looking then about,
> E're thou wert halfe got out,
> Wise child, did'st hastily returne,
> And mad'st thy Mothers wombe thine urne.
> How summ'd a circle didst thou leave man-kind
> Of deepest lore, could we the Center find![58]

While the infant in Pliny is an example of a monstrosity, in Jonson's poem he is praised as 'brave' and is enjoined to 'clear' his name in anticipation of those who would accuse it. The self-aborting infant conveys the image of a literary imagination which leaps to its own posterity in the very moment of its conception. Such a juxtaposition of birth and death testifies to a desire for immediate posterity and a rejection of the creative burden of birth, the burden of negotiating between creation (building, adding) and the threat of defacement: between 'raising' and 'razing'. Ironically, the 'razing' of the town of Saguntum by Hannibal enables and ensures that the town will be immortalized forever. Since the babe's coming forth and subsequent burial is intimately linked with the historically gigantic, 'prodigious' figure of Hannibal, both child and its town gain a kind of approximate fame. One may see in this small fragment a reflection of the authorial desire for fame and posterity, not through the long, wearying and even dangerous (if it involves following 'fierce undertakers') process of fabricating and building something new, but rather through the mingling and merging of the novel and the authoritative, in which the author 'raises' a monument out of the symmetrical threat of having his name 'razed'.

---

[58] Ben Jonson, *Underwood* (lxx), Herford and Simpson, vol. VIII, p. 242 (lines 1–8).

THE ENVIOUS READER: *POETASTER, OR HIS ARRAIGNMENT*

Corruption and interruption

For a study of envy in Jonson's plays two works which lend themselves naturally are *Every Man Out of His Humour* whose main character is the 'envious' Macilente, and *Poetaster, Or His Arraignment*. I have chosen *Poetaster* because it is a complex and varied representation of the way in which poets are confronted by and suffer the consequences of having their texts misread. Rather than focusing on Jonson's delineation of the humour or passion of envy in one or two specific characters (Macilente and Sordido), an examination of *Poetaster* aims to illustrate the extent to which the activity of writing is represented as a continual negotiation with envy and malice in the Jonsonian imaginary. The danger to literary reputation of envious calumny is shown to be frighteningly real and atemporal. At the same time, *Poetaster* reveals the extent to which literary creation is produced in confrontation with envy or 'bad' readers. *Poetaster* is set in ancient Rome, in order to show that even the now classic authors of antiquity were once, in their own lifetimes, the victims of the envy of contemporary readers. The play can be read as an elaboration of an early modern poet's fantasy of being, like the famed poets of antiquity, safe and secure from envy.[59]

In the Induction to this play, as we have seen briefly above, a nightmarish image of 'Envie', or the envious spectator and reader, appears on stage:

> TH'ARRAIGNMENT? I; This, this is it,
> That our sunke eyes have wak't for, all this while:
> Here will be a subject for my snakes, and me.[60]

The snakes, described a few lines later, which 'cling to my neck and wrists' (line 6), make 'Envie' a kind of fury or Medusa and her eventual defeat by the armoured Prologue reminds the reader of the defeat of the Medusa by Perseus, or the dragon by St George. The waking eyes of the monster attest to the importance of its gaze. It is she who has waited in her dark corner

---

[59] Joseph Loewenstein writes concerning envy in *Poetaster*: '*Poetaster* is a *cento* on envy, and texts from Martial shape it: after the final song of the play, the quarto quotes the final line from Epigrams, IX: 97, "*Rumpatur, quisquis rumpitur invidia*": let he who is bursting with envy burst.' Loewenstein, *Possessive Authorship*, p. 145 n. 33.

[60] Ben Jonson, Induction to *Poetaster*, Herford and Simpson, vol. IV, p. 203 (lines 3–5). Subsequent references to the Induction to *Poetaster* will be included in the text.

for the poet to give birth to his play and it is she who casts her eye upon it, interrupting the performance in order to 'blast' (line 23) the enjoyment of the other spectators:

> With wrestings, comments, applications,
> Spie-like suggestions, privie whisperings,
> And a thousand such promoting sleights as these. (lines 24–6)

To accomplish her maleficent designs she calls on the aid of her snakes:

> ... sting, and teare
> His worke, and him; to forge, and then declame,
> Traduce, *corrupt*, apply, enforme, suggest. [my emphasis; lines 52–4]

I would like to focus on the polysemic nature of the word 'corrupt': a word which underpins the Jonsonian idea of defacement. In this passage, corruption refers to the intriguing and secretive world of the court as it is mimicked in the theatre by the spectators. It also refers, however, to what Envie intends to do to the author and his 'worke'. The envious misreader intends to infect, rot and pervert or alter. The Latin root, 'corrumpere', not only implies putrefaction and depravation, it also implies the idea of 'breaking' in 'rumpere'. Corruption combines the ideas of *marring* and *spoiling* with the idea of *interruption* and this combination is an aspect of the idea of defacement. The Jonsonian suspicion of the spectator and reader may be attributed to their immense power to decide the fate of the author's fame as well, in the terms imagined within the justice system of early modern England, the frightening power of those to affect the poet's earthly fate as well. This distrust is enacted in *Poetaster* in a series of repetitive scenes in which the poetic stars of the ancient world are presented on stage, *interrupted* by malicious, spoiling voices while they are in the midst of writing the founding texts of antiquity. In other words, poets are represented as *corrupted* by envious readers.

Interestingly enough, the image of a poet, in the process of writing or commenting on his own wit before being suddenly interrupted or 'corrupted', repeats itself throughout Jonson's career. The opening of *Epicoene, Or The Silent Woman* (1609) is an example of such textual corruption: Clerimont is putting the final touches to a 'song', which is being sung, for the first time, by his page when the biting critic, Truewit, enters.[61] *Every Man Out of His Humour* opens with a scholar commenting upon the book he is reading, before being interrupted by the commenting of

---

[61] Ben Jonson, *Epicoene, Or The Silent Woman*, Herford and Simpson, vol. v, pp. 164–5 (1.i.1–22).

the chorus.⁶² *Bartholomew Fair* opens with John Littlewit, the aspiring writer and motions man, in the midst of complimenting himself on his 'Pretty conceit' and the fine art of quibbling before being interrupted by the entrance of his wife, Win. We see him happily imagining himself:

> [O]ne o' the pretty wits o' Pauls ... When a quirk, or a *quiblin* do's scape thee, and thou dost not watch, and apprehend it, and bring it afore the Constable of conceit: (there now, I speake *quib* too) let 'hem carry thee out o' the Archdeacons Court, into his Kitchin, and make a Iack of thee, instead of a John. (There I am againe la!) Win, Good morrow, Win. I, marry, Win!⁶³

When she can finally get a word in edgewise, Win tells her husband: 'Come, indeede la, you are such a foole, still!'⁶⁴ *The New Inn* begins with the Host boasting of his 'brayne-child', a poetic '*Rebus*' for the sign of his inn, which he explicates in detail to Lovel's servant, Ferret, before the entrance of Lovel himself.⁶⁵ In *Every Man In His Humour*, the *threat* of interruption is present in the lines by Knowell senior, 'but hear you sirrah, / If he be at his book, disturb him not'.⁶⁶ But it is in *The Case is Altered* that we find a similar rude interruption of a poet, while he is in the middle of composing, described specifically as 'corruption'. Act 1 opens with a young rustic singing pseudo-Spenserian verses:

> JUNIPER, *a Cobler is discovered, sitting at work in his shoppe, and singing.*
> JUNIPER. *You wofull wights, give ear a while,*
> *And mark the tenor of my style,*
> *Which shall such trembling hearts unfold,*
> *As seldom hath to-fore been told.*
> *Such chances rare, and doleful news,*
>   Enter Onion, *in haste*
> ONI. Fellow Juniper! Peace a God's name.
> JUN. *As may attempt your wits to muse.*
> ONI. Od's so, hear, man! a pox on you!
> JUN. *And cause such trickling tears to pass,*
>   *Except your hearts be flint, or brass:*

---

⁶² The play begins with Macilente presumably reading a Stoic author (Herford and Simpson claim the first line of the play to be an 'untraced quotation', IX, p. 424) and commenting on what he reads. He is 'interrupted' by the GREX. Ben Jonson, *Every Man Out of His Humour*, Herford and Simpson, vol. III, pp. 442–3.
⁶³ Ben Jonson, *Bartholomew Fair*, Herford and Simpson, vol. VI, p. 19 (line 1; lines 11–19).
⁶⁴ *Ibid.*, p. 19 (line 27).
⁶⁵ Ben Jonson, *The New Inn*, Herford and Simpson, vol. VI, p. 407 (I.i.6; 9). See the hilarious sign – also a rebus – Subtle makes for Drugger in *The Alchemist*, Herford and Simpson, vol. V, pp. 337–8 (II.vi.1–24).
⁶⁶ Ben Jonson, *Every Man In His Humour*, Herford and Simpson, vol. III, p. 304 (I.i.5).

ONI. Juniper! Juniper!
JUN. *To hear the news which I shall tell,*
 That in Castella once befel. –
S'blood, where didst thou learn to corrupt a man in the midst of a verse, ha?[67]

The interrupting voice of (the smelly) Onion corrupts the work of (the sweet-smelling) Juniper. Here, the poet character is first cut off in the midst of his singing, before he cuts himself off in mid-sentence to wonder: 'where didst thou learn to corrupt a man?' At the same time, Juniper is a buffoon, spouting bad verse. With a poet clown such as this, the reader finds himself identifying with the 'onion' who wishes 'a pox on you!' Both the poet and the corrupting censor are equally mocked in this passage. Nevertheless, the structure of the 'poet' interrupted and corrupted helps us understand other scenes in which the poet figure might be perceived as 'closer' to the figure of the author.[68]

If we turn to the first scene of *Poetaster*, we witness the great classical poet Ovid in the process of composing a poem. He is interrupted first by his servant and then by his father in quick succession. Like another Onion, Ovid's servant Luscus cries:

Young Master, master OVID, doe you heare? gods a mee! away with your *songs*, and *sonnets* ... These verses too, a poyson on 'hem, I cannot abide 'hem, they make me readie to cast, by the banks of *helicon*! Nay, looke, what a rascally untoward thing this *poetrie* is; I could teare 'hem now (1.i.5–11).

A few lines later, Ovid Senior, reading, comments scoffingly : 'Your name shall live, indeed, sir! ... Verses! Poetry! Ovid, whom I thought to see the pleader, become Ovid the play-maker!' (1.ii.1–9). 'Ovid' immediately incorporates these interrupting corruptions into what we discover is Elegy 15 from Book I of his *Amores*. We witness how Ovid names these scoffing interrupters 'Envie': 'Envie, why twist thou me, my time's spent ill? / And call'st my verse, fruits of an idle quill?'[69] The early modern writer thus shows that even the most important poetry of antiquity was forged in relation to the envious gaze and in spite of (or, because of) such interrupting

---

[67] Ben Jonson, *The Case is Altered*, Herford and Simpson, vol. III, p. 105 (1.i.1–14).
[68] The word and idea of 'corruption' is a very significant one in understanding Jonson. When Volpone and Mosca discuss Volpone's decision to 'play dead', Mosca considers the problem of the 'body':

 Mosca. But what, sir, if they ask
  After the body?
 Volpone. Say, it was *corrupted*.
 (my emphasis; *Volpone*, Herford and Simpson, vol. V, p. 112 (v.ii.77–9).
[69] Ben Jonson, *Poetaster*, Herford and Simpson, vol. IV, p. 207 (1.i.43–4). Subsequent references to the play will be included in the text.

and corrupting circumstances, the traces of which can be found in the work itself.⁷⁰

Not only does the opening scene in *Poetaster* theatricalize the writing of Elegy 15, it also performs the act of reading. The first words of the play proper are spoken by Ovid as he reads from 'his' *Amores*:

OVID. *Then, when this bodie falls in funerall fire,*
My name shall live, and my best part aspire.
It shall go so. (1.i.1–3)

Jonson represents the poet in the act of writing, an act defined immediately in terms of its specularity: he reads and comments on what he has written, passing judgement on his own lines, ('It shall go so'). There is a dialogue between Ovid, the writer, and Ovid, the reader of Ovid. Suddenly interrupted by his servant, the poet is left alone again a few lines later, to his great relief : 'I'm glad thou art gone; For thus alone, our ear shall better judge / the hasty errors of our morning muse' (40–2). Yet, even though the interrupting servant is gone, the judging author remains: we see Ovid oscillating between his own poem and his own judgement of it upon re-*reading* it. In other words, while envy in *Poetaster* is represented at first glance as coming from an outside source (Ovid's father, his servant) this scene shows us that poetic creation risks exposure to the distorting gaze of an envious reader, sometimes the writer himself, even at the moment of its birth. What these scenes of interruption show us is that the author regards his own work 'enviously' even at the moment he begins to create. I would suggest that the ubiquity of the references to 'envy' throughout Jonson's works is symptomatic of an authorial obsession with this defacing gaze upon his own text. This gaze, although projected upon a malicious exterior reader is, above all, the envious gaze of the writer confronted by the sight of his own work. The poet, in order to win durable fame, must justify and so modify his creation in light of his own initial invidious inquiry.

In *Poetaster*, then, the Jonsonian obsession with the threat of the envious reader is literally staged. The 'silent' authorial activities of writing,

---

⁷⁰ Joseph Loewenstein remarks on Jonson's staging of the writing of the *Amores*: 'At this point it might be ridiculous to wonder why Jonson chose to stage the composition of this, of all the *Amores* – we have reason enough already. But the choice had considerable force, for Ovid's poem begins with an apostrophe to Envy … In effect, then, the poem re-enacts the play's preliminaries, the armed theatrical Prologue who places his foot on Envie's head just as he is about to sink beneath the stage. The representation of Ovid's poem is not, however, simply an alternative opening. It operates under the mode of replacement, displacing theatrical display with a non-spectacular scribal event: it makes it a literary occasion.' 'Personal Material: Jonson and Book-burning' in Martin Butler (ed.), *Re-presenting Ben Jonson: Text, History, Performance* (New York: Macmillan Press, 1999), pp. 93–113; pp. 110–11.

reading and judging are performed out loud and physically enacted first by the voice of the poet composing, reading out loud and commenting on what he has just written and by the opening and closing of doors and the entrances and exits of envious (interrupting) characters. The sudden appearance on the stage of the critical and malignant censor confronts the spectator and the reader with the spectacle of the interior scene of writing; authorial stream-of-consciousness, centuries before Joyce, arrives on stage in 1601 in all its phantasmagoric power. Readers are the projections of the author's own distorting gaze, his own envious gaze upon his text. Narcissus, from *Cynthia's Revels, Or The Fountain of Self-Love* (1600) may be said to reappear in *Poetaster*, not as a character, but in the self-conscious gaze of the writer, represented first by Ovid, the author of the *Amores* and the *Metamorphoses*.

While *Poetaster* has been read as a late sixteenth-century *à clef* play or as a political statement concerning the Essex conspiracy, these interpretations need to be seen within the context of the play's obvious focus, since all the main characters are poets or would-be poets, on writing and reading.[71] There is no doubt that *Poetaster* represents, along with *Cynthia's Revels*, one of Jonson's contributions to what is commonly called the 'War of the Theatres'. This 'War' was a personal and professional feud mainly between Dekker and Jonson.[72] In *Poetaster*, Jonson, like Dekker a few weeks later in *Satiro-Mastix*, created characters who may be said to stand for the various writers engaged in this theatrical quarrel. According to critical opinion, each of the Roman poets stands for one of the combatants in the 'War': Horace stands for Jonson, Hermogenes for Marston, and Crispinus, the poetaster of the title, for Dekker. Others go further in speculating that Virgil is Shakespeare and so on. William Blissett notes that: '[T]he play is obviously topical, and most commentary has had more to do with London than with Rome.'[73] Indeed, the final scene in which Crispinus is made to vomit neologisms sheds light on the contemporary antagonism between members of different theatres and the controversies over linguistic novelties and new coinings.

---

[71] For a reading of the play in light of the Essex rebellion, see Tom Cain, '"Satyres, That Girde and Fart at the Time": *Poetaster* and the Essex Rebellion' in Julie Sanders, Kate Chedgzoy and Susan Wiseman (eds.), *Refashioning Ben Jonson: Gender, Politics, and the Jonsonian Canon* (Basingstoke: Macmillan, 1998), pp. 48–70.

[72] See James P. Bednarz, *Shakespeare and the Poets' War* (New York: Columbia University Press, 2001) and Shapiro, *Rival Playwrights*.

[73] William Blissett, 'Roman Ben Jonson' in Jennifer Brady and W. H. Herendeen (eds.), *Ben Jonson's 1616 Folio* (Newark: University of Delaware Press, 1991), pp. 90–110; p. 95.

Nevertheless, these contemporary debates are not the only ones with which the play engages. Underneath the 'War of the Theatres' is a battle within the poetic imagination between the act of creation and the necessity to submit and expose this creation to the eye and the ear of the reader. The play can be read as a series of confrontations between the poets of antiquity and their 'readers', precisely like that endured by Jonson's Ovid, interrupted in the act of writing. These readers are amply foreshadowed by the fabulous figure of Envy in the play's Induction who serves as an Ur-image of malignant reading. The Jonsonian suspicion of the spectator and reader is enacted in *Poetaster* through an all but oneiric repetition of scenes in which 'good' poets, cut off in the midst of their writing or reading, confront the slandering voices and traducing tongues of envious readers.

Poetaster is set in the court of Augustus Caesar around whom, anachronistically, Jonson brings together the three greatest Roman poets, Virgil, Horace and Ovid (ranked in that order in Dante's *Purgatorio*). Most modern readings assume that the author of the play is necessarily represented (and representable) by *one* of these three poets. There are, of course, reasons to see Horace as an ancient model for Jonson in terms of their shared poetic principles and Jonson's decision to translate Horace's *The Art of Poetrie*. Yet, the near automatic identification of Jonson with Horace has often led to a false interpretative denigration of the value, within the narrative economy of the play, of the other two poets, Ovid and Virgil. Alan Sinfield, for example, as a consequence, feels the necessity to add a caveat to Jonson's 'endorsement' of Horace by claiming 'there is no disrespect in *Poetaster* toward the writer of the *Aeneid*'.[74] Sinfield's doubling back reveals the critical bind this kind of hierarchization of the poets in the play entails and imposes. Besides creating an artificial hierarchy among the three, this attribution obscures a repetitive pattern within the play of similar scenes in which the poets might almost interchange roles. For it is not only the poet that is represented in this play, it is also very much a phantasmagoria of *reception* that is enacted. The narrative logic of the play insists upon a certain degree of equality among the three authors in terms of a common necessity (as writers) to defend themselves against the clamorous voices of those malicious readers whom they confront each in their turn. Their varying fates have less to do with who they are, in terms of posterity's ranking of them, than

---

[74] Alan Sinfield, 'Poetaster, the Author, and the Perils of Cultural Production', *Renaissance Drama*, n.s. 27 (1996), 3–18; p. 14.

with the way they negotiate those forces of power and authority that can either help or hurt them. Virgil and Horace successfully withstand the attacks of slander and envy by combining their poetic genius with (watchful) service to the state or, in the case of Horace, humility bound to unwavering honesty in the discovery of the evils and dangers which threaten the monarch. Ovid, on the other hand, represents, at some level, the refusal of poetic genius to submit itself to authority while it runs itself into a completely untenable position with regard to the dangers posed by calumny and envy.

The play, then, establishes a sequence of scenes in which Ovid, Horace and Virgil are exposed to slanderous attacks (based on their respective texts having been misread or in danger of being misread), with varying degrees of success in parrying these attacks.[75] The play resembles a series of masques, since the heroes are historical and even mythical, and the antiheroes are almost always (with the exception of Augustus) evil mechanicals. The play divides itself, for the most part, into panels devoted to a representation of a poet's voice interrupted by the clamorous and accusatory voices of slanderers. The narrative moves back and forth between these various scenes of interruption: Ovid is interrupted by his father, whom he calls 'Envie' (I.i.); Horace is bothered by the 'long-winded monster' Crispinus (III.i); Ovid is unjustly (according to both Horace and Maecenas) interpreted and banished by Augustus Caesar (IV.vi); Virgil is interrupted, while reading before Augustus, by a band of court conspirators who have come to accuse Horace of treason because they have misread Horace's 'embleme' (V.iii).[76] Scenes of envious interruption and corruption occur in different degrees, in different 'keys', all providing opportunities to comment upon the various forms the envious 'reader' can take and the relative harm they can wield. The long arm of misprision endangers a poet's fame, but also his life in very real ways. Banishment and hanging for treason are represented as possible consequences of *reading* in this play.

---

[75] M. Lindsay Kaplan's reading of *Poetaster* also focuses on the exposure of each of the classical poets to calumnious attacks. Kaplan's main line of inquiry is the problematic status of satire (often seen as synonymous with slander) in the early modern period. He argues that Jonson aims to show that the satirist – in attempting, like Horace in particular, to show the foibles and the follies of the time – was constantly in danger, if not of actual censorship, of nebulous and insidious accusations of slander and calumny.

[76] Virgil faces only one such scene and, interestingly enough, the interruption of Virgil is meant for Horace (in itself yet another form of misreading on the part of the slanderers). The play moves from minor to major scenes of confrontations with varying envious voices, capable of distorting poetic intention.

The envious prince

In *Poetaster*, to possess the ear of the prince is the common goal of poets and slanderers. He is the *princeps* in that he is both the origin of the court which surrounds him and the prince whose own fame necessarily elevates those who sit close to him. The poet attached to the prince receives fame in and through his connection with majesty. Yet, the prince has the power to banish into oblivion as well as ensure the fame of a poet who writes for the court. His *ear*, then, must be able to distinguish among all the *voices* around him in order to judge who will remain close to him, and achieve fame, and who will be pushed outside of the court and outside the circle of the elect. Through the figure of Augustus, the complicity of the ear, in receiving the slander of traducing tongues, completes the dramatic elaboration of the cycle of listening and reading. One listens to the voice of the actor or the voice that reads a book out loud and the ear opens itself to the poison of malice. It is no accident that Horace is denounced by an *actor* (though unwittingly because he is simply an empty vessel, a medium for others' words). Yet, the poet is defamed, banished, slandered, not simply by the voice of calumny, but by the ear which hears and accepts slanderous sounds. The banishment of Ovid by Augustus testifies to the incredible power of slander over even one of the greatest poets.[77] The figure of Augustus epitomizes the complicity between the slandering voice and the open ear of the prince. As Maecenas notes, voices themselves are ineffective without hearers, without those who will open their ears to the poison of slander. The complicity between the voice and the ear is such that the ear is as responsible for opening itself to slander and rumour as the voice is responsible for spreading it. Toward the end of Act IV, Maecenas expresses his opinion concerning the complicit ear of the Prince:

> Princes that will but heare, or give accesse
> To such officious spies, can ne're be safe:
> They take in poyson, with an open eare,
> And, free from danger, become slaves to feare. (IV.vii.57–60)

In the first lines of Shakespeare's *The Second Part of Henry the Fourth*, Rumour opens the play by exhorting the audience to open their ears: 'Open your ears; for which of you will stop / The vent of hearing when

---

[77] It is important to note that while the three poets of antiquity represented on the early modern stage in this play were 'poets', Ovid is banished by Augustus specifically for his part in a lascivious theatrical *play*.

loud Rumour speaks?'[78] The irony is, of course, that we have all heard and listened to the voice of Rumour at that precise moment. The necessity, as well as the difficulty, of 'stopping' the 'vent' of one's ears in order to judge wisely and make decisions of historic importance is a theme in Shakespeare's play.[79] In *Poetaster*, misreading is tangibly represented as a voice producing cacophonic sounds or distortions. Even the 'mispronounciation' of text is perceived as a type of defacement of it so that poets are always their own best readers. Only they can reproduce the intended sounds written on the page. Even the best readers cannot read a poet's work without distorting it somehow. This essentialist idea of the author as the only one able to pronounce his work correctly speaks to the same interpretative 'gap' between the author and the reader, between the one who can look 'straight' and the other who cannot but help look at the poetic text 'asquint'. The poet rereads the fruits of his first conception in order to defend against the voice of the envious and slandering reader, or even the fickle and potentially dangerous king.

The necessity for the writer to defend himself against defacement is staged in the last act of *Poetaster*, where Augustus Caesar invites Virgil to court. He wants to 'see' the poet's *Aeneid* (dedicated to him) and 'surfet on their sight' (v.ii.7). Virgil arrives, but is hesitant about showing the emperor his books, saying they are not worthy of 'Caesar's gracious eyes'; 'I would not shew them' (lines 7; 13). Caesar insists he would 'behold / A humane soule made visible in life' (lines 17–18). Yet, within the constraints of the stage world, this 'seeing' and 'reading' of text needs to be translated into something that the audience can 'hear'. Therefore, in order to 'see' the *Aeneid*, Caesar must read, but, oddly, he entreats the writer to read in his place:

> Read, read, thy selfe, deare VIRGIL, let not me
> Prophane one accent, with an untun'd tongue:
> 'Best matter, badly showne, shewes worse, then bad.'
> See then, this chaire, of purpose set for thee
> To reade thy *poeme* in: refuse it not. (v.ii.21–5)

Caesar insists that the poet read *himself*. Augustus insists that Virgil read his own work because he is afraid that his own 'untun'd' tongue would make a cacophony of the poet's verse. The emperor hints, flatteringly, that

---

[78] William Shakespeare, *The Second Part of Henry the Fourth* ('Induction', lines 1–2).
[79] See Mark Robson, 'Looking with Ears, Hearing with Eyes: Shakespeare and the Ear of the Early Modern', *EMLS*, 7.1, Special Issue 8 (May 2001), 10.1–23.

he does not wish to 'prophane' or defile the poet's sacred work.[80] Augustus 'stoops' to the poet, even to the point of giving him his chair, but he also gives him a pointed command: 'refuse it not'. Even while the prince is generous, the poet is represented as constrained to obey. When Virgil is shown the chair, he demurs:

> It will be thought a thing ridiculous
> To present eyes, and to all future times
> A grosse untruth; that any *poet* (void
> Of birth, or wealth, or temporall dignity)
> Should, with *decorum*, transcend CAESARS chaire. (v.ii.28–32)

The idea of transcendence to describe the taking of a chair may seem extreme, yet, this is precisely the point of this strange meeting between the ancient poet and his Caesar for the purpose of reading the poet's work. The scene shows the poet being offered the possibility of going beyond the limits imposed upon him by his station and his craft. In offering him his chair, Caesar has offered Virgil the possibility not only of going beyond but also of being *independent* of the emperor, even temporarily.[81] At the same time, transcendence is very much on Virgil's mind when he speaks of how 'future times' will view the 'scene' played in the last act of *Poetaster*, a scene in which Augustus offers Virgil, not only his chair, but also his 'name':

> Welcome to CAESAR, VIRGIL. CAESAR and VIRGIL
> Shall differ but in sound; to CAESAR, VIRGIL
> (Of his expressed greatnesse) shall be made
> A second sur-name, and to VIRGIL, CAESAR. (v.ii.2–5)

The scene in which Augustus Caesar offers his chair and gives his 'sur-name' to a poet may seem 'ridiculous' to 'present *eyes*', but will necessarily expand into a 'grosse untruth' for all future times. This, in effect, is Virgil's appraisal of the situation. What in the present is *ridiculous* becomes in the future grossly untrue. Virgil implies that this too is the problem with reading, since Caesar's indecorous 'chair' is the place from which he is to read. It is not only the reader's tongue that can untune the harmony of the book, the *place* from

---

[80] The word 'prophane' is a strong one. It is used frequently in Jonson to denote a profound kind of sacrilege, such as in the description of the anti-masque evils as having 'prophaner eyes' in *The Golden Age Restored*, Herford and Simpson, vol. VII, p. 422 (line 25). See Martin Butler and David Lindley, 'Restoring Astraea: Jonson's Masque for the Fall of Somerset', *ELH* 61 (1994), 807–27; p. 821.

[81] It would be tempting to see this gesture as the crowning of a Lord of Misrule. At the same time, this notion of transcendence is a theological one in which Virgil becomes independent of his earthly Caesar.

which one reads can also be problematic, especially if this place is that of an emperor, or within the purview of an emperor, who, in the previous scene, has just exiled the poet Ovid to the Black Sea in a fit of tyrannical rage.

Yet, the phrase 'present eyes' begs the question of what is the 'present', or, as the prologue 'Envie' puts it, the 'present state'?[82] The 'present eyes' are, as we know from the Induction, those of the early seventeenth-century audience watching the play named *Poetaster*, written in fifteen weeks by Ben Jonson, but they could also equally refer to those 'present' in the Roman past represented by the play, contemporary with Virgil and Caesar. Finally, the present could equally refer to the epoch of the audience (currently) watching or reading the play. In relation to the 'Romans' of the play, the seventeenth-century spectators are those 'future times' who will view an emperor offering his throne to a poet as a 'grosse untruth' and, in relation to both Rome and the seventeenth century, we, seeing the play entitled *Poetaster*, are that future.[83] In each scenario, the offer of the chair is either ridiculous or untrue. Like the 'ridiculous commentator' (v.iii.77), the wolvish Lupus, in the following scene, readers, whether they be Kings or wolves, are suspect.

Ultimately, the effect of Virgil's punning on 'present' and 'future' is to bring to the fore the relativity of the process of reading itself. By setting the play in Rome, as opposed to London, in the ancient past, as opposed to the present minute, the writer is opening up the space for his own poetic 'transcendence'. This transcendence may very well be achieved by accepting Caesar's chair and joining his name to his own. CAESAR, VIRGIL and VIRGIL, CAESAR shall have names that 'shall differ only in sound'. Caesar makes the poet an emperor and himself a poet. The identity between the two can be seen as mutually beneficial, mutually flattering. On the other hand, Caesar's gesture is not completely without a condition: the two *shall* 'differ' even if only by the 'sound'. This difference may seem small and yet the importance of 'sound', as accent, voice, tongue, in the act of reading and interpreting have been emphasized throughout the play. Differences in sound, through the voice of the actor, for instance, can change meanings,

---

[82] Many critics have put the question differently by wondering 'where' geographically, Rome or London? But this geographical marker occludes somewhat the historical dimension. Nowhere in the play is the word London mentioned, unlike, for instance, in *The Alchemist*. The 'present state' may very well be London as opposed to Rome, but more importantly, it is the *present* as opposed to the past and the future.

[83] I have not differentiated between future spectators and future readers in this discussion of the palimpsestic effect that the phrase 'present eyes' possesses. What is interesting is the way 'seeing' and 'beholding' for Caesar implies seeing the 'page' not the stage. We, as spectators of a play, 'behold' Virgil 'made visible in life' until we find after the enjambment: 'And more refulgent in a senseless paper' (v.ii.18–19).

distort texts, and prophane poetic works. Caesar's gesture can be seen as flattering, but is at the same time, grotesquely hyperbolic as well as potentially threatening for the poet.

Despite Virgil's initial protests, Caesar decides to choose a passage from Virgil's *Aeneid* to be read in public by resorting to the *Sortes Virgilianae*, the practice from medieval times of choosing at random any page in the *Aeneid* in order to know one's destiny. This blatant anachronism in a play set in ancient Rome, brings the future and its judgement into the past (or, in play time, the present). This same Virgil, putting aside the chair of Caesar, would become the equivalent of an oracle, a prophet and a guide and as such, ironically, Caesar, in choosing a page from Virgil's book, is instantly relegated to the role of the suppliant, seeking *his* destiny in the *poet's* work.

The page he turns to by chance was (and still is) one of the most famous in the *Aeneid*, recounting the secret 'marriage' between Dido and Aeneas, the cause of Dido's eventual downfall. The passage is also famed for Virgil's description of 'Fama'. Here, Fame is described as 'a fleet evill', 'a monster vast, / And dreadfull', full of 'waking eyes' and 'listning eares', 'covetous shee is of tales, and lies / As prodigall of truth' (v.ii.75ff.). Caesar has picked a passage about the monstrosity of 'Fame' and its multiplicity of tongues and eyes. He is shown again the danger that comes when, as Maecenas says to Horace regarding Augustus' judgment of Ovid: 'Princes … give accesse / To such officious spies' (iv.vii.57–8). Horace too rails against the banishment of Ovid attributing it to the 'clamorous tongues' of 'prodigious malice' (iv.vii.38; 50). Maecenas concurs, as we have seen, saying that Kings who listen to Rumour: 'take in poyson, with an open eare, / and, free from danger, become slaves to feare' (iv.vii.59–60). The passage Virgil reads to Caesar is, in fact, an image of the malice that has moved and swayed him, to which, in the previous act (in banishing Ovid) he had been, in Maecenas' word, a 'slave'. Envy, in the prologue, and Fame, in Virgil's *Aeneid*, turn out to be mirror images of each other.

The danger presented to the writer by the reader, then, is everywhere. Except for the ideal reader embodied in Maecenas, even Augustus Caesar himself is capable of defacing the author's text. The defences against such envious reading are represented as multiple. Virgil's acquiescence to his emperor's demands is in stark contrast to Ovid's utter disregard for imperial power in the pursuit of pleasure, but also in the pursuit of his own poetic gift. At the end of the play, we are naturally offered a 'third way'. Horace lies somewhere between Ovid, unprotected and interested only in poetry (and love), and Virgil, personally protected by the emperor himself, but at the cost of a certain conformism.[84] Horace, like Ovid, is open to slanderous attack, but is protected both by Maecenas and his own virtue. Horace sets his own 'virtue', but also his own 'voice', against those of his slanderers:

> A just man cannot feare, thou foolish *Tribune*;
> Not, though the malice of traducing tongues,
> The open vastnesse of a tyrannes eare,
> ...
> Should, in a point, meet all to take his life.
> His innocence is armour 'gainst all these. (v.iii.61–3; 66–7)

Innocence may be a kind of natural armour against malicious tongues and open ears, but in the scene following this declaration, Horace confronts, in a more practical way, the envious attacks of his readers. In the final act of the play, Horace is forced to explain the meaning of an *unfinished* emblem, which is maliciously interpreted by the envious reader, Lupus, as a treason against Augustus.[85] To each of Lupus' accusations, he counters with explanation and justification for his creation:

HORACE. With reverence to great CAESAR, worthy *Romans*,
Observe but this ridiculous commentator:
The *soule* to my *device*, was in this *distich*.
  Thus, oft, the base and ravenous multitude
  Survive, to share the spoiles of fortitude.
Which in this body, I have figur'd here,
A VULTURE –

LUPUS. A Vulture? I; now, 'tis a Vulture. O, abominable! monstrous! monstrous! ha's not your Vulture a beake? ha's it not legges? and tallons? and wings? and feathers?
...
HORACE. And therefore must it be an Eagle?
MECOENAS. Respect him not, good HORACE: Say your device.
HORACE. A VULTURE and a WOLFE—
LUPUS. A Wolfe? good. That's I; I am the wolfe. My name's LUPUS, I am meant by the wolfe. On, on, a Vulture, and a Wolfe. (v. iii.76–86; 88–94)[86]

---

[84] Alan Sinfield suggests that in 'establishing Virgil as the writer who figures the unity of the state and cultural production, Jonson gains space to suggest a different, emergent possibility: Horace as the voice of a critical authorial function.' Sinfield, 'Perils of Cultural Production', p. 8.

[85] Horace describes the 'libell in picture' (v.iii.47) – which is how Lupus refers to it – as 'the imperfect body of an embleme … I began for Mecoenas' (v.iii.57–8). This must mean that the part of the emblem that is still unfinished or unclear is the picture or image.

[86] Horace uses the word 'ridiculous' to describe his envious reader, associating Lupus, necessarily, with Virgil's appraisal of Augustus' gesture in giving the poet his chair.

Horace's 'embleme' for his patron Maecenas places Horace in the dangerous position of being accused of slandering Caesar. To defend himself, the poet reads out loud the 'distich' representing the 'motto', 'soule', or device of his emblem: 'Thus, oft, the base and ravenous multitude / Survive, to share the spoiles of fortitude' (lines 79–80). Then he goes on to explain that the image, or 'body' of the emblem is that of 'A Vulture' (line 81). The problem lies mainly with the image. Lupus mistakes the drawing of a vulture for an eagle, thereby skewing the interpretation of the constituent parts. If, in Lupus' prejudiced logic, the drawing is of an eagle, the bird representative of Caesar, this implies that Horace's emblem is a 'seditious libell' (line 47). That the drawing represents a vulture, not an eagle, is only Horace's word against Lupus'. Lupus, significantly, is represented as having interrupted Horace, just at the moment when he is about to complete the description of the emblematic *image*: it is a picture of a vulture and a wolf, the images of the 'base and ravenous multitude' (line 78). The envious reader interrupts the writer again to see himself in the image, which, ironically, though unintended as a portrait of Lupus himself, is precisely a mirror image of him, the wolf. Of course, what Horace does not explain is that in the Aesopic tradition, the wolf was emblematic of the cruel and tyrannical king. So, by situating the criticism in Lupus, the evil reader, the poet might be able to smuggle in a covert, seditious satirical allusion.

Only two solutions are offered to defend the poet from the envious reader: the author's continual presence (a physical impossibility) and/or a powerful protector, a risky enterprise for anyone familiar with the Tudor court milieu. The scene poignantly expresses Jonson's feeling of powerlessness, an almost tragic sense of the future abandonment of his works to the silence of future ages when he won't be there to control either the reading or the reader. Only the author's 'presence' can ensure proper interpretation. No image, no writing can be 'perfect', in other words, safely closed off from outside interpretation and misinterpretation.

In *Poetaster*, the danger of misreading and of traducing the poet's text is compared to the conspiracies and groups of slanderers in court who, by gaining the prince's ear, may ruin a career and even contribute to the banishment or death of a member of the court. In this play, however, the members of the court engage in no political action; rather, the factions loyal to the king or loyal to the upstarts are represented as factions in the court of poetic fame. They consist of those who are great poets and those who try to slander them. The conspiracies of the courtiers in Jonson's other Roman plays, *Sejanus* (1603) and *Catiline*, present a contrast to *Poetaster*.

The slanderous accusations against the author Cordus in *Sejanus* are eerily similar to those levelled against Horace by Lupus and his gang. But, in *Sejanus*, Cordus' self-defence wins him nothing and his books are summarily burnt with only Arruntius' voice to speak against the injustice. Cordus' reference to the way Augustus Caesar patronized Virgil is in stark and ironic contrast to Tiberius' disregard, fear and suspicion of poets. In *Catiline*, the political nature of these conspiracies may be seen as leavened with a heaping of fantasy about poetic fame, since the main figure is Cicero, the genius of rhetorical power as well as the defender of republican Rome.[87] Plays such as *Cynthia's Revels* and *Catiline* can be seen, like *Poetaster*, as the wishful response to the threat of defacement and an image of the author who tries to leap to his own posterity. The play serves as a testimony (and a testament) from the early modern author who knows the risks inherent in the gaze of the reader and knows he has to take action to both protect his work and control the way readers will read it. The relative immunity from envy, enjoyed by the classical poets of *Poetaster*, is something that Jonson may indeed have attempted to attain for himself through publication of the 1616 Folio.

---

[87] Cicero bridges perfectly the gap between poetic and political power, making him *the* ideal candidate for another play by the writer of *Poetaster*.

CHAPTER 4

Sanctuary: Jonson's prophylactic strategy

> But his chief safetie, shall be the not walking abroade; and his chief protection, the bearing the livery of your name, which (if much much good will do not deceive me) is worthy to be a sanctuary for a greater offender.
>
> (Sir Philip Sidney, 'To My Deare Ladie and Sister, The Countess of Pembroke', *The Countesse of Pembrokes Arcadia*, 1590)

A sanctuary is a holy place. It is a sacred place where fugitives from justice were formerly entitled to immunity from arrest. It is an asylum, a space of safety and refuge for the criminal. A sanctuary is also a piece of land or forest where wild animals, especially those hunted for sport, could take refuge from hunters in order to breed and reproduce. In sixteenth-century England, the jurist John Manwood's treatise on the laws of the forest describes a sanctuary as a '*silva sacrosancta*, a privileged wood for wild beasts to be safe in'.[1] Sanctuary describes places set aside for the preservation of both the human and beast. Like a hunted animal, the criminal places himself under the protection of the god of the sanctuary or within a special set of legal and juridical boundaries that create a magic space over which human law, temporarily, has no sway. In *The Masque of Queenes*, Ben Jonson identifies himself as the criminal seeking sanctuary. He is a fugitive, trying to escape the harsh judgement of the one who comes *after* him, the reader. In his dedicatory poem to the author of *The Rogue*, Jonson described the reader as one 'who *tracks* this Authors ... Pen', comparing the reader to a hound on a hunt and the author to its prey.[2] In the

---

[1] Also termed 'privilege of forest'. John Manwood, *A Treatise of the Laws of the Forest* (London, 1665 [1592]), p. 68. John Stow describes the privileges appertaining to sanctuary in his description of St Martins le Grand in Aldersgate Ward: 'Then in St Martins lane was of old time a fair and large college, of a deane and secular cannons or priests, and was called S. Martins le graund, founded by Ingelricus and Edwardus his brother in the year of Christ 1056. Confirmed by W. the Conqueror ... This colledge claymed great priviledges of sanctuary.' John Stow, *A Survay of London* (London, 1603 [1598]), p. 309.
[2] Ben Jonson, 'On the Author, Worke, and Translator' in *Ungathered Verse* (xxiv), Herford and Simpson, vol. VIII, p. 389 (line 1).

masque, the poet placed Queen Anne, his patron, in the company of twelve dead queens of antiquity as part of his programme to give his masque the necessary learning he felt it required. Yet, the spectacle of a living queen in the midst of a throng of 'dead' queens becomes the occasion for the poet suddenly to reconsider how this might appear to the tracking reader of the masque text. The writer anticipates censure and tries to deflect it in advance:

> But, here, I discerne a possible Objection agaynst mee, to which I must turne: As, *How can I bring* Persons, *of so different* Ages, *to appear, properly, together*? Or, *Why (which is more unnaturall) with* Virgil's Mezentius, *I joyne the living with the dead*? I answere to both these, at once, Nothing is more proper; Nothing more naturall: For these all live; and together, in their *Fame*; And so I present them. Besides, if I would fly to the all-daring Power of *Poetry*, Where could I not take Sanctuary? or in whose Poëme?[3]

The poet raises the spectre of the critical reader who objects to the writer's blatant anachronism in placing a living queen in the company of eleven 'dead' queens. The poet, anticipating this objection, compares himself to a monster. In Virgil's *Aeneid*, Mezentius was a king who would tie his enemies and prisoners to the corpses of the dead and let them die slow and painful deaths, bound to a corrupting body.[4] Why would the poet choose to compare himself with that ancient figure of horror, Mezentius? First, he recognizes that he has perpetrated a strange misalliance: joining a living queen with a group of effigies or yoking court flattery with poetic erudition. The poet portrays himself as one accused and defends himself by a rhetorical sleight of hand. The ancient queens are not dead, but alive in 'their Fame'. Yet, the problem seems to remain. Perhaps because the 'fame' of Queen Anne and the 'fame' of the queens of antiquity refer to different kinds of fame: a present fame, of rumour and gossip, opposed to the fame earned over the centuries, monumentalized and purified of the alloy of changing and changeable opinion. In the final analysis, the poet sees fit to place himself under the protection of 'Poetry' as if he were finding refuge in a sanctuary. Poetry, like sanctuary, seems to be where those who have been accused, even of robbery and murder, may enjoy certain privileges and protection.

Yet, who or what is pursuing the poet? The poet says that 'I discern a possible Objection' (line 670); then he notes 'I answer both these [objections], at

---

[3] Ben Jonson, *The Masque of Queenes*, Herford and Simpson, vol. VII, p. 313 (lines 670–9).
[4] In Book 8 of the *Aeneid*, Virgil describes the horrible deeds of the Etruscan King, Mezentius: 'He would even couple carcase / with living bodies as a form of torture. / Hand to hand and face to face, he made them / suffer corruption, oozing gore and slime / in that wretched embrace, and a slow / death.' Virgil, *The Aeneid*, trans. Robert Fitzgerald (New York: Vintage Books, 1984 [1981]), pp. 246–7 (lines 484–8).

once' (line 674). He seems to say, in the final sentence quoted above, that if he cannot convince his accuser(s) and decides to 'fly' instead, he will be sure to find sanctuary either in the abstract 'Power of *Poetry*' or in some particular author's poem (lines 677–9). Here we are reminded of Spenser's address 'To His Booke' prefacing *The Shepheard's Calendar*, in which, as we have seen, he urges his book to flee 'Envy' and seek the protection of Sir Philip Sidney:

> And if that Envy barke at thee,
> As sure it will, for succour flee
> Under the shadow of his wing.[5]

Spenser's urging his book to seek the protecting space under Sidney's 'wing' is echoed in Jonson's claim that he can find sanctuary in poetry. One might well argue that the 'all-daring Power of *Poetry*' may even be an indirect allusion to Sidney's *An Apologie for Poetrie* and that Jonson, like Spenser, sought figurative refuge in Sidney's *Apologie* and its eloquent defence of poetry and poets. It would be hard to overestimate the importance of the *Apologie* and the potent, even perhaps, talismanic effect of Sidney himself on the early modern poetic imaginary. Jonson's dedication of *The Alchemist* (1610): 'To the Lady, Most deserving of her name and bloud: Mary, La. Wroth' emphasizes her role as protectress-in-proxy for her uncle, Sir Philip Sidney: 'This, yet, *safe* in your judgment (which is a SIDNEYS) is forbidden to speake more' (my emphasis).[6] I would suggest that 'Envy' in Spenser's prefatory poem and the 'Objection' Jonson imagines might be raised against him describe the same menace. Moreover, both poets contemplate the same response to this menace, namely, flight to a refuge and, as we shall see a bit later, a form of 'fascinating' camouflage.

THE POET'S SANCTUARY: 'TO PENSHURST'

In his poem 'To Penshurst', the first poem in the collection *The Forrest*, Jonson places himself under the aegis of Sir Philip Sidney, finding sanctuary within the walls of the Sidney family home. 'To Penshurst' can be read as a representation of the poetic desire to find a safe haven for literary creation and the poetic name. I would argue that the house in the poem is a singularly powerful symbolic representation of a sanctuary that offers immunity to the author from the envious gaze of a judging posterity.

---

[5] Spenser, *The Shepheards Calendar*, 'To His Booke', n.p. (lines 5–7).
[6] Ben Jonson, *The Alchemist*, Herford and Simpson, vol. v, p. 289.

Penhurst, in short, may be seen as Jonson's objective correlative for a space sanctuarized against the gaze of envy.

As the prototype of a genre which praises the house of its owner, readers have seen the poem as praising a place where moral goodness and integrity hold sway in a corrupt world.[7] Raymond Williams was among the first to comment upon a 'double-edge' in Jonson's praise of Penshurst in the poem's insistent negative constructions and problematic hyperboles.[8] The critic highlights the strangeness of the lines in which the 'painted partrich … for thy messe, is willing to be kill'd' and comments: '[W]hat kind of wit is it exactly – for it must be wit; the most ardent traditionalists will hardly claim it for observation – which has the birds and other creatures offering themselves to be eaten?'[9] Similarly, Don Wayne's book-length examination of the poem in the Marxist terms first suggested by Williams' reading show that the Penshurst *ideal* can be viewed as possessing a darker social underside.[10] Katharine Eisaman Maus testifies to the strange conjunction of utopian and dystopian elements: 'the language of the non-material ideal collapses into the language of material abundance'; in other words, the spiritual and abstract good praised in the poem is disturbingly enmeshed in the language of hyperbolically corporeal and earthly goods.[11] Yet, readerly ideas about what is particularly 'ideal' about Penshurst range widely: social justice, aesthetic proportion, natural and social harmony and economic surplus are all included in the concept of the ideal world at Penshurst. If we see Jonson's Penshurst as a *sanctuary*, a certain number of contradictory elements in the poem begin to cohere. For, as a description of sanctuary, the poet would necessarily give voice to both the dangers and evils *outside* as well as the suspension of the ordinary operations of law and the quality of security *inside*. In *The Masque of Queenes*, when the poet says that he

---

[7] For articles on the country house poem as a genre see G. R. Hibbard, 'The Country House Poem of the Seventeenth Century', *JWCI* 19 (1956), 159–77; C. Molesworth, 'Property and Virtue: The Genre of the Country House Poem in the Seventeenth Century', *Genre* 1 (1968), 141–57 and the book-length study by William Alexander McClung, *The Country House in English Renaissance Poetry* (Berkeley: University of California Press, 1977). For articles on Penshurst as an emblem of moral goodness see Paul M. Cubeta, 'A Jonsonian ideal: "To Penshurst"', *Philological Quarterly* 42 (1963), 14–24; Gayle Edward Wilson, 'Jonson's Use of the Bible and the Great Chain of Being in "To Penshurst"', *SEL* 8 (1968), 77–89; Alastair Fowler, 'The "Better marks" of Jonson's "To Penshurst"', *The Review of English Studies* 95 (1973), 266–82.
[8] Raymond Williams, *The Country and the City* (New York: Oxford University Press, 1973), p. 29.
[9] *Ibid.*, p. 29.
[10] Don Wayne, *Penshurst: The Semiotics of Place and the Poetics of History* (Madison: Wisconsin University Press, 1984).
[11] Katharine Eisaman Maus, 'Facts of the Matter: Satiric and Ideal Economies in the Jonsonian Imagination' in Brady and Herendeen (eds.), *Ben Jonson's 1616 Folio*, pp. 64–89; p. 80.

will take 'Sanctuary' in the 'all-daring Power of *Poetry*', we may see him, in 'To Penshurst', flying to this sanctuary, finding refuge under the 'wing' of Sidney, sitting under the Muses' oak, safe from envy and censure.

Jonson begins his praise of Philip Sidney's ancestral home (as he began his praise of Shakespeare) by saying that Penshurst is *not* an object of envy:

> Thou are not, PENSHURST, built to envious show,
> Of touch, or marble; nor canst boast a row
> Of polished pillars, or a roofe of gold:
> Thou has no lanthrene, whereof tales are told;
> Or stayre, or courts; but stand'st an ancient pile.[12]

The restraint of Penshurst, the simplicity of its outlines, the naturalness of its materials and the proportion of its architecture are all in stark contrast to prodigy houses that were ornamented in an effort to outdo others in the spirit of envious rivalry with their neighbours. Yet, in its denial of envy, envy is paradoxically invoked. As a guest at Penshurst, the poet claims that he too is *not* an object of envy. Even the walls surrounding Penshurst are *not envied* by the people who built them or who live outside of them:

> And though thy walls be of the countrey stone,
> They're rear'd with no mans ruine, no mans grone,
> *There's none, that dwell about them, wish them downe*;
> But all come in, the farmer, and the clowne. [my emphasis; lines 45–8]

These walls, erected to separate (fostering envy and hate between classes), are magically porous even in a society founded on class divisions. At Penshurst, the clown can offer his daughter to the aristocrat: 'Some … send / By their ripe daughters, whom they would commend / This way to husbands' (lines 52–5). And a poet may even become, temporarily, a King:

> Nor, when I take my lodging, need I pray
> For fire, or lights, or livorie: all is there;
> *As if thou, then, wert mine, or I raign'd here*:
> There's nothing I can wish, for which I stay.
> That found King JAMES, when hunting late, this way. [lines 72–6; my emphasis]

William E. McCain addresses what he sees as 'Jonson's ambivalence about the poet's place in society', hinting at the fact that the poet portrays himself

---

[12] Ben Jonson, 'To Penshurst', *The Forrest* (ii), Herford and Simpson, vol. VIII, p. 93 (lines 1–5). All subsequent references will be to line numbers and will be included in the text.

as something of a scrounger.[13] He concludes that we should 'accept the poem itself as emblematic of what the poet contributes to his community', but he does not note the potentially radical and far-reaching ambition couched in the poetic fantasy of becoming King and surmounting his station and place in the community.[14]

So, even though 'To Penshurst' is marked by a repetitive chant of freedom from envy, Jonson's negative constructions tend to deny and admit envy simultaneously into Penshurst. Although the poem provides us with an image of bounty, it perpetually introduces, like the tombstone in the Arcadian landscape, the image of loss and lack. While the poem seems to describe the perfect hospitality of a gentleman and his wife, the house, '[W]here comes no guest' (line 61), seems eerily empty except for the poet who claims Penshurst as his. J. C. A. Rathmell argues:

> Contrary to what a too literal reading of the last line ['thy lord dwells' (line 102)] of that poem might suggest, Lord Lisle was only intermittently at home. The primacy which Jonson gives to his wife, Lady Barbara, in the poem is quite apposite; in the absence of her husband at court, the main responsibility for looking after Penshurst rested with her.[15]

There exists a kind of artificial, because it is problematically hyperbolic, 'fullness' everywhere, which finds its terminus in an empty room where a poet sits, eating gluttonously. If the poem is viewed in terms of artificial fullness and a symmetrical emptiness, it becomes clear that 'To Penshurst' shares, with *The Alchemist*, a fantasy of sanctuary in the house of the absent master. In *Poetaster*, the house of Maecenas is also a kind of sanctuary free from envy. For Horace, for instance, it is impossible:

> To thinke, there breathes a spirit beneath his roofe,
> Subject unto those poore affections
> *Of under-mining envie, and detraction,*
> Moodes, onely proper to base groveling minds:
> That place is not in *Rome*, I dare affirm,
> More pure, or free from such low, common evils.
> *There's no man greeved, that this is thought more rich,*
> Or this more learned; *each man hath his place,*
> And to his merit, his reward of grace,
> Which with a mutual love they all embrace.[16] [my emphasis]

---

[13] William E. Cain, 'The Place of the Poet in Jonson's "To Penshurst" and "To My Muse"', *Criticism* 21 (1979), 34–48; p. 35.
[14] *Ibid.*, p. 40.
[15] J. C. A. Rathmell, 'Jonson, Lord Lisle, and Penshurst', *ELR* 1 (1971), 250–60; p. 252.
[16] Ben Jonson, *Poetaster*, Herford and Simpson, vol. IV, pp. 241–2 (III.i.250–9).

According to Alan Sinfield, the house of Maecenas is a 'magical space', a 'detraction-free zone'.[17] These lines from *Poetaster*, where no one begrudges or is 'grieved' that another is 'more rich' or 'more learned', seem to echo the chant against envy in 'To Penshurst' and the careful hierarchy where 'each man hath his place'. In 'To Penshurst', *Poetaster* and *The Alchemist*, the poet envisions a space in which he can safely transcend class boundaries, make and imagine himself as more intelligent or creative and give himself an alternative identity or, in the case of Face, multiple identities. In such a sanctuary he can give free rein to his imagination (or proclivities), whether that takes the form of fantasizing himself as King James I or Horace. In *The Alchemist*, Face's ability to move himself up the social ladder from lowly butler to (potential) husband of the rich widow is contingent upon his having the use of Lovewit's house in the master's absence. In *Poetaster*, Horace's safety from slander and envy is due to Maecenas' patronage. The promotion of Ben Jonson, from starving writer to king, is also dependent upon the free use of Penshurst in the absence of its owner, at least within the poem itself: 'As if thou, then, wert mine, or I raign'd here' (line 74). Both the poet and Face lodge in the house of the absent master and 'raign' there whether for a brief moment or for all posterity.

We see the poet allowed 'to eate, / Without his feare' (lines 61–2) in the house of the great Philip Sidney, for Penshurst is not just an 'ancient', worthy, hospitable country house, it is foremost the house of Sir Philip Sidney, the literary predecessor and defender of poets. The poet, the 'I' of 'To Penshurst', becomes, for a time (within the duration of the narrative), for *all* time (within the life of the poem itself), a dweller in the house, which symbolizes the literary tradition represented by Sidney.[18] By placing himself at the Sidney table, eating without fear of comment or envy, the poet represents himself in a literary sanctuary from judgement. Inside the house, we find the poet, sitting alone, glutting himself:

> Where no guest, but is allow'd to eate,
> Without his feare, and of thy lords owne meate:
> Where the same beere, and bread, and self-same wine,
> That is his Lordships, shall also be mine.
> And I not faine to sit (as some, this day,
> At great mens tables) and yet dine away.

---

[17] Sinfield, 'Perils of Cultural Production', p. 12.
[18] The fantasy of being among the landed aristocracy and owning Penshurst is, of course, not a negligible part of the fantasy of placing himself in Penhsurst. However, the choice of Sidney's home and the poet's promotion to kingship, even fleetingly, implies a definite engagement with posterity for Jonson as a poet.

> Here no man tells my cups; not, standing by,
> A waiter, doth my gluttony envy:
> But gives me what I call, and lets me eate,
> He knows, below, he shall find plentie of meate. (lines 61–70)

The scene of the poet at the table is not simply a scene of satisfied hunger, because 'meate' in Jonson is not just 'food'. It is another word for learned invention and good poetry. In the preface to *Hymenaei*, Jonson takes pains to distinguish the light and frivolous 'shew' of the masque performance from the substantial literary invention of the poet's own 'meates':[19]

> I am contented, these fastidious *stomachs* should leave my full tables, and enjoy at home, their cleane emptie trenchers, fittest for such ayrie tasts: where perhaps a few *Italian* herbs, pick'd up, and made into a *sallade*, may find sweeter acceptance, than all, the most nourishing and sound meates of the world.[20]

Here, Jonson compares Inigo Jones' Italianate spectacle to a salad and erudition to meat. When he eats meat in Sidney's house we might see it as Jonson eating Sidney's 'nourishing' invention. Literary sanctuary for Jonson may be described, metaphorically, as eating the meat of former authors, borrowing or even stealing from them, in order to surround and enwomb his own text in citation and fill it with those ancient and contemporary poets' words. The poet fortifies himself and his own creation by eating another's food. This food, moreover, has already been consumed once, read and vetted and so becomes a kind of charm against envy. The same critical opinion which has pronounced Sidney a great poet will not be able to bring down judgement on the poet who finds sanctuary in Sidney's home and eats his *meat*.

Jonson makes it clear that the servant in the poem does not begrudge the poet this food. Penshurst is not governed by the rules of the zero-sum game in which one man's overindulgence leads to another man's lack. Yet, a question remains as to why the poet describes his eating as 'gluttony': 'No man tells my cups; nor … doth my gluttony envy' (lines 67–8). Gluttony, one of the seven deadly sins like envy, implies overindulgence, grossness and excessiveness. Yet, Jonson's references to his large girth often tend to be quite positive. Sometimes they imply 'weight', as in seriousness, 'volume', punning on himself as a kind of book, and 'prodigiousness', a word implying both portentousness as well as 'greatness'.[21] The glutton,

---

[19] Ben Jonson, *Hymenaei*, Herford and Simpson, vol. VII, p. 209 (lines 13, 28).
[20] *Ibid.*, p. 209 (lines 23–8).
[21] See, for instance: 'Though I seeme of a prodigious wast, / I am not so voluminous, and vast, / But there are lines, wherewith I might be embraced.' Ben Jonson, 'My Answer. The Poet to the Painter', *Underwood*, Herford and Simpson, vol. VII, p. 226 (lines 1–3).

in 'To Penshurst', may be one who devours, who enjoys and who wants as much out of life as possible. The waiter might have envied the poet not just how much food he is allowed to have but also how much he is capable of consuming. Gluttony may be the quality that makes the poet able to imagine that he is both the aristocratic lord who owns Penshurst and the king who visits it.

Penshurst, then, is the ultimate sanctuary for the fugitive from literary justice because he is given the invaluable Sidneyean 'meate' without any debt to pay. No one counts his cups, no one sees how much he eats and pours down his throat or reckons up the tab in authorial debt to the literary precursor. The dead poet does not begrudge him meat because there is surplus on the 'estate'. The Penshurst estate is where the poet may drink deep from the spring where 'all the *Muses* met' (line 14) and feel momentarily refreshed and complete. Like Face in the house of Lovewit, Jonson becomes, at least in his own fantasy, inheritor of the house where he played an alchemical confidence game. Without rival, without envy, the poet dwells in his poetic sanctuary for eternity.

AUTHORITY AND SANCTUARY

In the passage from *The Masque of Queenes*, quoted above, the reference to Mezentius describes a form of camouflage which the poet uses to help him flee for sanctuary. What Jonson does in *Queenes*, may be described, in Francis Bacon's words as *removing* 'the *Lot* (as they call it) and to lay it upon another'.[22] This means placing somebody or something in public view to fascinate the evil eye *in place of* the original target of envy. We have already seen that, according to Bacon, there are some 'so curious, as to note, that the Times, when the Stroke, or Percussion of an *Envious* Eye doth most hurt'; Bacon claims that it is when the person who is envied is perceived in the midst of 'Glory, or Triumph'.[23] In *The Masque of Queenes*, it is the poet who shows himself to be 'curious' exactly in this way; he actually records the moment when the envious eye strikes him in the midst of his own moment of poetic triumph (after having written a masque for the Queen). Jonson's spectral reader objects just at the moment the poet has been waxing eloquent on his own poems, just a few lines before: 'Of which, some may come forth with a longer *destiny*, than this *Age*, commonly, gives the best Births.'[24] Behind the reader's totem 'objection' to

[22] Bacon, 'Of Envy', *Essayes*, p. 47. [23] *Ibid.*, pp. 40–1.
[24] Ben Jonson, *The Masque of Queenes*, Herford and Simpson, vol. VII, pp. 312–13 (lines 666–8).

the mixing of the living and the dead is a perceived envy of the writer's 'longer *destiny*' and glory. This envy has the power to 'object' and call into question precisely the author's claim that his own poems might indeed survive his own epoch: a claim that implicitly condemns the ignorance of 'this Age' that is so miserly in rewarding true merit. Now that the spectre of the critical and envious reader has been raised, what must the writer do in order to deflect its gaze? Bacon describes the only cure for envy in counter-witchcraft:

> As we said in the beginning, that the Act of *Envy*, had somewhat in it, of *Witchcraft*; so there is no other Cure of *Envy*, but the cure of *Witchcraft*: And that is, to remove the *Lot* (as they call it) and to lay it upon another. For which purpose, the wiser Sort of great Persons, bring in ever upon the Stage, some Body, upon whom to derive the *Envy*, that would come upon themselves.[25]

Some object, effigy, or person must serve to encounter envy in the place of the intended victim. Bacon's idea of bringing 'upon the stage somebody, upon whom to derive the envy' resembles the apotropaic function of an amulet intended to fascinate the envious eye. These amulets needed to be striking, extremely gross or terrible to draw the harmful glance away from the intended victim. I would suggest that Virgil's king, Mezentius, serves the writer as a very powerful defence against envy because he provides the poet with the perfect example of 'somebody, upon whom to derive the envy that would come upon themselves'.[26] Mezentius fulfills the function of attracting the gaze perfectly. He is the epitome of the 'unnatural', a true tyrant and, in the early modern period, a highly visible degenerate.[27] While the eye of envy is fascinated by somebody grandly horrible like Mezentius, the poet will be running for sanctuary. The poet's setting the living beside the dead in his masque seems child's play in comparison.[28] So, the counter-magic employed by the poet to fend off envy involves fascinating the eye by presenting it with an attractive (i.e. horribly repellant) object. In the public

---

[25] Bacon, 'On Envy', *Essayes*, p. 47.
[26] The comparison between the poet and a king, even an evil one, is interesting in terms of the status the comparison confers upon the poet.
[27] Mezentius' habit of tying corpses to living bodies would feature in Renaissance emblematic literature as an image of the communication of syphilitic infection between spouses. In Alciati, Emblem 197 'Nupta contagioso' ('Married to an infected man') depicts the tyrant of the *Aeneid* ordering his men to tie a living victim to a dead body. The *subscriptio* compares this coupling to the work of a 'savage father' who gives a son 'consumed by the French pox and covered with horrible eruptions' in marriage. Andrea Alciati, *A Book of Emblems, The* Emblematum Liber *in Latin and English*, trans. John F. Moffitt (Jefferson: McFarland and Company, Inc., Publishers, 2004), p. 228.
[28] Yet, this same comparison between himself and the King of Virgil's *Aeneid* serves automatically to raise the poet to a certain legendary status as well.

realm of which he speaks, Bacon's 'cure' implies that people wanting to protect themselves from the gaze will display something in their place, even to the extent of using another person as a kind of charm to attract it away from themselves and so protect themselves by channelling envy toward their rival or enemy. Barring an historical example of the order of Mezentius, one begins to understand the cynical use of slander by one's enemies or rivals as a defence against ocular witchcraft. If one does not have an ancient tyrant at hand to display, one can always make someone into a fit morsel to serve up to public scrutiny as a kind of unwitting sponge for its irradiating rays.[29]

This moment where the 'stroke' or 'percussion' of the envious eye is felt must be seen as part of a continuous system of retrospection and interruption, defence and explanation from which *The Masque of Queenes* emerged as we see it today. It is the curiosity of the poet to note where and how the eye views his text so that he may counter the power of this eye, either by holding up an effigy of a monster or the body of the dead author of antiquity in the form of citation as a sop for envy. The work of revision and annotation, which is the work of *re*trospection, requires a constant process of 'eyeing' critically and 'inquiring' at every juncture to see if and when more explanation, more authorities and more commentary are appropriate and necessary. It is precisely the curious gaze of the writer that opens up the space in the text for the footnote.[30] Weaving itself through and around the poetry of the masque are quotations and citations from the dead. This call and response between the living poet and his dead models, between text and footnote, is the true mixing of the living and the dead, the real Mezentian legacy of *The Masque of Queenes*.

Self-defacement as sanctuary

The authorial need to 'fly' and seek out sanctuary speaks volumes concerning the fugitive status of the writer. Jonson's time in prison, for slurs against Scots in *Eastward Ho!* (1605), is just one example of his personal experience with the law. Yet, this direct experience with censorship and imprisonment is only one aspect, though it certainly colours the rest, of the potential risks the artist could run in the act of creation. Like many early modern poets and

---

[29] Bacon's list of those often used to publicly 'derive the *Envy*' includes 'Ministers, and Servants ... Colleagues and Associates; and the like; And for that turne, there are never wanting, some Persons of violent and undertaking Natures, who so they may have Power, and Business, will take it at any Cost.' Bacon, 'Of Envy', *Essayes*, p. 47.

[30] Anthony Grafton describes the origins of the footnote and its political and literary implications in *The Footnote: A Curious History* (London: Faber and Faber, 1997).

dramatists, Jonson was fully aware of the exposure attending personal poetic invention. The craft of playwriting was specifically attacked in the period as corrupt and immoral. Stephen Gossen, in *The School of Abuse*, and the Puritans vociferously blasted plays and playhouses for their contribution to the corruption of public morals. Leah Marcus notes: 'Enemies of the stage regularly charged that plays rested on lies and hypocrisy, reminding their readers that the Greek word hypocrite had meant both actor and pretender.'[31] Beyond the corruption of morals and traffic with deceit, the literary imagination risked meandering through uncharted paths led on, in Spenser, by 'Errour' and in Milton, by 'Fancy'.[32] Moreover, it hazarded at every turn creating literary monstrosity. The masque figure 'Phant'sie' in Jonson's *The Vision of Delight* asks spectators to imagine the 'offence it would be / For the Squirrel to see a Dog clime a tree', an image reminiscent of the opening of Horace's *Art of Poetrie* where the joining together of incongruous elements is criticized: 'If to a Woman's head a Painter would / Set a Horse-neck, and divers feathers fold … shapes, like sick-mens dreames, are fain'd so vaine, / As neither head, nor foot, one forme retaine.'[33] Yet, in *Timber*, Jonson testifies to the *pleasure* that attends the act of poetic creation:

For all that wee invent doth please us in the conception, or birth; else we would never set it downe. But the safest is to returne to our Judgement, and handle over againe those things, the easinesse of which might make them justly suspected. So did the best Writers in their beginnings; they impos'd upon themselves care, and industry. They did nothing rashly.[34]

Here, in this statement of the necessity of a return to judgement, to handle over the seductive but suspect fruits of the writer's first conception, is the poet's own recommendation for a form of self-censure. This censure is, significantly, in imitation of the 'best Writers' who, implicitly, earned their fame by the vigilant and constant use of retrospection. The poet equates excellence in writing with the censoring of a natural pleasure that comes with creation. This handling over is necessary because of their 'easinesse',

---

[31] Leah Marcus, *The Politics of Mirth: Jonson, Herrick, Milton, Marvell and the Defense of Old Holiday Pastimes* (Chicago: University of Chicago Press, 1986), p. 27.
[32] For 'Errour' see Spenser, *The Faerie Queene*, Book 1, Canto 1, 13ff.; for 'Fancy' see John Milton, *Paradise Lost*: 'Yet evil whence? … fancy … forms imaginations, airy shapes, / which reasons joining or disjoining, frames … Oft in her [reason's] absence mimic fancy wakes / To imitate her; but misjoining shapes, / wild work produces oft' (v.99–112) in Alastair Fowler (ed.) (London: Longman, 1968), pp. 261–3.
[33] Ben Jonson, *The Vision of Delight*, Herford and Simpson, vol. VII, p. 465 (line 79) and *Horace, His Art of Poetrie, Made English by Ben Johnson* [sic], Herford and Simpson, vol. VIII, p. 305 (lines 1–2; 9–10).
[34] Ben Jonson, *Timber, or Discoveries*, Herford and Simpson, vol. VIII, p. 616 (lines 1719–25).

implying both the ease with which they were first conceived and their openness to immediate (and thus circumspect) interpretation. This easiness would, furthermore, make them 'justly suspected' by the (implied and naturally) suspicious reader.

Jonson's famous criticism of Shakespeare's style, discussed briefly above, may be seen as one example of Jonson's imperative to judge creation and discipline nature. Jonson's pointing to the absence of this return to judgement in Shakespeare intimates, even, that creation may require some form of defacement:

> *I remember*, the Players have often mentioned it as an honour to *Shakespeare*, that in his writing (whatsoever he penn'd) he never blotted out line. My answer hath been, would he had blotted a thousand.[35]

Jonson condemns, not Shakespeare's invention or 'fancy', which are specifically complimented, but rather a subsequent lack of discipline. His critique is not directed toward what Shakespeare wrote, but rather what he did not *blot*, or revise upon better judgement. The act of blotting here describes Jonson's own ideal method of writing. He acknowledges the need for fertile and fanciful invention, but he distrusts that generative power of fancy which carries the threat of monstrosity. In the same way that he described the need to 'call former times into question; but make no parties with the present', Jonson argues for a middle way between creation and a form of useful self-defacement.[36] This injunction to *blot* is precisely the advice Jonson gave himself. His own method imagines a *furor poeticus* (or 'rage') that represents natural inspiration and, at the same time, possible monstrosity, succeeded by self-censorship or self-defacement. Jonson perceives some kind of initial blotting of 'fancy' to be necessary so that the creation can withstand the defacing forces outside of it. The birth of the monstrous is therefore not something to be avoided, for it is specifically pleasure in (monstrous) conception that drives the poet to 'set it down' in the first place. Rather, this initial monstrousness needs to be subsequently blotted, commented upon, noted and justified and so revised. In his elegy to Shakespeare, Jonson reflects on this idea of revision:

> Yet must I not give Nature all: Thy Art,
> My gentle *Shakespeare*, must enjoy a part,
> For though the *Poets* matter, Nature be,
> His Art doth give the fashion. And, that he,
> Who casts to write a living line, must sweat,

---

[35] *Ibid.*, p. 583 (lines 647–50).   [36] *Ibid.*, p. 627 (lines 2109–10).

> (Such as thine are) and strike the second heat
> Upon the *Muses* anvile: turne the same,
> (And himself with it) that he thinkes to frame. (lines 55–62)[37]

Jonson acknowledges Shakespeare's 'Nature', the equivalent of his 'excellent *Phantsie*; brave notions, and gentle expressions' in the passage from *Timber*.[38] He then turns to 'Art', which gives matter 'fashion'. Using the image of the 'Muses anvil' he describes how the writer/forger turns and sharpens his molten line, striking a 'second heat', the equivalent to the return to judgement or the handling over of Nature's 'matter'.[39] What is significant is the (seemingly redundant) addition of 'And himself with it' to the phrase 'turne the same'. In the passage from *The Masque of Queenes*, quoted at the start of this chapter, we have seen the poet do exactly this: 'turn' *himself* to confront an objection from the imagined reader.[40] This turning 'himself with it', then, is part and parcel of the process of striking a 'second heat' and rewriting a 'living line'. In the elegy to Shakespeare, Jonson sees both as integral parts of 'Art': the poet must turn his lines, but he must also turn himself, as author and as genitor, to act as defender of his own work. Jonson's frequent, 'autobiographical' use of 'I' in his works, speaks to this.

The complementary task of turning *himself*, in other words, defending himself and his work from readerly objection heralds an image of the artist who insists on forging a destiny for himself outside of patronage bonds, but also, consequently, outside patronage protection. This is not to say that Jonson felt himself beyond the need of patronage. Rather, I would argue that Jonson was trying to invent a new kind of protective power that would *supplement* that offered by traditional recourse to the figure of the patron. The efficacy of the sanctuary depends on the writer's own 'presence' at some level. The critical imperative to fend and explain leads to the introduction of a host of strategies and attitudes resulting in a vertiginous cycle of self-reflection and self-mirroring in which what has just been written needs to be examined, rewritten, blotted and filed, *but also* defended, explained and justified to a future reader or a future spectator. In this process we may see a statement of Jonson's particular

---

[37] Ben Jonson, 'To the memory of my beloved, The AUTHOR MR. WILLIAM SHAKESPEARE: And what he hath left us', *Ungathered Verse* (xxvi), Herford and Simpson, vol. VIII, p. 392.
[38] Ben Jonson, *Timber, or Discoveries*, Herford and Simpson, vol. VIII, p. 584 (lines 656–8).
[39] The image of the anvil is used by Horace: '… blot all: and to the anvile bring / Those ill-torn'd Verses, to new hammering'. Ben Jonson, *Horace, His Art of Poetrie*, Herford and Simpson, vol. VIII, p. 333 (lines 627–8).
[40] Ben Jonson, *The Masque of Queenes*, Herford and Simpson, vol. VII, p. 313 (line 671).

ars poetica. The passage in *Timber*, in which Jonson turns *himself* ('*I* had not told posterity this') to confront the accusation of the 'players', becomes a *mise-en-abyme* concerning the practice of 'Art' as described in the elegy to Shakespeare. In his answer to the 'players', the poet not only describes the need to 'blot' or, in the metaphor of the elegy, to 'strike the second heat', he also shows himself turning to face the accusation of malevolence for posterity.

If a sanctuary, then, is created in the space between the first and the second 'heat', between a 'turn' and 'counter-turn', in other words, in the saying and then submitting to judgement what is said, it seems no accident that Jonson found inspiration in the *choros* of ancient Greek tragedy and comedy, which functioned as a kind of commentary and response to what *had been said*.[41] In *Catiline*, he closely imitates Greek tragic choruses by having a unified group comment together on the action of each act. In *Every Man Out of His Humour*, *The Staple of Newes*, and *The Magnetic Lady*, the playwright's chorus (who are labelled in the Folio, by the Latin 'Grex', or the 'herd') consists of a group of spectators who sit upon the stage, observing and remarking during the play's interludes upon the action that unfolds before them. In these choral interludes, however, the spectators respond to the play in short dialogues with each other, sometimes from diametrically opposed points of view as in *The Magnetic Lady* where the 'Boy' attempts to instruct 'Master Probee' and 'Master Damplay', whose names, of course, refer to their critical functions, 'probing' and 'damning'. In these cases, the 'chorus' may be seen to function like the poet's imported 'objection' (made by a hypothetical reader) to which he will turn (in the form of an Asper or other figure) to explain and justify himself.[42]

In addition to choral interventions, within the plays, and many of the masques, there exist critical characters who, though actively participating in the actual plot (not a feature of the chorus), offer, in a choral manner, another voice in another register, on the tableau unfolding before them, whether to the audience in an aside or soliloquy, or in their dialogue with other characters. Surly in *The Alchemist* (1610) is an example of such another voice. Surly's critical stance toward the alchemical dream-world of Epicure Mammon and Subtle's highfalutin alchemical gibberish cannot

---

[41] Ley, *Greek Theater*, p. 32.
[42] Likewise, Jonson's interest in the Pindaric Ode form of 'turn', 'counter-turn', 'stand' (Jonson's own translation of the Greek 'strophe', 'anti-strophe', 'epode') might well be examined in light of his interest in *dramatic* choral forms.

be anecdotally reduced to an expression of the viewpoint of Ben Jonson, stern critic of alchemy, and the swindling confidence men the art has produced. Rather, Surly's interceptive critiques and asides should be seen as part of the necessary *turn* to create a sanctuary:

> [ENTER FACE.]
> SUBTLE. How now? What colour says it?
> FACE. The ground black, sir.
> MAMMON. That's your *crowes-head*?
> SURLY. Your cockscomb's, is it not?
> SUBTLE. No, 'tis not perfect. Would it were the *crow*. That worke wants some-thing.
> SURLY. [*Aside*.] O, I look'd for this. The hay is a-pitching.[43]

The voice of Surly may be seen as a form of protective authorial revision because a certain danger exists for the writer with classical aspirations in appropriating alchemy as a subject without adopting some kind of distance from it. Nevertheless, the highly scatological materials of alchemy exert a strong fascination for the writer, who has obviously read deeply in alchemical lore: 'Your broths, your *menstrues*, and *materialls*, / Of pisse, and egge-shells, women's terms, man's bloud, / Hair o' the head, burnt clouts, chalke, merds, and clay.'[44] The lines cited above represent both an authorial pleasure in monstrous language (and the strange alchemical language that mimics sex) and a judgement of it at the same time. In other words, if we consider this passage in the terms with which Jonson described Shakespeare's need to discipline initial invention, then the monstrous, but pleasurable conceptions of the poet are blotted by the judgement of a Surly. It is Surly's role as *blotter* which creates a refuge, a sanctuary in monstrosity and pleasure.

In *Sejanus, His Fall*, Arruntius is another example of a character whose role is one of observing and judging. Although in quite a different mode and tone from the critical asides of Surly, the observations of Arruntius in *Sejanus* upon the state of Rome and the people in it may also be seen as having a choral and slightly 'corrective' function. Arruntius, a citizen with strong republican leanings in a play about the dangers of tyranny, acts as an appropriate critic of the actions and characters witnessed in the play:

> Times? the men,
> The men are not the same: 'tis we are base,
> Poor, and degenerate from th' exalted streine

---

[43] Ben Jonson, *The Alchemist*, Herford and Simpson, vol. v, p. 323 (II.iii.67–71).
[44] *Ibid.*, p. 327 (II.iii.193–5).

> Of our great fathers ...
> ...
> Or where the constant BRUTUS, that (being proofe
> Against all charme of benefits) did strike
> So brave a blow into the monsters heart
> That sought unkindly to captive his country?[45]

The republicanism of Arruntius does not serve only to critique tyranny as a political alternative. It serves as well, in conjunction with the commentary of Cordus, to create a voice opposing the degenerate and unscrupulous protagonists of the play. Degeneracy in all of its forms is investigated repeatedly in this play, and then critiqued by characters such as Arruntius. The text is thus as free to revel in Roman decadence in *Sejanus* as it indulged in the sexualized and scatological language of alchemy, in turn censured by Surly.

Furthermore, in *Sejanus*, as in *The Alchemist, Catiline* and *Bartholomew Fair*, the writer engages in almost prurient meditations upon the mysteries of cosmetics and the secrets of the bedchamber and the boudoir. In *Sejanus*, he refers consistently to Agrippina, for instance, in terms of her womb. The text wallows in descriptions of ancient diviners contemplating the entrails of animals. It deals in intimate detail with the monstrous findings of the soothsayers, delighting in visions of enormous snakes emerging from a sacrificial body. These depictions of prodigies are balanced by commentators who, in effect, offer a retraction of the scene without it being struck from the record. The author's conception, even monstrous, remains, but already judged. Sejanus even, at one point in the play, takes on the role of the disabusing commentator when he observes, after a gory and graphically described divination scene:

> Be thou dumbe, scrupulous priest:
> And gather up thy selfe, with these thy wares,
> Which I, in spight of thy blind mistris, or
> Thy juggling mysterie, religion, throw
> Thus, scorned to the earth ...
> ...
> Avoid these fumes, these superstitious lights,
> And all these coos'ning ceremonies.[46]

Interestingly enough, these 'coos'ning ceremonies' are turned into an historical and anthropological 'note' in Jonson's marginalia for *Sejanus* to be recuperated subsequently and expanded upon in the text and the

---

[45] Ben Jonson, *Sejanus, His Fall*, Herford and Simpson, vol. IV, p. 358 (I.i.87–9; 93–6).
[46] *Ibid.*, pp. 443–4 (v.190–4; 199–200).

marginalia of *The Masque of Augurs*. The marginal descriptions of the activities of the 'Flamen' place the scene in yet another light, turning authorial indulgence in 'mysteries' into a kind of historical study of ancient Roman superstitions. *Sejanus* reveals a number of moments of this kind of sanctuarizing self-reflexivity. Sejanus, for instance, perfectly sums up Arruntius' role as the writer's censuring voice when he remarks to Tiberius, 'And ther's ARRUNTIUS too, he only talkes.'[47] Arruntius himself succeeds in encapsulating his function as mere observer when he says:

> We,
> That are the good-dull-noble lookers on,
> Are only call'd to keep the marble warme.[48]

Most hilariously, as the self-proclaimed judge of the monstrosities that inhabit *Bartholomew Fair*, Judge Adam Overdo moves about the Smithfield fair grounds in a disguise for the purpose of finding out 'enormities'. Like the Duke in Shakespeare's *Measure For Measure*, Adam Overdo's role may be perceived, at one level, as a way of passing judgement on the follies of the age. Yet, the choice of the Smithfield Fair as the site for holding up a mirror to the times is already suspicious. Characters such as Ursula, the Pig-Woman, Ezechiel Edgeworth, a cut-purse, Lanthorn Leatherhead, a hobby-horse seller or toyman, and Joan Trash, a gingerbread woman are created and described in all of their most monstrous and delightful detail before the disguised 'judge' performs the editorial function of the self-censuring author. Leatherhead and Trash are in adjacent booths at the Fair waiting for customers and are Judge Overdo's first glimpse of enormity:

LEATHERHEAD. The Fayre's pestilence dead, mee thinkes; people come not abroad, to day, whatever the matter is. Doe you hear, sister *Trash*, Lady o' the Basket? sit farther with your ginger-bread-progeny there, and hinder not the prospect of my shop, or I'll ha' it proclaim'd i' the Fayre, what stuff they are made on.
TRASH. Why, what stuff are they made on, Brother *Leatherhead*? nothing but what's wholesome, I assure you.
LEATHER. Yes, stale bread, rotten egges, musty ginger, and dead honey, you know.
OVERDO. I! have I met with enormity, so soon?[49]

By incorporating within itself a commentary upon itself, the text anticipates possible condemnations of the author's fascination with the lowest of the

---

[47] *Ibid.*, p. 384 (II.299). And we find Sejanus and Tiberius agreeing in this scene that it is precisely *because* he speaks freely that Arruntius is best left unmuzzled for fear of arousing suspicion against them. Arruntius protects them through his 'free' speech perhaps in the way he protects the writer.
[48] *Ibid.*, p. 393 (III.i.15–17).
[49] Ben Jonson, *Bartholomew Fair*, Herford and Simpson, vol. VI, p. 41 (II.ii.1–11).

low: rotten eggs and dead honey. The reader is at once encouraged to see through a judging eye and at the same time to laugh at the stupidity of the bumbling judge who never really understands what is going on. If the reader judges the play too harshly, he will be forced to identify himself with the idiotic critic that overdoes it. The censure of the reader upon reading the monstrous text is thus warded off by the inclusion of that same judging eye (in its grotesque and clownish form) within the play. The play reads, or in the words of Adam Overdo, 'brands' itself before the reader does.[50] This has the effect of a vaccine and degeneracy in all of its forms may be investigated *ad nauseam* and exposed to the curious and prying eye, but the author escapes the censure he imagines awaits his voyeuristic pleasure because everything is already pre-critiqued by a Surly, an Arruntius or an Adam Overdo.

'A sharper eye'

Prefaces, prologues, marginalia, commenting spectators, asides, critical characters as well as narrations and digressions are all part of the creation of a sanctuary for the poet from the judging gaze he posits everywhere and turns toward. These are incorporated into the body of the text toward the same end: to control the reception of the work to the greatest degree possible by creating a space for a sanctuary thereby anticipating and prophylactically fending off criticism. The danger of depleting the work through constant interruption and intervention does not seem to weigh much against the authorial intent to insure that the spectator, and later the reader, will not traduce the text. Algernon Charles Swinburne is a witness to Jonson's strategy to create a sanctuary for his work, which he characterizes as the poet's 'vigorous and vigilant devotion' in the writing of *Sejanus*:

> Had the study of Tiberius been informed and vivified by something of the same fervour [as *Volpone*], the tragedy of Sejanus might have had in it some heat of more than merely literary life. But this lesser excellence, the merit of vigorous and *vigilant devotion* or application to a high and serious object of literary labour, is apparent in every scene of the tragedy. That the subject is one absolutely devoid of all but historical and literary interest – that not one of these scenes can excite for one instant the least touch, the least phantom, the least shadow of pity or terror – would apparently have seemed to its author no argument against its claim to greatness as a tragic poem (my emphasis).[51]

Swinburne writes of a 'lesser excellence' which he attributes specifically, in his use of the word 'vigilant', to Jonson's unwavering gaze upon his play. The

---

[50] *Ibid.*, p. 136 (v.v.126).
[51] Algernon Charles Swinburne, *A Study of Ben Jonson* (New York: Worthington Co., 1889), p. 31.

author is vigilant in order to protect and defend, but, as Swinburne understood, this same vigilance could also ruin a work: 'We may say of Jonson's work in almost every instance that the picture would have been better if the artist had taken less pains.'[52] Perhaps not accidentally, Swinburne's description of the *poet* as 'vigilant', in relation to his own creation, appears throughout Jonson's works to describe *fathers* who watch over their sons, as Knowell does in *Every Man In His Humour*. Cicero, in *Catiline*, often describes himself as vigilant in his defence of Rome and, at the same time, his own fame. Vigilance, like envy, is bound up in obsessive looking. The writer's unsleeping eye judges his text and employs tactics to anticipate, protect and defend it from the envious gaze of the spectator and the reader. He prefers, as we shall see in the following chapter, even to turn it into a kind of stone to secure it from the envious gaze of posterity.

Moreover, mired in constant self-reference, the author refuses to let his creation speak for itself. He will interrupt it, explain it, defend it and even 'speak for it'. The author imposes his voice in the midst of and often in place of his creation. In the masques, this kind of authorial intervention is evident in the marginal references to the 'I' of the writer, interrupting and defending through learned citations and justifications of authorial choices. In the poems, it is often a question as to how much of the poem is devoted to its dedicatee and how much is devoted to the reflexive musings of the poet making a study of himself in the act of writing the poem. Stanley Fish, among others, has noted how Jonson's poems of praise often start with a succession of 'false starts', where the poet will 'consume' a good part of the poem 'searching for its subject'.[53] Katharine Eisaman Maus argues that Jonson 'pioneers a notion of authorship in which the poem continues, or ought to continue, to "bear the mark" of the poet, constantly referring its reader back to its source in the writer'.[54] In fact, in these prologues or prefaces, before beginning the poem proper (in other words, before beginning to write about the putative subject), the writer, it seems, is actually very often concerned with turning to face, explicitly or implicitly, some kind of accusation. Jonson's 'An Epistle to Master John Selden' is an example of

---

[52] *Ibid.*, p. 7.   [53] Fish, 'Authors-Readers', p. 233.
[54] Katharine Eisaman Maus, 'Fetish and Poem: Ben Jonson's Dilemma' in Linda Woodbridge (ed.), *Money and the Age of Shakespeare: Essays in New Economic History* (New York: Palgrave Macmillan, 2003), pp. 251–64; p. 261. Maus goes on to note that: 'Unlike most of his contemporaries Jonson eschews any pretence of *sprezzatura*, aggressively foregrounding his own poetic toil and the sheer difficulty of good writing: an emphasis that gains him some scorn but which I suspect he imagined would direct the readers' attention away from the poem and toward the poet' (p. 261). Again, I would emphasise the 'poet in the poem', rather than the literary-biographical poet.

how the poet not only writes about himself in the act of writing, but also how he defends himself against 'Suspition'.[55] From the very beginning of the poem dedicated to Selden, the poet begins with himself: 'I know to whom I write. Here, I am sure, / Though I am short, I cannot be obscure' (lines 1–2). He then goes through at least sixteen lines before he calls his 'Object' (the dedicatee) forth. These lines are, again, reminiscent of his turning toward the invisible objecting voice in *The Masque of Queenes*, when it appears that he has joined together the living and the dead:

> we see, before
> A many' of bookes, even good judgments wound
> Themselves through favouring what is there not found:
> But I on yours farre otherwise shall doe,
> Not flie the Crime, but the Suspition too:
> Though I confesse (as every Muse hath err'd
> And mine not least) I have too oft preferr'd
> Men past their termes, and prais'd some names too much,
> But 'twas with purpose to have made them such.
> Since, being deceiv'd, I turne a sharper eye
> Upon my self, and aske to whom? and why?
> And what I write? and vexe it many dayes
> Before men get a verse: much less a Praise;
> so that my Reader is assur'd, I now
> Meane what I speake: and still will keepe that Vow.
> Stand forth my Object, then. (lines 14–29)

The beginning of this section of the poem quoted above is consistent with Jonson's opening lines to Shakespeare and also his criticism of the players (and their misplaced praise of Shakespeare) in *Timber*. In both, as here, he addresses the manner in which badly placed praise can 'wound' (line 15) both the book being praised and the praiser by 'favouring what is there not found' (line 16). Here, he speaks of ignorant 'praise' as a 'Crime' (line 18). He will, in other words, 'flie the Crime' of wounding Selden's name with misplaced praise and he will 'flie … the Suspition too' (line 18). At one level, of course, the purpose of this digression is to assure Selden, as well as the reader, that his praise is neither facile nor thoughtless, but based upon careful judgement. Yet, the manner in which the poet goes about assuring both the dedicatee and the later reader of his sincerity is, never theless, quite revealing. He is eager to *clear* his name not only of a 'Crime'

---

[55] Ben Jonson, *Underwood* (xiv), Herford and Simpson, vol. VIII, p. 159 (line 18). Subsequent line references to the poem will be included in the text.

but even the suspicion of having committed it. In *Queenes*, the poet portrays himself as a criminal fleeing for sanctuary. In this poem, he creates his sanctuary in these sixteen lines by explaining himself and humbly submitting to self-correction. He freely 'confesses' his past crimes, namely praising some men too much who turned out to be unworthy.[56] He justifies himself, claims he was 'deceived' and promises a literary reformation by being more severe with himself: 'I turne a sharper eye / Upon my self' (lines 23–4). This means endlessly asking questions and 'vexing' it many days before putting pen to paper (line 25). All this time the poet has quite forgotten his subject, or placed it in the wings, to the extent that he needs to actively summon or reinvoke it saying: 'Stand forth my Object' (line 29). Again, these metaphors of crime and punishment may be seen as a rhetorically very effective form of praise, showing that what Jonson gives Selden is so much more precious as the poet has placed a kind of general moratorium upon himself. By line 61, the poet admits: 'I yeeld, I yeeld, the matter of your praise / Flowes in upon me, and I cannot raise / A banke against it' (lines 61–3). The poem ends with the poet counting the '[G]aine' (line 81) of the friendship between Selden and Selden's most appreciative reader, Hayward. Here, as in the *Cary-Morison Ode*, where he describes the 'fruit' and the 'harvest' of the friendship of Lucius Cary and Henry Morison, the poet sees a certain future benefit accruing to himself as praiser.[57] The end of the poem dedicated to Selden places the poet in the pole position: 'But here's no time, nor place, my wealth to tell, / You are both modest. So am I. Farewell' (lines 85–6). Just as the 'Ben / Jonson' of the *Cary-Morison Ode* inherits the posterity (and the 'harvest') of the 'dead son' or 'Morison', so too, he has been enriched by the friendship of Selden and Hayward ('O how I doe count / Amonge my commings in, and see it mount, / The Gaine', lines 79–81).[58] The poem 'To Selden' is throughout an uncannily accurate description of the writer's own fascination with himself in the act of creation, as well as his preoccupation with 'clearing' his *own* name in the eyes of the reader. He profits here, as in the masques, from the occasion lent him by his powerful patron or well-known friend to give himself a life in posterity.

To summarize then, Jonson's desire to build a sanctuary for his work against the defacing gaze of the spectator and reader manifests itself in

---

[56] Again, for a discussion of this poem and the problems such praise posed for the poet see Butler, 'Limits of Courtly Panegyric', p. 96.
[57] Ben Jonson, 'To the immortall memorie, and friendship of that noble pair, Sir Lucius Cary, and Sir H. Morison', *Underwood* (lxx), Herford and Simpson, vol. VIII, p. 247 (line 128).
[58] See 'Ben / Jonson', *ibid.*, p. 246 (lines 84–5).

repeated and varied strategies to gain control over the way his creation will be received. The interruptions within the Jonsonian text emerge from a will to forestall criticism, to insert himself within a tradition, to mask his role as a time-bound, isolated begetter, while placing himself under the aegis of antiquity and in the wake of his most revered predecessors. Jonson's attempt to deflect the criticism of contemporary (and, by extension, later readers) by continually interrupting his own creation, whether profitably in the creation of choral characters in the plays or in the more obstrusive positioning of himself to defend and explain his 'methods' can be seen as participating in the common goal of the creation of a space in which he can lie safely. These defences spring from the very first moments of the writing process, when, like a second Ovid in the first scene of *Poetaster*, the writer corrects his errors, and makes the work 'fortie-fold proof' against malignant reading.[59] These, at times, laborious efforts to fortify his works should be interpreted as a kind of *vigilant despotism* on the part of the author. The author may be said to work out of fear in his constant apprehension of how his words will be interpreted and how these interpretations will affect his posterity. This anxiety entails a tyrannical literary regime in which the author begrudges his own work a life and future of its own, imposing himself upon it through constant intercessions on its behalf. This unending process of incorporating interruption and turning toward objections creates works scarred by a rhetoric of discontinuity, a form of wilful self-fragmentation. The author strives to guard his creation, but, as Swinburne represented it, does so through an *excess* of vigilance. In fact, Jonson's constant allusions to his writing self throughout the works reveal a wish to inherit life from his own creation in a narcissistic desire to overtake his own issue. He seeks to be his own heir by being both legator and his own legatee.

THE ENVIOUS CREATOR

Significantly, we find the 'father' in many of Jonson's plays is voracious in his desire to disinherit the son and assume a position that allows him to become his own inheritor. The desire to inherit from himself reveals the kind of control over posterity that finds its *reductio ad absurdum* in the science of cloning: a dream that emerges out of the ancient envy of the old for the young, portrayed, in antiquity, as Saturn eating his offspring or the

---

[59] Ben Jonson, Prologue to *Poetaster*, Herford and Simpson, vol. IV, p. 205 (line 8).

Titans envying the Olympians. In *Catiline*, Jonson depicts the victory of the Olympians in the figure of the upstart Cicero. Yet, in this play, as in many others in which Jonson focuses on the friction between generations, Titans and Olympians do not range themselves into neat battle lines.[60] A writer partakes of both tradition and novelty. The first symptom of this problematic doubleness of writing (which we saw in Chapter 3 as the twin danger of defacing and being defaced) can be seen in Jonson's construction of a world in which fathers and sons often possess the same name. The plots and themes of Jonson's plays may be viewed as allegories for the creative activity of the writer, representing these two aspects. The writer is the envious father, who will not let go of his literary creation, or, as it is metaphorically referred to in so many of Jonson's plays, his *gold*. As son, he is the literary descendent who must sacrifice to the literary father (in the form of the citation, which is his debt to the father) in order to speak at all. As father, he envies his creation its due inheritance by attempting to guard what should be passed down to the son for himself. As son, the poet waits for the moment when he may finally gain his inheritance and throw off the mantle of the father. A number of Jonson's plays, throughout his career, involve confrontations between fathers and sons, specifically enacted through a dispute over money, and most particularly, inheritance. The avatars of the father are the dying man, the miser, the legator, the vigilant man, the judge, the king, the counterfeiter. The avatars of the son are the poet, the parasite, the apprentice, the trickster, the inheritor, the dead son and, significantly, the book. Their confrontation represents the confrontation between creator and his own envied creation, a confrontation which enacts the creator's censure of his own creation in advance of its censure by the reader.

In *Every Man In His Humour*, the father, Knowell senior, envious of his son, Knowell junior, is represented in terms of his desire to *track* his son's every move after his son runs away from home to escape, precisely, his father's vigilance and be among his literary friends in town. Knowell senior describes himself as a dragon watching over his 'fruit', his son: 'Why should he thinke, I tell my Apri-cotes? / Or play th' *Hesperian* Dragon, with my fruit, / To watch it?'[61] The envious gaze of the creator is represented

---

[60] I am describing *Catiline, His Conspiracy* as a play about the friction between generations because of the implicit analogy between Cicero's faction as Olympian and Catiline's as Titan in the passage translated from Claudian in the final lines of the play. While Catiline is probably not a generation older than Cicero, he is clearly aligned with an 'older order' of aristocrats threatened by a 'new man'.

[61] Ben Jonson, *Every Man In His Humour*, Herford and Simpson, vol. III, p. 309 (I.ii.103–5). Subsequent references to this play will be included in the text.

as an unsleeping eye. Like the dragon in the garden of the Hesperides, Knowell is all eyes, shadowing his son's every move, going so far as to disguise himself in order to better pursue his prey. The same kind of disguise and pursuit of the son by the envious father reappears, years later, in *The Staple of Newes* (1625). The father's hounding of his son in these plays is a literal manifestation of the authorial desire for complete control over his creation. He literally will not let it go. It is significant, in terms of the representation of the authorial phantasmagoria concerning the envious eye of the judging father, how Knowell junior attempts to escape from the gaze of his doting but suffocating father. Like so many son figures in Jonson's plays, Knowell junior has literary aspirations, and his desire to escape from the vigilant gaze may be seen as the enactment of the authorial fantasy of escape from the burden of the literary debt to the past and its authors, which manifests itself in the author's acute sense of justifying himself to his own hounding readers.

In the first Act of *Every Man In His Humour*, Knowell senior justifies opening a letter addressed to his son (but misdirected to him by his servant) by noting that, since both he and his son have the same name, Edward Knowell, the letter might well have been addressed to him:

KNOWELL. This letter is directed to my son:
   Yet, I am EDWARD KNOWELL too, and may,
   With the safe conscience of good manners, use
   The fellowes error to my satisfaction.
   Well, I will break it ope (old men are curious),
   Be it but for the style's sake and the phrase. (1.ii.61–6)

The possession of identical names creates, in the father's mind, ample justification for his voyeurism. It allows him to pass off the transgression against his son. What is his son's is also his. He may therefore read the letter in 'safe conscience' without violating any rule of etiquette, such is the fusion between father and son. The misdirected letter is particularly overdetermined: all 'writing' is ultimately the property of the father. All writing belonging to the son will, fatally, enter the purview of the father. In this respect, the authorial fear of creating novelty and defacing the texts of the older generation is acknowledged in the image of the envious father reading and judging the poetic son and his literary friends. Knowell reads and judges the letter from his son's literary friend, Wellbred, in terms of its style. His is the envious gaze of the father, watching over the son, opening his 'letters' and judging their contents and style. The fact that father and son possess the same name makes this scene of 'reading' a representation of the split in the author who is both son and father, letter (writer) and reader. The poetic self, in other words, is represented in the son, fearing the judgement of the father who, significantly, is both anterior *and* posterior, as reader, investing everything in controlling the movement of his creation.

Knowell is shocked by the contents of the letter, both in terms of its style and Wellbred's suggestion that Knowell, the son, 'leave thy vigilant father, alone' (lines 75–6). The father's condemnation of Wellbred's literary style is severe: 'From the *Burdello*, it might come as well; / The *Spittle*, or *Pict-hatch*' (lines 92–3). He finishes by noting the difficulty of being a father, no matter how carefully he counts 'his greene apricots' (line 76), the fruit, the offspring of his brain, his son:

> Well, my sonne, I' had thought
> Y'had had more judgment, t' have made election
> Of your companions, than t' have ta'en on trust
> Such petulant, geering gamsters, that can spare
> No argument or subject from their jest.
> But I perceive affection makes a foole
> Of any man *too much the father*. (my emphasis; 1.ii.105–11)

The phrase 'too much the father' is ambiguous. It implies that Knowell senior is too doting and affectionate, but it also implies that he is too vigilant and careful about the raising of his child, who, like his father, is also too affectionate and trusting of friends like Wellbred. The difficulty of being 'too much the father' resonates with Jonson's expression of rue in his elegy 'On My First Sonne' written about four years later in 1603: 'O, could I loose all father, now.'[62] The representation of the bond between father and son in the elegy bears a striking resemblance to that between Knowell senior and Knowell junior in *Every Man In His Humour*. I quote the elegy in full because it stands as a unique expression both of an hyperbolic expression of affection and, reciprocally, of the poet father's envy, not unlike Knowell senior's, of his own progeny, his physical creation, an envy, ultimately, of his own offspring, his own work, and himself:

> Farewell, thou child of my right hand, and joy;
> My sinne was too much hope of thee, lov'd boy,
> Seven yeeres thou wert lent to me, and I thee pay,
> Exacted by thy fate, on the just day.
> O, could I loose all father, now. For why
> Will man lament the state he should envie?

---

[62] Ben Jonson, 'On My First Sonne', *Epigrammes* (xlv), Herford and Simpson, vol. VIII, p. 41 (line 5). Subsequent references to the poem will be included in the text.

> To have so soone scap'd world's, and fleshes rage,
> And, if no other miserie, yet age?
> Rest in soft peace, and, ask'd, say here doth lye
> BEN. JONSON his best piece of *poetrie*.
> For whose sake, hence-forth, all his vowes be such,
> As what he loves may never like too much. (lines 1–12)

The author in this poem interposes himself, even while elegizing his own son. He uses the occasion of the death of his son, as he used the occasion of the destruction of the masque, to engrave his own name on his son's grave, earning the immortality of the memory (to 'my first son') symbolized by a stone set up for the future. The father literally usurps the son in the grave. In the epitaph inscribed within the elegy, '[H]ere doth lie / Ben Jonson', the author plays upon the identity between father and son. Yet the mourner uses this identity to create an emblem of the poet, divided into creator and his poetic creation, 'his best piece of poetry' (line 10). The son as a separate being is lost in the conflation of names and the pun on 'poetry'. It is Ben Jonson's *poetic creation* that lies in the grave and it is his creation, as well, printed on the page. The writer inherits his own name from his son precisely at the moment when he asserts his parental control over the child's reponse to the inquisitive passer-by: '*asked, say* here doth lie / Ben Jonson his best piece of poetry' (my emphasis). By 'burying' himself in his son's grave, the poet not only inherits from his own son, he may also be seen to create a sanctuary for himself in his son's grave. The father places himself in the grave of his child, calls that child his 'best *piece* of poetry' and, in so doing, profits his own name from the death of his son simply because this poem, putatively about the son, is also about the father, the maker and the poet.

As with the son, so with the book; as the poet finds sanctuary in his son's grave he also finds it when he imprints himself in his tome. Just as Spenser sees the book as a child, so Jonson's poem, 'To My Bookseller', recalls his elegy to his son.[63] In this epigram, the writer insists that his book should not be advertised by the bookseller. Rather, he wants it to 'lie upon thy stall, till it be sought' (line 5). In a sense, the future reader of the book is not unlike the future passer-by of the epitaph of the author's son. It lies, in peace, 'until it is sought' and 'asked for'. If the book does not sell, the author urges the bookseller to 'send it to *Bucklers-bury*, there 'twill, well' (line 13). Bucklersbury was the area in London where the grocers

---

[63] Ben Jonson, 'To My Bookseller', *Epigrammes* (iii), *ibid.*, p. 27. Subsequent references will be included in the text.

congregated, but Jonson literally means that the sheets may be used for wrapping food. Buried and entombed, the book, like the son, is buried and, through the monument above the grave, becomes a means of nourishing and regenerating the father's name. The poet will, in fact, inherit his own name again, from that of his son. He will borrow a life of his own posterity, of his own son, his own text. The perfect son then is the dead son because he is a monument, a tombstone, or a book upon which the father may en*grave* his name, and his fame.

An analogous relationship between father and son, author and book appears in Jonson's epigram, 'To My Book'.[64] The book, like the son, is 'named of me':

> It will be look'd for, booke, when some but see
> Thy title, *Epigrammes*, and nam'd of mee,
> Thou should'st be bold, licentious, full of gall,
> Wormewood, and sulphure, sharpe, and tooth'd withall;
> Become a petulant thing, hurle ink, and wit,
> As mad-men stones: not caring whom they hit.
> *Deceive their malice*, who could wish it so. [my emphasis; lines 1–7]

The author suspects the future reader of malice and envy and so instructs the book to become the image the reader possesses of the writer, full of 'wormwood' and 'gall' (lines 3–4). Thus, the writer deftly turns the image the reader would project onto the book back onto the reader: 'Deceive their malice, who could wish it so' (line 7). I would argue that this idea of deceiving and tricking refers to the apotropaic turning of the malice aimed at the writer back onto the reader. The book is given free rein to 'hurl ink, and wit, / As madmen stones' (lines 5–6): in other words, it is given licence to become a reflection of the evil aimed toward it, thus becoming itself an object with which to baffle the reader. So, the book throws back onto the reader the 'malice' the world assumes to be the writer's and in so doing 'deceives' or thwarts the reader's envy. To protect himself from the envy of the reader, then, the poet finds sanctuary in his book, which will face the audience and speak for him, *in his place*: 'And by thy wiser temper, let men know / Thou are not covetous of least selfe-fame, / Made from the hazard of anothers shame' (lines 8–10). The writer dissembles in projecting no desire for self-fame onto his book. The book speaks for itself and its contents, but also by proxy, it speaks for the 'me' accused of begrudging praise to others, of, in fact being full of gall and envy. It is up to the book to 'let men

---

[64] Ben Jonson, 'To My Book', *Epigrammes* (ii), *ibid.*, p. 27.

know' (line 8). The relationship between the poet, his book and his reader becomes particularly interesting in terms of the manner in which 'malice' is exchanged between reader and author. The poet acknowledges the image of himself in the eyes of his readers: 'It will be look'd for, booke, when some but see' (line 1), but in acknowledging it he turns it back on the reader. In addition, he has successfully wedged the 'book' as well as the word 'book' in the middle of the first line, between himself and the malicious reader.

As in Jonson's elegy to his son, it is the filial duty of the author's creation, the book, to speak for the writer. As in the elegy to his son, the book is 'nam'd of mee' (line 2). At the same time, the act of anthropomorphizing his own book creates the necessary gap between the poet and his work, enabling the writer to use the book to shield himself from the gaze of the reader. The book must defend itself (and by proxy the author) against the accusation that it is 'not covetous of least selfe-fame' (line 9) or desirous of the world's 'vaine gaze' (line 12). Similarly, by having the book, which is the analogue of the poet, but capable of occupying a future time, speak in defence against the accusations – which the author imagines will be levelled against both book and author – the poet prepares the ground for his own resurrection. Only the living author is prey to the malice and envy of his contemporaries. It is the book, or the buried son, that will speak to the future passer-by, but the writer will never be far away, because he shadows his book as he shadowed his son.

CHAPTER 5

Monument: turning the text to stone

JUSTICE OVERDO. How now? what's here to doe? friend, art thou the
  Master of the *Monuments*?
SHARKWEL. 'Tis a *Motion*, an't please your worship.
                                                                (*Bartholomew Fair*)[1]

Jonson's publication of his *Workes* in folio in 1616 marked not only a key moment in the career of the writer, but also a watershed in the history of print culture. Of course, his was not the first folio edition of a living poet's works to be published in England – Samuel Daniel and Thomas Heywood had both published in folio format before. What made Jonson unique was his implicit assertion that everything he wrote, including plays, was worthy of publication as *opera*. The only folio collections of plays, at the time, were those of classical playwrights such as Plautus or Terence. In producing the 1616 folio, Jonson was therefore 'engaged in an undertaking unprecedented in the world of contemporary drama'.[2] Furthermore, publishing himself meant the publication of a number of Jacobean court masques, a highly collaborative genre, as his *own* work. It might be said that Jonson created a new paradigm within his own epoch in giving a play or masque the same status as poetry.[3] For these reasons, Jonson has became a central figure in what Joseph Loewenstein has called the 'prehistory of copyright'.[4] The 1616

---

[1] Ben Jonson, *Bartholomew Fair*, Herford and Simpson, vol. vi, p. 117 (v.iii.1–3).
[2] Margery Corbett and Ronald Lightbown, *The Comely Frontispiece: The Emblematic Title-Page in England 1550–1660* (London: Routledge and Kegan Paul, 1979), p. 150.
[3] In *Timber, or Discoveries*, Jonson writes that 'hee is call'd a *Poet*, not hee which writeth in measure only; but that fayneth and formeth a fable, and writes things like the Truth. For, the Fable and Fiction is (as it were) the forme and Soule of any Poeticall worke, or *Poeme*.' Herford and Simpson, vol. viii, p. 635 (lines 2351–5). It would seem that this kind of logic on the part of the poet enabled him to justify printing *ephemera* such as plays and masques in a folio volume.
[4] Joseph Loewenstein, *The Author's Due: Printing and the Prehistory of Copyright* (Chicago: University of Chicago Press, 2002). 'The narrative of Jonson's career in England's public and published sphere is a constant scramble for vantage, from theater to press, from theater to banqueting house, from banqueting house to press, from quarto to folio – all of which can be described as a constant flight

folio and its publication, nearly a century before the first copyright law was passed in England, raises a number of issues surrounding intellectual property, ownership, authorship, collaboration and early modern print culture.[5] As Douglas A. Brooks has remarked:

> For many scholars, Jonson's folio stands as a singular achievement of emergent authorial awareness... Joseph Loewenstein asserts that 'the 1616 folio marks a major event in the history of what one might call the bibliographic ego'. Richard C. Newton singles out Jonson as the poet/author who 'in an important sense "invents" (discovers) the printed book by using the book to distinguish what is his.' For Harold Love, 'in the 1616 folio [Jonson] produced one of the great typographical monuments of his age'.[6]

Love's statement that the 1616 folio is a 'typographical monument' describes it as being like a Gütenberg Bible or Mercator's *Atlas*, representative of a moment in the history of the print. The word 'monument' is often used by scholars when evaluating and considering Jonson's folio. One does not need to look too far to find the reason. According to the authors of *The Comely Frontispiece*, many of the elements featured in the title-page visually suggest that its author intended the book to be seen as a monument or as monumental:

> The presence of the obelisks, which are monuments, and the laurels, the traditional crown of the poet, is surely to signify the author's desire that the folio may bring him a poet's immortality. The pictures of the ancient theatre and the sentences from Horace proclaim the allegiance to the revered models and precepts of the classical drama and classical poetry by which his works, too learned for the vulgar, have deserved eternal fame.[7]

Yet, the hubris of gathering one's theatrical production and placing it in a calf-bound mausoleum was too much for some of Jonson's contemporaries. Thomas Heywood alludes to Jonson's folio in his address 'To the Reader', prefixed to *The Fair Maid of the West*: 'Curteous Reader, my Plaeis have not beene exposed to the publike view of the world in numerous sheets, and a large volume; but singly (as thou seest) with great modesty,

---

from publicity to privacy... Jonson's obsessive and various self-display is a revealing historical phenomenon... he yearned to control his own reception; as a result his writing and his behavior register crucial adjustments in the economic and cultural organization of intellectual property' (pp. 93–4).

[5] See Jennifer Brady and W. H. Herendeen (eds.), *Ben Jonson's 1616 Folio* (Newark: University of Delaware Press, 1991) and Richard Dutton, *Ben Jonson: To the First Folio* (Cambridge: Cambridge University Press, 1983).

[6] Douglas A. Brooks, *From Playhouse to Printing House: Drama and Authorship in Early Modern England* (Cambridge: Cambridge University Press, 2000), p. 139.

[7] Corbett and Lightbown, *The Comely Frontispiece*, p. 150.

and small noise.'⁸ In a punning epigram an anonymous writer demands: 'Pray tell me *Ben*, where doth the mistery lurke, / What others call a play you call a work.'⁹ Richard Helgerson considers Thomas Dekker's condescending evaluation of Jonson's publication of his *Workes*:

> 'True poets,' Dekker wrote, 'are with Art and Nature crowned.' It is the passive construction, the 'are...crowned,' that particularly condemns Jonson. Unlike Dekker, Jonson obtruded himself on his work, manifestly seeking to make it an index of his laureate standing. As Owen Felltham was to charge some thirty years later, Jonson could never 'forbear [his] crown / Till the world put it on'. What Dekker, Felltham, and Jonson's many other critics fail to acknowledge is that given the poetic forms available to his generation he could attain the laurel only by reaching for it.¹⁰

As Helgerson aptly notes, Jonson's choice of literary forms did not lend themselves to his becoming a 'laureate' poet. As a writer for the public and private theatre and for the court, Jonson may be said to have been envied the appropriate genres with which to fashion himself in the image of the authors of antiquity. Theatre and masques were not bound in calf-vellum for the ages. Jonson did not write an epic, for instance, or philosophy or divinity like James I, whose folio was also published in 1616. With the exception of his books of poetry, the bulk of what Jonson wrote may be summed up in the word *ephemera*. The desire to imitate the ancients in their literary posterity led to an effort to transform the transitory into forms that possessed some kind of natural longevity. And this effort to change one species of writing into another finds its last stage, its final transmutation, in its publication in folio. Rather than allowing his fame to gestate in the womb of time, Jonson used all the alchemy at his disposal to hasten the process and induce the birth of his literary immortality within his own lifetime leaving as little as possible to the mercy of both contemporary and future readers' capriciousness.

Jonson clearly prepared a certain number of his works for their publication in the 1616 folio. According to Richard Dutton, he first selected the pieces he intended to include and then revised parts of them, such as the prologue to *Every Man In His Humour*, rewritten to emphasize its 'clear ancestry in Roman comedy'.¹¹ The general principle behind Jonson's editing

---

⁸ Thomas Heywood, *The Fair Maid of the West* (London, 1631), n.p.
⁹ Anon., *Wit's Recreation* [1640], sig. G3ᵛ.
¹⁰ Richard Helgerson, *Self-Crowned Laureates: Spenser, Jonson, Milton and the Literary System* (Berkeley: University of California Press, 1983), p. 101.
¹¹ Dutton, *Ben Jonson*, p. 12.

was 'the promotion of the image of himself as a serious poet – something very different from a mere playwright'.[12] Helen Ostovich also argues that Jonson regularized *Every Man Out of His Humour* for inclusion in the folio 'replacing its fluent and rhythmical stagecraft with a scenic structure that was more literary, controlled and fragmented. He thereby changed it from a play for *performing* to a text for *reading*' (my emphasis).[13] In the case of some of the masques, Jonson's revisions to make them more literary and learned had already been made at an earlier point in time, for their publication in quarto. The printed masques were not just *descrizione*, a kind of news-writing or eye-witness testimony of a particular event in time; they already, in quarto form, bear the marks of the monumental before their 'reprinting' in folio. By the time the 1616 folio was printed, four masques had already been published with copious paratextual material and marginalia in quarto; one, *The Masque of Queenes*, had already been published in a single-text volume, the others in collections.

What this tells us is that, for Jonson, building a monument did not *only* consist of collecting his poems, plays and masques into one volume, commissioning a neo-classical frontispiece with obelisks and identifying himself as the 'Author' of all. There was already a need to justify, not only in the apparatus of the 1616 Folio, but *within* the texts themselves, the weight and seriousness of what was to go inside the two covers of the folio. Scholars rightly emphasize the volume's status as an historical monument, yet, a too narrow focus on the monumentality of the 'book' itself falls short of the whole story of Jonson's engagement with posterity, which begins previous to his works' inclusion in the 1616 folio, even, in some cases, at the moment of their conception. We can see the poet adapting himself and his work to the exigencies of the monumental from the very choice of the location of a play to its typographical disposition on the printed page.

---

[12] *Ibid.*, p. 12.
[13] Helen Ostovich, '"To Behold the Scene Full": Seeing and Judging in *Every Man Out of His Humour*' in Martin Butler (ed.), *Re-presenting Ben Jonson: Text, History, Performance* (Houndsmills: Macmillan, 1999), pp. 76–92. I have quoted from Butler's summary of Ostovich's argument in his introduction to the volume, 'From *Workes* to Texts', p. 8. The editorial and bibliographic question as to how to edit Jonson's *Workes* for an audience today, addressed by the Jonson scholars in this volume, is a different issue from the one I am concerned with in this chapter. I aim to describe and examine what was clearly a very conscious authorial decision in 1616, one which, for better or for worse (depending on one's point of view), was (for certain texts, not all) an act of rewriting specifically conceived with an eye to posterity. It seems that important differences between quarto texts (whether more performable as Ostovich has argued concerning *Every Man Out* or historically marked as John Jowett has argued in the case of *Sejanus*) and folio would argue for, as David Bevington suggests, two-text editing for Jonson (as for *King Lear* (or *Hamlet*)), where the writer's changes to make a 'play' a 'work' are clearly visible to readers who would have the opportunity to compare the 'play' text with the more 'literary' text, both of which have their own validity.

The masques, for instance, arguably undergo a radical generic transformation in their new life in print; the writer can be seen to mix the plaster of spectacle with history, philosophy and learned commentary. In the descriptions of what the spectators saw, the (former) writer of a court masque becomes a kind of eye-witness historian of a unique historical spectacle: 'First, for the *Scene*, was drawne a Landschap, consisting of small woods, and here and there a void place fill'd with huntings.'[14] The masque in print includes descriptions of the masquers with notes both elaborating upon and rationalizing their costumes by citing classical authorities. The effect of this is odd, since the writer, originally inspired (with his set designer) by books such as Ripa's *Iconologia* in the creation of the masque and in the design of the costumes, ends up writing a kind of *Iconologia* of his own, *after the fact*, adding his own authorities and printing it as his own book. In other words, in addition to being a kind of documentary of the event, the masque in print becomes a miniature emblem book: 'OCEANUS, presented in a humane forme, the colour of his flesh, blue; and shaddowed with a robe of sea-greene; his head grey; and[h] horned; as he is described by the *Ancients*.'[15] Note *h*, in the margin on the left-hand side of the page, reads: 'The ancients induc'd *Oceanus* always with a bull's head: *propter vim ventorum, a quibus incitatur, & impellitur: vel quia Tauris similem fremitum emittat, vel quia tanquam Taurus furibundus, in littora ferature*, Euripid. in Oreste.'[16] Sometimes Jonson's notes parody the language of philological disquisition: 'Mentioned by *Homer Ilia*. Which many have interpreted diversely: Allegorically, *Pla. in Theaeteto*, understands it to be the *Sunne*, with which while he circles the world in his course, all things are safe, and preserved: others vary it. *Macrob*. (to whose interpretation, I am specially affected in my Allusion) considers it thus.'[17] In *The Masque of Augurs*, Jonson's obvious interest and knowledge of the Roman art of augury, like his understanding of the Roman marriage customs and rites he displays in *Hymenaei*, makes of the masque a kind of encyclopedia on Roman antiquities.

The process, then, of making a masque into something more 'solide', to use the word Jonson uses in the preface to *Hymenaei*, begins before its inclusion in the 1616 folio.[18] I hope to show that the process of making a monument, like the process of building a sanctuary, can be seen at very early and different stages in the process of writing. The possibility that

---

[14] Ben Jonson, *The Masque of Blacknesse*, Herford and Simpson, vol. VII, pp. 169–70 (lines 24–6).
[15] *Ibid.*, p. 170 (lines 44–7).   [16] *Ibid.*, p. 170 (note *h*).
[17] Ben Jonson, *Hymenaei*, Herford and Simpson, vol. VII, p. 221 (marginal note *i*).
[18] *Ibid.*, p. 209 (line 16).

his works will be defaced hangs like a sword of Damocles over the poet's head and acts as catalyst for the creation of sanctuary, for contemporary audiences and readers, and the construction of the monument, for the poet's posthumous life.[19] At the same time, the monument can be seen as the result of a certain authorial eagerness to *display* his own erudition and hoard he has amassed. This process is not without its side-effects. Like the excess of vigilance that leads to authorial self-defacement, the process of monument building can have a deadly effect upon the spontaneity of a work. At times, the desire to build a monument clashes with the necessity simply to *build* and the bricklayer leaves off construction with brick and mortar in favour of collecting or stealing pieces of antique marble and propping up his masonry with Corinthian capitals. The authorial pleasure involved in the collecting, arranging and cataloguing of these objects and fragments is not without an eventual price.

'IMMORTAL MONIMENT'

The relationship between poetry (or poems) and architecture was an important trope in the period. The comparison of poetry and architectural monuments dated back to antiquity and furnished a common *topos* of the sonnet sequences at the end of the sixteenth century in England. The block structure of the sonnet, like a kind of *stele*, aided in promulgating the conceit of the poem as a monument in miniature and sonnet writers often referred to their sonnets *as* monuments. Edmund Spenser in Sonnet 69 of the *Amoretti* writes: 'Even this verse vowd to eternity / shall be thereof immortall moniment; / and tell her prayse to all posterity.'[20] Samuel Daniel in Sonnet 37 of *To Delia* echoes this idea: 'Then take this picture which I heere present thee, / Limned with a Pensill not all unworthy…This may remaine thy lasting monument, / Which happily posteritie may cherrish.'[21] Shakespeare's Sonnet 55 uses the conceit of comparing a

---

[19] According to the *OED*, the Latin word *monumentum*, derived from the verb 'monere' ('to remind', but also to 'warn'), is precisely that: a reminder, a memorial, an act of commemoration. In the early modern period a monument could refer to an architectural memorial or a legally binding document. It referred to the place where the body itself was buried. It was also a written document or record and the *OED* notes John Foxe's *Acts and Monuments* under this definition, as, in effect, the recording of things said and done (*OED* s.v. 'monument' *sb*. 2). It is, as well, anything that 'by its survival commemorates a person, action, period or event', like the razing of the city of Saguntus (by Hannibal) in which the city itself is 'a grievous moniment to her truth, and faith to the Romans' (*OED* s.v. 'monument' *sb*. 4). Finally, it is an edifice, a structure in stone, a carved figure or statue that serves as a memorial and marker of people, deeds and events.
[20] Edmund Spenser, *Amoretti and Epithalamion* (London, 1595), p. 159.
[21] Samuel Daniel, *Delia and Rosamond augmented. Cleopatra* (London, 1594), sig. D3.

poem favourably to a monument, to argue the opposite, namely that his 'rime' is *more* lasting than any monument of stone or marble:

> Nor marble, nor the guilded monument,
> Of Princes shall out-live this powrefull rime,
> But you shall shine more bright in these contents
> Then unswept stone, besmeard with sluttish time.
> When wastefull warre shall *Statues* over-turne,
> And broiles roote out the worke of masonry,
> Nor *Mars* his sword, nor warres quick fire shall burne:
> The Living record of your memory.
> Gainst death and all oblivious enmity
> Shall you pace forth.[22]

Shakespeare follows Horace in his claim for a rhyme more powerful than 'marble'.[23] Stone monuments are liable to be 'besmeared' and 'warres' will inevitably 'over-turne' and 'broiles roote out the worke of masonry'. Instead, the poet offers a 'living record' from out of which the beloved shall 'pace forth' each time a reader reads the poem. The paradox of the 'living' outliving stone is a powerful commentary on the act of reading through time. It is the writer who gives the subject life through the midwifery of the future reader. As Helen Vendler has noted, the word 'live' is ensconced in the word 'ob*liv*ious', reinforcing the triumph of the poet over this defacing force, transforming 'a memorializing and commemorative impulse into a resurrective one'.[24]

While poets erected monuments in sonnet form to their subjects they also saw their poems as commemorative of their own names. In Sonnet 47 of *Idea*, Michael Drayton refers to himself as poet 'intomb'd' in the verse he writes:

> And though in youth my youth untimely perrish,
> To keepe thee from oblivion and the grave,
> Ensuing ages yet my rimes shall cherrish,
> Where I entomb'd, my better part shall save;

---

[22] William Shakespeare, 'Sonnet 55', *Shakespeare's Sonnets*, ed. Stephen Booth (Yale: Yale University Press, 1977), pp. 49–50 (lines 1–10).
[23] For the *aere perennis* topos referred to obliquely in Sonnet 55 (and, as we shall see, directly in Drayton's *Idea*) see Horace: 'Exegi monumentum aere perennius / regalique situ pyramidum altius': 'I have finished a monument more lasting than bronze and loftier than the Pyramids' royal pile.' Horace, *The Odes and Epodes*, trans. C. E. Bennett (Cambridge: Harvard University Press, 1946), pp. 278–9 (Ode xxx).
[24] Helen Vendler, *The Art of Shakespeare's Sonnets* (Cambridge: Harvard University Press, 1997), pp. 268–9.

> And though this earthly body fade and die,
> My name shall mount upon eternitie.[25]

Jonson similarly builds himself a monument while erecting one for his dedicatee, Elizabeth, Countess of Rutland:

> There like a rich, and golden *pyramede*,
> Borne up by statues, shall I reare your head.[26]

Gail Kern Paster remarks on the architectural importance of the 'pyramid' in the Renaissance as the architectural emblem of a monument and Jonson's appropriation of this symbol to represent his own poetry of praise. She comments on Jonson's symbolic substitution of a 'pyramede' for his own verse by noting that 'Jonson glorifies his own poetry by likening it to architectural splendor in an image which draws together the potentially heroic aspects of poetry and architecture.'[27] Jonson's description of his poem as equivalent to 'rearing' or, as in the Cary-Morison Ode, 'raising' a monument is in keeping with the *aere perennis* topos. Yet, the fact that Jonson was particularly interested in architecture as a craft or science necessarily lends a certain piquancy to this image of 'raising' a monument. Henry S. Turner draws attention to Jonson's underlinings in his copy of Vitruvius' *De Architectura*, of which he owned two copies with two different commentaries, 'both of which he read closely for their technical terms and annotated heavily with their English equivalents'.[28] That Jonson was interested enough, whether due to his collaboration with Jones, or his own obsession with fame and posterity or both, to procure copies of Vitruvius and develop a personal vocabulary out of the specialized language of architecture (as he did with 'alchemy' and the 'news'), goes far to inform us of his preoccupations.

Yet, in reading a poem such as Jonson's 'Elegie' on Lady Jane Pawlet, we begin to understand that the erection and the creation of monument

---

[25] Michael Drayton, *England's Heroicall Epistles. Newly Corrected. With Idea* (London, 1600), sig. Q3.
[26] Ben Jonson, '*Epistle*, To Elizabeth Countesse of Rutland', *The Forrest* (xii), Herford and Simpson, vol. VIII, p. 113 (lines 83–4). Cited in Gail Kern Paster, 'Ben Jonson and the Uses of Architecture', *Renaissance Quarterly* 27 (Autumn 1974), 306–20; p. 316.
[27] Paster, 'The Uses of Architecture', p. 316.
[28] Henry S. Turner, *The English Renaissance Stage: Geometry, Poetics, and the Practical Spatial Arts 1580–1630* (Oxford: Oxford University Press, 2006), p. 254. Turner's consideration of various passages of Jonson's works shows the extent to which Jonson was indeed interested in the language of the practical aspects of architecture. Turner's argument that this spatial and geometric language shaped Jonson's 'scenography' is fertile. See also Turner's source for his discussion of Jonson and Vitruvius: A. W. Johnson, *Ben Jonson: Poetry and Architecture* (Oxford: Clarendon Press, 1994). For a richly illustrated book on the symbolic language of craft 'tools' in the emblem literature of the sixteenth, seventeenth and eighteenth centuries see Irène Mainguy, *Symbolique des outils et glorification du métier* (Paris: Jean-Cyrille Godefroy, 2007).

in Jonson's work is not only the textual equivalent of a noble architectural project, but a strategic response to a specific terror. This terror is perhaps best described by Shakespeare's term 'oblivious enmity', an extremely evocative combination of the natural and malicious forces which join together to obliterate memory and against which the poet feels his 'powerful rime' must battle. While for Shakespeare, a kind of resurrection in and through the written word is achieved or at least hoped for, in Jonson a monument is *raised* through a *psychomachia* between the poet and those forces that would defeat him. The result is a form of prophylactic self-immolation or self-petrification in the face of this terror. In the first line of his poem to Lady Pawlet the poet is confronted by the 'gentle Ghost' of the dead woman.[29] He follows her as she beckons him and then finds himself suddenly filled with 'horrour': 'all my blood is steele! / Stiffe! stark! My joynts 'gainst one another knock!' (lines 8–9). Face to face with the dead, the writer finds himself turned to 'Marble' (line 13). Yet, this transformation into marble does not augur a kind of writerly impotence; rather, it becomes a means by which the writer can bypass a certain stage in the difficult work of creation by soliciting the fame that, in the normal order of things, should come *as a result of* the poem the poet is now writing: 'write the rest / *Thou wouldst have written*, Fame, upon my brest: / It is a large faire table, and a true' (my emphasis; lines 13–15). Instead of inventing, the poet becomes the gravestone / tablet that passively awaits the hand of fame (a surer writing hand) to write the epitaphic inscription. Of course, at the precise moment of his petrification into a marble 'table', the poet is *inculpated* of all responsibility concerning what he subsequently writes about the Lady for he attributes the poem not to his own hand, but to the hand of another writer, that of 'her Fame' (line 34).

Stanley Fish observes that this poem is the 'most complicated instance of the pattern' in which Jonson 'consumes' the first part of a number of poems before finally 'stumbling' on its subject.[30] While the poem is clearly an example of Jonson's self-reflexive habit of meditating on the writing of the poem before reaching the 'actual' subject, it is remarkable in how it reveals a Jonson representing himself as catatonic and numbed in the act of writing. The specular process by which we have seen the writer both judge and defend himself finds its *reductio ad absurdum* in this scene of

---

[29] Ben Jonson, 'An Elegie On the Lady Jane Pawlet, Marchion: of Winton', *Underwood* (lxxxiii), Herford and Simpson, vol. VIII, p. 268 (line 1). Subsequent references to the poem will be included in the text.
[30] Fish, 'Authors-Readers', p. 233.

petrification. In his essay 'Autobiography as De-facement', Paul de Man illuminates the danger inherent in the poetic use of the figure of *prosopopeia*. He writes about:

> the latent threat that inhabits prosopopeia, namely that by making the dead speak, the symmetrical structure of the trope implies, by the same token, that the living are struck dumb, frozen in their own death.[31]

Jonson's elegy to Lady Pawlet narrates the process by which the living (writer) is frozen in his own death. The poem is a visible reminder of and a warning concerning the threat of dealing in metaphor, figures and tropes. Bringing the dead into the world, clothed in words, hides, as de Man concludes, the 'defacement of the mind' that lies underneath the trappings of poetic figure and that the poet, from time to time, finds himself touching ('It is too neere of kin to heaven, the Soule, / To be describ'd! Fames fingers are too foule / To touch these Mysteries!'), only then to find himself frozen in the confrontation with that same defacement which he must cover and hide from view.[32] This threat of defacement is, in effect, the spectre of the inability to create. According to de Man: 'Milton speaks of the burden that Shakespeare's "easy numbers" represent for those who are, like all of us, capable only of "slow-endeavoring art".'[33] Jonson's response to the bereavement of his own fancy when confronted by the image of his own death might be described as, at best, a form of artful incapacity, at worst, a simulacrum of immobility.

'BORROWING A LIFE OF POSTERITY': MONUMENT AND THE COURT MASQUE

Such means of building a monument in response to the threat posed by the dead and death, can be seen throughout Jonson's works. They explain the recurrence of the figure of the gorgon, the monster that turns all it gazes upon to stone. These moments testify to Jonson's inherent fascination with mortality and immortality, with oblivion and with fame. Like the creation of sanctuary, the building of a monument is aimed at the poet's obsession with the threat of defacement and can be seen as representative of his vice-like grip on the reception of his works. Yet, monument-building can

---

[31] Paul de Man, 'Autobiography as De-Facement' in *The Rhetoric of Romanticism* (New York: Columbia University Press, 1984), pp. 61–81, p. 78.
[32] Ben Jonson, 'An Elegie On the Lady Jane Pawlet', Herford and Simpson, vol. VIII, p. 269 (lines 29–31)
[33] De Man, 'Autobiography as De-Facement', p. 81.

be distinguished from the creation of sanctuary in its particular fascination with death and ephemerality. Jonson's monument-building springs from a certain melancholic perception of his own mortality and the danger his mortality presents to his own work, a perception that emerges from his own interest in classical studies and antiquities of all kinds. He was prone to place himself and his own work within a larger historical framework particularly in relation to Roman history. It is within the context of speculation concerning the terms of his own mortality that we must see Jonson's particular interest in saving and recuperating his court masques. The inherent ephemerality of this form can only have sharpened his poetic resolve and determination to oppose what can only be seen in terms of intellectual waste. The poetic desire for control over death appears most distinctly in the gap between court performance and published text.[34] In Derridean terms, one might describe the gap between performance and text as the 'différance' which provides the 'jeu' for the emergence of a new piece of literature.[35] This gap, the lack constituted by envy and ignorance, constitutes the threat that propels the author to add a later hand, to rewrite and add to the original dialogues of the performance. Out of envy or lack, the writer thus carves out space within which to erect a monument, which, like a tablet, may be used to engrave his name. In many of Jonson's writings, it is the court masque which serves as the ultimate symbol of the swift transition from birth to death that marks theatrical performance. Masques 'vanish all away in a day'.[36] They are 'the short braverie of the night'.[37] Jonson, significantly, adopts an elegiac tone when he writes about the brevity of the masque. In his numerous prefaces to and commentaries on his own masques, he mourns the masque's inherent ephemerality and makes a point of insisting that it is the *duty* of the author to reconstruct the spectacular evening performance for posterity, in order to preserve the memory

---

[34] My emphasis on ephemerality needs to be distinguished from Jonas A. Barish's idea of Jonsonian 'anti-theatricality'. The notion of anti-theatricality has some serious shortcomings for a poet as dedicated and interested as Jonson in the theatre and the masque. I would argue that Jonson is, rather, obsessed with *defacement* as I have described it (which includes the perversion and misreading of the text through the actor's voice) rather than theatricality *per se*. For Jonson, it is the masque's inherent *ephemerality* and liability to distortion, not its inherent *theatricality* which presents a problem for the writer. It is this envious ephemerality that the writer attempts to overcome in the creation of the published texts. See Jonas A. Barish, *The Anti-theatrical Prejudice* (Berkeley: University of California Press, 1981).

[35] See Jacques Derrida, 'Différance' in *Margins of Philosophy*, trans. Alan Bass (Hemel Hempstead: Harvester Wheatsheaf, 1982), pp. 1–28.

[36] Ben Jonson, *Timber or, Discoveries*, Herford and Simpson, vol. VIII, p. 606 (line 1407).

[37] Ben Jonson, 'To Sir Robert Wroth', *The Forrest* (iii), Herford and Simpson, vol. VIII, p. 96 (line 10).

of it. In his 'reconstruction' of the masque *Hymenaei*, Jonson interrupts himself in the midst of a passage describing the beauty of the performance to mourn the inevitable passing of his and his collaborators' creation:

> Hitherto extended the first nights *Solemnitie*, whose grace in the execution, left not where to adde unto it, with wishing: I meane, (nor doe I court them) in those, that sustain'd the *nobler* parts. Such was the exquisite performance, as (beside the *pompe*, *splendor*, or what we may call *apparelling* of such *Presentments*) that alone (had all else been absent) was of power to surprize with delight, and steale away the *spectators* from themselves. Nor was there wanting whatsoever might give to the *furniture*, or *complement*; either in *riches*, or strangenesse of the *habites*, delicacie of *daunces*, magnificence of the *scene*, or divine rapture of *musique*. Onely the envie was, that it lasted not still, or (now it is past) cannot by imagination, much lesse description, be recovered to a part of that *spirit* it had in the gliding by.
>
> Yet, that I may not utterly defraud the *Reader* of his hope, I am drawne to give it those briefe touches, which may leave behind some shadow of what it was.[38]

The passage's repeated refrain is that nothing was lacking. As such, there is no place (for the poet) to 'adde unto it'. It was perfect, complete and whole: 'Nor was there wanting whatsoever.' Rhetorically, this list of the perfections of the masque leads perfectly to the final 'envie', the *one* lack, the one weak point, that, like the hole in the dyke, needs to be stopped up or filled. When the poet writes 'Onely the envie was', he is saying: 'all that was lacking to make the masque complete, whole and perfect', was that it was not lasting. It had everything: pomp, circumstance, splendour, beauty, the power to surprise, even the power to make the audience forget where they were. Yet, it was *envied* its immortality. It is therefore in clear opposition to (this) envy that the court masque writer finds his niche, his (new) role as *masque elegist* and thus the opportunity to reap a benefit, display himself, add and enlarge, speak at length from beyond the grave all the while coquettishly claiming that he does not want to 'defraud' the reader.[39] The poet makes much of his inability to describe the original spirit of the masque in printed words: 'It…cannot by imagination, much lesse

---

[38] Ben Jonson, *Hymenaei*, Herford and Simpson, vol. VII, p. 229 (lines 565–82).

[39] If we consider the author's 'new' role as masque elegist in Thomas Tanselle's terms, then Jonson's printed masques (quarto and folio version(s)) might *all* very well be considered the author's 'new intentions' as opposed to his 'final intentions' (the script for the actual performance). We lack the original performance script or 'final intentions' of the author for all but one masque. The 'wholly new conception of the work' which represents the masque in quarto or folio (some much more than others) is, interestingly enough, all that remains. Kevin Donovan, 'Forms of Authority in the Early Texts of Every Man Out of Humour' in Martin Butler (ed.), *Re-presenting Ben Jonson: Text, History, Performance* (New York: Macmillan Press, 1999), pp. 59–75, p. 70. G. T. Tanselle, 'The Editorial Problem of Final Authorial Intention', *Studies in Bibliography* 29 (1976).

description, be recovered to a part of that *spirit* it had in the gliding by.' And yet he does exactly that, to 'leave behind some shadow of what it was'. This Platonic 'shadow', ironically, becomes very materially published in quarto then folio, prefaced, with notes, commentaries and descriptions about the process of writing the masque, the ability of the performers and the reactions of the audience, as well as the musings of the writer upon the masque in performance. The writer may claim that he does not want to 'defraud the *Reader* of his hope', but he is equally interested in ensuring that posterity does not cheat the writer his part in creating this spectacle and, at the same time, appropriating the work of the set and costume designer, as well as the choreographer and musicians. In this passage, envy brings in its train the threat of death and oblivion. This threat is symbolically associated with fraud or with cheating the reader. Overcoming the threat and making up for envious 'lack' is, thus, implicitly represented as the writer honestly giving the reader the *change* due to him, while he profits from a situation in which he can produce the masque again, on his own terms, as his own work.

In his preface to *The Masque of Blacknesse*, Jonson goes so far as to associate the printing of the masque with certain economic benefits for both the reader and the writer. Here the reader could very well be, among others, a Royal.[40] In this preface the reader/Royal is not in danger of being 'defrauded' by the poet, rather, he or she is represented as in need of 'borrowing' from him:[41]

The honor, and splendor of these *spectacles* was such in the performance, as could those houres have lasted, this of mine, now, had been a most unprofitable worke. But (when it is the fate, even of the greatest, and most absolute births, to need, and borrow a life of posteritie) little had been done to the studie of *magnificence* in these, if presently with the rage of the people, who (as a part of greatnesse) are privileged by custome, to deface their *carkasses*, the *spirits* had also perished. In dutie, therefore, to that *Majestie*, who gave them their authoritie, and grace; and, no lesse then the most royall of predecessors, deserves eminent celebration for these solemnities: I adde this later hand.[42]

It remains unclear, perhaps consciously ambiguous, as to whether the 'profit' of the work belongs to the queen (or king) or to the poet: 'this of mine, now ... a most unprofitable worke'. What is even more astonishing

---

[40] See Chapter 3, n.9 concerning the ambiguity of the identity of the 'Majestie' referred to in the preface. I will therefore here again refer to the royal addressee in the gender neutral term 'Prince'.
[41] I quote again Jonson's preface to *The Masque of Blacknesse* quoted in Chapter 3.
[42] Ben Jonson, *The Masque of Blacknesse*, Herford and Simpson, vol. VII, p. 169 (lines 1–12).

is the position in which the poet places the Prince as 'needing' to 'borrow' a 'life of posteritie', something which the poet is quite clear (even in this syntactically tangled passage) is *his to lend*, just as it had already been lent to 'the most royal of predecessors', Elizabeth I. The poet describes himself as profiting as a result of the Prince's need to borrow. The poet may be seen as a kind of literary banker who lends a life to the Prince (and indirectly to himself at the same time) by adding a 'later hand'. Disturbingly, the poet extracts profit from the 'rage of the people' and the defacement of 'carkasses', because it is precisely the physical masque's destruction that gives him the *opening* he needs to save a part of what was lost. Jonson thus places the poet in the position, not only of writing a work (in the first instance) for his own and perhaps the profit of his Prince, but even of *lending* a life to the Prince in subsequently saving *his* masque from defacement. Jonathan Goldberg has noted the benefit Jonson receives from his monarch, in the form of a 'royal imprimatur':

> Jonson's decision to include the masques in his *Workes*, to transform scripts for performance into the permanence of print, provides one place of meeting between the monarch and the poet ... Printed, the masque gains an everlastingness, a royal imprimatur. In Jonson's masques, to celebrate the king means to reveal their shared status as writing. In the headnote to *Blacknesse* Jonson characteristically stresses the permanence of such representation. After presentation and performance comes re-presentation, 'a life of posterity' (line 4), nothing less than the eternal life of the text.[43]

Goldberg is correct in noting that the permanence of print offered the poet the kind of everlasting fame that Majesty possessed naturally. The imprimatur of the Royal seals the text. However, Goldberg has elided the way the poet portrays himself as the one able to give the Prince a life in posterity in his role as memorializer of royal '*magnificence*'. The economic language of the passage should make us pause. If the masque had lasted, the poet could not have profited: 'could those hours have lasted, this of mine, now, had been a most unprofitable work'. In his consideration of how the written masque is, by implication, profitable, the poet may be seen as a kind of speculator in futures. The calculation seems straightforward; the prince is in 'need' and the poet, alone, can lend him a life as a result. The loan of a posterity to Majesty enables the poet to gain in literary interest. While representing himself as writing for the profit of the Prince,

---

[43] Jonathan Goldberg, *James I and the Politics of Literature: Jonson, Shakespeare, Donne, and Their Contemporaries* (Baltimore: The Johns Hopkins University Press, 1983), pp. 57 and 59.

Jonson turns the masques into profit for his own literary fame by publishing them in his collected *Workes*. Jonson may be said to be Machiavellian in his solicitude for his own posterity. The publication of his plays, and especially the ephemeral masques, speaks to an intense desire to intervene in the establishment of his own posterity in a manner which reminds us of the Italian philosopher whom Jonson called 'St *Nicolas*', Niccolo Machiavelli.[44] According to Clement Rosset, for Machiavelli: 'the political problem of the Prince, more than one of efficiency is a problem of time; he must succeed in sustaining a state of things constitutionally transitory, unstable and fragile'.[45] By adding notes, comments and narrations of what happened, bearing witness to the novelty of the masque and at the same time justifying it with citations from authorized writers, the author turns the ephemerality of a light and splendid performance to profit for his own fame and a monument to his own name.

THE GORGON GAZE OF ENVY: *THE MASQUE OF QUEENES*

The Masque of Queenes (1609) is one of the most persuasive examples of Jonsonian monument-building. In the marginalia that surrounds and supports the text, we can literally see Jonson's negotiation with posterity and fame. In addition, the anti-masque and masque narrate a battle between the poet and the forces of envy against which he must build an everlasting monument to protect his name. In this masque, as in the 'Elegie to Lady Jane Pawlet', the poet is confronted by a similar 'terror' and, as we shall see, uses surprisingly similar strategies to confront it.

According to Ben Jonson, the sixteen-year-old Prince Henry of England asked him for an annotated version of *The Masque of Queenes* soon after it had been performed by the queen and her ladies at Whitehall on 2 February 1609.[46] Jonson in turn created a handwritten document for the Prince, carefully designing it to look like contemporary printed editions of the classical

---

[44] Ben Jonson, *Timber, or Discoveries*, Herford and Simpson, vol. VIII, p. 599 (line 1178).
[45] 'Le problème politique du Prince, avant d'être un problème d'efficacité, est un problème du temps; à faire durer un état de choses constitutionnellement provisoire, mouvant et fragile.' Clement Rosset, *L'Anti-nature* (Paris: PUF, 1973), p. 184.
[46] Jonson mentions the Prince's request in the dedication to Prince Henry of *The Masque of Queenes*: 'though it hath prov'd a work of some difficulty to mee to retrieve the particular *authorities* (according to your gracious command and a desire born out of judgment) to those things, which I writt out of fullnesse, and memory of my former readings; Yet, now I have overcome it, the reward that meetes mee is double to one act: which is that thereby, your excellent understanding will not only justifie mee to your own knowledge, but decline the stiffnesse of others originall Ignorance, allready arm'd to censure' (Herford and Simpson, vol. VII, p. 281, lines 32–41).

authors complete with footnotes and marginalia. *The Masque of Queenes* was printed later that year in Quarto 'to be sold at the Spred Eagle in Poules Church-yard. 1609.'[47] Like Jonson's earlier masques, it became a public document soon after it was performed. On sale in the largest market for books at St Paul's Church, Jonson clearly aimed to reach a larger readership. In addition to the dialogue and speeches of the masquers, the text includes descriptions of the decor, choreography and music on the night of the performance. It also includes detailed footnotes about witchcraft and magic from Jonson's study of both ancient and contemporary sources and numerous asides, written after the performance, justifying the moral and aesthetic underpinnings of his poetic methods and choices.[48] In fact, Jonson's text includes speeches which may not have been included in the original script and not spoken in actual performance. Its extraordinary array of citations and annotations makes one doubt whether they ever were actual sources for the original masque. The text is interspersed with authorial asides to the reader and commentary on the writer's own, as well as his collaborators', artistic decisions in the form of more quotations or elaborate explanations or both. Of these, many must have been added for posterity. We have no idea to what extent these are 'reconstructions' of the poet's thoughts when he wrote the masque for performance, even though this is what the writer has claimed he has done in his dedicatory letter to Prince Henry. Nor do we know to what extent they were conceived after the fact, in order to protect doubly and defend, while displaying, a text which the poet intends for the eyes of a larger audience and even a later one.

The print history of this text clearly shows that *The Masque of Queenes* is not the script of the masque performed at Whitehall.[49] The holograph Jonson produced for Prince Henry, reprinted in Herford and the Simpsons' edition,

---

[47] From the title page of the quarto, 1609, in Herford and Simpson, vol. VII, p. 278. See the facsimile of Jonson's handwritten version, the 'holograph', of the masque in vol. VII, facing page 290. Jonson possessed an original manuscript of his own, the 'archetype', which he sent to the printer to make the quarto. The holograph, now in the British Library, is a 'fair' copy of this original manuscript. Herford and Simpson note: 'The opportunity of printing a complete work of Jonson's exactly as he wrote it is unique. We have taken the holograph as our text and reproduced it *verbatim*' (vol. VII, p. 269).

[48] Jonson's footnotes concerning witches and their practices include references to ancient sources such as Aeschylus' *Oresteia*, Horace's *Odes* and Lucan's *Pharsalia*. Among Jonson's contemporary sources are King James' *Daemonologie* (1597), Reginald Scot's *The Discoverie of Witchcraft* (1584) (unacknowledged), contemporary folkloric beliefs and even, perhaps, echoes to the witches' chants from *Macbeth*, performed three years previously.

[49] Jerzy Limon astutely differentiates between what he calls the 'literary' masque and the masque as it was performed: 'By the term *masque* I mean two different phenomena. The first is the literary masque as a type of text that has survived in print or manuscript to the twentieth century. The second is the masque-in-performance, a theatrical text that can only be reconstructed on the basis

is actually the retrospective view of the writer on the masque. Instead of being read as a performance text, *The Masque of Queenes* needs to be read as the author's reflections on his own work *after* the performance. As such, it offers a fascinating example of authorial reflexivity. It is striking, then, that scholars attempting to understand the 'present occasions' of the masque borrow and quote from a post-performance text published later by the poet as his own work.[50] As we have seen, by rewriting the masque in retrospect, Jonson assumes property rights to a collaborative effort, extracting the maximum benefit for his own literary posterity. We can never know the exact nature and extent of what Jonson, as we have seen, called his 'later hand'.[51] The possibility must be considered that the writer modified the original script (of which we have no copy) or emphasized aspects of the scenario and even speeches suppressed in the original script. The holograph of *The Masque of Queenes* is at least a different and perhaps in part even a very consciously 'differing' and 'deferred' work from the original script used for the performance.[52] I would argue that reading *The Masque of Queenes* as a retrospective text will help illuminate a specifically Jonsonian poetic fantasy constructed around fame and envy. This will place into relief the poetic stakes of this post-performance text, eclipsed in readings which emphasize the masque in performance and the centrality of the king or other centres of power at court.[53]

---

of surviving contemporary sources.' *The Masque of Stuart Culture* (Newark: University of Delaware Press, 1990), p. 8.

[50] For the phrase 'present occasions' see the preface to *Hymenaei* in Herford and Simpson, vol. VII, p. 209 (line 17).

[51] See the preface to *The Masque of Blacknesse*, Herford and Simpson, vol. VII, p. 169 (line 12).

[52] I am again alluding to Jacques Derrida's concept of 'différance' which conflates the ideas of 'deferral' and 'difference'.

[53] For scholarship emphasizing the masque performance as a celebration of the centrality and power of the king see Orgel, *The Illusion of Power*; Stephen Orgel and Roy Strong, *Inigo Jones: The Theatre of the Stuart Court* (Berkeley: University of California Press, 1973); Jonathan Goldberg, *James I and the Politics of Literature: Jonson, Shakespeare, Donne, and their Contemporaries* (Baltimore: The Johns Hopkins University Press, 1983); Gordon Parry, 'The Politics of the Jacobean Masque' in J. R. Mulryne and M. Shewring (eds.), *Theatre and Government Under the Early Stuarts* (Cambridge: Cambridge University Press, 1993), pp. 87–117 and Leah Marcus in her discussion of the Jacobean masque in *The Politics of Mirth*. For studies emphasizing the 'occasion' of the masque and other centres of power at court see Butler and Lindley, 'Restoring Astraea'; David Lindley, 'Embarrassing Ben: The Masques for Frances Howard', *ELR* 16 (1986), 343–59 and for the contemporary political context J. Smith, 'Effaced History: Facing the Colonial Context of Ben Jonson's Irish Masque at Court', *ELH* 65 (1998), 297–321. For studies emphasizing the role of Queen Anne in the shaping of the masque see Leeds Barroll, *Anna of Denmark, Queen of England: A Cultural Biography* (Philadelphia: University of Philadelphia Press, 2001); Barbara Kiefer Lewalski, *Writing Women in Jacobean England* (Cambridge: Harvard University Press, 93); Suzanne Gossett, ' "Man-maid, begone!": Women in Masques', *ELR* 18 (Winter 1988), 96–113; Clare McManus, *Women on the Renaissance Stage: Anna of Denmark and Female Masquing in the Stuart Court (1590–1619)* (Manchester and New York: Manchester University

952   *Masques.*

10. *Ossa ab ore rapta ieiunæ canis,* Horace giues *Canidia,* in the place before quoted. Which *ieiunæ,* I rather change to Gard'ners, as imagining such persons to keepe Mastifes for the defence of their grounds,

10.

I, From the iawes of a Gardiners bitch,
Did snatch these bones, and then leap'd the ditch;
Yet went I backe to the house againe,
Kill'd the blacke Cat, and here's the braine.

whither this Hagge might goe also for *simples*: where, meeting with the bones, and not content with them, shee would yet doe a domesticke hurt, in getting the Catt's braines: which is another speciall *ingredient*; and of so much more efficacie, by how much blacker the Cat is, if you will credit *Agrip. cap. de suffitibus.*

11. These also, both by the confessions of Witches, and testimonie of Writers, are of principall vse in their witchcraft. The Toad mention'd in *Virg. Geo. lib.* 1. *Inuentusque cauis Bufo.* Which by Plinie is

11.

I Went to the Toad breedes vnder the wall,
I charm'd him out, and he came at my call;
I scratch'd out the eyes of the Owle before,
I tore the Batts wing; what would you haue more?

call'd *Rubeta, Nat. Hist. lib.* 32.*cap.*5. and there celebrated for the force in *Magick. Iuuenal* toucheth at it twice, within my memorie, *Satir.* 1. & 6. And of the Owles eyes, see *Corn. Agrip. de occult. Philos. lib.* 1. *cap.* 15. As of the Bats bloud, and wings there: and in the 25. chapter, with *Bapt. Porta, lib.* 2. *cap.* 26.

12. After all their boasted labors, and plentie of *Materialls* (as they imagine) I make the *Dame* not only to adde more, but stranger, and out of their means to get (except the first *Papauer cornutum*, which I haue touch'd at in the confection) as *Sepulchris cadrisicos eruitas, & cui ressos funebreis,* as Horace calls them, where he

12.
DAME.

YEs, I haue brought (to helpe our vowes)
Horned Poppie, Cypresse boughes,
The Fig-tree wild, that growes on tombes,
And iuice, that from the *Larch-tree* comes,
The *Basiliskes* bloud, and the *Vipers* skin:
And, now, our *Orgies* let's begin.

armes *Canidia, Epod. lib. Ode.* 5. Then *Agaricum Laricis,* of which, see *Porta. lib.* 2. *de Nat. Magi,* against *Plinie.* And *Basilici, quem & Saturni sanguinem vocant venefici, tantasq; vires habere ferunt. Cor. Agrip. de occult. Philos. lib.* 2. *cap.* 42. With the Viper, remembred by *Lucan. lib.* 6. and the skins of Serpents. *Innataq; rubris Æquoribus custos pretiosæ vipera conche, Aut viuentis adhuc Lybicæ membrana cerastæ.* And *Ouid, lib.* 7. *Nec defuit illis Squamea Ciniphei tenuis membrana chelidri.*

Here, the Dame put her selfe in the midst of them, and began her following Inuocation; wherein shee tooke occasion, to boast all the power attributed to Witches by the Ancients; of which, euery Poet (or the most) doe giue some: HOMER to CIRCE, in the Odyss. THEOCRITVS to SIMATHA, in Pharmaceutria; VIRGIL to ALPHESIBŒVS, in his. OVID to DIPSAS, in Amor. to MEDEA and CIRCE, in Metamorph. TIBVLLVS to SAGA; HORACE to CANIDIA, SAGANA, VEIA, FOLIA; SENECA to MEDEA, and the Nurse, in Herc. OEte. PETR. ARBITER to his SAGA, in Frag. and CLAVDIAN to MEGÆRA, lib. 1. in Rusinum; who takes the habit of a Witch, as these doe, and supplies that historicall part in the Poeme, beside her morall person of a Furie; confirming the same drift, in ours.

a These Inuocations are solemne with them, whereof we may see the formes, in *Ouid. Metam. lib.* 7. in *Sen. Trag. Med.* in *Luc. lib.* 6. which of all is the boldest and most horrid: beginning, *Eumenides, Stigiumq; nefas, paneq; nocentis, &c.*
b The vntying of their knots

YOu a *Fiends* and *Furies* (if yet any bee
Worse then our selues) you, that haue quak'd to see
These b knots vntied; and shrunke, when we haue charm'd.
You, that (to arme vs) haue your selues disarm'd,
And to our powers, resign'd your whips and brands,
When we went forth, the scourge of men and lands.

is, when they are going to some fatall businesse: as *Sagana* is presented by *Horace, Expedita, per totam domum Spargens Auernaleis aquas, Horret capillis, vt marinus asperis, Echinus, aut currens Aper.*

You,

Illustration 3. Facing pages from *The Masque of Queenes* in Ben Jonson, *Workes* (London, 1616).

You, that haue seene me ride, when HECATE
Durst not take chariot; when the boistrous sea,
Without a breath of wind, hath knock'd the skie;
And that hath thundred, IOVE not knowing why:
When we haue set the elements at warres,
Made midnight see the sunne, and day the starres;
When the wing'd lightning, in the course, hath staid;
And swiftest riuers haue run backe, afraid,
To see the corne remoue, the groues to range,
Whole places alter, and the seasons change,
When the pale *moone*, at the first voice downe fell
Poison'd, and durst not stay the second *spell*.
You, that haue oft, beene conscious of these sights;
And thou ᶜ *three-formed starre*, that, on these nights
Art onely powerfull, to whose triple name
Thus we incline, *once, twice,* and *thrise the same*;
If now with *rites* prophane, and foule inough,
We doe inuoke thee; darken all this roofe,
With present fogges. Exhale earths rott'nest vapors,
And strike a blindnesse through these blazing tapers.
Come, let a murmuring *charme* resound,
The whilst we ᵈ bury all, i'the ground.
But first, see euery ᵉ foote be bare;
And euery knee. HAG. Yes, *dame*, they are.

4. CHARME.

Deepe, ᶠ O deepe, we lay thee to sleepe;
We leaue thee drinke by, if thou chance to be dry;
Both milke, and bloud, the dew, and the floud.
We breathe in thy bed, at the foot, and the head;
We couer thee warme, that thou take no harme:
And when thou dost wake,
  Dame earth shall quake,
  And the houses shake,
  And her belly shall ake,
  As her backe were brake,
  Such a birth to make,
  As is the blue *drake*:
  Whose forme thou shall take.

ᶜ *Hecate*, who is called *Trinia*, and *Triformis*, of whom *Virgil. Æneid. lib. 4. Tergeminámq; Hecaten, tria virginis ora Dianæ.* She was beleeu'd to gouerne in witchcraft; and is remembred in all their inuocations. See *Theoc. in Pharmaceut.* χαῖρ Ἑκάτα. δασπλῆτι, *& Medea in Senec. Meis vocata sacris noctium sidus veni, Pessimos induta vultus: Fronte non vna minax.* And *Bricht. in Luc. Persephone, nostræq; Hecatis pars vltima, & c.*
ᵈ This *Rite*, of burying their Materials, is often confest in *Remig.* and describ'd amply in *Hor. Sat. 8. lib. 1. Vtq; Lupibarbam variæ cum dente colubræ Abdiderint furtim terris, &c.*
ᵉ The Ceremony also, of baring their feete, is expressed by *Ouid. Metamorph. lib. 7.* as of their haire. *Egreditur tectis vestes induta recinctas, Nuda pedem, nudos humeris insusa capillos.* And *Horac. ibid. Pedibus nudis passáq; capillo.* And *Senec. in Traged. Med. Tibi more Gentis, vinculo soluens comam Secreta nudo nemora lustraui pede.*

ᶠ Heere they speake as if they were creating some new feature, which the *deuill* perswades them to be able to do, often, by the pronouncing of words, and powring out of liquors, on the earth. Heare what *Agrip.* saies *De occult. Phil. lib. 4.* neer the end. *In euocationibus vmbrarum fumigamus cum sanguine recenti, cum ossibus mortuorum, & carne, cum ouis, lacte, melle, oleo, & similibus, quæ aptè mediis tribuunt animabus, ad suurenda corpora*; and a little before. *Namq; animæ cognitis medijs, per quæ quondam corporibus suis coniungebantur, per similes vapores, liquores, nidoresq; facile alliciuntur.* Which doctrine he had from *Apuleius*, without all doubt, or question, who in *lib. 3. de Asin. aureo.* publisheth the same. *Tunc decantatis spirantibus fibris litat vario latice; nunc rore fontano, nunc lacte vaccino, nunc melle montano, libat & mulsa. Sic illos capillos in mutuos nexus obditos, atque nodatos, cum multis odoribus dat viuis carbonibus adolendos. Tunc protinus inexpugnabili Magicæ Disciplinæ potestate, & cæca numinum coactorum violentia, illa corpora quorum fumabant stridentes capilli spiritum mutuantur humanum, & sentiunt, & audiunt, & ambulant. Et qua nidor suarum ducebat exuuiarum veniunt.* All which are meere arts of *Sathan*, when either himselfe will delude them with a false forme, or troubling a dead body, makes them imagine these vanities the meanes: as in the ridiculous circumstances that follow, he doth daily.

Like the publication of his masques with marginalia and commentary, Jonson's dedication of *The Masque of Queenes* to Prince Henry may best be read as yet another aspect of the author's negotiation with posterity rather than just a piece of courtly flattery. Elsewhere, Jonson states that it was the Prince who asked him to dilate upon his own work: 'his Highnesse command, to have mee adde this second labor of annotation to my first of Invention'.[54] Yet, the act of annotating and expanding upon the 'original' masque and then publishing it in quarto was precisely what the author had done with his previous masques.[55] Jonson writes that the Prince 'was curious to examine her [Poetry] with your eye, and inquire into her beauties, and strengths'.[56] The identification of the Prince as 'curious' necessarily has an ambivalent flavour. The Prince, in effect, is depicted as possessing the curious, prying eye of certain censorious critics. Yet, this description of the Prince's eye also aptly describes the curious eye of the poet with regard to his own work, a curiosity that bordered on a kind of obsessional inquisitiveness concerning how his work would be received. The poet hopes that the Prince's approval of the poet's work will 'decline the stiffeness of others' originall Ignorance, allready arm'd to censure'.[57] Here, Jonson effectively enlists the Prince in the poet's ongoing battle against present and future readers, whose 'censure' would, in effect, have the power to pervert and deface the writer's text. Jonson adroitly transforms the young Prince's wish for annotations into a means of 'declining' the judgement of the reader. In other words, Jonson attributes his own desire to publish the masque to the Prince's command to see it. The poet thus transforms the specific demands of his patron into the foundation upon which to build his monument.

Press, 2002), M. Wynne-Davies, 'The Queen's Masque: Renaissance Women and the Seventeenth-Century Court Masque' in M. Wynne-Davies and S. Cerasano (eds.), *Gloriana's Face: Women, Public and Private, in the English Renaissance* (Detroit: Wayne State University Press, 1992), pp. 79–104 and Kathryn Schwarz, 'Stranger in the Mirror: Amazonian Reflections in the Jacobean Queen's Masque' in *Tough Love: Amazonian Encounters in the English Renaissance* (Durham and London: Duke University Press, 2000), pp. 109–33.

[54] Ben Jonson, Dedication [of *The Masque of Queenes*] to Queen Anne, Herford and Simpson, vol. VII, p. 279 (lines 10–11). According to Herford and Simpson, the poet 'explains...his reasons for dedicating the quarto to Prince Henry rather than to her' (vol. VII, p. 269).

[55] Jonson had already published four masques with notes and prefaces by 1609. Is it a result of chance or a perfect sympathy of wills that the Prince should ask the poet for exactly the kind of thing the poet would have planned on doing anyhow? The Prince mirrors the poet's own desire, by commanding him to do what he knew he would be interested in doing. On the other hand, it remains plausible that the poet interpreted the princely request so as to do much more than he had been asked for.

[56] Ben Jonson, Dedication to Prince Henry in Herford and Simpson, vol. VII, p. 281 (lines 31–2).

[57] *Ibid.*, (lines 39–40).

The whole of *The Masque of Queenes* may be read as we read Jonson's dedication to Prince Henry. The masque places both King James I and Queen Anne in the forefront, while at the same time the scenario and its accumulation of notes and marginalia is constructed around a literary battle against the defacing forces of time and judgement. As we have argued, these forces often find expression in Jonson's works in the polysemic word 'envy'. A closer examination, both of the scenario and the annotations of *The Masque of Queenes*, will reveal that the anti-masque of witches, the violent beheading of Terror and the subsequent erection of a monument to literary authority are all part of a sequence of events which narrate both the poet and the king's confrontation and victory over envy. Jonson uses the spectacular occasion of the masque to graft his own struggle for fame onto the *topos* of the historical-heroical accession of James I to the throne of England. In the case of the poet, the forces of envy are those that threaten the author's fame. In the case of King James I, these envious forces are composed of the witches and queens who once threatened his accession to the throne of England.

'A new Gorgon'

The transformation scene of *The Masque of Queenes* represents simultaneously a break with the previous action on stage and a link with the masque to come, the erection of the House of Fame and the parade of ancient queens and their equally ancient citations. The figure of Heroique Virtue, armed like Perseus for his battle with the Gorgon, comes forward to explain the sudden disappearance of the witches of the anti-masque:

> So should, at FAMES loud sound, and VERTUES sight
> All poore, and envious Witchcraft fly the light.
> ᑫ· I did not borrow *Hermes* wings, nor aske
> His crooked sword, nor put on *Pluto's* caske,
> Nor, on mine arme advauncd wise *Pallas* sheild,
> (by which, my face avers'd, in open field
> I slew the *Gorgon*) for an empty name:
> When *Vertue* cut off *Terror*, he gat *Fame*.
> And, if when *Fame* was gotten, *Terror* dyde
> What black *Erynnis*, or more Hellish pride
> Durst arme these Hagges, now she is growne, and great,
> To think they could her Glories once defeate?
> I was her Parent, and I am her Strength.

> *Heroique Virtue* sinkes not under length
> Of yeares, or Ages, but is, still, the same
> While he preserves, as when he got *good Fame*.[58]

The main characters in this masque are emblematic: 'Fame', 'Virtue', 'Terror'. While the source of this passage lies in ancient accounts of the myth of Perseus slaying Medusa, the emblematic figures of 'Virtue' and 'Envy', in the guise of a gorgon, were already represented in the emblematic literature of the period.[59] It is clear that in a masque performed before the king at Whitehall, 'good Fame' and 'Virtue' would flatteringly represent attributes of the king. Many critics of the masque have read 'Fame' as the king's fame and Fame's 'parent', Heroique Virtue, as a representation of King James I, armed against forces that would disturb his 'soft peace' (line 144) and reign. Virtue banishing envious witchcraft would have been taken by the spectators as a pointed reference to James I's particular interest in witches. Yet, I would argue that Heroique Virtue's Fame is also very much literary fame, specifically the fame of the poet who sees his own posterity threatened by another kind of 'poore, and envious Witchcraft' (line 369), namely that of slander and envy. Virtue, for instance, assures the audience that he did not engage in combat 'for an empty name' (line 374). There is always the danger of the vessel holding reputation leaking and emptying if the poet is not vigilant. The unexplained resurgence of the Erinnyes in pursuit of Virtue's Fame implies that preserving one's personal fame is a never-ending task.

The problem of protecting a poetic reputation from envy was also the subject of *Poetaster*, written four years earlier. Heroique Virtue's banishment of the envious witches in *The Masque of Queenes* may be seens as a reenactment of the battle between the poet and the envious reader staged at the opening of the play. In the Induction to *Poetaster*, as we have seen above, the very masque-like character, 'Envie', is defeated by an 'armed *Prologue*', the figure of the male author, who places his 'bolder foot' upon her snaky head. This mock battle resembles a masque in miniature and demonstrates how the poet needs to protect himself from envious misreaders who want to 'damne the Authour'; the writer must arm himself against envy 'fortie-fold proofe' and put on a 'forc't defence' to protect his 'Scenes'.[60]

Terror in *The Masque of Queenes* and Envie in *Poetaster* closely resemble each other, both in the way they are connected to envy and in their need to

---

[58] Ben Jonson, *The Masque of Queenes*, Herford and Simpson, vol. VII, p. 302 (lines 368–83). Subsequent references to *The Masque of Queenes* will be included in the text.
[59] See Emblem XIX, 'Vir Bonus Invidiae Securus', Jean-Jacques Boissard, *Emblematum Liber* (Frankfurt: Theodore de Bry, 1593), fig. 2.
[60] Ben Jonson, 'Prologue' in *Poetaster*, Herford and Simpson, vol. IV, p. 205 (lines 6–11).

be 'cut off' in order for things to begin, whether it be the birth of Fame or the commencement of a play. Heroique Virtue, like *Poetaster's* battle-ready Prologue, may be seen as representing the poet in his own literary fight with envious readers. The emblematic figure of Virtue in *The Masque of Queenes*, therefore, represents not only the virtuous king in his war against witchcraft, but also the virtuous poet in his struggle against envy, namely the misreader who would cheat him of his rightful posterity. In both cases, the problem of 'succession', whether to literary fame or the throne, is at issue.

The moment of 'crisis' when Virtue 'cuts off' Terror describes a particularly violent birth sequence. The fate of Terror in *The Masque of Queenes* combines a number of antique myths involving not just the decapitation of a monster but also the intricate link between cutting and generation, as well as blood-guilt against the mother. Most of these myths are familiar ones. First, the gorgon, pregnant by Poseidon when Perseus decapitated her, is said to have given birth at the moment of her beheading to Pegasus and Chrysaor. Pegasus, with a stamp of his hoof, later engendered the fountain of the Muses. Jonson's masque follows the logic of these myths: Terror's 'cutting off' leads to the birth of another avatar of poetry, Fame, whose house is built upon columns of 'Men-making *Poets*, and those well made *Men*, / Whose strife it was, to have the happiest pen / Renowme them to an after-life.'[61] The masque also alludes to the myth of the birth of Athena out of the head of Zeus in the birth of the daughter Fame out of her male parent. The parthenogenic emergence of Athena, like Fame, may be seen as an abridgement of the laws of generation itself, the male fantasy of generation directly out of the male, without recourse to the problematically untrustworthy feminine body.

Jonathan Goldberg has noted the similarity of the masculine worlds of *Macbeth* and *The Masque of Queenes* and their suspicion of the feminine:

The hypermasculine world of *Macbeth* is haunted – as is *The Masque of Queenes* – by the power represented in the witches; masculinity in the play is directed as an assaultive attempt to secure power, to maintain success and succession, at the expense of women.[62]

In Jonson's plays, a husband's anxiety about his wife's unfaithfulness is often representative of the poet's anxiety about envious misreadings that cheat the poet out of his posterity. Jonson, in imitation of the iconography

---

[61] Ben Jonson, *The Masque of Queenes*, Herford and Simpson, vol. VII, pp. 302–3 (lines 386–8).
[62] In 'Speculations: *Macbeth* and Source' in Jean E. Howard and Marion F. O'Connor (eds.), *Shakespeare Reproduced: The Text in History and Ideology* (New York: Methuen, 1987), pp. 242–64; p. 259.

of the period, represents envy as the gorgon, whose petrifying gaze imitates the noxious gaze of envy. For instance, Jonson uses the gorgon in an early play, *Every Man Out of His Humour*, to represent the unfaithful wife, aptly named Fallace. She is displayed to her horrified husband, like another gorgon, by Macilente: 'Why, how now, signior DELIRO? has the wolfe seene you? ha? hath GORGONS head made marble of you?'[63] Macilente effectively cuts off and displays the gorgon's head of the false wife much like Heroique Virtue cuts off and displays the head of Terror in *The Masque of Queenes*.

In *Epicoene, Or The Silent Woman*, the link between women's faithlessness and anxiety about succession is also represented in the image of the gorgon. Yet, in this play, the gorgon, while an emblem of women's adulterous nature, is represented in literary terms as the unstoppable flow of words and 'tales'. Like Deliro, Morose is confronted by the gorgonic monstrosity of woman, but (second-hand so to speak) in the form of misogynistic literature. Truewit, the new Perseus, describes how he turned Morose into stone with words:

I...turned him into a post, or a stone, or what is stiffer, with thundring into him the incommodities of a wife, and the miseries of marriage. If ever GORGON were seene in the shape of a woman, hee hath seene her in my description.[64]

The gorgon Medusa's power to arrest and to freeze is frequently described as the power to render the spectator dumb or mute as in *Macbeth* (1606) when Macduff describes the 'horror' within – the sight of the regicide: 'Approach the chamber, and destroy your sight / With a new Gorgon. Do not bid me speak; / See, and then speak yourselves.'[65] Macduff's challenge to future viewers of the spectacle to 'see' and then to 'speak' is perceived as an impossible sequence; a glimpse of Duncan's body will not only 'destroy sight', but will render the spectator *speechless* or incapable of describing what they have

---

[63] Ben Jonson, *Every Man Out of His Humour*, Herford and Simpson, vol. III, p. 594 (v.xi.2–4).

[64] Ben Jonson, *Epicoene, Or The Silent Woman*, Herford and Simpson, vol. V, p. 188 (II.iv.12–17). In a brief essay, 'Medusa's Head', Freud argues that: 'To decapitate = to castrate. The terror of Medusa is thus a terror of castration that is linked *to the sight of something*' (my emphasis). Sigmund Freud, 'Medusa's Head (1922)' in *The Standard Edition of the Complete Psychological Works of Sigmund Freud*, ed. James Strachey, 24 vols. (London: The Hogarth Press, 1955), vol. XVIII, pp. 273–4; p. 273. Neil Hertz's reading of the Commune's perception of the French Revolution and Terror is inspired by Freud's essay; he argues that the figure of the Medusa represents a political threat as a sexual threat: the terror of the guillotine becomes a kind of castration anxiety. 'Medusa's Head: Male Hysteria under Political Pressure', *Representations* 4 (1983), 27–50. While Freud's reading of decapitation and castration could be very easily brought to bear on Jonson's description of Morose turned to stone, I have tried to avoid reading Jonson here in purely psychoanalytic terms.

[65] William Shakespeare, *The Tragedy of Macbeth* (II.iii.70–3).

seen.⁶⁶ In *The Queen of Corinth* (1647), the queen, perceiving the silence of her followers demands: 'What new Gorgon's head / Have you beheld, that you are all turn'd statues? / This is prodigious! Has none a tongue / To speak the cause?'⁶⁷ This inability to speak is defended by Leonidas when he states that if he spoke at all: 'You'll say I am *too eloquent*, and wish / I had been born without a tongue' (my emphasis).⁶⁸ Eloquence, in other words, would bring back the horror by creating a picture in the queen's imagination of the sight that had originally turned her followers into stone.⁶⁹ In effect, the gorgon of eloquence produces the effect of dumbness or silence. While Morose is being petrified by the (loquacious) gorgon in Truewit's misogynistic monologue, he paradoxically describes himself as having had his own throat cut by Truewit, 'here has bin a cut-throate with me'.⁷⁰ It is as if Morose had *become* a Medusa rather than having been turned to stone by one. In fact, Truewit later tells Dauphine how *he* (Truewit) has been '[S]trooke into stone, almost, I am here, with tales o' thine uncle! There was never such a prodigie heard of.'⁷¹ Morose is *both* confronted by the terror that is woman (the never-ending flow of words, the gorgon of eloquence) and, at the same time, becomes the feminized spectacle of this terror, *cut off*. Morose's search for the 'silent woman' is not only a search for a faithful wife, but also the search for the safe sterility that comes with the stopping up of words. In *The Masque of Queenes*, as we shall see, Jonson, may be said, perversely, like Morose, to *cut his own throat*. In other words, he may be seen to cut the imaginative and excessive flow of words which inevitably opens the writer up to the danger of being misread and substitute a monumental, petrified text/tablet in its place: a text of citations and quotations from male

---

⁶⁶ For the Gorgon in *Macbeth* see Marjorie Garber, 'Macbeth: The Male Medusa', *Shakespeare's Ghost Writers: Literature as Uncanny Causality* (New York: Methuen, 1987). Reprinted in Marjorie Garber and Nancy J. Vickers (eds.), *The Medusa Reader* (New York: Routledge, 2003), pp. 249–57.
⁶⁷ Francis Beaumont and John Fletcher, *The Queen of Corinth* in *Comedies and Tragedies* (London, 1647), p. 20 (v.ii.65–8).
⁶⁸ Ibid., (v.ii.75–6), p. 20.
⁶⁹ Henry Peacham describes the ability of eloquence to paint a picture in the mind's eye: 'The Oratour... may set forth any matter with a goodly perspicuitie, and paint out any person, deede, or thing so cunningly with these coulours that it shall seem rather a lyvely Image paynted in tables, then a reporte expressed with the tongue.' In the dedicatory 'Epistle' to *The Garden of Eloquence* (London, 1577), sig. A3. This description of words' ability to 'paynt' and create a 'lyvely image' seems apropos to *Macbeth*, a play involved in the problem of hallucination, spectres and the power of the imagination to create forms.
⁷⁰ Ben Jonson, *Epicoene*, Herford and Simpson, vol. v, p. 183 (II.ii.154).
⁷¹ Ibid., p. 170 (I.ii.2–3).

authors of antiquity concerning the good women of antiquity.[72] The text of *The Masque of Queenes* becomes, essentially, Morose's silent woman.[73]

The cutting off of Terror in *The Masque of Queenes* may be seen, then, as Jonson's version of the male fantasy that finds expression in *Macbeth*, what Janet Adelman calls the 'fantasy of exemption from woman':

> The ambivalence that shapes the portrayal of Macduff is evident even as he reveals to Macbeth that he 'was from his mother's womb / Untimely ripp'd' (v.8.15–16): the emphasis on untimeliness and the violence of the image suggest that he has been prematurely deprived of a nurturing maternal presence; but the prophecy construes just this deprivation as the source of Macduff's strength. The prophecy itself both denies and affirms the fantasy of exemption from women: in affirming that Macduff has indeed had a mother, it denies the fantasy of male self-generation; but in attributing his power to his having been untimely ripped from that mother, it sustains the sense that violent separation from the mother is the mark of the successful male.[74]

The Caesarean birth of Macduff, 'ripped' from his mother's womb, implies, though it isn't expressed directly in *Macbeth*, the subsequent death of the mother. By 'ripping' or 'cutting', the fantasy of success and succession in both *Macbeth* and *The Masque of Queenes* appears to be represented as the act of extracting the child from the grip of the mother, Terror. In *The Masque of Queenes*, after the cut, the male takes over the role of the mother in the act of generation. It is Virtue who 'gat' Fame, giving birth, ironically enough, to a daughter who will never supplant the father as a son naturally would. The consequence of the act of cutting out the mother from the process of birth, replacing and exempting her from her proper role, is that the child Fame is pursued by the Erinnyes. These furies attack the child, who is guilty of mother-murder in the act of being born: 'And, if when *Fame* was gotten, *Terror* dyde / What black *Erynnis*… think they could her Glories once defeate?' (lines 376–9). If the hags who pursue Heroique Virtue's daughter are Erinnyes, the birth of Fame must then be seen to involve some kind of blood-guilt against the mother. The Erinnyes are inevitably linked with the tragedy of Orestes in the second play of the *Oresteia* by Aeschylus. Fame herself is guilty, like Orestes, of mother murder if she is being pursued by the shadows of the justice-

---

[72] See Ben Jonson, *The Masque of Queenes*: 'These (in their lives, as fortunes) crown'd the choyse / Of Woman-kind and 'gaynst all opposite voyce / Made good to Time.' Herford and Simpson, vol. VII, p. 303 (lines 410–12).

[73] *Epicoene* and *The Masque of Queenes* were both performed in 1609.

[74] Janet Adelman, *Suffocating Mothers: Fantasies of Maternal Origin in Shakespeare's Plays, 'Hamlet' to 'The Tempest'* (New York: Routledge, 1992), p. 144.

seeking mother. The implicit allusion to Oresteian guilt in this masque is particularly interesting in terms of the king whose own filial 'guilt' against the mother we shall consider later. As for the poet, the question posed by the appearance of the Erinnyes is at what point one has achieved sanctuary and what methods may be necessary to achieve and hold on to such literary safety.

'A master of Terror'

For Jonson, one way of keeping the furies of envy at bay is by erecting a barricade of ancient authorities. Within a dense forest of eloquence and authority, the writer can hide himself from the envious gaze of a judging posterity. In the margins of *The Masque of Queenes* Jonson explicitly places his art under the aegis of two ancient authors, Hesiod and Apollodorus:

> So should, at FAMES loud sound, and VERTUES sight
> All poore, and envious Witchcraft fly the light.
> q. I did not borrow *Hermes* wings, nor aske
> His crooked sword, nor put on *Pluto's* caske,
> Nor, on mine arme advauncd wise *Pallas* sheild,
> (by which, my face avers'd, in open field
> I slew the *Gorgon*) for an empty name.[75]

The interruption of the footnote marker *q*, inserted in the text just before the word 'I', of the line, 'I did not borrow *Hermes* wings' signals Jonson's claims to classical authority:

The Antients expressed a brave, and masculine *virtue*, in three figures. (Of *Hercules*, *Perseus*, and *Bellerophon*) of which I chose that of *Perseus*, armd, as I have him describ'd out of *Hesiod*. Scuto Hercul. See *Apollodor*. the *Gram-arian*, of him. lib. ij.[76]

---

[75] *The Masque of Queenes*, Herford and Simpson, vol. VII, p. 302 (lines 368–74).

[76] *Ibid.*, p. 302 (note *q*). The marginal note in question, *q*, appears side by side with the text of Heroique Virtue's speech. Thus, the 'I' of the footnote (the poet) and the 'I' of the masque speech (Heroique Virtue), are directly side by side in the printed text. Both 'I's are concerned, at the same moment in the text, with the problem of 'arming'. In the footnote, the authorial 'I' states, 'I chose ... Perseus, armd, as I have describ'd him out of *Hesiod*'. In the speech, the 'I' of the masque character, Heroique Virtue, states 'I did not borrow *Hermes* wings ... nor put on *Pluto's* caske ... for an empty name.' The 'I' of the author and the 'I' of the character are linked on the page typographically. No argument may rest on this observation of a certain typographic doubling. I would simply like to note a possible mirroring between the 'author' of the note (the poet) and 'author' of the speech (Heroique Virtue). Heroique Virtue echoes the poet's own concern, evident in the dedication to Prince Henry, that the poet must be armed in order to protect his *name*. Interestingly, in some editions of the

The footnote is precise. Not only does Jonson specify the three ancient figures of 'masculine virtue' from among whom he chose Perseus, he also specifies which ancient *version* of the Perseus story he primarily alludes to: '*Perseus...* out of *Hesiod. Scuto Hercul.*' In *The Shield of Heracles*, Hesiod vividly describes the moments *after* Perseus has just cut off the head of the Gorgon:

> The head of a terrible monster, the Gorgon, covered his whole back; a pouch ran around it, a wonder to see, made of silver; shining tassels hung down from it, made of gold. The terrible helmet of Hades was set around the king's temples and held the dread darkness of night. Perseus himself, Danae's son, was outstretched, and looked as though he were hastening and shuddering. The Gorgons, dreadful and unspeakable, were rushing after him, eager to catch him; as they ran on the pallid adamant, the shield resounded sharply and piercingly with a loud noise. At their girdles, two serpents hung down, their heads arching forward; both of them were licking with their tongues, and they ground their teeth with strength, glaring savagely. Upon the terrible heads of the Gorgons rioted great Fear.[77]

The hero is running, 'outstretched', shuddering with horror and fear. He is running so quickly that his feet do not touch the shield. Hesiod depicts Perseus running in absolute terror after he has decapitated the Medusa. The ancient writer adds a terrifying touch to the ekphrasis by describing how 'the shield resounded sharply and piercingly with a loud noise' as the Gorgons ran over it. This version of the Perseus myth is unique in classical literature in that it portrays Perseus at just the moment after the decapitation, but before the hero becomes 'the master of Terror' as Jean-Pierre Vernant puts it in his description of Hesiod's account:

> Medusa has death in her eyes; the one who will be able to put the head of Medusa in his pouch and hide it there will be declared a master of Terror, *mestor phoboio*, lord over death.[78]

Perseus has achieved his aim; he is in possession of the decapitated head of the Medusa and it is within its sack. Yet, in Hesiod, he runs in terror because he is not yet the master of Terror. Heroique Virtue, similarly, has cut off Terror, but is still pursued by the furies of Terror. Jonson's Heroique Virtue may be seen as a portrait of the artist as terrified hero, one who does not see himself as

---

1616 Folio, the 'I' in footnote q is a 'we' or a 'wee'. The Herford and Simpson copy has 'I' both in the text and in the margin as I have described.

[77] Hesiod, *The Shield, Catalogue of Women, Other Fragments*, ed. and trans. Glenn W. Most (Cambridge: Harvard University Press, 2007), pp. 19–21 (lines 216–36).

[78] Jean-Pierre Vernant, 'Death in the Eyes' and 'In the Mirror of Medusa' in Froma I. Zeitlin (ed.), *Mortals and Immortals: Collected Essays* (Princeton: Princeton University Press, 1991), pp. 111–50; p. 145.

having achieved mastery and is in search of some kind of sanctuary from the furies of envy and misreading. Poetic mastery only comes with a posterity free and clear of staring eyes and envying Erinnyes, when Virtue is 'still the same / While he preserves, as when he got *good Fame*'.[79]

I would suggest that Jonson chose Perseus out of Hesiod because Hesiod gave back the poet his own image of Terror, one that combined the fear of the petrifying gaze (associated with the Gorgon in the sack) with the pursuit of a band of unforgiving furies. Terror is the never-wearying gaze upon the writer's text, whose counterpart is the vigilant, gorgonic gaze of the poet attempting to protect himself from exposure. This poetic gaze is, as we have said, divided between an 'eye' which looks curiously at its own creation and an 'I' which defends the same creation from the harmful eye of its own envy. Jonson is both the writer seeking sanctuary from the gorgonic gaze of envy and the vigilant, petrifying gaze of this same gorgon. The writer seeks sanctuary from the furies of envy in the authority of antiquity, folding his work in an envelope of citations and annotations. It is the writer's envy that opens up the lack in the text, only to fill it with layer upon layer. The writer paradoxically creates the discontinuous, uniquely fragmentary Jonsonian text which, rather than obeying the laws of literary generation, abridges and perverts them, cutting in order to generate (like Heroique Virtue), petrifying (like the Medusa), in order to save.

'Our Labor dies'

In *The Masque of Queenes*, Terror is not simply a synonym for the Medusa. Terror is at the heart of a poetic phantasmagoria intimately connected with envy of the writer and his work. Terror may be seen as a fury haunting the poet, questioning artistic decisions and choices. Terror also represents the spectre of creative impotence, painfully visible when the poet is expected to produce (a masque) for the king (or queen). The plot of *The Masque of Queenes* explicitly mirrors the process of literary creation itself. The anti-masque narrates the strain of giving birth and frustration with the slow process of literary generation. The transformation scene represents the Jonsonian narrative device of cutting, bypassing natural labour in favor of the instant raising of monument, through quotation and citation of authors from antiquity.

The witches of the anti-masque are described in the masque as 'Opposites' (line 133) to fame and glory. The Dame of the anti-masque, or head witch, commands

---

[79] *The Masque of Queenes*, Herford and Simpson, vol. VII, p. 302 (lines 382–3). Subsequent references to the masque will be included in the text.

the other witches to: 'Shew ourselves truely envious' (line 135). Their purpose, as befits the envious, is to destroy, break down and spoil. They vow to:

> blast the light;
> Mixe Hell, with Heaven; and make *Nature* fight
> Within her selfe; loose the whole henge of Things;
> And cause the Endes to runne back into their Springs. (lines 146–9)

The Dame is described as a kind of fury or an emblem of envy:

> naked arm'd, barefooted, her frock tuck'd, her hayre knotted, and folded with vipers; In her hand, a Torch made of a dead-Mans arme, lighted; girded with a snake. (lines 95–8)

Yet, while the witches are envious and want to turn Nature against herself, the anti-masque, paradoxically, relates their efforts to create. The Dame leads the group in collecting the 'materials' to generate their 'Magick-feature' (line 286).[80] She herself brings a 'horned poppie' and 'Cypresse boughes' (line 200); 'a Figg-tree wild' (line 201); '*Basiliskes* blood' and 'Vipers skin' (line 203). The last two animals are connected with the Gorgon, since one is a monster with the same petrifying gaze, the other, a snake. It seems that the materials of creation are found in the basket of envy, and are, like Jonsonian creation, constantly energized by the threat of envy. The Dame commands the witches to 'bury' all their materials and sing a 'Charme' (lines 244–5). The witches bury their ingredients and sing the following lullaby-like spell:

> Deepe, ô, deepe, We lay thee to sleepe;
> Wee leave thee drinke by, if thou chance to be dry;
> Both milke, & blood, the dew, and the flood.
> We breath in thy bed, at the foote, and the head;
> We cover thee warme, that thou take no harme:
> And, when thou do'st wake,
>   Dame Earth shall quake
>   And the Houses shake,
>   And her Belly shall ake,
>   As her Back were brake,
>   Such a birth to make,
>   As is the blew Drake,
>   Whose forme thou shalt take. (lines 249–61)

The witches are midwives to 'Dame Earth' who will give birth to a 'blew Drake'. Yet, in subsequent charms, the process is shown as difficult and

---

[80] For 'materials' see *ibid.*, p. 294 n. 12.

frustrating: the 'Sage' is rotten (line 270); they try more heat, they sing more charmes, but according to the Dame: 'All our *Charmes* do nothing winne / Upon the night; Our Labor dies! / Our Magick-feature will not rise; / Nor yet the Storme!' (lines 284–7). They repeat the process. They beat the ground with snakes, a very phallic image evoking conception, 'till it sweate' (line 289). More charmes, curses and threats in a strangely repetitive sequence. The Dame finally invokes the highest threat, one against Nature herself:

> I'll speake a *charme*
> Shall cleave the ground, as low as lies
> Old shrunke-up *Chaös*; and let rise,
> Once more, his darke, and reeking head,
> To strike the World, and *Nature* dead
> Untill my Magick birth be bred. (lines 310–15)

The contrast between striking 'Nature dead' and breeding is part of the paradox of envious creation, beautifully portrayed as the creativity of a witch. The witches destroy Nature in order to give birth.[81] They are involved in a frustrating and antithetical process of midwifery. The Dame threatens to use a 'rusty knife' (line 309) to wound herself and 'speake a *charme*' to dig up the phallic 'shrunke-up *Chaös*' whose 'reeking head' will then 'strike' the world. While it may be all very well for Jonson to describe his anti-masque as a 'spectacle of strangenesse' (line 20), it is clear to any close reader that the 'spectacle' is birth and the 'strangenesse' is the difficulty in giving it. The witches have gathered exotic ingredients and materials and, by burying them in the ground, hope to give birth to something new. Their efforts end in abject failure and the Dame's reaction is rage. At the same time, the process of repeating charms and bursting out in fury results in nothing but frustration and ennui. Like the blowing up of *The Staple of Newes* or the sudden explosion in *The Alchemist*, Heroique Virtue's 'cutting off' of the witches' efforts to transform a batch

---

[81] See *Catiline:* 'The ruine of thy countery: Thou wert built / For such a worke.' Herford and Simpson, vol. v, p. 436 (Act I, lines 45–6); we see, as well, Jonson's play on the idea of ruin in his dedication of *Sejanus, His Fall* to Esmé, Lord Aubigny: 'My Lord, If ever any ruine were so great, as to survive; I thinke this be one I send you: The Fall of Sejanus.' Herford and Simpson, vol. IV, p. 349. The conflation and consequent ambiguity between the *subject* of the work, the historical Sejanus, and the play written by Ben Jonson, makes the early modern poet's art equivalent to a 'ruin', which the author hopes, in part by dedicating it to Aubigny and in part by including it in his monument/folio, will 'survive'. The idea of 'ruin' is even more full of significance, of course, with respect to those works of Jonson's inspired directly from antiquity, like the Roman tragedies.

of mysterious materials into real 'birth' is the narrative equivalent of an admission of failure to (poetically) generate successfully.[82]

The witches' long and exhausting attempt at birthing, ending suddenly in the turning of the anti-masque into masque, is emblematic of Jonson's method. Instead of development, Jonson generates newness by 'cutting'. The act of cutting off the witches indeed serves to generate something new, if by a more radical means. Giving birth to more narrative is accomplished by inexplicably supplanting one narrative by another. Some may argue that this sudden 'transformation' is simply in the nature of the masque. But the reason Ben Jonson created the form known as the anti-masque is that this moment of cutting off one narrative in favour of another is an integral part of Jonson's creative method. The masque form itself is based in the Jonsonian *rhetoric of discontinuity* linked to envy. The scene turns, the anti-masquers disappear and Heroique Virtue makes his speech. The Dame's attempt to give birth is cut off and completed by a male figure who, quickly, efficiently and artificially (like Zeus to Athena or Dionysus) gives birth to his own Fame. The cutting off of the witches amounts to curtailing an exhausted theme, even a frustrating method of creation, representative of the labour of writing itself, consisting of gathering materials and trying to create something new. The text of *The Masque of Queenes* reveals the poet's abandonment of this kind of literary creation in favour of emblematic posturing coupled with exegesis in the form of quotations from antiquity. Instead of narrative, Jonson turns to emblem; instead of romance, the poet strives for a monument. All that is 'born' in the narrative of *The Masque of Queenes* is Fame herself, parthenogenetically out of her father Heroique Virtue, at the moment of the death of her mother, Terror.

Yet, even Fame is not new. The birth of Fame, I would suggest, may be seen as the rebirth of the gorgon Terror. Fame, 'described, in Iconolog. di Cesare Ripa' (line 448), possesses a 'sharpe eye' (line 467), but even more, she is the terrifying monster in the description from Virgil's *Aeneid* that Jonson specifically cites. Jonson notes that his model for 'her state, it was as *Virgil*' describes her, at the full, her feete on the Ground, and her head in the Cloudes' (lines 453–4). The note sends the reader to the margin to see 'Æneid. Lib. 4'. Virgil's description of Fame in Book 4 of the *Aeneid* is the same one Jonson chose to translate and put into the mouth of Virgil in

---

[82] See *The Staple of Newes*: 'Our Staple is all to pieces, quite dissolved ! ... Shivered, as in an earth-quake! heard you not / The cracke and ruine? We are all blowne up!' Herford and Simpson, vol. vi, p. 366 (v.i.39–41); and *The Alchemist*: 'O sir, we are defeated! all the workes / Are flowne in fumo: every glass is burst.' Herford and Simpson, vol. v, p. 378 (iv.v.57–8).

Poetaster. It seems worthy of notice that Virgil read this same description of Fame before Augustus Caesar, just as the early modern poet presents it in a masque before *his* king, James I:

> Fame, a fleet evill, then which swifter none:
> …
> With feet on ground, her head doth pierce a cloud!
> …
> Shee was last sister of that Giant race…
> …a monster vast,
> And dreadfull. Looke, how many plumes are plac't
> On her huge corps, so many waking eyes
> Sticke underneath: and (which may stranger rise
> In the report) as many tongues shee beares,
> As many mouthes, as many listning eares.
> …
> As covetus shee is of tales, and lies,
> As prodigall of truth: This monster, &c.[83]

Fame is represented, even in *The Masque of Queenes*, where she is 'good Fame', as the source and purveyor of falsehood and slander, exactly those elements, which made up an aspect of her mother Terror:

> She [good Fame], that enquireth into all the world,
> And hath, about her vaulted *Palace*, hoorl'd
> All rumors, and reports, or true or vayne,
> What utmost Landes, or deepest Seas contayne: (lines 390–3).

Fame, like Envie in *Poetaster*, is watchful and ready to spread rumour and slander. To understand the extent to which Fame's 'eye' perpetuates the terrifying gaze of the Gorgon, one can look at the original summary of the plot of *The Masque of Queenes*. This 'Argument' gives us a unique glimpse into the genetics of the masque. Originally, in place of 'Farre-sighted *Eagles*' (line 467) on Fame's chariot, Jonson's 'Argument' envisions *panthers*, followed by eagles and lions, drawing the chariot. The panther, like the basilisk, was believed to have the power to petrify with the eye, just like the Gorgon. Fame's chariot, therefore, was originally conceived as being drawn by beasts that were, perhaps, too close in kind to the monster who had just been exiled from the masque. Just as Cicero's vigilant gaze is the obverse of Catilinian envy, so too the emergence of the eye of Fame from out of the decapitated head of envious Terror reveals the

---

[83] *Poetaster*, Herford and Simpson, vol. IV, pp. 296–7 (v.ii.75ff.).

extent to which the writer's own obsessive vigilance with regard to how he will be read becomes just another version of the envious gaze he fears upon his own creation.

The petrifying gaze of Fame, born out of the gorgon gaze of Terror, turns the text into a monument. Just as Perseus returned to the court of King Acrisius and displayed the head of the Medusa before the court, Jonson turns the fatal gaze of Fame full upon his own text, petrifying it by means of allusion, quotation and catalogue. The text generated out of the decapitation of the envious gaze becomes, in turn, a petrifying text. The eye of Fame paralyzes and petrifies anyone who tries to equal the giants of antiquity or stand beside them in the House of Fame. The frozen text cannot give birth to anything new. It can only list, quote, cite, allude and accuse itself of mixing the 'living with the dead'.[84] The text, frozen by the gorgon, Fame, is intended to function as a new gorgon. *The Masque of Queenes* is a text aimed at turning the reader to stone when confronted by its bulk of dry-as-dust commentaries from antiquity and the frigid, monumental queens. In certain versions of the Medusa story, the gorgon turns herself to stone after catching a glimpse of her own reflection in Perseus' shield. By creating a mimetic reflection of Fame, in the form of the host of citations from the famed authors of antiquity, the author intends to use it as an apotropaic charm turned full upon the reader, who will then petrify him or herself in the very act of reading.[85] The image of perfect eloquence, the citations and marginalia from the great texts of the classical period, is intended to silence malice and deflect judgement.

The king's terror

Literary monument is conceived in this masque as contrary to the process of invention and natural inspiration. This opposition between fame and birth may also be seen in the problematic of royal succession, a process which, in English history, featured, among other things, virginity and barrenness, decapitation and blood-guilt. Grafted onto the literary and authorial problematic of creation, generation and literary succession, the royal problem of succession is equally terrorized by the figure of the envious mother and female predecessor, both needing to be 'cut off'. I

---

[84] See Chapter 4, 'Sanctuary', for the reference to King Mezentius and the joining of the 'living and the dead' in *The Masque of Queenes*.

[85] Not unlike the reader who, licking his finger to turn the page, poisons himself while reading the book in Umberto Eco's *The Name of the Rose*.

would now like to address one spectral Terror, haunting not the poet, but the Oresteian king himself: the Catholic Terror embodied in Mary Stuart, whose beheading enabled her son James to succeed Elizabeth on the throne of England. After surmounting the obstacles of mother and virgin queen, James I's accession was threatened by witchcraft, according to his own account in *Daemonologie*. James I claimed the English throne not only after the death of a powerful queen with no heir and thanks to a beheaded mother, but also subsequent to his self-publicized rescue from a group of witches. All the elements of James I's accession story are mapped onto the story of the poet's own terror and fantasy of literary succession in *The Masque of Queenes*.

The figure of Terror in Jonson's masque may be seen, from the perspective of the king, as the ghost of Elizabeth I, only six years dead at the time *The Masque of Queenes* was performed. The dead queen haunted not only the buildings and the palaces occupied by the new king and queen, but also the pens of those poets and their predecessors who had spent so much of their imaginative energy creating the myths of virginity and chastity as well as power attributed to Queen Elizabeth I. The dead queen's ghost haunts Jonson's *Masque of Queenes* in the form of the goddess Hecate. She is transported into the masque by Jonson's allusion to what Philippa Berry calls Chapman's 'obscure narrative poem', 'The Shadow of Night'.[86] Jonson's Dame, or head witch, invokes the goddess Hecate in language clearly allusive of the language with which Chapman, as Berry shows, transformed Elizabeth/Cynthia into the witch Hecate:

The most disturbing metamorphosis of the Cynthia figure occurs at the end of the poem, where she assumes the aspect of Hecate, goddess of death and witchcraft...Cynthia is presented here as prototype both of the magician and the witch, the practiced executor of occult ritual as well as an expert in the lore of deadly herbs.[87]

Following is the passage Berry quotes from Chapman describing this 'disturbing metamorphosis' of Cynthia into Hecate:

> Slip everie sort of poisoned herbes, and plants,
> And bring thy rabid mastiffs to these hants.
> Look with thy fierce aspect, be terror-strong;

---

[86] Philippa Berry, *Of Chastity and Power: Elizabethan Literature and the Unmarried Queen* (London: Routledge, 1989), p. 139.
[87] *Ibid.*, p. 142.

> Assume thy wondrous shape of halfe a furlong:
> Put on thy feet of Serpents, viperous hayres,
> And act the fearefulst part of thy affaires:
> Convert the violent courses of thy floods,
> Remove whole fields of corne, and hugest woods,
> Cast hills into the sea, and make the starrs,
> Drop out of heaven.[88]

Berry notes that some of the aspects of the goddess Chapman attributes to Cynthia include her Titan enormity, 'halfe a furlong', her expertise in the lore of deadly herbs, and her power to change the natural order of things, 'convert the violent courses of thy floods, / Remove whole fields of corne'. In *The Masque of Queenes*, Jonson may well have been alluding specifically to Chapman when his Dame boasts of *her* power to change the natural course of Nature:

> When we have set the Elements at warres;
> Made Mid-night see the Sunne; and Day the starres;
> When the wing'd Lightning, in the course, hath stayd;
> And swiftest Rivers have runne back, afrayd
> To see the Corne remove, the Groves to range
> Whole Places alter, and the Seasons change. (lines 228–33)

Like Chapman's Hecate, Jonson's Dame possesses the power to control the revolutions of the sun, moon, stars and seasons, keep lightning from striking, and change the topology of rivers, fields and woods. Both Jonson's Dame and Chapman's Cynthia/Hecate 'remove' the 'corne'. The 'hugest wood', like Birnam wood in *Macbeth*, can suddenly change its place in Chapman; in Jonson's description, the power of the Dame's sorcery may also owe something to the sorcery and magic of the protean masque set, the architectural magic, at once black and white, of Inigo Jones. Like Chapman's Hecate, Jonson's Dame can make 'Whole Places alter', but the language of moving groves and changing seasons also creates the strange effect of the former queen as a kind of ghost in the machine. Like the witches in *Macbeth*, calling upon Hecate to present herself to the Scottish king who searches for his destiny, the Dame too invokes her:

> And thou, c· *three-formed Starre*, that on these nights
> Art only power-full, to Whose triple Name

---

[88] George Chapman, 'Hymnus in Cynthiam', *The Shadow of Night: Containing Two Poetical Hymnes* (London, 1594), sig. E2ᵛ. Chapman glosses this section in the final entry of his 'Gloss': 'All these are proper to her as she is *Heccate*.' Sig. E4ᵛ. There is no space in my discussion at the moment to consider what seem to be numerous other echoes of both of Chapman's Hymns in Jonson's *Masque of Queenes*.

> Thus wee incline; *Once, twise,* and *thrise-the-Same*:
> If, now, with *rites* profane and foule inough,
> Wee doe invoke thee; Darken all this roofe,
> With present fogges. Exhale Earths rott'nest vapors;
> And strike a blindnesse, through these blazing tapers. (lines 237–43)

The reference to 'blazing tapers' and the 'roofe' is an allusion to the masquing hall. The Dame powerfully and poetically invokes darker spirits to enter the hall, where the king and his court are sitting, to 'darken' it. Hecate seems to be associated both with black magic and the specific magic of the masque form: 'thou … that on these nights / Art only power-full'.[89]

It seems that, through his witch, Jonson invites the uninvited guest to the feast, the late virgin queen. The dead queen, as the 'three-formed Starre' Hecate, is invited to enter the masquing hall and, Medusa-like, 'strike a blindnesse' upon the assembly, gathered for Queen Anne's masque. The envious witches of the anti-masque invoke the dead queen, whose place in panegyric has been usurped, to blind the spectators in the hall. This power of blinding may be considered part of the typical attributes of the gorgonic powers of Queen Elizabeth, duly celebrated in panegyric.[90] Jonson may here be utilizing a conceit which was commonly associated with the cult of Elizabeth and which is prominent in Chapman's 'Hymnus in Cynthiam'. This was the power, as we have seen, of the queen's gaze to purge evil and envy. Chapman's own 'Hymnus' begins with an address to Cynthia: 'Nature's bright eye-sight, and the Night's faire soule' and a few lines later describes the 'beames' of Cynthia's eyes in their 'All-ill-purging puritie'. The dazzlingly pure beams from the queen's eye have the power to purge evil and this evil was often associated with envy. The queen's gaze, like Plato's *pharmakon*, is the beneficial version of the harmful rays of a Medusa or of the envious. Elizabeth's power to purge is both the poison and its antidote. She is both gorgon and the most effective apotropaic defence against the petrifying gaze of envy.

In his 'Hymnes of Astraea', Sir John Davies dedicates the last poem, 'To Envie' (Hymne xxvi), in the sequence entitled 'Hymnes of Astraea in

---

[89] 'Hecate is constantly associated with the operations of black magic or sorcery in the Renaissance… she was a fairly mysterious figure even in antiquity … in late traditions, Hecate was made into the mother of Circe who was herself Medea's aunt, which gives the impression of a tightly knit family of evil-doers.' François Laroque, 'Magic in Macbeth', *Cahiers Élisabéthains* 35 (April 1989), 59–84, pp. 65–6.

[90] The history of queenly 'blinding' goes back to Helen, who blinded Stesichorus after he referred to her as a prostitute and restored his sight after he wrote his *palinode*, or apology and panegyric.

Acrosticke Verse', to the power over envy the writer has acquired by writing about Elizabeth:

> E nvie go weepe, my Muse and I
> L augh thee to scorn; thy feeble Eye
> I s dazled with the glorie
> S hining in this gay poesie. (lines 1–4)[91]

Davies tropes on the queen's gaze and its innate power to 'dazzle' the eye of envy. The queen's eye, in other words, blinds the envious eye, much in the same way as envy, like the Gorgon, 'dazzles' the eye that beholds it. Davies plays on this same trope in an earlier poem in the 'Hymnes of Astraea' called 'Of Her Phantasie' (Hymne xviii). Again, as in all the poems in the sequence, the queen's name is spelled out of the first letter of each line:

> E xquisite curiositie,
> L ooke on thy self with judging eye,
> I fought be faultie leave it,
> S o delicate a phantasie
> A s this, will straight perceive it; (lines 1–5)

'Exquisite curiositie' may here be seen as another way of describing the envious eye, delving into what is hidden in order to find fault and to judge. Jonson's description of Prince Henry as 'curious to examine her [Poetry] with your eye' must be seen as an ambiguous form of praise. As Elizabeth's eye blinds the envious by dazzling them in turn, so too the queen's imagination or 'phantasie' will immediately 'perceive' the curious gaze of the judging eye. In this respect, the queen, again in this poem, appropriates the dangerous and harming power of an envious or curious eye, and turns it back upon itself.

By bringing Chapman's Hecate into the masque, *The Masque of Queenes* invokes a gorgonic, envious Terror in the form of the dead royal predecessor. This ghost of the dead queen poses a specific threat to King James I, Queen Anne and their ceremonies, as well as to the creative power of the poet who comes after all those poets who celebrated Elizabeth. Like a second Perseus, the writer holds aloft the gorgon heads of the two *dead* queens who lie entombed in the text. Just as the Dame has called on Hecate/Elizabeth to blind the assembly with her terrifying gaze, the writer raises the 'reeking head' of the dead virgin queen and decapitated mother before the court of James I. At the same time, the 'living' Queen Anne,

---

[91] Sir John Davies, 'To Envie' (Hymne xxvi), 'Hymnes of Astraea' in Robert Krueger (ed.), *The Poems of Sir John Davies* (Oxford: Oxford University Press, 1975); p. 86.

very possibly wearing Elizabeth's clothing on the stage in the masque would have been, in a sense, implicitly associated with her dead predecessor.[92] As such, the particular danger Elizabeth's gaze had presented would, in part, have been transferred to the new queen. This gaze, as we have seen in the chapter previous, was underlying the 'Objection' raised suddenly by the writer concerning his having effectively murdered Queen Anne by binding her, metaphorically, to the corrupting bodies of the dead queens of antiquity and, at a deeper level, by alluding to her predecessor in an implicit *prosopopeia*, making the living dead by bringing the dead to life.

In so doing, Jonson defends his masque, twice over, both for posterity and for the present. Not only does Jonson turn the petrifying gaze of fame onto his own text, turning it into an undefaceable slab of marble monument, seemingly impervious to judgement, swaddled in its padding of classical quotations, the poet also finds sanctuary from the terrifying gaze of his royal patrons by holding up before them the heads of Elizabeth I and Mary Stuart. While the poet uses the king's battle against the forces of envy to both mask and supplement his own poetic phantasmagoria, he appropriates the gorgon power of Terror to protect himself apotropaically against those judging eyes upon him, those of the past and the present. This may be what the poet refers to when he refers to the 'all-daring Power of *Poetry*': a power to bring the living together with the dead and a Machiavellian ability to conceal his own poetic power in the presence of power.

THE MEDUSA OF ELOQUENCE: *CATILINE, HIS CONSPIRACY*

Only two years after *The Masque of Queenes*, Jonson returns to the powerful tale of the Gorgon's decapitation and exhibition on the public stage in *Catiline, Or His Conspiracy*. In *Catiline*, the historical combat between Cicero and Catiline is emblematized in a struggle between forces very similar to those in *Queenes*. *Catiline* thematizes the power of eloquence to silence opposition, which is conceived as the conspiracy that threatens both Rome and Cicero's fame. In the last lines of the play, Cicero, after having discovered and thwarted the Catilinian conspiracy against the

---

[92] James Knowles has noted how 'Jonson's text [*A Particular Entertainment of the Queen and Prince to Althorpe* (1603)] suggests how the image of Elizabeth haunted the Jacobean polity' and argues that Anne of Denmark actively 'drew upon her predecessor's imagery far more than has been recognised'. James Knowles, '"To Enlight the Darksome Night, Pale Cinthia doth Arise": Anna of Denmark, Elizabeth I and the Images of Royalty' in Clare McManus (ed.), *Women and Culture at the Courts of the Stuart Queens* (London: Palgrave Macmillan, 2003), pp. 21–48; pp. 21–2.

Roman republic, listens to a messenger's report describing the death of Catiline in battle:

> Then he [Catiline] fell too...
> And as, in that rebellion 'gainst the gods,
> MINERVA holding forth MEDUSA's head,
> One of the gyant brethren felt himselfe
> Grow marble at the killing sight, and now,
> Almost made stone, began t'inquire, what flint,
> What rocke it was, that crept through all his limmes,
> And, ere he could thinke more, was that he fear'd;
> So CATILINE at the sight of *Rome* in us,
> Became his tombe: yet did his looke retayne
> Some of his fiercenesse, and his hands still mov'd,
> As if he labour'd, yet, to graspe the state,
> With those rebellious parts.[93]

Jonson took this description of the death of 'one of the gyant brethren' directly from Claudian's *Gigantomachia*, a late Latin poem whose subject is the mythological battle between the Olympian gods and the Titans. In the play, the followers of Cicero, loyal to the republic, are indirectly compared to the young Olympian gods, while Catiline and his followers, restive aristocrats left over from the reign of Sylla, are compared to the old race of the Titans or giants. The 'gyant' petrified at the sight of the *gorgoneion* on Minerva's breastplate is a model for Catiline feeling himself '[G]row marble at the killing sight'. This 'sight' is glossed a few lines later by Jonson as the 'sight of *Rome* in us' – a mysterious phrasing. Minerva is described as 'holding forth' the head of the Medusa closely following Claudian's description where she rushes forward 'presenting her breast' upon which 'glittered the Gorgon's head'.[94] Yet, moving beyond his allusion to the Latin poet, Jonson clearly offers an analogy between the 'killing sight' of 'MEDUSA's head' and the 'sight' (or the *site*) 'of *Rome* in us'. The consequence of this analogy is

---

[93] Ben Jonson, *Catiline, His Conspiracy*, Herford and Simpson, vol. v, p. 548 (Act v, lines 676–88). All subsequent references to the play will be included in the text.

[94] 'Tritonia virgo / prosilit ostendens rutila cum Gorgone pectus.' Claudian, *Shorter Poems*, trans. Maurice Platnaeur 2 vols. (Cambridge: Harvard University Press, 1963), vol. II, pp. 281–91; p. 287 (lines 92–3). It may be useful here to draw the reader's attention to the fact that the ancient sources are not perfectly in agreement concerning the *way* the Medusa petrified her victims or the way her victims petrified themselves by looking at her. Was it necessary to cross the Medusa's gaze to be turned immediately into stone, or was a simple glimpse of any part of the Medusa's head enough to kill immediately? This question is linked to the different (subsequent) versions of how Perseus actually cut off Medusa's head. In some versions, he is depicted turning his head away and looking at a weakened version of her image in his shield; in other versions, it is the Medusa who, seeing *herself* in his mirror, turns herself into stone just after Perseus has cut off her head.

slightly disturbing. Rome is compared to the monstrous and horrific sight of the Medusa. Even if the Medusa that is Rome is used to defeat sedition, the image is highly problematic. It raises the question not only of what Rome *is*, but who *they* are, represented by 'us', who are willing to make use of the ultimate instrument of power and terror to crush their enemies. In *Catiline*, as in *Epicoene*, the Medusa is emblematic of an eloquence that petrifies, speech or citation that turns the interlocutor to stone. By silencing Catiline with the Medusa's head of his own oratorical art, Cicero may be seen as embodying the homeopathic principle in which *like* cures *like*, showing the extent to which, for Jonson, Cicero and his famous interlocutor Catiline are in many ways equivalent 'furies'.

In the ancient tradition which inspired Jonson's image of Minerva holding aloft the Gorgon's head (both directly and by way of Renaissance commentators), Homer describes Athena preparing herself for battle arming herself with the 'tasselled aegis, fraught with terror, all around which Rout is set as a crown, and on it is Strife, on it Valor, and on it Assault, that makes the blood run cold, and on it is the Gorgon head of the terrible monster'.[95] In Lucan's *Pharsalia*, Pallas is described as scattering 'the Gorgon tresses over all her aegis'.[96] Later, in Book 7 of the *Pharsalia*, Julius Caesar is compared to 'Bellona brandishing her bloody scourge … when with fierce blows he lashes on his steeds terrified by the aegis of Pallas'.[97] The representation of a Medusa's head on a cavalier's shield was an extension of this conception of the Medusa as the ultimate weapon of mass destruction, the shield acting simultaneously as a defensive and offensive weapon.

Allegorical interpretations of the Medusa's head in the iconologies and mythographies of the sixteenth century reveal the Gorgon to be closely associated with language and speech. Cesare Ripa's *Iconologia* (1593), Natalis Comes' (or Conti's) *Mythologia* (1551) and Vincenzo Cartari's *Imagini* (1556) all provided interpretations and exegeses of varying ancient versions of the mythological tale of Perseus decapitating the Medusa in order to show what its hidden meaning was. Cartari moralizes on the image of Minerva arming herself for battle with the head of the Medusa:

---

[95] Homer, *Iliad: Books 1–12*, trans. A. T. Murray and William F. Wyatt (Cambridge: Harvard University Press, 1999), p. 261 (5.738–41).
[96] Lucan, *Pharsalia* (*The Civil War*), trans. J. D. Duff (New York: G. P. Putnam's Sons, 1928), pp. 380–81 (Book 7, line 149).
[97] Ibid., pp. 410–11 (Book 7, lines 568–70). See Lucan's subsequent description of Libya, filled with the snakes born from the blood of the Medusa (Book 9, line 700 ff.).

These things show the power of knowledge and prudence, which through wonderful works and wise counsels can *astonish* men and *render them like stone with amazement*, so that it can obtain whatever it wishes, provided it can suitably expound it; it is language that is expressed by that terrible head [my emphasis].⁹⁸

Cartari fuses the image of Minerva, armed to the hilt for war, with her aspect as the goddess of wisdom, allegorizing the 'terrible head' as language and Minerva as the dexterous manipulator of it. Yet, as Nancy Vickers has pointed out, this particular allegorization of the Medusa as language that petrifies was originally derived from Plato's *Symposium*.⁹⁹ Socrates, having just heard Agathon speak, admiringly flatters him:

> For his speech so reminded me of Gorgias that I was exactly in the plight described by Homer: I feared that Agathon in his final phrases would confront me with the eloquent Gorgias' head, and by opposing his speech to mine would turn me thus dumbfounded into stone.¹⁰⁰

This idea of a petrifying eloquence finds a powerful visual elaboration in the engraved frontispiece of a treatise on eloquence from 1641. In *L'École du silence: le sentiment des images au XVIIe siècle*, Marc Fumaroli discusses the iconography of the frontispieces of a number of Jesuit treatises of eloquence from 1594–1641.¹⁰¹ In these frontispieces, rhetorical skill and oratorical eloquence are represented by the various signs and symbols associated with eloquence in the period. The frontispiece of the treatise *Palatium Reginae Eloquentiae*, by P. Gérard Pelletier, S.J., published in Paris in 1641, is particularly striking.¹⁰² In the background, Mercury, so often associated with eloquence, is depicted instructing two noble youths, Enghien and Conti Condé, before one of the portals of the *Palatium Reginae Eloquentiae*, the palace of eloquence.¹⁰³ In the foreground, the goddesses Minerva and Diana are shown in battledress, attacking with their weapons, including

---

⁹⁸ Vincenzo Cartari, *Imagini* (Padua, 1571), p. 384. Cited in Stephen Orgel, 'Jonson and the Amazons' in Elizabeth D. Harvey and Katharine Eisaman Maus (eds.), *Soliciting Interpretation: Literary Theory and Seventeenth-Century English Poetry* (Chicago: University of Chicago Press, 1990), p. 129.
⁹⁹ Nancy Vickers, '"The blazon of sweet beauty's best": Shakespeare's *Lucrece*' in Patricia Parker and Geoffrey Hartman (eds.), *Shakespeare and the Question of Theory* (London: Methuen, 1985), pp. 95–115, p. 110.
¹⁰⁰ Plato, *Lysis, Symposium, Gorgias*, trans. W. R. M. Lamb (Cambridge: Harvard University Press, 1925), p. 163.
¹⁰¹ Marc Fumaroli, *L'École du silence: le sentiment des images au XVIIe siècle* (Paris: Flammarion, 1994), pp. 325–42. For Fumaroli, these frontispieces are a kind of *mise-en-abyme* of his own examination of eloquence in the visual arts since they are engravings which 'show' and 'depict' visually the spoken eloquence that is the subject of the treatises they introduce.
¹⁰² *Ibid.*, p. 341.
¹⁰³ Fumaroli notes that the two Condé sons were students of the Jesuits. *Ibid.*, pp. 340–1.

Illustration 4. Frontispiece from P. Gérard Pelletier, S. J., *Palatium Reginae Eloquentiae* (Paris, 1641).

the open-mouthed visage of a Medusa on Minerva's shield, a writhing crew of men, who represent 'heresies and passions'.[104] The pitched battle in the foreground and the scene of quiet instruction in the background are linked by a feminine figure, the 'queen' of Eloquence who stands beside Minerva and gestures toward Mercury and the entrance into the palace. Minerva and the horrible Medusa on her shield are the dramatic centre of the frontispiece. The open mouth of the fury is in contrast to the earnest gaze of Minerva intent on defeating her enemy. Here, Eloquence, represented in the figure of Minerva brandishing her Medusa, has no compunction in using *vehemence* to achieve her purpose.[105] In utilizing the iconography of Minerva with her Medusa's head, eloquent vehemence is indeed likened to a kind of rage, the terror and heart-freezing fury of Minerva in battle.

Minerva displaying the gorgon's head in the frontispiece of the *Palatium Reginae Eloquentiae* may be seen as part of the iconography of 'vehement' and forceful eloquence in the seventeenth century. In *The Garden of Eloquence*, Henry Peacham also describes a kind of 'vehement' eloquence that baffles and silences its enemies. However, to illustrate this eloquence, Peacham does not use Minerva brandishing the Medusa's head, but *the historic emblem of eloquence in the period: the ancient orator Cicero*. Peacham describes the ornament he calls 'Amplification' and its uses:

> whatsoever is very pleasant or very lamentable, whatsoever is thought deare and precious, profitable, admirable, detestable or dangerous, may minister matter to Amplification: and finally all such things as *cannot be heard without a great motion of minde*: Examples whereof are plentifull and almost everywhere to be found in the *orations of Tully*. He doth amplifie the theftes, the sacrileges, the robberies, the lecherous life of Verres... the drunkennesse, the bold presumptions, the prodigalitie, and other such like wicked offences of Antony... he doth vehemently invey... against Clodius, but *most vehemently of all against Catiline*... The orations of this Orator are plentifully replenished with these exornations... by his eloquence he oft cast downe his adversaries from their estate and dignitie, oftentimes by his copious speech and vehemencie of pleading, he frayed most excellent Orators from their frends defence... and *made Catiline (a most audacious traitor) dumbe in the Senate.* (my emphasis)[106]

It was a commonplace of the period to link Cicero (or 'Tully') and eloquence. Nevertheless, Peacham's description of Cicero's oratorical ability to blast his interlocutor by amplifying the nature and extent of their deeds and

---

[104] *Ibid.*, p. 340. [105] *Ibid.*, p. 341.
[106] Henry Peacham, *The Garden of Eloquence* (London, 1593), p. 122.

crimes finds its culmination in the implied petrification of Catiline in the Senate by Cicero's *amplification* or torrent of words.[107] If we turn back, now, to the end of *Catiline* and the petrification of its eponymous anti-hero by 'the sight of Rome in us' we realize that the Catiline who finds himself turning to stone is like one of the writhing heretics on the floor before Pelletier's *Palace of the Queen of Eloquence*. He is also the figure in Peacham's treatise, struck 'dumbe' by the implied gorgon of Ciceronian eloquence. This in turn reminds us again of Terror in *The Masque of Queenes*, where envy and the envious are represented as being cut off and silenced by a torrential flood of authorities, citations and glosses. The *pharmakon* of antique eloquence in *The Masque of Queenes* defeats envious witchcraft just like the terrifying gorgon on the shield of Minerva in the Jesuit frontispiece. Catiline too is a 'passion', a 'heretic' and an 'audacious traitor' defeated by the petrifying gaze of the Medusa as eloquence. There is ample evidence to interpret the Medusa's head held aloft by Minerva at the end of *Catiline, His Conspiracy*, as the Ciceronian eloquence powerful enough to exile or execute Rome's enemies. We could even read Jonson's play itself as a kind of 'treatise' on eloquence testifying to the power of oratory, even in the early modern author's translation, to move and persuade to defend the legitimate regime.

As many critics have noticed, the doubling of Cicero and Catiline in Jonson's play goes against a simple and unambiguous 'victory' of one over the other. We have seen that Rome, under Cicero's consulship, is compared in the final scene to something monstrous. The description of Catiline 'inquiring' and wondering what is happening to him as the marble courses through his veins has a different effect upon the reader of this play than the same description has upon a reader of the *Gigantomachia* by Claudian. The Titan in the poem is an unknown soldier, one of many brutes on a battlefield. Yet, Claudian's description is a moving one and, appropriated by Jonson for Catiline, elicits sympathy in the reader. Catiline is easily the most subtly drawn character in Jonson's play (along with Caesar), a balance between the exaggeratedly bloodthirsty (though highly entertaining) Cethegus and the pompously clean and self-important figure of Cicero which Jonson derived, in part, from Plutarch, and whose eloquence, according to Juvenal in Satire 10, was the root cause of his downfall: 'Tullie's owne wit cut off his head and hands.'[108] Catiline and Cicero

---

[107] In the early modern period, force in eloquence is often described as a 'flood' or a torrent. *Ibid.*, p. 4.
[108] Juvenal, *That Which Seemes Best is Worst, Exprest in a Paraphrasitical Transcript of Juvenal's Tenth Satyr*, trans. W.B. (London, 1617), sig. [A6ᵛ]. Jonson's play is based on Sallust's account of the Catilinian conspiracy, but, as Bruce Boehrer has noted, the playwright has incorporated a number of 'anti-

are mirror images, giving similar exhortatory speeches to their followers, secretly admiring and hating one another and finally becoming, in the eyes of posterity, symbiotically attached one to the other. In treatises on eloquence as well as in Latin school books, Tully would, as Jonson well knew, be forever linked with his Catiline. This historical association is, in fact, alluded to in the play by Caesar, who attributes it to Cicero's own 'art', which, he argues, *needs* to create a 'monster' in Catiline so that Cicero can become a 'Herculean actor in the scene' by defeating his 'hydra' (III.i.96–100). Caesar implies that the 'new man', Cicero, cannot hope to become a Roman hero unless he cuts off the heads of a hydra of his own making (Catiline). In this respect, we see the extent to which Jonson perceives *like* curing *like*. The gaze of Fame in *Queenes* is nothing other than the gaze of Terror, reversed and used against itself. In *Catiline*, the petrifying eloquence of Tully is the antidote for the envious gaze of Catiline. The parallelism between Cicero and Catiline is constantly emphasized. Jonson's play continuously stages how Catiline's plots nourish Cicero's fashioning of himself as the selfless and ever 'vigilant' protector of Rome. Peacham, as we have seen above, shows how Cicero amplifies Catiline's excessiveness, boldness, ambition and rebelliousness in order to silence him. Yet, at the same time, Cicero's heavy-handed use of amplification can be seen in Jonson's play to implicate Cicero in Catiline's monstrosity, as the marginal commentary of Caesar upon the scene of 'Hercules' with his 'hydra' seems to indicate. Cicero is excessive. He and other demagogues ('popular men') are exactly like Catiline in Caesar's view: they 'must sweat no lesse / To fit their properties, then t'expresse their parts' (III.i.100–1).

The *gorgoneion* is an effective talisman because it acts as a prophylactic charm against the fatal glance which the Medusa was believed to have possessed. It is for this reason that it was painted and carved on shields as the ultimate form of protection, baffling the enemy with its glance. Its power is a homeopathic one, turning against the enemy a version of its own face in order to defeat it. Ciceronian eloquence, held aloft like a Medusa's head, may very well be a version of Catilinian fury used to defeat that fury. Even in the *Symposium*, the reputation of Gorgias as a model of eloquence, like that of Cicero, was not wholly unproblematic. The editor of an eighteenth-century edition of the *Symposium* (or *The Banquet*) glosses Socrates' reference to Gorgias so that his readers will not be tempted to take a 'Superficial

---

Sallustian' elements. Bruce Boehrer, 'Jonson's *Catiline* and Anti-Sallustian Trends in Renaissance Humanist Historiography', *Studies in Philology* 94 (Winter 1997), 85–102. Plutarch is notoriously critical of Cicero. Juvenal's Satire 10 is one Jonson quoted at length in his previous 'Roman' play, *Sejanus*; Juvenal describes Cicero as an orator who perished because of his excessive eloquence.

View of this Passage', namely one which would interpret Socrates as having bestowed a sincere compliment on Agathon:

> But under the Compliment lies concealed a Piece of Satyrical Humour. For Gorgias was the first who *corrupted* Oratory with the injudicious and unlimited Use of Antitheses, Paritys, and those other still lesser ornaments of Style... He was fond of them to such a Degree, that when the Great Fathers of Criticism, Plato and Aristotle, had, by their excellent Rules, established a better Taste in Style... from that time, falling into disrepute with all Men of Sense, they obtained the Name of 'Gorgiasms' of which Agathon's speech is full.[109]

Gorgias' reputation places Socrates' comparison of Gorgias to a gorgon in a new light. It reveals that for Socrates the Medusa's head is a kind of shorthand for excess in speech.

Jonson may be said to oppose another kind of 'eloquence' to that of the excessive Cicero in this play: the Machiavellian manoeuvering, secret whispering and well-timed silence of Caesar, a figure of James I perhaps. It is Caesar who will, eventually, be rewarded, only a few years after the events of the play are finished, with an offer of ultimate power and whose account of the *Gallic Wars* would also, like Ciceronian rhetoric, become a model for good writing in the early modern period. The ambiguous nature of the play's ending and its problematic eloquent 'hero' – depicted as self-important, self-flattering and mocked constantly by the politically canny Caesar – was most likely the reason it was judged a complete and utter disaster by its first audiences, even while Jonson himself believed it to be among his best works.[110]

Catiline helps us to understand better the strategy involved in the Jonsonian *pharmakon*, in which the terror the reader represents to the writer can only be defeated by the ambivalent use of another kind of terror. The play helps us distinguish the mechanisms of Jonson's phantasmagoria in a masque such as *The Masque of Queenes*, in which the gorgon represents both the envy of the reader and the talismanic eloquence of antiquity used to ward off that envy. Jonson is, in many ways, a Ciceronian figure holding aloft the gorgon of eloquence before the reader. The texts considered in this chapter all show the extent to which the idea itself of monumental 'fame' serves as a *pharmakon* to protect the writer from defacement.

---

[109] Plato, *The Banquet, A Dialogue of Plato concerning Love. The second part*, trans. Floyer Sydenham (London, 1767), p. 122 n. 96.

[110] In the dedication of *Catiline, his Conspiracy* to the Earle of Pembroke, Jonson writes that the play 'is the first (of this race) that ever I dedicated to any person, and had I not thought it the best, it should have been taught a lesse ambition'. What the play's 'race' was in Jonson's mind is not perfectly clear although he is most likely saying that he thought it is the best of his 'Roman' plays. Herford and Simpson, vol. v, p. 431 (lines 10–12).

CHAPTER 6

Being posthumous

> Thou wrapt and Shrin'd in thine own sheets, wilt ly
> A Relick fam'd by all Posterity.
> (Henry King, 'To my dead friend Ben: Johnson')[1]

The Staple of Newes (1625) was the first play to be written after the poet's ten-year absence from the public stage and, even more significantly, the first play to be written after the poet's publication of his collected *Workes* in 1616. By the time the play was performed, Jonson had the bulk of his career behind him, had been honoured with a poet laureateship, an honorary degree from Oxford, and was still a writer of the court's masques, which he had continued to write throughout his absence from the public stage. One of these masques, *News From the New World Discover'd in the Moone* (1620), can be seen as Jonson's original 'sketch' for the later *Staple*, for in the masque we already find a 'Staple of newes', the dream of an enterprising 'Factor' who describes himself as 'one that otherwise take [*sic*] pleasure i' my Pen'.[2]

The *Staple* was also the first of what John Dryden was to call Jonson's 'dotages', now referred to, less prejudicially, as his 'late plays'.[3] The recent rethinking of 'late Jonson' has encouraged more critical and scholarly work on these understudied texts. Anne Barton's argument that Jonson's plays written after the death of Shakespeare (in 1616) reflect a certain nostalgia

---

[1] Henry King, *Poems, Elegies, Paradoxes, and Sonnets, 1657* (London: A Scolar Press Facsimile, 1973), p. 94 (lines 59–60).
[2] Ben Jonson, *News From the New World Discover'd in the Moone*, Herford and Simpson, vol. VII, p. 514 (line 34). This 'Factor' describes himself as 'neither Printer, nor Chronologer, but one that otherwise take pleasure i' my Pen: A Factor of newes for all the Shieres of *England*' (lines 33–5).
[3] Jonson's 'late plays' are considered to be those written after the publication of the 1616 Folio *and* Jonson's ten-year absence from the public stage. So, *Bartholomew Fair* (1614) and *The Devil is an Ass* (1616) are not included in this list of late plays, even though they were not published in folio in 1616. *The Staple of Newes* (1625), *The New Inn* (1629), *The Magnetic Lady* (1632), *A Tale of A Tub* (1632), *The Sad Shepherd* and *The Fall of Mortimer* (these last two, published posthumously for the first time in Jonson's *Workes* in 1640) are all considered 'late'.

for a lost Elizabethan world (embodied presumably in Shakespeare's plays) may indeed reflect a certain critical nostalgia, one felt by Jonson's contempories as well. The speculation that Jonson had become less acerbic, more tolerant in his later plays reveals yet again the critical difficulty of breaking free of certain entrenched ideas, for at some level it echoes Dryden's more direct diagnosis of senility. To avoid such global pronouncements, even if partly true, it seems important to approach 'late Jonson' first in terms of its continuities with earlier Jonson before coming to conclusions about what is new or different about his 'late' period. It is important, for instance, to see a later play such as *The Magnetic Lady, Or Humours Reconciled* as part of Jonson's continuing scholarly and literary interest in 'humoural theory' in *Every Man in His Humour* and *Every Man Out of His Humour*. *The Sad Shepherd, Or A Tale of Robin Hood* (in *Workes*, 1640) demonstrates again an authorial interest in witchcraft previously seen in *The Masque of Queenes*. There is also evidence, in the latter part of his career, of Jonson's intellectual associations with some of the greatest thinkers of his day, his possible connection with Gresham College as a lecturer in rhetoric, his association (testified to by John Aubrey, in his *Brief Lives*) with the Great Tew circle of intellectuals around the 2nd Viscount of Falkland in Oxfordshire as well as his nomination in 1618 for the proposed 'Academ Roial', an association under James I which anticipated the formation of the Royal Society. These connections, as Martin Butler has shown, all argue for a reevaluation of Jonson's 'late period', not as a period of, at best, nostalgia, at worst, dearth, but of novelty and renewal.[4] If, for instance, Jonson's involvement in and fascination with magnetism reflects a line of inquiry with strong precedents in the humoural theory of his early works, the leap from humours to magnetism may also be seen to engage certain new intellectual currents of his time in a continuing search for a means of representing 'character'. This chapter will argue in relation to *The Staple of Newes*, that the late plays, masques and poems cannot be studied in isolation from Jonson's previous work since they return, repeat and refer to it, both implicitly and explicitly. At the same time, Jonson's late works are uniquely marked by the self-cannibalizing nature of the authorial *bricolage*. There is a new drive to sack, pillage, borrow, allude to and repeat *verbatim* his own previous works in a manner unseen before. The fact of writing in the shadow of his own 1616 Folio, writing, so to speak, from 'beyond the grave', as well as with his intellectual engagement

---

[4] Martin Butler, 'Late Jonson' in Gordon McMullan and Jonathan Hope (eds.), *The Politics of Tragicomedy: Shakespeare and After* (London: Routledge, 1992), pp. 168–88.

with the 'new science', may be seen to mark a kind of renewal and break with a certain past in 1616.[5]

THE PATCHED MANTLE OF FAME: *THE STAPLE OF NEWES*

The Staple of Newes cannot be fully appreciated without reference to Jonson's decision to print and publish his works during his own lifetime. In collecting his writings, up to that point, Jonson enfolioed himself, so to speak, as a dead classical author. Jonson's self-publication in folio has been accounted an historical and literary innovation. However, writing from *beyond* this self-made monument, after one's own literary entombing, may also be said to be a novelty. This paradoxical situation was not lost on Jonson's contemporaries, some of whom insisted that he 'leave the stage' even 'die' since he had already erected a monument to himself and garnered his laureate.[6] It was understood that the aging playwright could no longer produce anything to rival his *Alchemist* or *Volpone* and that he should gracefully desist. Douglas M. Lanier states, with reference to the ambient hostility in late Jacobean London toward Jonson's self-renewal on the public stage, that the Folio had proved to be 'too successful, for it not only set the terms of Jonson's reputation but also became the measure by which all Jonson's subsequent stagework was to be judged … Jonson would have to compete with his own *Workes*.'[7] Jonson would have to compete with *himself*, or, more precisely, the self in his *Workes*, in order to continue to write and build a career.[8] I would argue that this 'competition', even

---

[5] I have argued that certain speeches and aspects of *The Magnetic Lady* come into relief if we see them as representative of Baconian 'errors' or 'distempers' of learning. 'This is a piece / Of Oxford science': Jonson's *The Magnetic Lady, Or Humours Reconciled* given at The Maison Française, Oxford (March 2007).

[6] Nicholas Oldisworth writes in 'A Letter to Ben. Johnson. 1629':

> DIE: seemes it not enough, thy Writing's date
> Is endlesse, but thine owne prolonged Fate
> Must equall it? For shame, engrosse not Age,
> But now, thy fifth Act's ended, leave the stage,
> And lett us clappe.

Herford and Simpson, vol. XI, p. 397 (lines 33–7).

[7] Douglas M. Lanier, 'The Prison-House of the Canon: Allegorical Form and Posterity in Ben Jonson's *The Staple of Newes*' in J. Leeds Barroll (ed.), *Medieval and Renaissance Drama in England* (New York: AMS Press, Inc., 1985), vol. II, pp. 253–67; p. 254. Lanier also cites Herford and Simpson when he notes that 'it is significant that *The Staple of Newes* had to compete with the growing reputation of Jonson's own work in repertory, notably *The Alchemist* at court in 1623 and *Volpone* in 1624'. *Ibid.*, p. 265 n. 7.

[8] Lanier argues that Jonson addressed the problem of his canon by turning to allegory: 'Jonson consciously chose to eliminate as much as possible those details that would mark him as a dramatist of his age. Instead he chose allegory, a deliberately universalized form, a timeless mode in which he might cast the characteristic themes of the 1616 Folio for all ages' (Lanier, 'Prison-House of the

'strife', between his past self, entombed in the 1616 Folio, and his 'new' self, the post-1616 writer, is staged in *The Staple of Newes* in the conflict between father, uncle and son. The father, disguised as a beggar, clothed in rags and tatters, pursues his son and heir, whose new news-making machine is his latest rage. The father, believed dead, comes back to life when he throws off his ragged coat, coincidentally at the same time the magical news-making staple blows up. The prodigal son effects a reconciliation with his angry father by showing himself to be as good at 'plotting' and eventually is allowed to share the favors of Pecunia with his father. The role of woman, of reproduction, even of sexual generation and desire between the sexes has all but evaporated in this play, to an even greater extent than hitherto in Jonson's works. This near emptying of woman is at the service of a genetics of creation which privileges, not sexual union, but rather cutting (as Perseus begets his daughter Fame out of cutting off the head of Terror) and the piecing together of poetic fragments. Like the alchemical furnace at the centre of *The Alchemist*, the staple, the engine of production and distribution at the centre of the play, is run by men.[9] Yet, there is a crucial difference between the earlier, alchemical, and the later, news engine: while the sexual union of man and woman is imitated in a limbeck, the staple simply *vents*, of itself, discrete items, pieces of news. The necessity of securing a position in the staple office for Thom, the barber, becomes an emblem of the cutting function in the Jonsonian literary genetics of which the staple is an apt representation. The legator, the writer of the 1616 folio volume, and his legatee, the writer of *The Staple of Newes*, the first of the 'late plays' (plays first performed *after* 1616), may thus be seen as reconciled in this highly self-reflexive and self-allusive play.[10] As a mannerist allegory

---

Canon', p. 257). Lanier's emphasis on the importance of the 1616 Folio in Jonson's subsequent writing of the *Staple* is well taken. However, his suggestion that Jonson chose to write in a 'timeless mode', eliminating details that would mark him as a dramatist of his age, is difficult to conceive after reading *The Staple of Newes*.

[9] According to Karen Newman: 'By dubbing his new office a "staple", he [Jonson] emphasizes the interdependence of news and the marketplace since a staple was a principal place of business for a class of goods, an emporium or mart, sometimes a town, even a country, appointed by royal authority in which a group of merchants had exclusive right of purchase to goods destined for sale or export... Staple also came to mean the merchants themselves so privileged, and subsequently a depot or storehouse of provisions, especially war materials. Finally, staple has the common meaning of a staple commodity... In choosing to dub his news office a staple, Jonson emphasizes the news as goods, regulated by the state, produced for a market, sold for a price, and consumed by the public.' Karen Newman, 'Engendering the News' in A. C. Magnusson and C. F. McGee (eds.), *The Elizabethan Theatre XIV: Papers given at the International Conference on Elizabethan Theatre held at the University of Waterloo, Ontario in July 1991* (Toronto: P. D. Meany, 1996), pp. 49–70; pp. 51–2.

[10] *Bartholomew Fair* was produced by Lady Elizabeth's Men and performed at the Hope Theatre in 1614; *The Devil is an Ass* produced by the King's Men, was performed at Blackfriars in 1616. As mentioned

of his own authorial 'self', divided into three parts, each emblematic of a stage in the authorial 'career', *The Staple of Newes* can be seen as a singular effort at renovation and an attempt at poetic reengendering.

In recent years, *The Staple of Newes* has primarily been read against the backdrop of the early seventeenth-century English news business and the news world's epistemological links with gossip and rumour.[11] One of the mainstays of this play is the way it marks an interest in the newly emerging newsbooks at the beginning of the seventeenth century. *The Staple of Newes* can certainly be read, in the words of Marchette Chute, as 'a lively and topical satire on the current London interest in Newspapers', and on the novelty in the 1620s of a regular, weekly newsbook in London.[12] Following the lead of Dutch journalists in 1620, London publishers replaced the occasional and unreliable pamphlets of the time, full of 'wonderful strange Newes' with a regular paper, *The Weekly Newes*, published by Nathaniel Butter.[13] Readings of Jonson's *Staple* as a satirical or even moral piece on the emerging medium reveals its clear engagement – and that of its author – with the very *idea* of news: its problematic connections to gossip and slander, its status as a product to be bought and sold at an international emporium and its innate tendency to become almost immediately obsolete.[14] This last characteristic is one which has led at least one critic to suggest that the *Staple*'s satiric view of news reflects the anxiety the now monumentalized poet may have felt about the very security

---

above, neither appeared in the 1616 Folio, but were published for the first time in folio in 1631.

[11] The insights the play can provide historians of seventeenth-century newsbooks has served to renew scholarly interest in Jonson's *Staple*. In addition to Karen Newman, 'Engendering the News', cited above, articles emphasizing Jonson's interest in seventeenth-century news and the topicality of Jonson's play include: Mark Z. Muggli, 'Ben Jonson and the Business of News', *SEL* 32 (1992), 323–40; Stuart Sherman, 'Eyes and Ears, News and Plays: The Argument of Ben Jonson's *Staple*' in Brendon Dooley and Sabrina Baron (eds.), *The Politics of Information in Early Modern Europe* (London: Routledge, 2001), pp. 23–40; Julie Sanders, 'Print, Popular Culture, Consumption and Commodification in *The Staple of News*' in Julie Sanders, Kate Chedgzoy and Susan Wiseman, *Refashioning Ben Jonson: Gender, Politics, and the Jonsonian Canon* (Basingstoke: Macmillan, 1998), pp. 183–207; Donald F. McKenzie, '*The Staple of News* and the Late Plays' in William Blisset *et al.* (eds.), *A Celebration of Ben Jonson* (Toronto: Toronto University Press, 1973), pp. 83–128. See also Joad Raymond, *The Invention of the Newpaper: English Newsbooks 1641–1649* (Oxford: Clarendon Press, 1996) and *Pamphlets and Pamphleteering in Early Modern Britain* (Cambridge: Cambridge University Press, 2003).

[12] Chute, *Ben Jonson of Westminster*, p. 297.   [13] *Ibid.*, pp. 297–8.

[14] Douglas M. Lanier notes that 'Jonson…seems to recognize that plays themselves, the latest dispatches from the poet's brain, are also regarded as a sort of news. The gossip Tattle, at the theater for entertainment and not moral instruction, specifies that "your *Newes* be new, and fresh, *Mr. Prologue*, and untainted".' Lanier, 'The Prison-House of the Canon', pp. 257–8. Joad Raymond similarly observes, 'Jonson implicated himself, recognizing that the dramatist and poet, as well as the journalist, was involved in the business of selling news.' Raymond, *Invention of the Newspaper*, p. 2.

of print to ensure his fame.¹⁵ Yet, I would argue that the writer of the 1616 Folio made no such associations between that volume and the ephemeral fragments of gossip, slander and news that invaded London in printed form. I have argued in the previous chapter that the building of an enduring monument was not simply based on its being *in print*, but in the creation of sanctuary. It seems unlikely that Jonson was anxious concerning the status of the works in the Folio. On the other hand, he may well have been anxious concerning those works he was writing afterwards. Works which were, suddenly, 'news' in relation to what had gone before. These new works were perhaps even more defaceable by public opinion than those written before 1616 *because* they were written in the shadow of the Folio, a possibility which the comments by contemporaries might seem to demonstrate. The ten-year-old publication of a folio edition of his works and his 'fame' as the writer of *The Alchemist*, *Volpone*, and *Bartholomew Fair* necessarily changed the manner in which the poet eyed his own subsequent creative efforts. Both the structure and themes of *The Staple of Newes* reveal a new perspective of the poet upon his work. Ten years after the publication of his collected *Workes* in folio, the poet's envious gaze on his own work is here imagined as emanating from his former writing self. The entombed self is imagined to have his eye fixed firmly and critically on the upstart creator of *The Staple of Newes* (who, paradoxically, is the elder in years to the enfolioed self of 1616) to see if he meets the standards of the previous 'age'. Like Knowell senior vigilantly surveying the movements of Knowell junior, the author of the 1616 Folio acts as censor and tracker of the new, emerging Jonson. In regarding his own new work in relation to his previous output, Jonson reproduces with his former self the relationship he had with the ancient authors from the past. In order to propitiate the critical gaze he imagines will (as always) be watching the play, he employs the same defensive gestures as before, only now, Jonson's former works serve as the authority with which to defend the text against envy. The writer parasites himself and cites himself just as he did the authors of antiquity. Poetic self-plagiary and self-allusion act to fill up the new 'lack' in the text, a lack which is present in relation to a new version of the father, the former poetic self, buried, in the folio volume, but rearing its head and critical eye like the fathers of former plays.

The distinct evidence of a more than usual amount of reference and allusion to former plays (both his own and, significantly enough, Shakespeare's)

---

¹⁵ Lanier, 'The Prison-House of the Canon', pp. 256–7.

as well as a phenomenon of self-citation in *The Staple of Newes* reveals how the poet's own former work becomes the means of buoying up and sanctioning his new work like the citations of other, mostly classical authors, served to buoy up his former texts. The method hasn't changed, only the sources have.[16] The writer's allusion to and citation of his former texts has the double effect of conferring on the *Staple* a certain legitimacy already possessed by the writer of *The Alchemist* and *Bartholomew Fair*. On the other hand, this same process confers upon the cited text a new authority in its metamorphosis into citation or allusion. Like the writings of antique authors, Jonson's own former writing acquires a kind of monumental and monumentalizing status *within* the new and younger text.[17] Jonson's previous work begins to possess the intrinsic soundness of a text which is both quotable and recognizable by the spectator and reader. By quoting and citing himself, he finds a new way of creating a sanctuary, again with the aid of the literary father, but *himself* as literary father. He may fly now and find sanctuary, not only under the shadow of Sidney's wing, but under his own wing. Jonson's former works have acquired new virtue through, precisely, his citation and reference to them. As will be apparent, the play contains more direct citations of the poet's former works, as well as more direct references to the *historical* figure of the playwright himself, than any other play preceding it. The *Staple* marks an interesting permutation in the nature of Jonsonian literary creation as it has been described in the previous chapters, because the spectre of the envious gaze of the father is here projected on the writer's own former literary self, which now occupies a position of literary validity. The plot of the play enacts meta-textually the *reconciliation* between the writer of the authoritative text and the writer of the new, parasitic text, who attempts to inherit from the former and acquire an independence of his own. It is for this reason that even while the play seems highly 'allegorical' in the manner of contemporary plays such as *A Pleasant Comedy Shewing the Contention betweene Liberalitie and Prodigalitie* (1602), Richard Barnfield's *Lady Pecunia, Or the Praise of Money Also A Combat betwixt Conscience and Covetousnesse* (1605) and *The London Prodigall* (1605)

---

[16] Anne Barton has noted this change in Jonson's practice. Jonson began 'to use selected Elizabethan authors, Marlowe, Sidney and Shakespeare in the way that he had long been accustomed to use Horace, Virgil, Seneca or Quintilian: as guides to right ways of thinking and feeling'. Anne Barton, 'Harking Back to Elizabeth: Ben Jonson and Caroline Nostalgia', *ELH* 48 (1981), 706–31; p. 724. My own argument differs from Barton's as to the reason *why* Jonson began to make use both of these authors and himself.

[17] And so does Shakespeare's: Jonson had begun burying Shakespeare and himself in the *Staple* as 'antique' sources.

attributed to Shakespeare when it was 'added' to the 'impression' of the Third Folio of 1664, the allegory of *The Staple of Newes* must be seen as highly mannerist, because the allusions are self-reflexive and meta-theatrical. The allegorical characters in the *Staple* are not universal types, but rather pseudo-anthropomorphized forms of literary citation.[18]

The Staple of Newes is parasitic of old structures, themes and even texts of Jonson's works. The inclusion of a 'chorus' of women marks a return to the form of *Every Man Out of His Humour*. What is new and notable is that the spectatorial commentators are four female 'Gossips' instead of male wits or critics, none of whom may be said to 'speak' for the author. Additionally, in a remarkable emblem of his career-long fascination with cant languages, Jonson creates a 'Canters Colledge' in the *Staple*.[19] The final dissolution of the staple repeats the sudden explosion and dissolution of the alchemical 'laboratory' in *The Alchemist*. There are, furthermore, definite similarities between the family 'house' in which the staple is erected and the family 'house' of the alchemists. Thom, the barber, recalls Cutbeard of *Epicoene*; *The Staple of Newes* is compared to the House of Fame from *The Masque of Queenes*; the almanac, a recurring element in previous plays, becomes a character, Almanach, in the *Staple*; the Gossips make complimentary references to the writer of *The Devil is an Ass* as well as a reference to the *Bartholomew Fair* character, Zeal-of-the-Land Busy. It seems no accident that the Gossip, Mirth, describes the poet as having 'two heads, as a Drum has; one for making, the other repeating, and his repeating head is all to pieces'.[20]

These references to his former works as well as auto-allusions and auto-citations serve to link the new play with the already authorized productions of the author, in exactly the way references to (and repetitions from) Ovid, Horace or Pliny served the former writer by giving his text a kind of authenticity and propitiating the reader's gaze. An allusion to a previous work, and the recollection of the former work in the mind of the reader, is key to a reconciliation between the writer and his future reader or spectator, who is no more than a paranoid projection of the self-critical gaze of the poet onto his interpreter. The spectator or reader's recognition of the allusion parallels the (reading) father's recognition of his (writing) son. It is

---

[18] For Jonson's sources in the morality play tradition as well as the *Plutus* of Aristophanes, see Arthur Bivins Stonex, 'The Sources of Jonson's *The Staple of News*', *PMLA* 30 (1915), 821–30. See the title page of the 1664 Folio: 'Mr. William Shakespear's comedies, histories and tragedies published according to the true original copies: and unto this impression is added seven plays never before printed in folio, viz *Pericles, Prince of Tyre, The London prodigall.*'
[19] Ben Jonson, *The Staple of Newes*, Herford and Simpson, vol. VI, p. 360 (IV.iv.125).
[20] *Ibid.*, p. 281 (lines 68–70).

important to understand that it is, ultimately, the future reader alone who is capable of conferring upon the writer his posterity or literary inheritance. While this may seem to reverse the normal process of inheritance we must remember that the later reader is in a position perfectly symmetrical to that of the writer's predecessor because the writer *as reader* projects his own envy of former writers upon the reader who will be reading him.[21] So, it is the reader who is in the position to recognize the writer in the way the envious father gives up his envy and recognizes the son. The envy of the dead and the envy of the yet-to-be-born reader are symmetrical: yet, only the future reader will be in a position to give the author the posterity due to him and withheld by the envious father.

In this play, as in *Epicoene* and *Bartholomew Fair*, the recognition and reconciliation between father and son is enacted through the transfer of a piece of writing, a deed ensuring the son his inheritance. The securing of this deed and the extraction of the heritor's signature is an important aspect of the paradigmatic struggle between father and son figures in the plays. To this, *The Staple of Newes* is no exception:

> PENI-BOY JUNIOR. Where is the deed? hast thou it with thee?
> PICKLOCKE. No,
>   It is a thing of greater consequence,
>   Then to be borne about in a blacke boxe.[22]

The 'blacke boxe' echoes another box at the centre of one of Jonson's most successful plays, *Bartholomew Fair*. The black box in *Staple* may be seen as a direct allusion to the container in which the all-important marriage licence (and thus the inheritance of a dowry of 6,000 pounds) is passed from hand to hand in *Bartholomew Fair*.[23] The reader's recognition of this allusion to *Bartholomew Fair* automatically changes his perspective on *The Staple of Newes* in at least two crucial ways. First, if the paper in the *Staple* is too important to be carried in a box, the logical assumption is that what is in *The Staple of Newes* is of 'greater consequence' than what was in *Bartholomew Fair*. Secondly, the way in which the paper is subtly tricked out of the hands of Picklocke and into the hands of the son, through

---

[21] This refers us back to the usefulness of a concept of an 'anxiety of reception', which accounts for the continuum between past and future and the incessant shuttling back and forth between the 'gaze' of the past and the future inherent in the act of writing.

[22] *Ibid.*, p. 367 (v.i.86–9).

[23] See for instance: 'QUARLOUS...I would ha' you get away that boxe from him, and bring it us. EDGWORTH. Would you ha' the boxe and all, Sir? Or onely that, that is in it? I'le get you that, and leave him the boxe, to play with still.' Ben Jonson, *Bartholomew Fair*, Herford and Simpson, vol. VI, pp. 79–80 (III.v.248–52).

the son's ingenious plotting, contrasts significantly with the rather clumsy awkwardness of the physical travels of Littlewit's black box through the fairgrounds of *Bartholomew Fair*. The father's compliment to the son on the ingenuity of his plot represents the fantasy of having lived up to the father's standards. The reconciliation between the writer of *Bartholomew Fair*, who can appreciate the plot engendered by his 'inheritor', i.e. the writer of *The Staple of Newes*, is made through the allusion to a box and mirrored in the reader's understanding of this allusion.

Yet, at the same time, the black box of the *Staple* is indirectly related to another dramatic container, and as such, creates an interesting tissue of allusion returning ultimately to one of the most important plays for Ben Jonson's career, *The Spanish Tragedy* (1592). The black box in *Bartholomew Fair* is itself an echo of the similarly empty box in Thomas Kyd's play, which Pedringano believes contains his pardon. *The Staple of Newes* then necessarily places *Bartholomew Fair* on a referential par with *The Spanish Tragedy*, for it is equally likely that the deed in *Staple* is also of 'greater consequence' than the supposed contents of Pedringano's black box. Furthermore, the mere physical theatricality of the device of a black box, bordering on slapstick in *Bartholomew Fair*, and a stagey device to inform the audience of Pedringano's fate, is ridiculed by a character who is an element in a sophisticated *theatrum absurdum*, where the need for such devices as black boxes has gone the way of the 'flesh and blood' romantic love interest and any attempt at adherence to physical or metaphysical laws. The play appropriates some of the unmotivated magic logic of the masque and flaunts the old rules of the theatre to which even its author earlier conformed.

Like this allusion to *Bartholomew Fair*, the text of *The Staple of Newes* is filled with self-reflexive allusions and borrowings from Jonson's previous works. Moreover, this patchwork of former works is even emblematized in the play. The reconciliation between father and son in *The Staple of Newes*, effected through the exchange of the piece of paper, the deed, is paralleled in their exchange of a ragged cloak. The ragged cloak, in *The Staple of Newes*, may be seen as a highly self-referential symbol of the transfer of inheritance from father to son. Believed dead, the father is in fact disguised as a beggar in a patched cloak: 'hee's a wise old Fellow, / Though he seeme patch'd thus, and made up o' peeces'.[24] This cloak serves as a powerful image of a conglomeration of remnants of the poet's own former works. The cloak is a covering, a mantle, even an investiture, but one significantly

---

[24] Ben Jonson, *The Staple of Newes*, Herford and Simpson, vol. VI, p. 296 (I.v.94–5).

made up of fragments of the poet's most successful *pieces*. It signifies a collection of phrases and passages which possess a sanctuarizing virtue. This virtue inherent in the cloak is emblematized in references to coats-of-arms, created and sanctioned by the suitably named character, Pyed-mantle. The protective origin is not now derived from another writer, another father figure in the form of notes or glosses. There is no need, in this play, to cover over the lack of the writer with scraps from the tables of other authors: this lack is covered by the previous texts of Jonson. Within the Jonsonian literary economy, the cloak is an image even of the creative power of writing itself: it is the mantle of the predecessor. Gossip Mirth remarks that the figure of the father, the Canter, is 'a kin to the Poet'.[25] And Gossip Expectation, exasperated with the 'Catastrophe', rails at the playwright and his resurrection of the Canter, who, for the whole of the play has been believed by the son and everyone else to be dead: 'Absurdity on him for a huge overgrowne *Playmaker*! why should he make him live again, when they, and we all thought him dead? If he had left him to his ragges, there had beene an end of him.'[26] Expectation is referring to the 'Canter', but the Canter is, as Mirth has argued, a 'kin' of the Poet, namely his former, enfolioed self. The 'ragges' of the Canter are like the 'leaves' of a book, the 'sheets' of the folio volume. The poet is condemned (by his disapproving female spectators) 'to stand in a skin of *parchment* ... And those fill'd with newes!'[27] In this way, the 'ragges' worn by the Canter are paralleled perfectly by the 'sheets' the poet wears, or the 'skin of parchment': they are 'kin' in the same way that cloth rags and sheets of paper are 'kin'.[28]

This cutting and piecing together of a play from remnants of the poet's old plays to serve as a kind of mantle and investiture is taken up in the often oneiric unfolding of the plot. The poet's *former* self is divided into *two* father figures, Peni-boy, the Father and Canter, and Peni-boy, the Uncle and Usurer.[29] The writer of *The Staple of Newes* is represented in the newly born heir, Peni-Boy, 'the Sonne, the heire and Suiter'. Peni-boy, the Canter, is described as a 'Myne' man, 'bred i' the *Mines*' and Peni-boy, the Usurer is depicted as a hermit and miser.[30] One is representative of inexhaustible abundance, a land of plenty like the 'rich *Peru* ... the golden mines, / Great

---

[25] *Ibid.*, p. 362 (lines 4–5).   [26] *Ibid.*, p. 362 (lines 8–11).   [27] *Ibid.*, p. 364 (lines 71–2).
[28] It is useful to remember that, as Linda Woodbridge notes, 'the technology of writing has a long intimacy with cloth. Paper, invented in China, was made of rags (the ideogram for paper includes the radical for cloth).' Linda Woodbridge, 'Patchwork: Piecing the Early Modern Mind in England's First Century of Print Culture', *ELH* 23 (Winter 1993), 5–45; p. 37.
[29] Ben Jonson, 'The Persons of the Play', *The Staple of Newes*, Herford and Simpson, vol. VI, p. 278.
[30] *Ibid.*, p. 292 (1.iii.57–9).

SALOMON's *Ophir*' of the house within which Mammon, the incarnation of the greedy pursuit of gain, will chase his alchemical dream to turn all into gold in *The Alchemist*.³¹ When Peni-boy asks the Canter (his father disguised as a beggar and, ironically the *source* of the boy's own new-found wealth) if he needs any money the Canter cries:

> Who, Sir I?
> Did I not tell you I was bred in the *Mines*,
> Under Sir *Bevis Bullion*? P. JUNIOR. That is true,
> I quite forgot, you *Myne-men* want no money,
> Your streets are pav'd with 't: there, the molten silver
> Runns out like cream, on cakes of gold. P. CANTER. And Rubies
> Doe grow like Strawberries. P. JUNIOR. 'Twere brave being there!
> Come *Thom*, we'll go to the *Office* now. P. CANTER. What *Office*?
> P. JUNIOR. *Newes Office*, the *New Staple*; thou shalt goe too,
> 'Tis here i' the house, on the same floore, *Thom*. sayes.
> Come, *Founder*, let us trade in Ale, and nutmegges.³²

The previous generation was rich in the mines. The younger generation can only imagine what it might have been like. On the other hand, there is something 'new', a 'new staple' where the son and his barber companion will 'trade' in 'Ale' and 'nutmegges'. To this office the Canter is invited, to glimpse a new world of plenty unlike anything his own generation could imagine. On the other hand, the image of the Usurer and uncle, unlike the Canter or 'myne-man', is one of deprivation at the hands of a miserly force. This earlier period manifests the prevalence of the melancholic figure of the miser, which finds its almost tragic culmination in the figure of Volpone. The period of the 'mynes' brings into eminence the availability of plentiful material thanks to the treasury of lingoes and cants. It is the period of the greatest plays. I would suggest that the 'myne-man' and the 'miser' offer a symbolic characterization of two creative veins, each of which, inseparable though they are, dominates a period of the poet's career. These two veins are personified in the figure of a father usurer and a father canter. Canter is the one who thrives off ready-made languages and prefabricated material. He fits the image of the writing force dominating *The Alchemist* and *Bartholomew Fair*, the Jonsonian golden age of the rich and inexhaustible mines of language lying in the womb of the earth. The figure of the usurer, the elder Peni-boy, may be seen as a reinvention, through a number of allusions, of the miserly father of the early plays: Jaques, of *The Case is Altered*,

---

³¹ Ben Jonson, *The Alchemist*, Herford and Simpson, vol. V, p. 314 (II.i.2–4).
³² Ben Jonson, *The Staple of Newes*, Herford and Simpson, vol. VI, p. 292 (I.iii.55–62).

Sordido of *Every Man Out*, Volpone and Morose of *Epicoene*. The links with *Volpone* are particularly strong : Peni-boy, the Usurer and Volpone both keep their *pecunia* in a dark place, safe from others' sight; they are both wrapped in 'furs' and live in a kind of squalor of self-deprivation.[33] Volpone is entertained by his bastard troupe of misbegotten children, Peni-boy Senior plays with his two dogs, Blocke and Lollard, as if they were his children. This miserly uncle is also beset by a group of jeerers, who torment him as Morose was tormented by Truewit and his friends on his wedding-night. Peni-boy, the Uncle and Usurer, may also be seen as a version of Sordido, who, before his miraculous transformation, is also beset by jeerers who revile him for his penny-pinching ways. The transformation scene of Peni-boy, the Usurer, at the end of *Staple* may be compared with the transformation of Sordido in *Every Man Out of His Humour*.[34] The *Staple of Newes* attempts to reconcile three creative periods and types, the two father figures, Peni-boy Canter, Peni-boy Usurer, and the son, Peni-boy Junior. I believe that the split of the father figure into two polarities, one positive and one negative permits this symbolic reconciliation. Thus, the plot offers a family of two generations of men all of the same name who vie for the possession of a strange currency, the bland Pecunia, a very insubstantial woman who acts as a mere substitutive symbol for the desired and invidious creative power to produce and increase.[35]

A closer look at the plot will show how this (self-literary) reconciliation is accomplished. The piece of 'News' around which the play turns, is the news of the death of the father. This piece of information is passed on to the heir by the father himself, disguised as a beggar. It is for this reason that the 'heir' dubs the beggar 'Founder' because: 'He brought me the first newes of my fathers death, / I thanke him, and ever since, I

---

[33] 'And there hee sits like an old *worme of the peace*, / Wrap'd up in furres, at a square table, screwing, / Examining, and committing the poor curres, / To two old cases of close stooles, as prisons; / The one of which, he calls his *Lollard's* tower, / Th' other his *Blocke*-house, 'cause his two dogs names / Are *Blocke*, and *Lollard*.' Ben Jonson, *The Staple of Newes*, Herford and Simpson, vol. VI, pp. 373–4 (v.iii.37–43).

[34] In *Every Man Out of His Humour*, Sordido claims that he is 'by wonder chang'd' and one of the Rustics states (in one of many references to John Foxe's *Book of Martyrs*), that he will 'get our clarke put his *conversion* in the Acts, and Monuments' (my emphasis). Herford and Simpson, vol. III, p. 520 (III.viii.55; 61–2); In *The Staple of Newes*, Peni-boy Senior (the Uncle and Usurer), thanks his brother for having 'altered me' after having been 'sent from the dead'. Herford and Simpson, vol. VI, p. 380 (v.vi.32–3).

[35] Newman describes her as 'a pseudo-centre; she facilitates homosocial relations between men, as do her household, but they play no active part in the news or the allegory'. Newman, 'Engendering the News', p. 66.

call him *Founder*.'³⁶ This piece of news in turn gives the heir the right to spend money without his father's vigilant eye upon him. Peni-boy Junior is invested with the marks of his coming of age at the very beginning of the play. These marks consist of a new set of garments symbolizing his coming into his inheritance.

Garment imagery appears prominently in Jonson as a symbol for the transmission between father and son. One of the most symbolically significant transfers of clothing occurs when Face in *The Alchemist* decides that Drugger must acquire a Spanish suit and decides that 'HIERONYMO's old cloake, ruffe, and hat will serve'.³⁷ The symbolic importance of Kyd's *Spanish Tragedy* for Jonson cannot be underestimated. Jonson referred to Kyd's play as a kind of byword for that which was old-fashioned in early modern drama. In his Induction to *Bartholomew Fair*, he identifies as fairly staid those in the audience who 'sweare, *Jeronimo*, or *Andronicus* are the best playes, yet, [he] shall pass unexcepted at, heere, as a man whose Judgment shewes it is constant, and hath stood still, these five and twenty, or thirty yeeres'.³⁸ In this remark concerning both Kyd and Shakespeare lies an uneasiness concerning the continuing success of the fathers' plays. The phenomenal success of *The Spanish Tragedy* is underlined even more when one considers that Jonson was commissioned to renovate this very popular drama by writing additions to the play. Moreover, *The Spanish Tragedy* is a sort of 'fathering' play itself. Other playwrights, such as Shakespeare in *Hamlet*, drew upon it for their own work and, as we have already seen, the 'blacke boxe' of the *Staple* and *Bartholomew Fair*, may have its origins in *The Spanish Tragedy*. References to Kyd's tragedy in *The Alchemist* highlight Jonson's own renewal of the drama, for Face's original name, Jeremy, may well be an Anglicization of Hieronimo.³⁹ The cloak of Hieronimo, of Kyd's *Spanish Tragedy*, is (eventually) acquired by Face himself, in the hopes that it will 'serve' him in his attempts to possess the woman meant for Subtle. In putting on the mantle of Hieronimo, Face will eventually capture the widow. Ann Rosalind Jones and Peter Stallybrass have noted the extent to which this particular costume is replete with significance:

---

³⁶ Ben Jonson, *The Staple of Newes*, Herford and Simpson, vol. VI, pp. 290–1 (1.iii.19–20).
³⁷ Ben Jonson, *The Alchemist*, Herford and Simpson, vol. V, p. 385 (IV.vii.71).
³⁸ Ben Jonson, *Bartholomew Fair*, Herford and Simpson, vol. VI, p. 16 (lines 106–9).
³⁹ More striking even is the fact that Jonson's one major role as a young actor was the part of Hieronimo, the mad father: Jonson may be said to have literally donned the mantle of the father, the cloak of Hieronimo, at a very early stage in his dramatic career.

The costume here hovers between a fetishized identity from the past (the specific role of Hieronimo) and its new possibilities once it has been appropriated, that is, its generalized nature as a disguise and as a sign of 'Spanishness'.[40]

Yet, the quality of this cloak as fetishized object is only fully comprehensible when we consider the meta-theatrical nature of the exchange between Drugger and Face:

FACE. Thou must borrow, a *Spanish* suit. Hast thou no credit with the players?
DRUGGER. Yes, sir; did you never see me play the foole?[41]

If 'foole' is indeed, as some scholars have noted, a reference not only to the ridiculous character of Drugger in *The Alchemist*, but also to the actor Robert Armin, who played Drugger and who always played the jester or fool for the King's Men, then the cloak truly does become even more than its signification as a 'sign of "Spanishness"'. The mantle signifies a transfer from theatrical generation to generation, both in terms of the plot of the play, as well as in the milieu of the theatre itself, where the costume for Kyd's Hieronimo is recycled, recirculated and, perhaps, even 'robbed' like other literary citations for use in the present play.[42] Under the mantle of Hieronimo, Face will acquire the father's literary power, and it is through the return of the mantle, the fragmentary citation, that the father (Lovewit) will acquire the means of his own alchemical rejuvenation, although this rejuvenation, significantly enough, is not effected by his becoming a father or parent. The importance and significance of the widow in Jonson's plot needs to be considered, it seems, in terms of a certain narrative desire for renewal through the acquisition of the accoutrements and the talismanic objects of the older text.[43]

The image, then, of the young heir throwing off his gown and putting on a 'rich' suit made specially for him by his tailor at the very beginning of the first, post-1616 Folio play, *The Staple of Newes*, may be seen in the same light as the acquisition of Hieronimo's mantle by Face. In *The Alchemist*, this transfer enables Face to inherit from Kyd's play; in *The Staple*, we can see the

---

[40] Jones and Stallybrass, *Renaissance Clothing*, p. 195. Jones and Stallybrass refer to the 'materiality of memory' in their discussion of clothing in the theatre (p. 13), what Peter Holland refers to as 'performance memory'. See Peter Holland (ed.), *Shakespeare, Memory and Performance* (Cambridge: Cambridge University Press, 2006). See also Will Fisher, *Materializing Gender in Early Modern English Literature and Culture* (Cambridge: Cambridge University Press, 2006).
[41] Ben Jonson, *The Alchemist*, Herford and Simpson, vol. v, p. 384–5 (IV.vii.67–9).
[42] For the play on 'robe' and rob' see Jones and Stallybrass, *Renaissance Clothing*, p. 231.
[43] For a discussion of Hieronimo's cloak within the context of the rivalry between father and son, see my 'Jonson and the Alchemical Economy of Desire: Creation, Defacement and Castration in *The Alchemist*', *Cahiers Élisabéthains* 62 (October 2002), 47–64.

rich suit of the heir as a Jonsonian shorthand for an authorial desire for the 'death' of the father, namely the monumentalized author of the Folio.

In *Every Man Out of His Humour*, Fungoso, the son of Sordido, the utterly miserly father, is a student, who: 'followes the fashion a farre off, like a spie. He makes it the whole bent of his endevours, to wring sufficient meanes from his wretched father, to put him in the Courtiers cut.'[44] The disease of the son is 'nothing but the *fluxe* of apparell', a humour to change one costume for another.[45] This sartorial imagery and interest in clothing, disguise, the tailor and the cloak condenses in itself an aspect of great importance in the Jonsonian imaginary system. For the change of clothing, as shown most clearly in the very first speech of *The Staple of Newes*, enacts and symbolizes the actual transfer, from the father to the son, of his posterity and inheritance:

> …The houre is come
> So long expected! There, there, drop my wardship,
>   [*He throws off his gowne.*]
> My pupill age and vassalage together.[46]

The opening scene of *The Staple of Newes* presents the image of an heir throwing off a gown, and with it his 'pupill age'. Having a new set of clothes tailored for him is highly symbolic of the acquisition, not only of his inheritance, but of a whole new identity represented by his clothing. The hyperbolic reaction of the young Peni-boy to the tailor being late is a reflection of his anger and impatience to be free of the yoke of his father. Peni-boy Junior needs his Tailor to make him a man:

> Not come? Not yet? – [*He goes to the doore, and lookes.*] Taylor, thou
>   art a vermine,
> Worse than the same thou prosecut'st, and prick'st
> In subtill seame – (Go too, I say no more –)
> Thus to retard my longings: on the day
> I doe write man.[47]

Strangely, Peni-boy's 'Not come? Not yet?' echoes the frustrated attempts of the Dame and her hags in *The Masque of Queenes* to give birth to their 'magick feature'.[48] Yet, as becomes evident at the climatic moment at the end of Act IV, when his believed-to-be-dead father reveals himself to his

---

[44] Ben Jonson, *Every Man Out of His Humour*, Herford and Simpson, vol. III, p. 425 (lines 72–4).
[45] *Ibid.*, p. 560 (IV.viii.128)
[46] Ben Jonson, *The Staple of Newes*, Herford and Simpson, vol. VI, p. 284 (I.i.14–16).
[47] *Ibid.*, p. 285 (I.i.23–7).
[48] Ben Jonson, *The Masque of Queenes*, Herford and Simpson, vol. VII, p. 298 (line 296).

son, Peni-boy Junior is only, like Face of *The Alchemist*: 'All that the taylor has made'.[49] The father has followed the son in a ragged cloak, before eventually throwing off the 'patch'd' disguise and revealing himself to the son, taking away Pecunia (in other words, his inheritance), accomplishing precisely what Subtle threatens to do to Face, 'marre / All that the taylor has made'.[50] The son and the father exchange places in the ethical and monetary economy of the play: the cloak possesses a kind of hidden virtue, for in his newfound, lowly estate, the heir rises to a moral position above that of the father, who, in the end becomes reconciled to him: 'Put off your ragges, and be your selfe againe.'[51] Clothing, then, in Jonson's system, becomes a signifier not only for a change of rank, or a change of position in life – which clothing reflected in English society at this time to a very specific degree, since sumptuary laws dictated one's ability to wear clothing of a certain type in the streets – but more specifically the wish to obtain land, goods and a posterity from the father.

Interestingly, just after Peni-boy Junior acquires his new set of clothes, it appears, later in the first Act, that the apparel indeed still has to be paid for. There is a debt between the young man and his outfitters who, as the providers of the metonyms of his new body, become avatars of the father. Now, the mediator between the young man and the tailor and haberdasher to whom he owes money, is Peni-Canter in the disguise of the Founder. He is the one who actually gives the heir the money to settle the debt, ruefully observing that ''tis nobly done, to cherish Shop-keepers/ And pay their Bills, without examining, thus'.[52] The subsequent discovery that the Founder is the boy's real father may be seen as representing the impossibility of paying one's debt to the dead father. Here the father is diluted into a mixture of beggar and rich man, of stranger and parent, a combination which fuels an attenuated phantasmagoria of rebirth. The Founder is a fairly positive figure. He is associated with the mines of a golden age, not with the miser figured by the Uncle. The staple, which emblematizes the son's machinery of easy creation, 'dissolves' when the beggar reveals himself to be the father and disinherits him. Thom brings the boy the news:

> Our *Staple* is all to pieces, quite dissolved…
> Shiver'd, as in an earth-quake! heard you not

---

[49] Ben Jonson, *The Alchemist*, Herford and Simpson, vol. v, p. 295 (1.i.10).
[50] Ibid., p. 295 (1.i.9–10).
[51] Ben Jonson, *The Staple of Newes*, Herford and Simpson, vol. vi, p. 373 (v.iii.22).
[52] Ibid., p. 291 (1.iii.44–5).

> The crack and ruines? We are all blowne up!
> ...
> I, and my fellow melted into butter,
> And spoyl'd our Inke, and so the *Office* vanish'd.
> The last *hum* that it made, was, that your Father,
> And *Picklocke* are fall'n out, the *man o' Law*.[53]

The sudden apparition of the father plunges the young heir into a culpable gloom and he dissolves into tears at the same time as the so far well-oiled machinery of the news-generating staple dissolves. The absolute melancholy of the 'son', and the dissolution of the wonderful language-creating machine offers a representation of the process of Jonsonian literary creation *interrupted* by the apparition of the envious and critical eye of the more powerful father. The father, Peni-boy Canter, steals Pecunia away from the boy, an allegory of the son's loss of his inheritance and literary virility and creativity.

At the start of Act V, the stage directions, of which there are many in the Folio margins of this play, tell the reader that Peni-boy Junior 'comes out in the patchd cloak his father left him' intending to write a 'penitent Epistel' to his father.[54] The lawyer, Picklocke, informs the 'velvet-*heyre*' that there exists a deed which would prevent him from being defrauded of his inheritance, a deed signed in front of Picklocke by Peni-boy Canter.[55] Picklocke vows that he can be trusted, yet it turns out that he plans to double-cross both father and son; the boy, however, manages to intercept the deed and have it brought into his own hands instead of Picklocke's. With the writing in hand, the father congratulates the son on his good 'plotting' and agrees to a partial reconciliation. Full reconciliation between all the images only occurs when their correlative characterizations visit Peni-boy elder in his musty house and manage to secure Pecunia by promising him that he can keep Pecunia's less liquid parts: Mortgage, Wax, Statute and Band. In this scene, Peni-boy Canter acts as a go-between and an intercessor between the young inheritor and the elder Peni-boy. He lies between the youthful creator and the miser father, who would keep the creative power to himself. Peni-boy Canter occupies a space between the generations, and between generosity and envy: only when the heir has proven his ability to obtain the 'writing' does the envious gaze disappear and the reconciliation between the youngest generation and the oldest one begins to become possible.

---

[53] *Ibid.*, p. 366 (v.i.39–52).
[54] *Ibid.*, p. 365; p. 368 (v.i.95). [55] *Ibid.*, p. 366 (v.i.60–1).

The playwright's projection of the critical eye upon two versions of his own previous writing selves, results in an importation, never seen to such an extent before in Jonson's works, of the writer's *own* work to fill the gaps of the new work. In *The Staple of Newes*, one is confronted with fragments and pieces from the 1616 monument which in turn serve as the *new* authorities with which to appease the envious gaze of the future spectator and reader. A natural continuation of the work of building monument, auto-reference and auto-citation effectively transform the former work into the equivalent of a living classic. The irony is that this further work of monumentalization takes place first on the theatrical stage where the cloak of 'Hieronimo' is donned once again.

EPILOGUE: FAME IN THE AGE OF PRINT

The Staple of Newes was entered on the Stationers' Register on 14 April 1626. In the printed version in the 1631 Folio, Jonson inserts a short note addressed, 'To the Reader', just after 'the second Intermeane after the second *Act*' and just before the opening of Act III, to prepare them for what they are about to read:

To the Readers
In this following *Act*, the *Office* is open'd, and shew'n to the *Prodigall*, and his *Princesse Pecunia*, wherein the *allegory*, and purpose of the *Author* hath hitherto beene wholly mistaken, and so sinister an interpretation beene made, as if the soules of most of the *Spectators* had liv'd in the eyes and eares of these ridiculous Gossips that tattle between the *Acts*. But hee prayes you thus to mend it. To consider the *Newes* here vented, to be none of his *Newes*, or an reasonable mans; but the *Newes* like the times *Newes*, (a weekly cheat to draw mony) and could not be fitter reprehended, then in raising this ridiculous *Office* of the *Staple*, wherin the age may see her owne folly, or hunger and thirst after publish'd pamphlets of *Newes*.[56]

This is the first time Jonson as 'Author' addresses 'Readers' directly in the middle of a play text, rather than in the preliminaries or in an epilogue like the 'Dialogue' he attached to *Poetaster*. This type of interruption by the author can be found, rather, in the printed masque, where the writer comments retrospectively on the performance *explicitly for a reader*. In the *Staple*, Jonson makes use, yet again, of the 'diffe*r*ance' between performance and print to intervene on behalf of his own posterity hoping, as he wrote in a note to the 'Reader' in *Poetaster* in 1601 that '[P]osteritie may

[56] *Ibid.*, p. 325 (lines 1–13).

make a difference'.⁵⁷ In the *Staple*, the 'Author' seems to enlarge artificially the gap between performance and reading by castigating the spectators in their appreciation of the play, casting the reader into the role of an ally. 'Most' of the spectators were 'wholly mistaken' in their interpretation of the play, and the 'Author' compares their interpretive skills to those of the *ridiculous* Gossips who 'tattle between the Acts'.⁵⁸ The writer objectifies the threat to his meaning in an historical, theatre-going body. It is not the 'implied reader' or 'implied spectator' who may or may not raise an 'objection' or a 'suspicion' against the writer. Here, the writer locates envious *misprision* specifically in the spectators of the play during a performance. The writer then turns toward the reader to *repair* bad spectatorial interpretation, to 'mend' interpretation, and thereby, sew up the torn text.

Jonson's direct plea to the 'Reader' to 'mend' the defaced text can be seen as a new means of building sanctuary. While the author has always *implicitly* turned to the reader in the hope that he or she will intervene on his behalf, never has the writer so explicitly invested himself in an alliance of trust with the reader. This moment in *The Staple of Newes* may be said to mark a turn in Jonson's work in his future investment in the reader. This investment is accompanied by a clear demonization of the spectator. The title page of the *The New Inn*, printed in octavo in 1631 may be read as an aesthetic manifesto on the part of the 'late' writer:

The New Inne, Or, *The light Heart*. A COMOEDY. As it was never acted, but most negligently play'd, by some, the Kings Servants. And more squeamishly beheld, and censured by others, the Kings Subjects. 1629. Now, at last, set at liberty to the Readers, his Majesties' Servants, and Subjects, to be judg'd. 1631. By the Author, B. Jonson.⁵⁹

This manifesto does not represent a break from Jonson's images either of the spectator or the actor. He has already 'tax'd' them both in *Bartholomew Fair* and *Poetaster*, respectively.⁶⁰ Nevertheless, a new authorial investment in the 'reader' is clearly seen here in the gap between performance as captivity and print as 'liberty'. The phrase 'set at liberty to the Readers' implies a conscious choice of the reader as an ally and print as a source of sanctuary. He flatters the reader's judgement by contrasting him to the spectator

---

⁵⁷ Ben Jonson, 'To the Reader', *Poetaster*, Herford and Simpson, vol. IV, p. 317 (line 7).
⁵⁸ The word 'ridiculous' is also the word Horace uses to describe the calumniator, Lupus, in *Poetaster*, Herford and Simpson, vol. IV, p. 299 (v.iii.77).
⁵⁹ From the title-page to *The New Inn*, Herford and Simpson, vol. VI, p. 395.
⁶⁰ Ben Jonson, 'Induction', *Bartholomew Fair*, Herford and Simpson, vol. VI, pp. 15–17; *Poetaster*, Herford and Simpson, vol. IV, p. 321.

and explicitly trusting in his power to mend. He holds up the image of the 'ridiculous Gossips' to encourage the Reader to read differently. In 'The Dedication, to the Reader' of *The New Inn*, Jonson goes a step further in his flattery of his reader: 'If thou bee such, I make thee my Patron, and dedicate the Piece to thee.'[61] Whereas before Jonson described himself as craving 'leave to stand' in his dedicatee's 'light' or described a patron, such as Sir Francis Stuart, to whom he dedicates *Epicoene*, as possessing 'the authority of a Judge', he has never before described his reader as his *patron*.[62] Again, he uses this dedication to set the reader apart and elevate him by representing the spectators as 'fastidious impertinents, who…never made piece of their prospect the right way' and who rose 'between the Actes, in oblique lines'.[63] The spectators are described in terms of their visual ability: they cannot pull the lines of perspective together in such a way as to make a whole of the 'piece'. Like the Gossips 'tattling between the *Acts*', the spectators file in 'oblique lines' between the Acts. Here we see Jonson locating that conflation of the envious eye and the calumnious tongue in the spectator. In his new battle with the envying and gossiping public of the stage, the 'Author' seeks an alliance with 'Readers' who in his dedication replace traditional aristocratic patrons. The idea that the play is now 'set at liberty to the Readers' invites the reader to feel flattered, complacent and perhaps, as a result, generously inclined toward the author in comparison to the evil spectators. Here we are witnesses, perhaps, to Jonson's fresh investment in print and renewed hope in a reader who could offer the writer the posterity he desired. Yet, I would suggest that we should not be too quick to perceive Jonson letting down his guard against readers in these lines; instead, we may well be witnesses to the author brandishing the gorgon of spectatorship as a final talisman against the envious gaze of his reader. The peculiarly terrible image of the spectator who moves obliquely through the theatre is ritualistically turned against the reader who may well make as little effort to overcome his or her *own* natural inclinations, making it impossible to look the right way rather than awry.'

---

[61] Ben Jonson, *The New Inn*, Herford and Simpson, vol. VI, p. 397 (lines 1–2).
[62] Ben Jonson, Dedication to 'The Most Noble William, Earle of Pembroke', *Catiline*, Herford and Simpson, vol. V, p. 431; *Epicoene*, Herford and Simpson, vol. V, p. 161 (line 10).
[63] Ben Jonson, *The New Inn*, Herford and Simpson, vol. VI, p. 397 (lines 5–6; 12).

Select bibliography

Adelman, Janet, *Suffocating Mothers: Fantasies of Maternal Origin in Shakespeare's Plays, 'Hamlet' to 'The Tempest'* (New York: Routledge, 1992).
Agnew, Jean-Christophe, *Worlds Apart: The Market and the Theater in Anglo-American Thought, 1550–1750* (Cambridge: Cambridge University Press, 1986).
Alciati, Andrea, *A Book of Emblems, The* Emblematum Liber *in Latin and English*, trans. and ed. John F. Moffitt (London: McFarland & Company, 2004).
Anon., *Wit's Recreation* [1640].
Aristotle, *The 'Art' of Rhetoric*, trans. John Henry Freese (London: William Heinemann, 1926).
  The Nicomachean Ethics, trans. H. Rackham (London: William Heinemann, 1926).
Aubrey, John, *Miscellanies Upon the Following Subjects* (London, 1696).
Auray, Christophe, *Magie et sorcellerie dans les fermes bretonnes* (Rennes: Editions Ouest-France, 2006).
Bacon, Sir Francis, *The Essayes or Counsels, Civill and Morall* (London, 1629).
  Sylva Sylvarum: Or, A Naturall History (London, 1651).
  The Two Bookes of Francis Bacon, Of the Proficience and Advancement of Learning (London, 1605).
Baltrusaitis, Jurgis, *Aberrations: essai sur la légende des formes* (Paris: Flammarion, 1995).
Bar, Virginie, *La Peinture allégorique au Grand Siècle* (Dijon: Editions Faton, 2003).
Barbour, Richmond, '"When I Acted Young Antinous": Boy Actors and the Erotics of Jonsonian Theater', *PMLA* 110 (1995), 1006–22.
Barish, Jonas A., *The Anti-theatrical Prejudice* (Berkeley: University of California Press, 1981).
  Ben Jonson and the Language of Prose Comedy (Cambridge: Harvard University Press, 1960).
  'Feasting and Judging in Jonsonian Comedy', *Renaissance Drama* 5 (1972), 3–35.
Barish, Jonas A. (ed.), *Ben Jonson: A Collection of Critical Essays* (Englewood Cliffs: Prentice Hall, 1963).

Barroll, Leeds, *Anna of Denmark, Queen of England: A Cultural Biography* (Philadelphia: University of Philadelphia Press, 2001).
Barton, Anne, *Ben Jonson: Dramatist* (Cambridge: Cambridge University Press, 1984).
  Essays, Mainly Shakespearean (Cambridge: Cambridge University Press, 1983).
  'Harking Back to Elizabeth: Ben Jonson and Caroline Nostalgia', *ELH* 48 (1981), 706–31.
  'The New Inn and the Problem of Jonson's Late Style', *ELR* 9 (1979), 395–418.
Baskervill, Charles Read, *English Elements in Jonson's Early Comedy* (New York: Gordian Press, Inc., 1967).
Bateman, Stephen, *A Christall Glasse of Christian Reformation* (London, 1569).
Beaumont, Francis and John Fletcher, *Comedies and Tragedies* (London, 1647).
Bednarz, James P., *Shakespeare and the Poets' War* (New York: Columbia University Press, 2001).
Bernand, André, *Sorciers grecs* (Paris: Fayard, 1991).
Berry, Philippa, *Of Chastity and Power: Elizabethan Literature and the Unmarried Queen* (London: Routledge, 1989).
Bevington, David, 'Review Article: Varieties of Historicism: "Beyond the Infinite and Boundless Reach"', *Modern Philology* 81 (August 1995), 73–88.
Blagrave, Jonathan, *The Nature and Mischief of Envy* (London, 1693).
Bland, Mark, 'William Stansby and the Production of *The Workes of Beniamin Jonson*, 1615–16', *The Library*, Sixth Series, 20 (March 1998), 1–33.
Blissett, William, 'Roman Ben Jonson' in Brady and Herendeen (eds.), *Ben Jonson's 1616 Folio*, pp. 90–110.
Bloom, Harold, *The Anxiety of Influence: A Theory of Poetry* (Oxford: Oxford University Press, 1973).
Bloom, Harold (ed.), *Modern Critical Interpretations: Ben Jonson* (New York: Chelsea House Publishers, 1988).
Bloomfield, Morton W., *The Seven Deadly Sins: An Introduction to the History of a Religious Concept, with Special Reference to Medieval English Literature* (Michigan: Michigan State University Press, 1967 [1952]).
Boaistuau, Pierre, *Le Théâtre du monde* [1558], ed. Michel Simonin (Genève: Droz, 1981).
Boehrer, Bruce Thomas, *The Fury of Men's Gullets: Ben Jonson and the Digestive Canal* (Philadelphia: University of Pennsylvania, 1997).
  'Jonson's *Catiline* and Anti-Sallustian Trends in Renaissance Humanist Historiography', *Studies in Philology*, 94 (Winter 1997), 85–102.
  'The Poet of Labor: Authorship and Property in the Work of Ben Jonson', *Philological Quarterly* 72 (1993), 289–312.
Boissard, Jean-Jacques, *Emblematum Liber* (Frankfurt: Theodore de Bry, 1593).
Bond, Ronald B., 'Supplantation in the Elizabethan Court: the Theme of Spenser's February Eclogue', *Spenser Studies* 2 (1981), 55–65.
  'Vying with Vision: An Aspect of Envy in *The Faerie Queene*', *Renaissance and Reformation*, n.s. 8 (1984), 30–8.

Bradbrook, M.C. 'Social Change and the Evolution of Ben Jonson's Court Masques', *Ben Jonson: Studies in the Literary Imagination* 6 (April 1973), 101–38.
Braden, Gordon and William Kerrigan, *The Idea of the Renaissance* (Baltimore: The Johns Hopkins University Press, 1989).
Brady, Jennifer, "Noe fault, but Life': Jonson's Folio as Monument and Barrier' in Brady and Herendeen (eds.), *Ben Jonson's 1616 Folio*, pp. 192–216.
  'Progenitors and Other Sons in Ben Jonson's *Discoveries*' in James Hirsh (ed.), *New Perspectives on Ben Jonson* (London: Associated University Press, 1997), pp. 16–34.
Brady, Jennifer and W.H. Herendeen (eds.), *Ben Jonson's 1616 Folio* (Newark: University of Delaware Press, 1991).
Brooks, Douglas A., *From Playhouse to Printing House: Drama and Authorship in Early Modern England* (Cambridge: Cambridge University Press, 2000).
Brown, Peter, 'Sorcery, Demons, and the Rise of Christianity from Late Antiquity into the Middle Ages' in Mary Douglas (ed.), *Witchcraft, Confessions, and Accusations* (London: Tavistock, 1970).
Burckhardt, Jacob, *The Civilisation of the Renaissance in Italy*, trans. S. G. C. Middlemore, 2 vols. (New York: Harper and Row, 1959).
Burt, Richard, *Licensed by Authority: Ben Jonson and the Discourses of Censorship* (Ithaca: Cornell University Press, 1993).
Burton, Robert, *The Anatomy of Melancholy* (Oxford, 1621).
Butler, Martin, 'Ben Jonson and the Limits of Courtly Panegyric' in Kevin Sharpe and Peter Lake (eds.), *Culture and Politics in Early Stuart England* (Basingstoke: Macmillan, 1994), pp. 91–115.
  'Late Jonson' in Gordon McMullan and Jonathan Hope (eds.), *The Politics of Tragicomedy: Shakespeare and After* (London: Routledge, 1992), pp. 168–88.
Butler, Martin and David Lindley, 'Restoring Astraea: Jonson's Masque for the Fall of Somerset', *ELH* 61 (1994), 807–27.
Butler, Martin (ed.), *Re-presenting Ben Jonson: Text, History, Performance* (New York: Macmillan Press, 1999).
Byrne, Muriel St Clare (ed.), *Lisle Letters*, 6 vols. (London, 1983 [Chicago, 1981]).
Caillois, Roger, *Méduse et Cie* (Paris: Gallimard, 1960).
Cain, Tom, '"Satyres, That Girde and Fart at the Time": Poetaster and the Essex Rebellion' in Sanders *et al.* (eds.), *Refashioning Ben Jonson*, pp. 48–70.
Cain, William E., 'The Place of the Poet in Jonson's "To Penshurst" and "To My Muse"', *Criticism* 21 (1979), 34–48.
Cairns, D.L., 'The Politics of Envy: Envy and Equality in Ancient Greece' in Konstan and Rutter (eds.), *Envy, Spite and Jealousy*, pp. 235–52.
Callisen, S.A., 'The Evil Eye in Italian Art', *The Art Bulletin* 19 (September 1937), 450–62.
Campbell, John Gregorson, *Witchcraft and Second Sight in the Highlands and Islands of Scotland: Tales and Traditions Collected Entirely from Oral Sources* (Glasgow: James MacLehose and Sons, 1902).

Campbell, Lily B., *Shakespeare's Tragic Heroines: Slaves of Passion* (Magnolia, MA: Peter Smith, 1960).
Campbell, Thomas, *Specimens of the English Poets*, 7 vols. (London: John Murray, 1819).
Cartari, Vincenzo, *Imagini* (Padua, 1571).
Cartelli, Thomas, 'Bartholomew Fair as Urban Arcadia, Jonson Responds to Shakespeare', *Renaissance Drama*, n.s. 14 (1983), 151–72.
Cast, David, *The Calumny of Apelles: A Study in the Humanist Tradition* (New Haven: Yale University Press, 1981).
Castelain, Maurice, *Ben Jonson, l'homme et l'oeuvre* (Paris: Hachette, 1907).
Cave, Richard Allen, *Ben Jonson* (Basingstoke: Macmillan, 1991).
Chapman, George, *The Georgicks of Hesiod: Translated Elaborately out of the Greek* (London, 1618).
  The Iliads of Homer, Prince of Poets (London, 1611).
  The Shadow of Night: Containing Two Poetical Hymnes (London, 1594).
Chaucer, Geoffrey, *The Riverside Chaucer*, ed. Larry D. Benson (Oxford: Oxford University Press, 1987).
Cheney, Patrick, 'Jonson's The New Inn and Plato's Myth of the Hermaphrodite', *Renaissance Drama* 14 (1983), 173–94.
Chew, Samuel, *The Pilgrimage of Life* (New Haven: Yale University Press, 1962).
Chute, Marchette, *Ben Jonson of Westminster* (New York: E. P. Dutton & Co., 1953).
Clair, Jean, *Méduse: contribution à une anthropologie des arts du visuel* (Paris: Gallimard, 1989).
Claudian, *Shorter Poems*, trans. Maurice Platnaeur, 2 vols. (Cambridge: Harvard University Press, 1963), vol. II.
Corbett, Margery and Ronald Lightbown, *The Comely Frontispiece: The Emblematic Title-Page in England 1550–1660* (London: Routledge and Kegan Paul, 1979).
Cottegnies, Line, 'Modernité du XVIIème siècle: la naissance de l'écrivain en Angleterre', in *Confluences VI: Ecriture(s) et modernité* (Nanterre: Université Paris X–Nanterre, 1993), pp. 57–76.
Cowley, Abraham [attributed to], *The Foure Ages of England* (London, 1648).
Cubeta, Paul M., 'A Jonsonian Ideal: "To Penshurst"', *Philological Quarterly* 42 (1963), 14–24.
Cunningham, Dolora, 'The Jonsonian Masque as a Literary Form', in Barish (ed.), *Ben Jonson: A Collection of Critical Essays*.
Dällenbach, Lucien, *The Mirror in the Text*, trans. Jeremy Whiteley and Emma Hughes (Cambridge: Polity Press, 1989).
  Le Récit spéculaire: Essai sur la mise en abyme (Paris: Editions du Seuil, 1977).
Daniel, Samuel, *A Defence of Ryme* (London, 1603).
  Delia and Rosamond Augmented. Cleopatra (London, 1594).
Davies, John, *Microcosmos* (London, 1603).
Davies, Sir John, *The Poems of Sir John Davies*, ed. Robert Krueger (Oxford: Oxford University Press, 1975).
De Luna, B. N., *Jonson's Romish Plot: A Study of Catiline and its Historical Context* (Oxford: Clarendon Press, 1967).

De Man, Paul, 'Autobiography as De-Facement' in *The Rhetoric of Romanticism* (New York: Columbia University Press, 1984), pp. 61–81.

Dekker, Thomas, *The Magnificent Entertainment* (London, 1603).
The Seven Deadly Sins of London (1606).
Troia-Nova Triumphans. London Triumphing (London, 1612).
The Dramatic Works of Thomas Dekker, ed. Fredson Bowers (Cambridge: Cambridge University Press, 1958).

Derrida, Jacques, *Margins of Philosophy*, trans. Alan Bass (Hemel Hempstead: Harvester Wheatsheaf, 1982 [1972]).
Dissemination trans. Barbara Johnson (London: Continuum, 1981 [1972]).

Desan, Philippe (ed.), *Humanism in Crisis: The Decline of the French Renaissance* (Ann Arbor: University of Michigan Press, 1991), pp. 10–17.

Dickie, Matthew W., 'Invidia', *The Classical Review*, n.s. 49 (1999), 363–4.

Donaldson, Ian, *Jonson's Magic Houses: Essays in Interpretation* (Oxford: Clarendon Press, 1997).
'Looking Sideways: Jonson, Shakespeare, and the Myths of Envy', *Ben Jonson Journal: Literary Contexts in the Age of Elizabeth, James, and Charles*, 8 (2001), 1–22.

Donovan, Kevin, 'Forms of Authority in the Early Texts of *Every Man Out of His Humour*' in Butler (ed.), *Re-presenting Ben Jonson*, pp. 59–75.

Drayton, Michael, *England's Heroicall Epistles. Newly Corrected. With Idea* (London, 1600).

Duncan, Douglas, *Ben Jonson and the Lucianic Tradition* (Cambridge: Cambridge University Press, 1979).

Dundee, Alan, 'Wet and Dry, the Evil Eye: An Essay in Indo-European and Semitic Worldview' in *Interpreting Folklore* (Bloomington: Indiana University Press, 1980), pp. 93–133.

Dunford, Terrance, 'Consumption of the World: Reading, Eating, and Imitation in *Every Man Out of His Humour*', *ELR* 14 (1984), 131–48.

Dutton, Richard, *Ben Jonson: To the First Folio* (Cambridge: Cambridge University Press, 1983).
'The Comedy of Errors and The Calumny of Apelles: An Exercise in Source Study' in Dutton and Howard (eds.), *A Companion to Shakespeare's Works, Volume III, The Comedies*, pp. 307–19.

Dutton, Richard and Jean E. Howard (eds.), *A Companion to Shakespeare's Works, Volume III, the Comedies* (Oxford: Blackwell Publishing, 2003).

Eco, Umberto, *The Limits of Interpretation* (Bloomington: Indiana University Press, 1990).
The Name of the Rose, trans. William Weaver (San Diego: Harcourt Brace Jovanovich, 1983).

Eliot, T. S., *Elizabethan Dramatists* (London: Faber and Faber, 1963 [1934]).

Elworthy, Frederick Thomas, *The Evil Eye: The Origins and Practices of Superstition* (New York: The Julian Press, Inc., 1958).

Elyot, Thomas, *The Dictionary of Sir Thomas Eliot Knight* (London, 1638).

Epstein, Joseph, *Envy: The Seven Deadly Sins* (New York: Oxford University Press and The New York Public Library, 2003).
Evans, Robert C., *Ben Jonson and the Politics of Patronage* (Lewisburg: Bucknell University Press, 1989).
   Habits of Mind: Evidence and Effects of Ben Jonson's Reading (Lewisburg: Bucknell University Press, 1995).
   Jonson, Lipsius and the Politics of Renaissance Stoicism (Wakefield: Longwood Academic, 1992).
Fineman, Joel, 'More About "Medusa's Head"', *Representations* 4 (Fall 1983), 57–63.
   The Subjectivity Effect in the Western Literary Tradition: Essays Toward the Release of Shakespeare's Will (Cambridge: Harvard University Press, 1991).
Finkelstein, Richard, 'Ben Jonson on Spectacle', *Comparative Drama* 21 (Summer 1987), 103–14.
Fischlin, Daniel, 'Political Allegory, Absolutist Ideology, and the "Rainbow Portrait" of Queen Elizabeth I', *Renaissance Quarterly* 50 (Spring 1997), 175–206.
Fish, Stanley, 'Authors-Readers: Jonson's Community of the Same' in Greenblatt (ed.) *Representing the English Renaissance*, pp. 231–64.
Fisher, Will, *Materializing Gender in Early Modern English Literature and Culture* (Cambridge: Cambridge University Press, 2006).
Foley, D. K., 'Resource Allocation and the Public Sector', *Yale Economic Essays* 7 (1967), 45–198.
Forster, Leonard, *The Icy Fire: Five Studies in European Petrarchism* (Cambridge: Cambridge University Press, 1969).
Foster, George M., 'The Anatomy of Envy: A Study in Symbolic Behavior', *Current Anthropology* (April 1972), 165–202.
Foucault, Michel. *The Order of Things: An Archaeology of the Human Sciences* (New York: Random House, 1970).
   'Qu'est-ce qu'un auteur?' in Arnold I. Davidson and Frédéric Gros (eds.), *Philosophie: anthologie* (Paris: Gallimard, 2004), pp. 290–318.
   'What is an Author?' in Josue Harari (ed.), *Textual Strategies: Perspectives in Post-Structuralist Criticism* (Ithaca: Cornell University Press, 1979).
Fowler, Alastair, 'The "Better marks" of Jonson's "To Penshurst"', *The Review of English Studies* 95 (1973), 266–82.
Foxe, John, *Actes and Monuments* (London, 1596).
Freehafer, John, 'Leonard Digges, Ben Johnson [sic], and the Beginning of Shakespeare Idolatry', *Shakespeare Quarterly* 21 (Winter 1970), 63–75.
Freud, Sigmund, *The Standard Edition of the Complete Psycholological Works of Sigmund Freud*, ed. James Strachey, 24 vols. (London: The Hogarth Press, 1955).
Frommand, Johannes Christian, *Tractatus de Fascinatione* (Nuremberg, 1674).
Fumaroli, Marc, *L'École du silence: le sentiment des images au XVIIe siècle* (Paris: Flammarion, 1994).

Garber, Marjorie, 'Macbeth: The Male Medusa', *Shakespeare's Ghost Writers: Literature as Uncanny Causality* (New York: Methuen, 1987), pp. 87–123. Reprinted in Garber and Vickers (eds.), *The Medusa Reader*, pp. 249–57.
'"What's Past Is Prologue": Temporality and Prophecy in Shakespeare's History Plays' in Barbara Kiefer Lewalski (ed.), *Renaissance Genres: Essays on Theory, History and Interpretation* (Cambridge: Harvard University Press, 1986), pp. 301–31.
Garber, Marjorie (ed.), *Witches, Cannibals and Divorce: Estranging the Renaissance* (Baltimore: Johns Hopkins University Press, 1987).
Garber, Marjorie and Nancy J. Vickers (eds.), *The Medusa Reader* (New York: Routledge, 2003).
Gellrich, Jesse M., 'The Art of the Tongue: Illuminating Speech and Writing in Later Medieval Manuscripts' in Colum Hourihane (ed.), *Virtues & Vices: The Personifications in the Index of Christian Art* (Princeton: Department of Art and Archaeology, 2000), pp. 93–119.
Genette, Gérard, *Seuils* (Paris: Éditions du Seuil, 1987).
Gifford, Edward S. Jr, MD, *The Evil Eye: Studies in the Folklore of Vision* (New York: Macmillan, 1958).
Gifford, William, *The Works of Ben Jonson, With Notes Critical and Explanatory and a Biographical Memoir in Nine Volumes*, ed. F. Cunningham (London: Bickers and Son, 1875).
Gilbert, Allan H., *Dante's Conception of Justice* (New York: AMS Press, Inc., 1965).
The Symbolic Persons in the Masques of Ben Jonson (Durham: Duke University Press, 1967).
Gill, R. B., 'The Renaissance Conventions of Envy', *Mediaevalia et Humanistica*, n.s. 9 (1979), 215–30.
Gilman, Ernest B., *The Curious Perspective: Literary and Pictorial Wit in the Seventeenth Century* (New Haven: Yale University Press, 1978).
Iconoclasm and Poetry in the English Reformation: Down Went Dagon (Chicago: University of Chicago Press, 1986).
Girard, René, *A Theater of Envy: William Shakespeare* (New York and Oxford: Oxford University Press, 1991).
Shakespeare: Les Feux de l'envie (Paris: Bernard Grasset, 1990).
Goffen, Rona, *Renaissance Rivals: Michelangelo, Leonardo, Raphael, Titian* (New Haven: Yale University Press, 2002).
Goldberg, Jonathan, *James I and the Politics of Literature: Jonson, Shakespeare, Donne, and Their Contemporaries* (Baltimore: The Johns Hopkins University Press, 1983).
'Speculations: Macbeth and Source' in Jean E. Howard and Marion F. O'Connor (eds.), *Shakespeare Reproduced: The Text in History and Ideology* (New York: Methuen, 1987), pp. 242–64.
Gordon, D. J., *The Renaissance Imagination: Essays and Lectures by D. J. Gordon*, ed. Stephen Orgel (Berkeley: University of California Press, 1975).

Gossett, Suzanne, '"Man-maid, begone!": Women in Masques', *ELR* 18 (Winter 1988), 96–113.
Gott, Samuel, *An Essay of the True Happiness of Man* (London, 1650).
Gower, John, *Confessio Amantis*, ed. Russell A. Peck and trans. Andrew Galloway (Kalamazoo: Medieval Institute Publications, 2003).
  Mirour de l'Omme, trans. William Burton Wilson (East Lansing: Colleagues Press, 1992).
Grafton, Anthony, *The Footnote: A Curious History* (London: Faber and Faber, 1997).
Greenblatt, Stephen, *Renaissance Self-Fashioning: From More to Shakespeare* (Chicago: University of Chicago Press, 1980).
  Shakespearean Negotiations: The Circulation of Social Energy in Renaissance England (Oxford: Clarendon Press, 1988).
Greenblatt, Stephen (ed.), *Representing the English Renaissance* (Berkeley: University of California Press, 1988),
Greene, Thomas, 'Ben Jonson and the Centered Self', *SEL* 10 (1970), 325–48.
  The Light in Troy: Imitation and Discovery in Renaissance Poetry (New Haven: Yale University Press, 1982).
Hackel, Heidi Brayman, *Reading Material in Early Modern England: Print, Gender and Literacy* (Cambridge: Cambridge University Press, 2005).
Hamon, Philippe, *Du descriptif* (Paris: Hachette, 1993).
Hamou, Philippe (ed.), *La Vision perspective (1435–1740): l'art et la science du regard de la Renaissance à l'âge classique* (Paris: Editions Payot & Rivages, 1995).
Harington, John, *Orlando Furioso in English Heroical Verse* (London, 1591).
Harris, M. A., 'The Origin of the Seventeenth-Century Idea of Humours', *MLN* 10 (1895), 44–6.
Harvey, Elizabeth D. and Katharine Eisaman Maus (eds.), *Soliciting Interpretation: Literary Theory and Seventeenth-Century English Poetry* (Chicago: University of Chicago Press, 1990).
Hassoun-Lestienne, Pascale (ed.), *L'Envie et le désir: les faux frères* (Paris: Autrement, 1998).
Hayes, Tom. *The Birth of Popular Culture: Ben Jonson, Maid Marian and Robin Hood* (Pittsburgh: Duquesne University Press, 1992).
Haynes, Jonathan, *The Social Relations of Jonson's Theater* (Cambridge: Cambridge University Press, 1992).
Helgerson, Richard, *Self-Crowned Laureates: Spenser, Jonson, Milton and the Literary System* (Berkeley: University of California Press, 1983).
Hertz, Neil, 'Medusa's Head: Male Hysteria under Political Pressure', *Representations* 4 (1983), 27–50.
Hesiod, *The Shield, Catalogue of Women, Other Fragments*, ed. and trans. Glenn W. Most (Cambridge: Harvard University Press, 2007).
  Theogony, Works and Days, Testimonia, ed. and trans. Glenn W. Most (Cambridge: Harvard University Press, 2006).
Heywood, Thomas, *The Fair Maid of the West* (London, 1631).

Hibbard, G. R., 'The Country House Poem of the Seventeenth Century', *JWCI* 19 (1956), 159–77.
Hirsh, James (ed.), *New Perspectives on Ben Jonson* (London: Associated University Press, 1997).
Holland, Peter (ed.), *Shakespeare, Memory and Performance* (Cambridge: Cambridge University Press, 2006).
Homer, *Iliad*, trans. A. T. Murray and William F. Wyatt (Cambridge: Harvard University Press, 1928).
Horace, *The Odes and Epodes*, trans. C. E. Bennett (Cambridge: Harvard University Press, 1946).
  Satires, Epistles and Ars Poetica, trans. H. Rushton Fairclough (Cambridge: Harvard University Press, 1926).
Huet, Marie-Hélène, *The Monstrous Imagination* (Cambridge: Harvard University Press, 1993).
Jackson, Gabriele Bernhard, *Vision and Judgement in Ben Jonson's Drama* (New Haven: Yale University Press, 1968).
James I, *Daemonologie* (1597).
Jay, Martin, *Downcast Eyes: The Denigration of Vision in Twentieth-Century French Thought* (Berkeley: University of California Press, 1993).
Johnson, A. W., *Ben Jonson: Poetry and Architecture* (Oxford: Clarendon Press, 1994).
Jones, Ann Rosalind and Peter Stallybrass, *Renaissance Clothing and the Materials of Memory* (Cambridge: Cambridge University Press, 2000).
Jones-Davies, Marie-Thérèse, *Ben Jonson* (Paris: Aubier Montaigne, 1980).
  Inigo Jones, Ben Jonson et le masque (Paris: Petit, 1967).
Jonson, Ben, *Ben Jonson*, ed. C. H. Herford and Percy and Evelyn Simpson, 11 vols. (Oxford: The Clarendon Press, 1925–52).
Juvenal, *That Which Seemes Best is Worst, Exprest in a Paraphrasitical Transcript of Juvenal's Tenth Satyr*, trans. W. B. (London, 1617).
Kant, Emmanuel, *The Metaphysics of Morals* in *The Cambridge Edition of the Works of Immanuel Kant: Practical Philosophy*, trans. M. Gregor (New York: Cambridge University Press, 1996).
Kaplan, Lindsay M., *The Culture of Slander in Early Modern England* (Cambridge: Cambridge University Press, 1997).
Karagiannis-Mazeaud, Edith, 'Sur la rime vie/Envie: Jalons pour une histoire de l'Envie et de ses représentations au XVIe siècle: Ronsard, Du Bellay, Jodelle, Peletier du Mans' in Fabrice Wilhelm (ed.), *L'Envie et ses figurations littéraires* (Dijon: Editions Universitaires de Dijon, 2005), pp. 95–118.
Kastan, David Scott, *Shakespeare and the Book* (Cambridge: Cambridge University Press, 2001).
Kastan, David Scott and Peter Stallybrass (eds.), *Staging the Renaissance: Reinterpretations of Elizabethan and Jacobean Drama* (New York: Routledge, 1991).
Kay, W. David, *Ben Jonson: A Literary Life* (Basingstoke: Macmillan, 1995).
  'The Christian Wisdom or Ben Jonson's "On My First Sonne"', *SEL* 11 (1971), 125–36.

Kernan, Alvin, (ed.), *Two Renaissance Mythmakers: Christopher Marlowe and Ben Jonson* (Baltimore: The Johns Hopkins University Press, 1977).
Kerrigan, William, 'Ben Jonson Full of Shame and Scorn', *Ben Jonson: Studies in the Literary Imagination* 6 (April 1973), 199–218.
King, Henry *Poems, Elegies, Paradoxes, and Sonnets, 1657* (London: A Scolar Press Facsimile, 1973).
Klein, Melanie, *Envy and Gratitude: A Study of Unconscious Sources* (London: Tavistock Press, 1957).
Klibansky, Raymond, Erwin Panofsky and Fritz Saxl, *Saturn and Melancholy: Studies in the History of Natural Philosophy, Religion and Art* (London: Nelson, 1964).
Knights, L.C., *Drama and Society in the Age of Jonson* (London: Chatto and Windus, 1937).
Knowles, James, '"To Enlight the Darksome Night, Pale Cinthia doth Arise": Anna of Denmark, Elizabeth I and the Images of Royalty' in McManus (ed.), *Women and Culture at the Courts of the Stuart Queens*, pp. 21–48.
Konstan, David, *The Emotions of the Ancient Greeks: Studies in Aristotle and Classical Literature* (Toronto: University of Toronto Press, 2006).
Konstan, David and N. Keith Rutter (eds.), *Envy, Spite and Jealousy: The Rivalrous Emotions in Ancient Greece* (Edinburgh: Edinburgh University Press, 2003).
La Rochefoucauld, François de, *Maximes, 1678* (Paris: Bordas, 1992).
Lacan, Jacques, 'Of the Gaze', *The Four Fundamental Concepts of Psychoanalysis*, trans. Alan Sheridan (New York: W.W. Norton and Company, 1981).
Laing, R.D., *The Divided Self: An Existential Study in Sanity and Madness* (Harmondsworth: Penguin Books, 1965).
Lambert, Sheila, 'State Control of the Press in Theory and Practice: The Role of the Star Chamber before 1640' in Robin Myers and Michael Harris (eds.), *Censorship and the Control of Print in England and France, 1600–1910* (Winchester: St Paul's Bibliographies, 1992), pp. 1–32.
Lanier, Douglas M., 'The Prison-House of the Canon: Allegorical Form and Posterity in Ben Jonson's *The Staple of Newes*' in J. Leeds Barroll (ed.), *Medieval and Renaissance Drama in England* (New York: AMS Press, Inc, 1985), vol. II, pp. 253–67.
Laquer, Thomas. *Making Sex: Body and Gender from the Greeks to Freud* (Cambridge: Harvard University Press, 1984).
Laroque, François, 'Magic in *Macbeth*', *Cahiers Élisabéthains* 35 (April 1989), 59–84.
   Shakespeare's Festive World: Elizabethan Seasonal Entertainment and the Professional Stage, trans. Janet Lloyd (Cambridge: Cambridge University Press, 1991).
Lee, Jongsook, *Ben Jonson's Poesis: A Literary Dialectic of Ideal History* (Charlottesville: University of Virginia Press, 1983).
Leggatt, Alexander, *Ben Jonson: His Vision and His Art* (London: Methuen, 1981).
Levin, Harry, '*The Staple of Newes*, The Society of Jeerers, and Canters' College', *Philological Quarterly* 44 (1965), 445–53.

Levin, Richard, '"No Laughing Matter": Some New Readings of *The Alchemist*', *Ben Jonson: Studies in the Literary Imagination* 6 (April 1973), 85–99.
Lewalski, Barbara Kiefer, 'Anne of Denmark and the Subversions of Masquing', *Criticism* 3 (1993), 341–55.
  Writing Women in Jacobean England (Cambridge: Harvard University Press, 1993).
Ley, Graham, *A Short Introduction to the Ancient Greek Theater*, rev. edn (Chicago: University of Chicago Press, 2006).
Limberis, Vasiliki, 'The Eyes Infected by Evil: Basil of Caesarea's Homily, "On Envy"', *The Harvard Theological Review* 84 (April 1991), 163–84.
Limon, Jerzy, *The Masque of Stuart Culture* (Newark: University of Delaware Press, 1990).
Lindley, David, 'Embarrassing Ben: The Masques for Frances Howard', *ELR* 16 (1986), 343–59.
Llasera, Margaret, *Représentations scientifiques et images poétiques en Angleterre au XVIIe siècle: à la recherche de l'invisible* (Paris: CNRS Editions, 1999).
Lockwood, Tom, *Ben Jonson in the Romantic Age* (Oxford: Oxford University Press, 2005).
Loewenstein, Joseph, *The Author's Due: Printing and the Prehistory of Copyright* (Chicago: University of Chicago Press, 2002).
  Ben Jonson and Possessive Authorship (Cambridge: Cambridge University Press, 2002).
  'Personal Material: Jonson and Book-burning' in Butler (ed.), *Re-presenting Ben Jonson*, pp. 93–113.
  'Printing and the 'Multitudinous Presse': The Contentious Texts of Jonson's Masques' in Brady and Herendeen (eds.), *Ben Jonson's 1616 Folio*, pp. 168–91.
  Responsive Readings: Versions of Echo in Pastoral, Epic, and the Jonsonian Masque (New Haven: Yale University Press, 1984).
  'The Script in the Marketplace' in Greenblatt (ed.), *Representing the English Renaissance*, pp. 265–78.
Love, Harold, *The Culture and Commerce of Texts: Scribal Publication in Seventeenth-Century England* (Amherst: University of Massachusetts Press, 1993).
Lovejoy, Arthur O. *The Great Chain of Being: A Study of the History of an Idea* (Cambridge: Harvard University Press, 1936).
Loxley, James, *The Complete Critical Guide to Ben Jonson* (London: Routledge, 2002).
Lucan, *Pharsalia (The Civil War)*, trans. J. D. Duff (New York: G. P. Putnam's Sons, 1928).
Lucian, *Lucian* (I), ed. A. M. Harmon (Cambridge: Harvard University Press, 1913).
Lumiansky, R. M. and David Mills (eds.), *The Chester Mystery Cycle* (London and Oxford: Oxford University Press, 1974).
Lykiardopoulos, Amica, 'The Evil Eye: Towards an Exhaustive Study', *Folklore* 92 (1981), 221–30.

Macfarlane, Alan, *Witchcraft in Tudor and Stuart England: A Regional and Comparative Study* (London: Routledge and Kegan Paul, 1970).
Magnusson, A. C. and C. F. McGee (eds.), *The Elizabethan Theatre XIV: Papers given at the International Conference on Elizabethan Theatre held at the University of Waterloo, Ontario in July 1991* (Toronto: P. D. Meany, 1996).
Mainguy, Irène, *Symbolique des outils et glorification du métier* (Paris: Jean-Cyrille Godefroy, 2007).
Manwood, John, *A Treatise of the Laws of the Forest* (London, 1665[1592]).
Marcus, Leah, *The Politics of Mirth: Jonson, Herrick, Milton, Marvell and the Defense of Old Holiday Pastimes* (Chicago: University of Chicago Press, 1986).
Marienstras, Richard, *New Perspectives on the Shakespearean World* [*Le Proche et le Lointain*], trans. Janet Lloyd (Cambridge: Cambridge University Press, 1985).
Marin, Louis, *Détruire la peinture* (Paris: Flammarion, 1997).
Marotti, Arthur F., 'All About Jonson's Poetry', *ELH* 39 (1972), 208–37.
Massing, Jean-Michel, *Du texte à l'image: la calomnie d'Apelle et son iconographie* (Strasbourg: Presses Universitaires de Strasbourg, 1990).
Masten, Jeffrey A., 'Beaumont and/or Fletcher: Collaboration and the Interpretation of Renaissance Drama', *ELH* 59 (1992), 337–56.
Maus, Katharine Eisaman, *Ben Jonson and the Roman Frame of Mind* (Princeton: Princeton University Press, 1984).
  'Facts of the Matter: Satiric and Ideal Economies in the Jonsonian Imagination' in Brady and Herendeen (eds.), *Ben Jonson's 1616 Folio*, pp. 64–89.
  'Fetish and Poem: Ben Jonson's Dilemma' in Woodbridge (ed.), *Money and the Age of Shakespeare*, pp. 251–64.
  Inwardness and Theater in the English Renaissance (Chicago: Chicago University Press, 1995).
McCanles, Michael, *Jonsonian Discriminations: The Humanist Poet and the Praise of True Nobility* (Toronto: University of Toronto Press, 1992).
McClung, William Alexander, *The Country House in English Renaissance Poetry* (Berkeley: University of California Press, 1977).
McDonald, Peter D., 'Implicit Structures and Explicit Interactions: Pierre Bourdieu and the History of the Book', *The Library*, Sixth Series, 19, no. 2 (1997), 105–21.
McKenzie, Donald F., '*The Staple of News* and the Late Plays' in William Blisset et al. (eds.), *A Celebration of Ben Jonson* (Toronto: Toronto University Press, 1973), pp. 83–128.
McManus, Clare, *Women on the Renaissance Stage: Anna of Denmark and Female Masquing in the Stuart Court (1590–1619)* (Manchester and New York: Manchester University Press, 2002).
McManus, Clare (ed.), *Women and Culture at the Courts of the Stuart Queens* (Basingstoke: Palgrave Macmillian, 2003).
McPherson, David, 'Jonson's Library and Marginalia: An Annotated Catalogue', *Studies in Philology, Texts and Studies Series* 71.5 (1974).

Meagher, John, *Method and Meaning in Jonson's Masques* (Notre Dame: University of Notre Dame, 1966).
Meskill, Lynn S., 'Jonson and the Alchemical Economy of Desire: Creation, Defacement and Castration in *The Alchemist*', *Cahiers Élisabéthains* 62 (October 2002), 47–64.
  'Optique et Anamorphose dans *Le Paradis perdu* de John Milton', *Revue de la Société d'Etudes Anglo-Américaines des XVIIe et XVIIIe Siècles* 61 (November 2005), 53–70.
Miles, Rosalind, *Ben Jonson: His Life and Work* (London: Routledge and Kegan Paul, 1986).
Miller, David Lee, 'Writing the Specular Son: Jonson, Freud, Lacan, and the (K)not of Masculinity' in Valeria Finucci and Regina Schwartz (eds.), *Desire in the Renaissance: Psychoanalysis and Literature* (Princeton: Princeton University Press, 1994), pp. 233–60.
Milton, John, *Paradise Lost* [1667], ed. Alastair Fowler (London: Longman, 1968).
Molesworth, C., 'Property and Virtue: The Genre of the Country House Poem in the Seventeenth Century', *Genre* 1 (1968), 141–57.
Montaigne, Michel de, *Essais*, 3 vols., ed. Pierre Michel (Paris: Gallimard, 1965).
Montrose, Louis Adrian, 'Celebration and Insinuation: Sir Philip Sidney and the Motives of Elizabethan Courtship', *Renaissance Drama*, n.s. 8 (1977), 3–35.
More, Thomas, *The Complete Works of St. Thomas More*, Anthony S. G. Edwards *et al.* (eds.) (New Haven: Yale University Press, 1997).
Most, Glenn W., 'Epinician Envies' in Konstan and Rutter (eds.) *Envy, Spite and Jealousy*, pp. 123–42.
Muggli, Mark Z., 'Ben Jonson and the Business of News', *SEL* 32 (1992), 323–40.
Murray, Timothy, *Theatrical Legitimation: Allegories of Genius in Seventeenth-Century England and France* (New York: Oxford University Press, 1987).
Myers, Robin and Michael Harris (eds.), *Censorship and the Control of Print in England and France, 1600–1910* (Winchester: St Paul's Bibliographies, 1992).
Newlyn, Lucy, *Reading, Writing, and Romanticism: The Anxiety of Reception* (Oxford: Oxford University Press, 2000).
Newman, Karen, '"City Talk": Femininity and Commodification in Jonson's *Epicoene*', *ELH* 56 (1989), 503–18.
  'Engendering the News' in Magnusson and McGee (eds.), *The Elizabethan Theatre XIV*, pp. 49–70.
Newton, Richard C., 'Ben/Jonson: The Poet in the Poems' in Kernan (ed.), *Two Renaissance Mythmakers*, pp. 165–95.
  'Jonson and the (Re-) Invention of the Book' in Summers and Pebworth (eds.), *Classic and Cavalier* pp. 31–55.
Nichols, John Gordon, *The Poetry of Ben Jonson* (London: Routledge and Kegan Paul, 1969).
Nohrnberg, James, *The Analogy of The Faerie Queene* (Princeton: Princeton University Press, 1976).
Orgel, Stephen, *The Illusion of Power: Political Theatre in the English Renaissance* (Berkeley: University of California Press, 1975).

'Jonson and the Amazons' in Harvey and Maus (eds.), *Soliciting Interpretation*, pp. 119–39.
The Jonsonian Masque (Cambridge: Harvard University Press, 1965).
Orgel, Stephen and Roy Strong, *Inigo Jones: The Theatre of the Stuart Court*, 2 vols. (Berkeley: University of California Press, 1973).
Ostovich, Helen, ' "So Sudden and Strange a Cure": A Rudimentary Masque in *Every Man Out of His Humour*', *ELR* 22 (1992), 315–32.
' "To Behold the Scene Full": Seeing and Judging in *Every Man Out of His Humour*' in Butler (ed.), *Re-presenting Ben Jonson*, pp. 76–92.
Ovid, *The First Five Bookes of Ovids Metamorphosis*, trans. George Sandys (London, 1621).
The Fyrst Four Bookes of P. Ovidius Nasos worke intitled Metamorphosis, translated out of Latin into English meter by Arthur Golding Gentleman, trans. Arthur Golding (London, 1565).
Parfitt, George. *Ben Jonson: Public Poet and Private Man* (London: Dent, 1976).
Parker, Patricia, *Literary Fat Ladies: Rhetoric, Gender, Property* (London: Methuen, 1987).
Parker, Patricia and Geoffrey Hartman (eds.), *Shakespeare and the Question of Theory* (London: Methuen, 1985),
Parry, Gordon, 'The Politics of the Jacobean Masque' in J. R. Mulryne and M. Shewring (eds.), *Theatre and Government Under the Early Stuarts* (Cambridge: Cambridge University Press, 1993), pp. 87–117.
Paster, Gail Kern, 'Ben Jonson and the Uses of Architecture', *Renaissance Quarterly* 27 (Autumn 1974), 306–20.
Partridge, Edward B., *The Broken Compass: A Study of the Major Comedies of Ben Jonson* (New York: Columbia University Press, 1958).
Peacham, Henry, *The Garden of Eloquence* (London, 1593).
Peacock, John, *The Stage Designs of Inigo Jones: The European Context* (Cambridge: Cambridge University Press, 1995).
Pelletier, P. Gérard, SJ, *Palatium Reginae Eloquentiae* (Paris, 1641).
Peterson, Richard, *Imitation and Praise in the Poems of Ben Jonson* (New Haven: Yale University Press, 1981).
'Virtue Reconciled to Pleasure: Jonson's "A Celebration of Charis" ', *Ben Jonson: Studies in the Literary Imagination* 6 (April 1973), 219–68.
Petrarch, *Lyric Poems: The 'Rime Sparse' and Other Lyrics*, trans. Robert M. Durling (Cambridge: Harvard University Press, 1976).
Phillips, Edward, *The New World of English Words, 1658* (Menston: The Scolar Press Limited, 1969).
Pierce, Thomas, *The Law and Equity of the Gospel, or, The Goodness of our Lord as a Legislator* (London, 1686).
Pigman III, G. W., 'Versions of Imitation in the Renaissance', *Renaissance Quarterly* 33 (1980), 1–32.
Plato, *The Banquet, A Dialogue of Plato concerning Love. The second part*, trans. Floyer Sydenham (London, 1767).

Lysis, Symposium, Gorgias, trans. W. R. M. Lamb (Cambridge: Harvard University Press, 1925).

Plutarch, *The Philosophie Commonlie called, The Morals, Written by the learned Philosopher Plutarch of Chaeronea, Translated out of Greek into English* (London, 1603).

Polizzi, Gilles, 'L'Enfant désallaité: Envie et création dans la fiction humaniste de la première Renaissance' in Wilhelm (ed.), *L'Envie et ses figurations littéraires*, pp. 119–45.

Poole, Joshua, *The English Parnassus, 1657* (Menston: The Scolar Press Limited, 1972).

Pope, Alexander, 'Mr. Pope's Preface' in Edmond Malone (ed.), *Plays and Poems of William Shakespeare in Ten Volumes*, (London, 1790).

Prescott, Anne Lake, 'Jonson's Rabelais' in James Hirsh (ed.), *New Perspectives on Ben Jonson*, pp. 35–54.

Probst, Neil P., 'A Topical Index to Jonson's Discoveries', *The Ben Jonson Journal* 3 (1996), 153–77.

Puttenham, George, *The Arte of English Poesie* (London, 1589).

Ramus, Peter, *A Compendium of the Art of Logick and Rhetorick in the English Tongue* (London, 1651).

Rathmell, J. C. A., 'Jonson, Lord Lisle, and Penshurst', *ELR* 1 (1971), 250–60.

Rawls, John, *A Theory of Justice*, rev. edn (Oxford: Oxford University Press, 1999 [1971]).

Raylor, Timothy, *The Essex House Masque of 1621: Viscount Doncaster and the Jacobean Masque* (Pittsburgh: Duquesne University Press, 2000).

Raymond, Joad, *The Invention of the Newpaper: English Newsbooks 1641–1649* (Oxford: Clarendon Press, 1996).

Pamphlets and Pamphleteering in Early Modern Britain (Cambridge: Cambridge University Press, 2003).

Rebhorn, Wayne A., 'The Crisis of the Aristocracy in Julius Caesar', *Renaissance Quarterly* 43 (1990), 75–111.

Redwine, James D., Jr, 'Beyond Psychology: The Moral Basis of Jonson's Theory of Humour Characterization', *ELH* 28 (1961), 316–34.

Riddell, James A. and Stanley Stewart, *Jonson's Spenser: Evidence and Historical Criticism* (Pittsburgh: Duquesne University Press, 1995).

Riggs, David, *Ben Jonson: A Life* (Harvard: Harvard University Press, 1989).

Ripa, Cesare, *Iconologia* (Padua, 1611).

Robson, Mark, 'Looking with Ears, Hearing with Eyes: Shakespeare and the Ear of the Early Modern', *EMLS* 7.1/ Special Issue 8 (May 2001), 10.1–23 URL.

Rollin, Roger B., 'The Anxiety of Identification: Jonson and the Rival Poets' in Summers and Pebworth (eds.), *Classic and Cavalier*, pp. 139–56.

Ronan, Clifford J., 'Snakes in *Catiline*', *Medieval and Renaissance Drama in England* 3 (1986), 149–63.

Rosset, Clement, *L'Anti-nature* (Paris: PUF, 1973).

Rowe, George W., *Distinguishing Jonson: Imitation, Rivalry, and the Direction of a Dramatic Career* (Lincoln: University of Nebraska Press, 1993).

Rowe, Katherine and Mary Floyd-Wilson (eds.), *Reading the Early Modern Passions: Essays in the Cultural History of Emotion* (Philadelphia: Pennsylvania University Press, 2004).
Sacks, Peter M., *The English Elegy: Studies in the Genre from Spenser to Yeats* (Baltimore: Johns Hopkins University Press, 1985).
Sanders, Julie, 'Print, Popular Culture, Consumption and Commodification in The Staple of News' in Julie Sanders *et al.*, *Refashioning Ben Jonson*, pp. 183–207.
   Kate Chedgzoy and Susan Wiseman (eds.), *Refashioning Ben Jonson: Gender, Politics, and the Jonsonian Canon* (Basingstoke: Macmillan, 1998),
Schneider, Michel, *Voleur de mots: essais sur le plagiat, la psychanalyse et la pensée* (Paris: Gallimard, 1985).
Schwarz, Kathryn, 'Stranger in the Mirror: Amazonian Reflections in the Jacobean Queen's Masque' in *Tough Love: Amazonian Encounters in the English Renaissance* (Durham and London: Duke University Press, 2000), pp. 109–33.
Scodel, Joshua, 'Genre and Occasion in Jonson's "On My First Sonne"', *Studies in Philology* 86 (1989), 235–59.
Scot, Reginald, *The Discoverie of Witchcraft* (1584).
Shakespeare, William, *The Riverside Shakespeare*, G. Blakemore Evans and Herschel Baker (eds.), 2nd edn (Boston: Houghton Mifflin Company, 1997).
   Shakespeare's Sonnets, Stephen Booth (ed.) (Yale: Yale University Press, 1977).
   The Works of Mr. William Shakespeare in Six Volumes, Nicholas Rowe (ed.) (London, 1709).
   Plays and Poems of William Shakespeare in Ten Volumes, Edmond Malone (ed.) (London, 1790).
Shapiro, James, *Rival Playwrights: Jonson, Shakespeare, Marlowe* (New York: Columbia University Press, 1991).
Sherman, Stuart, 'Eyes and Ears, News and Plays: The Argument of Ben Jonson's *Staple*' in Brendon Dooley and Sabrina Baron (eds.), *The Politics of Information in Early Modern Europe* (London: Routledge, 2001), pp. 23–40.
Shoeck, Helmut, *Envy: A Theory of Social Behavior* (London: Secker and Warburg, 1966).
Sidney, Sir Philip, *An Apologie for Poetrie* (London, 1595).
   Astrophil and Stella [1591], in *Sir Philip Sidney* ed. Katharine Duncan Jones (Oxford: Oxford University Press, 1989).
   The Countess of Pembrokes Arcadia (London, 1590).
Siebers, Tobin, *The Mirror of Medusa* (Berkeley: University of California Press, 1983).
Silberman, Lauren, 'To Write Sorrow in Jonson's "On My First Sonne"', *John Donne Journal* 9 (1990), 149–55.
Sinfield, Alan, 'Poetaster, the Author, and the Perils of Cultural Production', *Renaissance Drama*, n.s. 27 (1996), 3–18.
Slights, William W. E., *Ben Jonson and the Art of Secrecy* (Toronto: University of Toronto Press, 1994).

'The Edifying Margins of Renaissance English Books', *Renaissance Quarterly* 42 (1989), 682–716.

Smith, J., 'Effaced History: Facing the Colonial Context of Ben Jonson's Irish Masque at Court', *ELH* 65 (1998), 297–321.

Smith, Lacey Baldwin, *Treason in Tudor England: Politics and Paranoia* (London: Pimlico, 2006).

Smith, Lucy Toulmin (ed.), *York Plays: The Plays Performed by the Crafts or Mysteries of York on the Day of Corpus Christi in the 14th, 15th, and 16th Centuries* (New York: Russell & Russell, 1885).

Snuggs, Henry L., 'The Comic Humours: A New Interpretation', *PMLA* 62 (1947), 114–22.

Spenser, Edmund, *Amoretti and Epithalamion* (London, 1595).

The Faerie Queen[e]: The Shepheards Calendar: Together with the Other Works of England's Arch-Poët (London, 1611).

Stallybrass, Peter and Allon White, *The Politics and the Poetics of Transgression* (Ithaca: Cornell University Press, 1986).

Steggle, Matthew, *Wars of the Theatres: The Poetics of Personation in the Age of Jonson* (Victoria, BC: University of Victoria, 1998).

Stevens, Edward B., 'Envy and Pity in Greek Philosophy', *The American Journal of Philology* 69 (1948), 171–89.

Stonex, Arthur Bivins, 'The Sources of Jonson's *The Staple of News*', *PMLA* 30 (1915), 821–30.

Stow, John, *A Survay of London* (London, 1603 [1598]).

Sullivan, Garret A., Jr, *Memory and Forgetting in English Renaissance Drama: Shakespeare, Marlowe, Webster* (Cambridge: Cambridge University Press, 2005).

Summers, Claude J. and Ted-Larry Pebworth (eds.), *Classic and Cavalier: Essays on Jonson and the Sons of Ben* (Pittsburgh: University Of Pittsburgh Press, 1982).

Sweeney, John Gordon, *Jonson and the Psychology of Public Theatre: To Coin the Spirit, Spend the Soul* (Princeton: Princeton University Press, 1985).

Swinburne, Algernon Charles, *A Study of Ben Jonson* (New York: Worthington Co., 1889).

Tanselle, G.T., 'The Editorial Problem of Final Authorial Intention', *Studies in Bibliography* 29 (1976), 167–211.

Thomas, Keith, *Religion and the Decline of Magic: Studies in Popular Beliefs in Sixteenth and Seventeenth-Century England* (London: Penguin Books, 1971).

Tribble, Evelyn A., *Margins and Marginalia: The Printed Page in Early Modern England* (Charlottesville: University Press of Virginia, 1993).

Trimpi, Wesley, *Ben Jonson's Poems: A Study of the Plain Style* (Stanford: Stanford University Press, 1962).

Turner, Henry S., *The English Renaissance Stage: Geometry, Poetics, and the Practical Spatial Arts 1580–1630* (Oxford: Oxford University Press, 2006).

Van den Berg, Sara, *The Action of Ben Jonson's Poetry* (Newark: University of Delaware Press, 1987).

Varian, H., 'Distributive Justice, Welfare Economics, and the Theory of Fairness', *Philosophy and Public Affairs* 4 (1975), 223–47.
'Equity, Envy, and Efficiency', *Journal of Economic Theory* 9 (1974), 63–91.
Veblen, Thorstein, *The Theory of the Leisure Class: An Economic Study of Institutions* (New York: Macmillan, 1915 [1899]).
Vendler, Helen, *The Art of Shakespeare's Sonnets* (Cambridge: Harvard University Press, 1997).
Vernant, Jean-Pierre, 'Death in the Eyes' and 'In the Mirror of Medusa' in Zeitlin (ed.), *Mortals and Immortals*, pp. 111–50.
Vickers, Nancy, '"The blazon of sweet beauty's best": Shakespeare's *Lucrece*' in Patricia Parker and Geoffrey Hartman (eds.), *Shakespeare and the Question of Theory* (London: Methuen, 1985), pp. 95–115.
[Villiers, George, second Duke of Buckingham], *Poetical Reflections on a Late Poem entitled Absalom and Achitophel By a Person of Honour* (London, 1682).
Virgil, *Eclogues, Georgics, Aeneid I–VI*, trans. H. Rushton Fairclough (Cambridge: Harvard University Press, 1999).
The Aeneid, trans. Robert Fitzgerald (New York: Vintage Books, 1984 [1981]).
Waddington, Raymond B., 'Moralizing the Spectacle: Dramatic Emblems in *As You Like It*', *Shakespeare Quarterly* 33 (Summer, 1982), 155–63.
Walcot, Peter, *Envy and the Greeks: A Study of Human Behaviour* (Warminster: Aris and Phillips, Ltd., 1978).
Wall, Wendy, *The Imprint of Gender: Authorship and Publication in the English Renaissance* (Ithaca: Cornell University Press, 1993).
Wayne, Don, *Penshurst: The Semiotics of Place and the Poetics of History* (Madison: Wisconsin University Press, 1984).
'Poetry and Power in Ben Jonson's *Epigrammes*: The Naming of "Facts" or the Figuring of Social Relations?', *Renaissance and Modern Studies* 23 (1979), 79–103.
Webster, John, *The Displaying of Supposed Witchcraft* (London, 1677).
Whetstone, George, *The English Myrror. A Regard Wherein al estates may behold the Conquests of Envy* (London, 1586).
Whitney, Geffrey, *A Choice of Emblemes And Other Devises* (Leyden, 1586).
Wilhelm, Fabrice (ed.), *L'Envie et ses figurations littéraires* (Dijon: Editions Universitaires de Dijon, 2005).
Williams, Raymond, *The Country and the City* (New York: Oxford University Press, 1973).
Wilson, Edmund, 'Morose Ben Jonson', *The Triple Thinkers* (New York: Charles Scribner's Sons, 1948), pp. 213–32.
Wilson, Gayle Edward, 'Jonson's Use of the Bible and the Great Chain of Being in "To Penshurst"', *SEL* 8 (1968), 77–89.
Wilson, Thomas, *The Arte of Rhetorique, 1560*, ed. G. H. Mair (Oxford: Clarendon Press, 1909).
Wither, George, *A Collection of Emblemes, Ancient and Moderne* (London, 1635).
Womack, Peter, *Ben Jonson* (Oxford: Basil Blackwell, 1986).

Woodbridge, Elisabeth, *Studies in Jonson's Comedy* (New Haven: Yale Studies in English, 1898).
Woodbridge, Linda, 'Patchwork: Piecing the Early Modern Mind in England's First Century of Print Culture', *ELH* 23 (Winter 1993), 5–45.
Woodbridge, Linda (ed.), *Money and the Age of Shakespeare: Essays in New Economic History* (New York: Palgrave Macmillan, 2003),
Wright, Peter M., 'Jonson's Revision of the Stage Directions for the 1616 Folio Workes', *Medieval and Renaissance Drama* 5 (1991), 257–85.
Wynne-Davies, Marion, 'The Queen's Masque: Renaissance Women and the Seventeenth-Century Court Masque' in M. Wynne-Davies and S. P. Cerasano (eds.), *Gloriana's Face: Women, Public and Private, in the English Renaissance* (Detroit: Wayne State University Press, 1992), pp. 79–104.
Yates, Frances A., *The Art of Memory* (Chicago: Chicago University Press, 1966).
Young, R., 'Egalitarianism and Envy', *Philosophical Studies* 52 (1987), 261–76.
Zeitlin, Froma I. (ed.), *Mortals and Immortals: Collected Essays* (Princeton: Princeton University Press, 1991),

Index

Aeschylus, 154n.48, 164
Alciati, Andrea, 16n.54, 119n.27
Anne of Denmark, 75, 77n.9, 111, 159, 175, 176–7
Apelles, 84, 87
Aquinas, St Thomas, 48
Aristotle, 19, 44, 45n.9, 46, 55, 63, 69
Armin, Robert, 200
Aubrey, John, 56, 57, 187
Augustine, St, 47, 62

Bacon, Francis, 22, 36, 53, 55–7, 61, 78, 90–1, 118, 119–20
Banister, John, 67
Barish, Jonas, 149n.34
Barnfield, Richard, 192
Barton, Anne, 186, 191n.16
Basil, St, 46–7, 62
Bateman, Stephen, 50n.38, 52
Beaumont, Francis, 163
Beaumont, John, 35
Bernand, André, 45
Berry, Philippa, 173–4
Blagrave, Jonathan, 62–4
Blanchot, Maurice, 8
Bland, Mark, 81–2
Blisset, William, 99
Bloom, Harold, 4, 5–6
Bloomfield, Morton, 48
Boaistuau, Pierre, 61
Boehrer, Bruce, 4
Boissard, Jean-Jacques, 54
Bond, Ronald B., 13, 56, 60
Bosse, Abraham, 30
Breton, Nicholas, 26, 35
Brooks, Douglas A., 140
Brown, Peter, 47
Bunyan, John, 50n.38
Burt, Richard, 22
Burton, Robert, 43, 51–2, 61, 63
Butler, Martin, 187
Butter, Nathaniel, 190

Cairns, D. L., 15, 19
Callimachus, 66
calumny, *see* slander
Campbell, Lily B., 19
Campbell, Thomas, 2
Carleton, Dudley, 76n.7
Cartari, Vincenzo, 179–80
Cartelli, Thomas, 6
Catullus, 65–6, 87
censorship *see* defacement
Chapman, George, 43, 67, 173–4, 175, 176
Chaucer, Geoffrey, 48–9
Church Fathers, The, 46–7
Chute, Marchette, 190
Cicero, 177–85
Claudian, 178, 183
Clifford, Lady Anne, 55
Comes, Natalis, 179
Corbett, Margery, 140
Cort, Cornelis, 55
Cowley, Abraham, 52
Cyprian, 46, 47

Dällenbach, Lucien, 74
Daniel, Samuel, 67, 88, 139, 144
Dante, Alighieri, 48, 100
Davies, John (of Hereford), 52, 62, 64
Davis, Sir John, 175–6
defacement: and censorship, 78, 79, 80, 82–83, 89, 111; and masques, 75–78; as misreading, 39, 78, 86–9, 95–109, 131, 205; and monument, 92, 148; and novelty, 91; as physical destruction, 78, 80–1; and self-defacement, 90–3, 122, 144; and typographical errors, 81–2
Deguileville, Guillaume de, 50n.38
Dekker, Thomas, 50n.38, 59, 65, 67, 92, 99, 141
Del Moro, Battista, 55
Della Porta, Jean-Baptiste, 30
De Man, Paul, 148

226

Index

Democritus, 30
Derrida, Jacques, 71n.122, 149, 155n.52
Devereux, Robert, second Earl of Essex, 99
Devereux, Walter, first Earl of Essex, 55
Donaldson, Ian, 21–2, 26
Donne, John, 23, 30
Drayton, Michael, 27, 145
Dryden, John, 1, 186, 187
Dunbar, William, 51
Dutton, Richard, 141

Eliot, T. S., 10–1
Elizabeth I, 13, 59–61, 77n.9, 152, 173–7
eloquence, 177–85
Elyot, Thomas, 53n.59
emulation, 7, 8, 14–16, 35, 42–3, 62–4, 74
  see also envy
Evagrius, 47
envy: in the classical tradition, 42; as deadly sin, 47–9, 50n.38, 51; as disease, 44, 52–3, 59; and emulation, 42–3; etymology of, 17, 29; as *invidia*, 46; and jealousy, 16–19; literary characters, 13, 16, 18, 20–1, 46, 50, 50–1, 59, 70–2, 94; as *Livor*, 51; as male, 84n.32; as *phthonos*, 19, 42–6; physical characteristics of, 51–2; as prefatory *topos*, 28–9, 68, 94, 100; representations of, 16n.54, 18, 50n.38, 53–5, 59; with slander, 84–8, 206; and snakes, 53–5, 94; social, 12, 14; and virtue, 55
Essex House Masque, The, 30
evil eye, 1, 8, 23, 29–35, 36, 45–7, 55–8, 65–6, 118

fame, 18, 44, 55, 106, 111, 147, 148, 155, 159–60, 161, 165, 167, 170–2, 184, 189, 193
Felltham, Owen, 141–189
Fischlin, Daniel, 61
Fish, Stanley, 24, 26, 129, 147
Fletcher, John, 163
Foster, George, 38
Foucault, Michel, 9
Freud, Sigmund, 4, 5, 7n.23, 162n.64
Frommand, Johannes Christian, 53
Fulwell, Ulpian, 60
Fumaroli, Marc, 180

Galilei, Galileo, 31
gaze: envious, 8, 11, 22, 35, 36, 39, 113, 118, 119, 120, 192, 206; oblique, 5, 21, 22, 26, 27, 35, 36, 45, 51, 56, 67, 87, 103, 206; rays, 29–30, 56–8, 65–7, 78, 120; of spectator or reader, 23, 24, 31, 73
Genette, Gérard, 5
Gide, André, 74
Gifford, William, 1–2, 38
Gilbert, Allan H., 87

Gilman, Ernest, 80
Giotto, 53
Girard, René, 15
gluttony, 117–18
Goldberg, Jonathan, 152, 161
Gorgon, 20, 30, 31, 35, 40, 59, 159–67, 170, 177–85 *see also* Medusa
Gossen, Stephen, 121
Gossip, 50, 79, 89, 111, 190, 193
Gott, Samuel, 52n.53
Gower, John, 49
Greenblatt, Stephen, 9
Greene, Thomas, 5, 6
Gregory the Great, (Pope), 48

Hackel, Heidi Brayman, 27–9, 67
Harington, John, 67, 88
Helgerson, Richard, 141
Henry, Prince of Wales, 153, 154, 158–9, 176
Herrick, Robert, 28
Hesiod, 42–3, 62, 63, 165–7
Heywood, Thomas, 139, 140
Homer, 8, 64, 67, 179
Horace, 45, 99, 100–1, 102, 107–9, 121, 145, 145n.23, 154n.48
Huet, Marie-Hélène, 58

Jay, Martin, 46
James I (James VI of Scotland), 85, 141, 159, 160, 171, 173, 176, 185
jealousy, 14, 16–19
Jones, Ann Rosalind, 199
Jones, Inigo, 75, 117, 174
Jonson, Ben: admiration for Bacon, 90; authorial specularity, 73–4, 98, 123–4, 133, 147, 155, 167; auto-citation, 189, 193, 195–8, 204; critical reputation, 3–5; envy of Shakespeare, 1–3, 21–2, 38–9; *Jonsonus Virbius*, 3; and masques, 139, 142, 143, 148–53; obsession with envy, 11; paratexts, 8, 28, 72–3, 80, 82, 91–2, 126, 128, 129, 143, 159, 165–7, 154–8; perception of spectator or reader, 5–9, 22, 25–7, 29, 37, 79, 100; rhetorics of discontinuity, 7, 82, 95–9, 132, 167, 170; vigilant, 128–9, 144, 167, 171, 172
works:
The Alchemist, 115, 116, 124–5, 126, 169, 188, 189, 191, 192, 193, 196, 197, 199–200, 202; *Bartholomew Fair*, 4, 89, 90, 96, 126, 127–128, 139, 192–5, 197, 199, 205; *The Case is Altered*, 96–7, 197; *Catiline, His Conspiracy*, 18, 89, 108, 109, 124, 126, 129, 133, 177–85; *Cynthia's Revels*, 99, 109; *The Devil is an Ass*, 193; *Eastward Ho!* 120;

Jonson, Ben (*cont.*)
'Elegie on Lady Jane Pawlet', 146–8, 153; *Epicoene*, 95, 162, 163–4, 179, 193, 194, 198, 206; 'An Epistle to Master John Selden', 129–31; 'An Epistle to Sir Edward Sacvile, Now Earl of Dorset', 55; *Every Man In His Humour*, 18, 96, 129, 133–5, 141, 187; *Every Man Out of His Humour*, 18, 20, 59, 94, 95, 124, 142, 162, 187, 193, 198, 201; 'An Execration upon Vulcan', 78; *Hymenaei*, 27, 76, 117, 143, 150–1; 'In Authorem', 21, 26, 27, 88; *The Magnetic Lady*, 124, 187; *The Masque of Augurs*, 127, 143; *The Masque of Beauty*, 20, 70, 72; *The Masque of Blacknesse*, 9, 20, 30, 70–2, 75–7, 78, 79, 92, 151–2; *The Masque of Queenes*, 20, 39, 40, 72, 110–11, 113, 118–20, 123, 130, 131, 142, 153–77, 177, 183, 185, 187, 193, 201; *The New Inn*, 4, 96, 205–6; *News From the New World Discover'd in the Moone*, 186; 'Ode To Himself', 79; 'On My First Son', 135–8; *Part of the Kings Entertainment in Passing to his Coronation*, 91, 92; *Poetaster*, 20, 87, 94–5, 97–109, 115–16, 132, 160–1, 171, 204, 205; *The Sad Shepherd*, 187; *Sejanus, His Fall*, 75, 108–9, 125–7, 128; *The Staple of Newes*, 41, 124, 134, 169, 170n.82, 186–204, 204–5; *Timber, Or Discoveries*, 38, 89, 90, 121, 130; 'To Elizabeth, Countess of Rutland', 146; 'To My Book', 137–8; 'To My Bookseller', 136; 'To Penshurst', 20, 112–18; 'To the Immortall Memorie, and Friendship of that Noble Paire, Sir Lucius Cary, and Sir H. Morison', 93, 131, 146; 'To the Reader', 43; 'A Vision of Ben Jonson, On the Muses of His Friend M. Drayton', 27; *A Vision of Delight*, 121; *Volpone*, 4, 188, 191, 197; *Workes* (1616 Folio), 40, 55, 81, 89, 109, 139–44, 153, 186, 187, 188–9, 191
Juvenal, 183

Kant, Emmanuel, 12n.38
Kaplan, Lindsay M., 86
Kastan, David Scott, 28
Kepler, Johannes, 30
Kerrigan, William, 4
King, Henry, 186
Klein, Melanie, 14, 15
Konstan, David, 17
Kyd, Thomas, *The Spanish Tragedy*, 195, 199–200

La Rochefoucauld, François de, 16
Laing, R.D., 23

Lanier, Douglas M., 188
Limberis, Vasilikos, 47
Limon, Jerzy, 154n.49
Lightbown, Ronald, 140
Lodge, Thomas, 67
London Prodigall, The, 192
Loewenstein, Joseph, 23, 139, 140
Love, Harold, 23, 140
Lucan, 179, 154n.48
Lucian, 84, 87
Lucretius, 30
Lydgate, John, 50n.38

Macfarlane, Alan, 58
Machiavelli, 61, 153
Malone, Edmond, 2
Manwood, John, 110
Marcus, Leah, 121
Marston, John, 99
Mary Stuart (Queen of Scots), 85, 173, 177
Maus, Katharine Eisaman, 113, 129
McCain, William E., 114
Medusa, 16, 23, 30, 31–2, 40, 45, 46, 54, 55, 59, 71–2, 87, 94, 160, 162, 167, 172, 175–7, 177–85, 178n.94 *see also* Gorgon.
Milton, John, *Paradise Lost*, 13, 29, 31, 121
Montaigne, Michel de, 25, 56–8
Montrose, Louis, 60
monument, 40, 92–3, 139–85, 188
More, St Thomas, 51
Moseley, Humphrey, 80n.19

Newlyn, Lucy, 6–7
Newman, Karen, 189n.9, 198n.35
Newton, Richard C., 140

oblivion, 77n.10, 84, 86
Oldisworth, Nicholas, 188n.6
Orgel, Stephen, 155n.53
Ovid, 16, 45, 49, 51–2, 97–8, 99, 100–1, 102

Palmer, Thomas, 35
Paré, Ambroise, 58
Paster, Gail Kern, 146
Peacham, Henry, 155, 182–3, 185
Pelletier, Gérard, 180–2, 183
Petrarch, Francesco, 59
pharmakon, 59, 65, 71n.122, 74, 175, 183, 185
Phillips, Edward, 53n.59
Pierce, Thomas, 56
Pindar, 44, 144n.8
Plato, 65n.105, 71n.122, 83, 175, 180, 184–185
Plautus, 139

Index

Pliny, 58
Plutarch, 43, 44, 45, 64
Poole, Joshua, 53
Pope, Alexander, 1n.1
Poulet, Georges, 8
Prynne, William, 82n.26
Puttenham, 86, 86n.40

Rabelais, François, 4
Raleigh, Walter, 77n.10
Ramus, Peter, 61, 63
Rathmell, C. A., 115
Raymond, Joad, 190n.14
Rebhorn, Wayne A., 7
Ripa, 17, 21, 18n.62, 143, 170, 179
Rosset, Clément, 153
Rowe, Nicholas, 1
rumour, 50, 79, 89, 103, 106, 111

Sackville, Sir Edward, second Earl of Dorset, 55
sanctuary, 40, 110–38, 167, 192, 205
Sandys, George, 45
Sallust, 183n.108
Scève, Maurice, 30, 79
Schoeck, Helmut, 15
Scot, Reginald, 57n.71, 154n.48
Secundus, Johannes, 66
Selden, John, 35
Shakespeare, William: his art, 122–3; construction of fame, 2; envied by Jonson, 1–3; *Hamlet*, 83–4, 199; Jonson's elegy to, 36–9; *The London Prodigall*, 193; *Macbeth*, 161, 162, 164, 174; *Measure For Measure*, 127; nostalgia for, 186, 187; *Othello*, 13; portrait in 1623 folio, 43; *Richard II*, 22n.78, 83; *The Second Part of Henry the Fourth*, 102–3; *The Sonnets*, 144–5, 147; *The Tempest*, 76; *Titus Androncius*, 199
Sidney, Philip, 3, 66, 68, 74, 83, 110, 112, 114, 116, 117
Siebers, Tobin, 34
Sinfield, Alan, 100, 116

slander, 29, 46, 49, 65, 78, 79, 83–90, 101, 108, 120, 190, 191 *see also* Apelles
Smith, Lacey Baldwin, 19–20
Spenser, Edmund, 13, 50n.38, 60–1, 68–9, 84–5, 112, 121, 144
Stallybrass, Peter, 199
Stansby, William, 25, 81
Stevens, Edward B., 44
Stow, John, 110n.1
Swinburne, Algernon Charles, 128–9

Terence, 139
Thomas, Keith, 57
Tribble, Evelyn A., 91

Vendler, Helen, 145
Vernant, Jean-Pierre, 166
Vickers, Nancy, 180
Villiers, George, second Duke of Buckingham, 56n.69
Virgil, 18, 46, 99, 100–1, 103–6, 111, 119, 170
Vitruvius, 146

Walcot, Peter, 14, 62
Wall, Wendy, 69
War of the Theatres, 21n.71, 99–100
Wayne, Don, 113
Webster, John, 57, 67
Whetstone, George, 64
Whitney, Geffrey, 54
Wilhelm, Fabrice, 14, 15
Williams, Raymond, 113
Wilson, Edmund, 4
Wilson, Thomas, 53n.59
witchcraft, 46, 56–8, 71, 119, 154, 160, 167–70
Wither, George, 49, 86n.39
Woodbridge, Linda, 196n.28

Zoilus, 28, 67
Zuccari, Federico, 55